D0407506

America Ascendant

ALSO BY STANLEY B. GREENBERG

It's the Middle Class, Stupid!

*Dispatches from the War Room: In the
Trenches with Five Extraordinary Leaders*

*The Two Americas: Our Current Political
Deadlock and How to Break It*

*The New Majority: Toward a Popular
Progressive Politics*

*Middle Class Dreams: Building the New
American Majority*

*Legitimating the Illegitimate: State, Markets
and Resistance in South Africa*

*Race and State in Capitalist Development:
Comparative Perspectives*

*Politics and Poverty: Modernization and
Response in Five Poor Neighborhoods*

**America ascendant : a
revolutionary nation's
path to addressing its
deepest problems and
leading the 21st century**

6an   02/18/16

AMERICA
ASCENDANT

A Revolutionary Nation's Path to
Addressing Its Deepest Problems
and Leading the 21st Century

STANLEY B. GREENBERG

THOMAS DUNNE BOOKS
ST. MARTIN'S PRESS
NEW YORK

THOMAS DUNNE BOOKS.
An imprint of St. Martin's Press.

AMERICA ASCENDANT. Copyright © 2015 by Stanley B. Greenberg. All rights reserved. Printed in the United States of America. For information, address St. Martin's Press, 175 Fifth Avenue, New York, N.Y. 10010.

www.thomasdunnebooks.com
www.stmartins.com

Design by Jonathan Bennett

The Library of Congress Cataloging-in-Publication Data is available upon request.

ISBN 978-1-250-00367-6 (hardcover)
ISBN 978-1-4668-8699-5 (e-book)

St. Martin's Press books may be purchased for educational, business, or promotional use. For information on bulk purchases, please contact the Macmillan Corporate and Premium Sales Department at 1-800-221-7945, extension 5442, or write to specialmarkets @macmillan.com.

First Edition: November 2015

10 9 8 7 6 5 4 3 2 1

To
Rosa L. DeLauro

and

Rigby Maya Zentner
Sadie Liberty Delicath
Teo Isaac Zentner
Jasper Samuel Delicath

CONTENTS

1 AMERICA AT A TIPPING POINT

America is poised to lead the twenty-first century, as it led the twentieth. That will happen because America is at a tipping point in its own renewal, a renewal that will allow it to be the exceptional nation again.

America led the Industrial Revolution that changed human history, produced once-in-a-century disruptive changes in where and how families lived and worked, and created a rising prosperity unheard of before the late nineteenth century. It was made possible by the steam engine, the railways built coast to coast, the massive immigration, the concentration of populations in burgeoning cities, and the governments that supported the new industrial monopolies. America became a magnet to the world and was poised to be the leading economic, cultural, and military power of the twentieth century.

But those revolutionary changes left a lot of blood, and they came with a high social cost. The desperate working conditions and teeming tenements, exploitation of women, government corruption, and the inequality of the Gilded Age put it all at risk. It was the two-decade struggle for progressive reforms and government activism to mitigate those costs and renew America that allowed the twentieth century to become America's century.

America emerged ascendant by the turn of the twentieth century, when it became the largest industrial power. By the end of World War II, America would account for almost a half of the global economy. It became the country that produced the highest per capita income and eventually the country with the largest middle class. It remained the country where people all across the globe sought to emigrate, and the country that produced the highest per capita income and largest middle class by 1980. Starting with Presidents Teddy Roosevelt, Woodrow Wilson, Franklin Roosevelt, and Harry Truman, America invested in U.S. military defenses and technology and projected a global presence in support of American interests and values. And America emerged exceptional because of what Joseph Nye called its growing "soft power"—its openness to technology and innovation and to a robust popular culture and civil society.[1]

Well, America is being transformed today by revolutionary changes that are fueling the country's growing economic and cultural dynamism. These revolutions are producing seismic changes to our economy, culture, and politics as well as disruptive, once-in-a-century changes in where we live, our way of life, the structure of families, and what are considered the ascendant values. But those revolutionary changes come with powerful contradictions: they come with a high human cost, stark inequalities, and political dysfunction. People live the contradictions, and increasingly they insist on a bold politics that can mitigate the social costs and create human possibility. That is why reformers have the opportunity to renew America and make it possible for America to be exceptional again.

This is a very different picture than the one offered by those who are averse to government or those who think America is in decline or those who believe we are so deeply gridlocked that it cannot begin to tackle its great problems.

America's economy is on the move. It is being fueled by revolutions in energy, immigration, innovation, big data, and advanced manufacturing, by revolutions in the metropolitan areas. Each is disruptive and they feed on each other to produce accelerating changes across the economy and society. America is increasingly energy independent, sending shock waves across the energy market, lowering energy costs, and making progress on climate change at the same time. America's support of basic research, great research universities, and openness to innovation have allowed it to take advantage of the digital revolution, big data, and advanced manufacturing to attract investment from around the world and foster whole new industries.

Just as important to America's emerging standing are the social transformations that are making the country ever more racially and culturally diverse, younger, a home to immigrants, and located in the big metropolitan centers that are host to the rising economic and cultural dynamism. While most other countries struggle profoundly and sometimes violently with their immigrant populations and religious and racial differences, America's path to a unified, multicultural identity makes it truly exceptional.

America's revolutions have produced a country where 38 percent are racial minorities and 15 percent of new marriages are interracial. Adding to the racial and cultural diversity is the influx of immigrants. The globe has witnessed a massive, growing migration, and fully one in five migrants has ended up in the United States. The foreign-born now comprise about 40 percent of the residents of New York City and Los Angeles and half of Silicon Valley's engineers. America's revolutions have produced a country where a growing number of people are secular, though America remains uniquely a country where 40 percent still attend religious services each week.[2]

Just think of the scale of social change over the past two decades. America has grown more diverse and racially tolerant at an impressive and accelerating rate, particularly among the Millennials. The proportion of African Americans, Hispanics, and Asians in the presidential electorate has doubled to 30 percent. Millennials will be more than a quarter of the 2016 presidential electorate and 40 percent of the eligible voting population in the election after that.[3]

America is emerging as a racially blended, multinational, multilingual, religiously pluralistic society. And while these revolutions are tilting America's trajectory upward, they are also producing sudden, sweeping, and accelerating social changes, evident in the decline of the traditional family and the struggles of working-class women and men. For all the problems, that multiculturalism grows more central to our national identity. And today's major national leaders in politics, civil society, and big companies have accepted the call to find unity in diversity.

Religious observance has plummeted across the spectrum of religious denominations, except for white Evangelicals. Over one in five Americans is secular with no religion, and they now outnumber the mainline Protestants. And with the exception of the Evangelicals, people of all faiths now accept premarital sex and gay marriage.[4]

The traditional family has given way to a country relaxed about the pluralism of family types and a revolution in the role of women. Women are pouring into the universities, where they are now a growing majority of the graduates. Three-quarters of women are now in the labor force, and two-thirds are the principal or cobreadwinner. Fully half of Americans are now not married, and 40 percent of the households include only a single person.[5]

The metropolitan areas have been turned on their heads. The exurbs, Levittowns, strip malls, and automobiles are being forsaken as people move to the cities, attracted by the urbanism, the major businesses, universities and research institutions, culture, and the influx of immigrants and racial diversity. Two-thirds of the college-educated Millennials now live in the fifty-one largest cities and are moving into the close-in neighborhoods. They identify with the new way of life in these cities and are contributing to the new kind of localism.[6]

So America's revolutions have America on the move in impressive ways and they are setting off waves of change that are the main story for a generation.

But these economic and social transformations are also creating stark problems for people and the country that leave the public seething, frustrated, and pessimistic about the future of the country. That sentiment is also fostering a growing reform movement that wants to expose the dark side of America's progress and demands political leaders take up the country's deepest problems in order to be taken seriously.

To begin with, this new, wondrous economy produces no wage gains for anyone except for those at the top. People distill that into a first economic principle: jobs in the new economy don't pay enough to live on. People are on the edge financially as they cope with stagnant wages and pay cuts. This leads people to put together multiple jobs to get by. Since they are on the edge, they think they face an endemic cost-of-living crisis. They feel powerless in the face of the inexplicably high costs of child care and student debt, which can send them into ruin.

Aspirations have been recalibrated to the times that are dramatically different. The younger generations think hardworking people can set their sights on a "more comfortable life," but that middle-class dreams are only for the older ones.

To add income or ease the constraints of the new economy, a growing number of people are working independently as service providers, consultants, freelancers, or in their own small businesses, though most never succeed in escaping the low-pay economy.

And while ordinary people are scrambling, the CEOs of big businesses make 295.9 times the pay of the average worker and have emerged as the face of America's inequality. They broke the social compact with their employees and their country. These big businesses executives use Super PACs and lobbyists to make sure government works for them. Their companies got bailed out, while ordinary people struggled and lost their homes or businesses.[7]

At the same time, all these revolutions in the American economy and around the globe are producing the most vexing contradiction of all—climate change and its resulting, and now foreseeable, economic and human costs. The poor will certainly pay the highest price.

And the social transformations that make America exceptional also come with a high price and create a lot of uncertainty about how to proceed. Social conservatives are still contesting the sexual revolution and the changes to gender roles and the traditional family. In that context, how do you begin the discussion about the surge in the number of unmarried households and children raised by a single parent? How do you deal with the social consequences of the very real demise of the traditional family and the male breadwinner role?

The debate in the 1960s over the "crisis in the Negro family" and the mounting number of children raised by single parents was smothered by the unsettled debates over civil rights and affirmative action. At that time, the proportion of children born to single parents among blacks was 23 percent, but now the rate is higher for all races and has risen to 44 percent across the white working class.[8]

The consequences of that change could not be more important. Children raised by a single parent learn fewer skills and important values at an early age and are much more likely to end up in poverty and face huge blockages to upward mobility. While middle-class men and women have been adapting by marrying later and settling into more egalitarian parenting roles, many more children are being raised by working-class single parents—mostly women.

At the same time, working-class men have been left marginalized. In the boom decades after World War II, many of these men would have had the primary responsibility for supporting the family and its 3.8 children, the peak average in 1956. Now, with most looking at earning dramatically less than prior generations, working-class men are not rushing to get more education and many are pulling back from the labor force and marriage.[9]

Working women, on the other hand, have been left on their own. America has witnessed a revolution in women's roles in the economy and the family. Yet working mothers are managing work and family without the barest help on child care, paid sick days, and family leave. Women have obtained more education and moved into more skilled jobs. But they still dominate the lowest-paid occupations, face a wage gap relative to men, and receive lower benefits in retirement. And all of these problems are just multiplied for the majority now unmarried.

Working women are on the edge of revolt and poised to demand reform, though it is not clear yet whether the single working-class mothers raising children on their own or the men who are being marginalized will rise up and demand help.

People are living these changes and adapting to the new economy and society, but they are also judging leaders and parties on whether they "get it" and whether they will address these accumulating problems. Is their agenda relevant and bold enough for these times? And that is why it seems like the country is at a tipping point very much like the one it came to in 1900 that led America's leaders to move over two decades toward progressively bolder reforms in our economy, society, and politics and that allowed the twentieth century to become America's century.

America led the global economy in the last two decades of the nineteenth century because it was better able to translate technological discoveries into economic practice than England, Germany, or France. The steam engine and portable power fueled the Industrial Revolution like computers and the Internet fuel the digital revolution today, Walter Isaacson writes. Economic output tripled, and America would soon lead the world in the "age of oil, automobiles, and aircraft."[10]

To fuel the steam-powered economy, America sucked in immigrants from all across Europe to work in the mines and factories and build the railroads from coast to coast. A country where two in every three people were employed in agriculture fell to four in ten as people rushed to America's cities. New York City's population grew to 2.5 million in 1890, and Chicago grew from a "prairie town" to the home of 1.7 million by the turn of the century, more than three-quarters of them first-generation immigrants. With poverty and starvation the backdrop, the Irish led the rush of one in five in Great Britain who immigrated to America, followed by the Germans and Scandinavians, Italians and eastern Europeans.[11]

But the surging populations were jammed into tenements that were often swept by contagious diseases. Factories and housing were built shoddily as building codes were often ignored and local party bosses were bought off to cater to businesses' needs.

The new working-class people that crowded into the cities were recruited as families, and the roles of men and women in the family were changed abruptly and radically in the process. The husband was the breadwinner and the unions and reformers worked for a family wage that could support the new family. Single women worked in the lowest-paid jobs, where the hours were long. Married women were expected to wash clothes, raise children, sell rags, do piecework from home, and handle boarders to help the family get to bare subsistence.[12]

Beyond the teeming slums and inhumane working conditions, America's Industrial Revolution also produced political corruption on a massive scale, market monopolies, squeezed incomes for laborers and farmers, and a level of inequality not seen before in America.

Atop this new economic order stood the industrialists, such as Andrew Carnegie, John D. Rockefeller, and John Pierpont Morgan. These entrepreneurs created huge trusts to eliminate competitors and used their monopoly power to set prices. The trusts were products of corrupt deals between business and government at the highest and lowest levels. The federal government used tariffs to protect these industries from foreign competition, and their market power meant rigged prices for farmers and consumers. Before the turn of the century, "muckraking" investigative journalists would expose special deals between businessmen and local party bosses that corrupted both parties.

During America's first century, the top 1 percent owned between 25 and 32 percent of the country's wealth, but that doubled to 45 percent between 1870 and 1910. That earned this era the name "Gilded Age."[13]

With rising opposition to the new industrial order, industrialists mobilized to defend tariffs, trusts, and the big banks in the 1896 presidential election. The Republicans raised more money as a percent of GDP than has ever been raised on a U.S. campaign to maintain control of the federal government. That might even embarrass the billionaire donors in the post–*Citizens United* era, now that the U.S. Supreme Court has given billionaires legal permission to make unlimited contributions to the new Super PACs.[14]

America first began to confront the dark side of its growth from the bottom up. Factory workers organized, and local charities, settlement houses, and parishes began to grapple with the overwhelming social cost of growth; investigative journalists—"muckrakers"—forced leaders to address the worst abuses, and ultimately the reform-minded leaders in cities and states came to power and created models of reform. They consciously expanded the role of government, and made gradual steps to reform democratic participation so it could not be captured by powerful business interests. It would take not

one but four elections and three presidents to achieve the bold reforms necessary for America's renewal at the turn of the twentieth century. And ultimately,
it would take President Franklin Roosevelt and the New Deal to establish
legal protections for labor unions and to create a system of social insurance.

Teddy Roosevelt achieved some reforms during his time as president, and
by 1912, when he ran as an independent, he was insisting we "must drive the
special interests out of politics"—an evil he put on the same level as slavery. He
embraced the whole emerging progressive agenda of minimum wages, maximum workweeks, workplace safety regulations, graduated income, workmen's
compensation, child labor laws, tariff reform, direct Senate elections, voter referendums and recalls, inheritance taxes, public disclosure of campaign donations, and even environmental conservation.[15]

When Woodrow Wilson and the Democrats swept out the conservatives
in the 1912 elections, they confronted the problems of the time head-on. The
Republican Party remained the party of the industrialists and continued to
protect the trusts and fight limits on working hours and child labor. The conservative Republicans had to be decisively defeated before the progressives
could limit the workweek, pass real antitrust laws, regulate railway rates,
slash high trade tariffs to favor farmers and consumers, introduce direct
primaries to defeat the party machines, require the direct election of U.S.
senators, bar corporate contributions to campaigns, introduce an income
tax, and give women the right to vote.

The conservative Supreme Court overturned legislation passed in 1916
barring the use of child labor in manufactured products intended for interstate commerce. This and other progressive reforms would have to wait
until a more thoroughgoing defeat of the conservatives and the next wave of
reform under the New Deal and the post–World War II national investments
that produced the American middle class. Nonetheless, the two-decade era
of progressive reform that began with Teddy Roosevelt and ended with Woodrow Wilson fundamentally changed the path of American capitalism and
democracy and allowed America to dominate the century.

Today, America is at another tipping point, and Democrats are leading the
battle for reform because, quite simply, they are aligned with the ascendant
trends and because the Republicans are fighting those trends with growing
ferocity. Surging racial and immigrant diversity, the sexual revolution, gay
marriage accepted constitutionally, growing secularism, and radically changing family structures have moved conservatives to join a counterrevolution
to reverse these trends before it is too late for the country. The modern Republican Party's raison d'être is to keep the new American majority from
governing successfully.

But this battle against America's ascendant trends and values has put the
Republican Party into a death spiral that it can only hope to slow. Despite its
constitutional advantages in the Congress and its success mobilizing voters in

off-year elections, the Republican Party is deeply unpopular nationally, and fewer and fewer voters identify themselves as Republican. It is the party of the oldest, most rural, most religiously observant, and mostly married white voters. It is barely up for consideration with the Millennials, the secular, the foreign-born, and anyone with a trace of color or an accent, and it does not compete in the country's most dynamic metropolitan areas.

Voters have given Democrats the political stage because they embrace America's multiculturalism as a unifying concept and welcome the seismic changes that have upended the traditional family, accelerated racial and immigrant diversity, and reshaped the metropolitan areas. With Republicans digging in and contesting these changes, Democrats more explicitly defend the values of equality, equal rights, and fairness; they place more emphasis on empathy and protecting people from harm; they place a high premium on openness to diversity and acceptance of differences; they celebrate an individualism rooted in individual autonomy; and they uphold education and science rather than religion as paths to discoverable truths.

Having the political stage, however, is not the same as stepping up to push for the reforms that can renew America. That requires putting America's economic and social contradictions at the top of the public agenda, even as powerful conservative forces mobilize to defeat them. And progressive reformers will have to make the case for government activism, even as it joins the even more difficult battle to reform a deeply corrupted government dominated by special interests. It is not certain that Democrats will be willing to confront those contradictions without growing pressure in civil society, growing protest movements, and electoral battles within the Democratic Party.

Importantly, the Republicans' intensifying mobilization against the ascendant trends over the past decade has allowed them to win control of the U.S. Congress and historic numbers of state legislatures. They now govern almost unopposed in nearly half of the states. That will delay America addressing its greatest challenges.

Republicans sustained high off-year turnouts in 2010 and 2014 by constantly raising the specter of President Barack Obama and the grave risks to the country's traditional values if Democrats hold office. By stoking fears about Obamacare, illegal immigrants, and gay marriage, they have raised the stakes for conservatives and built their turnout. Every election is national when you are battling to block the new American majority.

And with the electoral and constitutional bias in favor of rural areas, Republicans have joined the battle for traditional values with great success. Those battles, however, only further alienate the Republicans from the burgeoning new electorate.

Even more consequential and polarizing is the Republican strategy to hold off the deluge by building a conservative base in the race-conscious and religiously observant South, the Appalachian Valley, across the rural Plains states, and in the Mountain West. It has won nearly total control in twenty states by fighting Obamacare, eliminating aid for the poor and the unemployed, making a last-ditch effort to end abortion, and defending traditional marriage. By winning big in this GOP conservative heartland, the Republicans can govern as conservatives in twenty states and take for granted nearly forty Senate seats, even though the party's regional base counts for only a quarter of the national presidential electorate.[16]

The problem for the Republicans is that the more they succeed in animating and solidifying their support in the GOP conservative heartland, the more the rest of the country views them as out of date and out of touch.

It also creates forbidding odds against the Republicans in national elections and in the Electoral College. Democrats are aligned with the current trends, only expanding their Electoral College map while Republicans fight these battles.

This recent history has left America profoundly polarized into red and blue America—and it only grows worse as the economic and cultural revolutions seem ever more certain. The deep red-blue polarization is not a sign that Republicans will prevail. Indeed, it portends the opposite.

Republicans increasingly say it is important for them to live with people who share their religious faith and political views, while Democrats say they want to live in neighborhoods with people of different racial and ethnic backgrounds. Each holds increasingly negative views of the other party, though Republicans' contempt for Democrats is in a league of its own: 72 percent of consistent conservatives hold a very unfavorable opinion of Democrats, while just 53 percent of consistent liberals hold a similarly intense negative view of Republicans. Increasingly, they each think that if the other party wins and gets to promote its values, the country is at risk. This intensifying polarization is hardly symmetric, as Republicans grow more alienated from the ascendant values.[17]

As the national odds grow longer for conservatives, that only increases the urgency to defend their values and translate them into politics.

The Republican battle for American values is also a battle for policies that they advance in the GOP-controlled states, the U.S. Congress, and the U.S. Supreme Court when they can. They think the social safety net itself, including food stamps and unemployment benefits, is the primary cause of idleness and poverty. They oppose immigration and making gay marriage legal. They oppose further equal-employment protections for women and gays. They are determined to ban abortions. They are an antitax party that cuts corporate and top tax rates as a matter of principle. They cut public spending for education and science. With large financial contributions from the energy companies and banking sector, they promote fossil fuels and battle to protect the coal industry while opposing action to limit greenhouse gas emissions. They want to lift regulations of business and Wall Street banks. They believe campaign spending by the very rich and by corporations counts as constitutionally protected free speech.

These are the policies Republicans enact, and thus, defeating and marginalizing Republicans and conservatives is the only way to fully proceed with a reform agenda for these times.

It is already happening. Many of the reforms to address the dark side of our economic growth and social transformations are starting to gain momentum in civil society. Initial reformist steps are being taken at the local and state levels that may show the path for enacting much bolder ones nationally.

If you think this is fanciful, consider what happened in California.

In 2008, the California budget was in crisis and faced shattering deficits and drastic cuts in public programs. "Political paralysis gripped the Capitol and left the state starved for cash," *The Los Angeles Times* observed. The population was leaving and many stories talked about California as no longer the pioneer of change for the country. The citizens of the state despaired of its future, and more than half said the state faced structural problems that would not ease when the national economy recovered. Four of every five voters said the state was on the wrong track going into the 2010 elections. With the deficit projected to reach $60 billion in 2010 and a $27 billion shortfall expected the next year, Jay Leno joked, "California is so broke that I saw a going-out-of-business sign at a meth lab."[18]

The gridlock was painfully familiar. The voters via state initiative had limited state property tax increases and blocked the legislature from raising taxes without the support of two-thirds of the legislature. In any event, the Republican caucus in the Assembly and Senate voted to kill any revenue increase to address the crisis. Between 2008 and 2013, the state's prestigious universities were cut by $900 million and per-pupil school spending was slashed by 29.3 percent. The voters ignominiously recalled the Democratic governor, Gray Davis, after just ten months in office and rated Republican Arnold Schwarzenegger so poorly he dared not run for reelection in 2010.[19]

But California embodies many of the trends in this book, and voters turned against the gridlock and against candidates who were increasingly hostile to spending and taxes, immigration, abortion, and action on climate change. In 2010 voters elected Democrats to every statewide office, and in 2012 they passed a referendum that raised the income tax on the wealthy to fund education. In the general election they gave the Democrats super majorities that ended the Republicans' ability to veto tax increases. Progress was premised on taking power away from Republicans, not a return to bipartisanship. Reporting on our bipartisan poll for *The Los Angeles Times*, I observed, "Only in the context of California can you imagine coming out of that scenario and describe it as going more smoothly."[20]

The California budget came into surplus in 2013 and is projected to reach $4.2 billion in fiscal year 2015–2016. The surpluses have been devoted to spending for schools and universities, to a rainy-day fund, and to paying down liabilities. Rather than California going bankrupt and shutting off the lights, Standard & Poor's upgraded California's' bond rating to A+, the state led the country in jobs created, and its economy grew 4 percent in 2014, stronger than the national economy. In its own show of confidence, Boeing announced it was returning some engineering jobs to California.[21]

While putting its budget in order, growing the economy, and creating jobs, California also made the state a better place for working families by increasing the minimum wage in 2013, and employers will be required to pay their employees at least $10 an hour by 2016. At the same time, many California cities are proposing and passing even higher minimum wages. California became one of three states to require certain employers to offer paid sick days and has expanded its paid family leave insurance program to include caring for an ill family member. The governor has reached levels of popularity not seen for decades and was reelected in a landslide in 2014.[22]

And what is the "best state for business? Yes, California," according to data compiled by Bloomberg and reported in *Bloomberg View*. California-based companies over the past four years outperformed the S&P 500 by 23 percent. They delivered returns of 134 percent—2.5 times the returns for companies based in Texas.[23]

The United States, too, will soon have a political moment that allows it to transcend the dysfunction and move on to tackle its huge challenges. A lot of people will sigh, finally. A lot of people around the world who need America to be exceptional will be reassured it can renew itself and represent progress again. The plate-shifting changes taking place in the economic realm along with the social and cultural transformations are setting the stage for new leaders—leaders who identify with the new realities, understand its contradictions, and are prepared to fight so all Americans can share in the rewards of America's ascendant trends.

There is no evidence in the California story that the specter of extinction brings out Republican leaders ready to join the battle for reform. If anything, the party became more conservative. The conservative columnist David Brooks beseeches his party "to declare a truce on the social safety net" and insists, "They need to assure the country that the net will always be there for the truly needy." But how do conservatives get there when they believe the safety net is the cause of poverty and idleness?[24]

Perhaps a shattering national defeat like the Democrats faced in 1984 or progressives gaining control of the judiciary and Supreme Court will allow the modernizers to gain the upper hand in the Republican Party.

Until then, Democrats will have the role of addressing the contradictions and dark side of our progress.

Just as there was building reaction to the trends of the Gilded Age, there is momentum for reform brewing in America today. People are at work in their communities and with their churches to help struggling families; journalists are finding new forms of media and using technology to speak truth to power and to challenge people to act; companies are forming coalitions with nonprofits to pass important legislation that invests in people; and leaders seeking to make bold policy reforms are being promoted in their cities and states. It is becoming clear that America has the capacity to bring the big changes that are necessary for its ascent. America is not paralyzed.

Just look at what is happening in the cities and states. The political liberation of California, for example, is made possible by the dynamic, diverse, and growing cities and metropolitan areas that refuse to wait for the smoke of national gridlock to clear. California cities as well as metropolitan areas all over the country, even in the conservative heartland, are urgently proceeding with progressive reforms, much as leading cities and states did after the turn of the twentieth century. Cities are beginning to address the issue of low wages, the need for more union organizing, the challenges of balancing work and family, and the need for universal pre-K education to raise social mobility and push back against the rising tide of inequality.

Cities are taking action because they cannot wait to tackle even the most difficult challenges. Just as an illustration, mayors are taking on the responsibility of addressing climate change. Impatient with "the continuing absence of tangible outcomes from inter-governmental efforts to reduce greenhouse gases," New York City's former mayor Michael Bloomberg organized the mayors of the world's greatest cities in the C40 Cities Climate Leadership Group to take "concrete actions that demonstrate that preventing catastrophic climate change is possible." Under that banner, San Francisco is taking steps to reduce emissions to 25 percent below 1990 levels by 2017, with the ultimate goal of an 80 percent reduction by 2050.[25]

As the United Nations was convening for the first time to consider the issue, New York City mayor Bill de Blasio pledged that New York would become the largest city to meet the U.N. target of reducing greenhouse gas emissions by 80 percent from 2005 levels. That is comparable to taking 700,000 vehicles off the road. "Climate change is an existential threat to New Yorkers and our planet," de Blasio declared, and "New York City must continue to set the pace and provide the bold leadership that's needed." His proposal accepts and builds on the $20 billion plan of his immediate predecessor, Bloomberg, to mitigate the effects of a thirty-one-inch rise in sea levels with vast storm protection, floodwalls, bulkheads, and new building codes. Bloomberg asserted, "If anyone is up to the task of defending and adapting the city they love, it's New Yorkers."[26]

States are also acting. Oregon and Washington have taken dramatic steps to block America's potential coal-export boom by denying permits that would allow the shipment of coal mined in Wyoming and Montana from their Pacific

Coast ports to Asia. Export plans have been blocked by what Ronald Brownstein calls "America's coal-fired divide." These states champion the EPA's efforts to limit new coal-fired plants nationally while shutting down their own. With California implementing its own cap-and-trade law and requiring zero-emission vehicles, the West Coast is rapidly turning to alternative energy and a greenhouse-gas-free future.[27]

America's progressive cities and states will serve as models for future national action to address climate change, the struggles of working women and families, and jobs that don't pay enough. The actions being taken by city and state leaders will teach the country that it can address the deepest problems holding America back.

Of course many of the changes in the country are just becoming the new orthodoxy and part of our shared national character—they go unchallenged, or if questioned, there is pushback.

Millions were moved by Coca-Cola's Super Bowl commercial featuring seven young women singing "America, the Beautiful" in different languages, because this diversity is something we have integrated into our national identity. When an outspoken few took to Twitter and conservative talk radio to express their discomfort with the ascendant populations, Coca-Cola doubled down and extended their ad buy to the Sochi Winter Olympics, signaling to the world that these angry voices do not speak for America or corporate America.

In spite of the polarized country and U.S. Congress, we have seen impressive coalitions forming to advance the needed reforms at the national level. The U.S. Chamber of Commerce, industry trade associations, and leading high-technology companies joined together with advocacy groups, churches, and unions in support of comprehensive immigration reform, large-scale and long-term investment to renew America's infrastructure, and the adoption of universal pre-K education.

The Catholic Church, too, is challenging the priorities of those who resist reform, denying them any religious standing for their economic values. Pope Francis shook up the agenda when his apostolic exhortation found the "free market" sinful: "Just as the commandment 'Thou shalt not kill' sets a clear limit in order to safeguard the value of human life, today we also have to say 'thou shalt not' to an economy of exclusion and inequality. Such an economy kills." That is a powerful call to action in all areas, but also to politicians.[28]

Democrats will have to make the case for government activism at the national level.

The reader will soon appreciate that America's economic and cultural ascent was made possible by government, though it is hard to unpack that amid the dysfunction and gridlock, brinksmanship, stop-and-go politics, contradictory policies, and lack of long-term thinking. But our shambolic politics has managed to further America's promising economic transformations. It ranged from the Defense Department's financing of new technology to direct government support for universities, science programs, and research and development to pluralistic policy approaches to energy and immigration that basically said "all of the above." Mayors and governors stepped in where the federal government was stymied.

Pluralistic political control set the stage for the revolution taking place in energy. It could not have happened without Congress passing tax credits for investment and exploration for unconventional sources of natural gas, together with the light hand of regulation in pro-oil states. But the energy industry was revolutionized when the federal government negotiated and legislated successive and dramatic increases in the required fuel-efficiency standards for American cars and trucks. The federal government created tax credits and investment funds for alternative energy, and half the states now require a growing proportion of state power generation to come from these new energy sources. It is this uniquely American and seemingly contradictory combination of government actions that proved transformative.

The same is true of immigration. A Great Society–era law reopened America's gates to immigrants, and nearly all of them came from Spanish-speaking and Asian countries. Legal immigration was more than matched by the growing generations of the undocumented, including foreign students and visitors that stayed. Republican president Ronald Reagan signed the law granting amnesty to millions, though a reluctant Congress demanded tougher enforcement at the Mexican border. The increased risk of being sent home led growing millions of undocumented immigrants, ironically, to remain in the United States and to move out of the border areas of the Southwest and settle permanently in cities all across the country. That roughly 40 percent of the megacities and almost 30 percent of California residents are foreign-born are very much products of these contradictory government policies.[29]

America's leadership in new industries and innovative technologies is rooted in a half century of steady investment in R & D, Defense Department spending on basic research and weapons technology, and federal support for great research institutes and universities. The recent gridlock has slowed spending on research and education, but Congress continues to prioritize Defense Department funding, and each year at the midnight deadline, it inevitably extends the R & D tax credits for companies that conduct research in the United States.

So America has managed to advance these transformations through the political pluralism and chaos. But that is surely at its limit.

For the country to take full advantage of these revolutions and the ascendant economic trends, government must do a lot better. It must educate dramatically better and use resources more equitably. It must educate kids at the earliest ages and support parenting. It must help black and white working-class men get off the margins and give support and greater equality for working women and working mothers. It must support unions as they find new ways to speak out on behalf of working people. And for America to address the big contradictions at the heart of its economic progress, including the growing inequality and failure to produce economic gains for most people in the country, government itself needs to become transformative.

Our sense of the possible should be shaped by remembering the economic policies enacted and pursued by President Bill Clinton, when government policy raised wages, moderated inequality, and gave relief to the poor. At the outset of his first term, President Clinton passed an economic plan that reduced America's deficits mainly by cutting defense spending and raising taxes in nearly equal measure. His plan raised the top tax rate from 31 to 36 percent for individuals with income above $150,000 and established a new tax rate of 39.6 percent for incomes over $250,000, and critically, it taxed income from capital gains and work equally. It subjected all income above $135,000 to the Medicare tax of 3.8 percent. It raised the tax rate for corporations from 34 to 35 percent. At the same time, Clinton's plan expanded the earned income tax credit for low-wage workers and indexed it for inflation, and later he expanded health care coverage for poor children. He would embrace the child tax credit that was part of the conservative policy wheelhouse. That combined with full-employment policies and welfare reform in his second term.

President Ronald Reagan and President George W. Bush had a different mix of policies, and their failure is obvious. The rate of income growth in the Clinton economic period was 16.8 percent, double the average for the Republican presidents (8.3 percent). And that is using the calculations of conservative academics that take into account reduced family size, income transfers, food stamps, tax credits, and subsidies for health insurance![30]

The top 5 percent in the country saw a 15.1 percent gain in income in the Clinton period—and importantly, they gained just a touch less than the middle class, who had gained 16.8 percent. But the Clinton policy mix brought gains for the poor and those on the bottom fifth of the income ladder as well. The income of this bottom quintile went up 23.2 percent during the Clinton economic period, but only 0.4 percent under Reagan and 2.2 percent under George W. Bush. The great expansion of the earned income tax credit along with increasing wages allowed the bottom 20 percent to make real gains. In fact, only in the Clinton period did one see an improvement in the Gini coefficient, the standard measure of inequality.[31]

Clearly government policy matters and can make a difference on the issues America must address. We can have fewer people in poverty, can push wages up for the middle class, and can have a more broadly shared prosperity. The challenges in 2016 and beyond are much greater than in 1992, but government policy can still push against the arc of inequality.

Consider the Affordable Care Act, which came into full effect at the outset of 2014. America stood out in the Western world with its 15 percent of the population without health insurance seemingly in perpetuity, a moral outrage that came with such a high human cost in illness and lost peace of mind as well as a high economic price as cost shifting made the whole system unaccountable. But look at the graph below and what happened to the line tracking the percent uninsured in the months since the new health care law came into effect. Look at the bars and the dramatic drop in the numbers of people who face financial stress from dealing with health care costs.[32]

The new health care law is surely imperfect, and it almost fell victim to the ferocious Republican opposition determined to repeal it and limit where it can be fully implemented. The dramatic drop in that graph line and bars tells you why. It says government has the power to effect transformative social and economic changes.

To tackle the huge issues America will require a new politics, and that, too, is possible, as we hope to prove in this book.

The stage is set for contemporary Democratic leaders to play such a role in the face of today's greatest problems, if they take up the challenge.

In 2008, the citizenry elected Barack Obama, who attacked "hyperpartisanship" and promised to "change the culture of Washington." But the country knows this is a different moment. The president's determination to reach

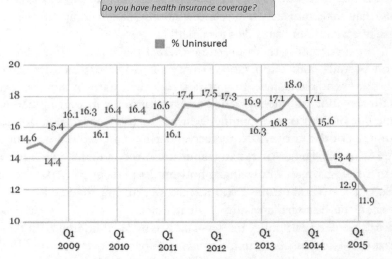

Percent without health insurance in the United States

Do you have health insurance coverage?

■ % Uninsured

Jenna Levy, "In U.S., Uninsured Rate Sinks to 13.4% in Second Quarter," *Gallup*, July 10, 2014.

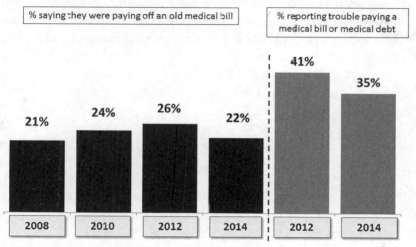

Percent reporting financial hardship from health care costs down since implementation of the Affordable Care Act

% saying they were paying off an old medical bill				% reporting trouble paying a medical bill or medical debt	
21%	24%	26%	22%	41%	35%
2008	2010	2012	2014	2012	2014

Elisabeth Rosenthal, "How the High Cost of Medical Care Is Affecting Americans," *New York Times*, December 18, 2014.

a compromise exposed the recalcitrance of the conservatives and why Democrats have no other option than to win the argument and champion bold reforms to mitigate the inequality and social costs that hold America back. While America has a long way to go and conservative resistance is strong, President Obama will have achieved near-universal health care coverage, substantially lowered carbon emissions, and legalized the "DREAMers," those who came to the United States as minors under age sixteen, so America will be enriched even more by its immigrant diversity.

President Obama himself made a personal turn in his 2015 State of the Union address as the country began to see robust macroeconomic growth. He continued to describe the "state of the union" as very strong and overstate how many lives have been touched by the recovery. Nonetheless, he stopped to signify this time of building imbalances and injustices. At "every moment of economic change throughout our history, this country has taken bold action to adapt to new circumstances," enacting bold reforms. At this moment, he called for the country to turn to "middle-class economics"—the abiding idea "that this country does best when everyone gets their fair shot, everyone does their fair share, and everyone plays by the same set of rules."[33]

He set the stage for the next Democratic president. We do not know whether he or she will act gradually and pragmatically, like the early Teddy Roosevelt, or will take up the full banner of reform, like Teddy Roosevelt under the New Nationalist banner, or will govern as a partisan to vanquish the conservatives and finally enact what the country has longed to see, like Woodrow Wilson did upon taking office.

The public is very conscious of the economic and social transformations that are changing the country. While they identify with the revolutions that are changing America in exceptional ways, they are acutely aware of the contradictions that make life a daily struggle for so many. They are ready to join the struggle to tackle the downside of our progress and join the battle for bold reforms. It is just such an American renewal that will allow America to lead in this twenty-first century.

Part I

AMERICA: THE EXCEPTIONAL NATION

2 AMERICA'S ECONOMIC ASCENDANCY

America's economy is dynamic and on the rise. And it is being renewed as a model for the aspirant here and for America's admirers around the world.

The underlying economy is churning, and the global financial crisis revealed our comparative resiliency among the advanced economies, despite the serious economic toll taken by America's political dysfunction and home-grown austerity policies. Even the smoke over Washington cannot obscure the transformative changes that are under way and already putting America onto a trajectory very different from almost every other country.

America's ascent is being fueled by revolutions in energy, immigration, innovation, big data, and advanced manufacturing, by revolutions in the metropolitan areas and among Millennials, and perhaps even by a revolution in health care. The use of the term "revolution" is not hyperbole. These are each disruptive, accelerating changes that undermine the pessimistic assumptions about America's economic future. They produce an America that is growing economically—one that will soon be energy independent but also more sustainable in the face of climate change. It is an America that is best able to take advantage of game-changing innovations, lower energy costs, big data, and advanced manufacturing technologies to create new industries and attract long-term global investment. They also produce an America that is renewed as an ever more culturally diverse, younger, immigrant, and urban country where the big metropolitan centers create a new and productive dynamism.

None of this will impress the "declinists" and China watchers because they view the country's long-term budget deficits and dependence on Asian creditors as America's core vulnerability. But as America has begun to tame health care costs, the most inefficient and bloated sector of the economy, those deficit projections are falling sharply. They will be revised downward again and again with improved economic performance and the enactment of comprehensive immigration reform, which greatly expands the working and taxpaying population in the United States.

America's current patterns of economic ascent and growth will produce winners that include many more than the top 1 percent. It includes those in the growing number of professional service careers, in STEM fields, and in new cutting-edge industries. It could include postgraduates and many of those with four-year college degrees, particularly women. Many African Americans, Hispanics, and new immigrant groups have a certain faith that a rising America will mean a better future for them. That will be particularly true in diverse, high-growth cosmopolitan areas such as Portland, Washington, D.C., Denver, San Jose, San Francisco, and Seattle, where many residents identify with their dynamic and distinctive cities.

But, as we shall see in the coming chapters, America must do dramatically better to tackle the country's greatest challenges, and that requires the ascendant political forces and leaders to champion a whole new political project. That is possible because those people aligned with the ascendant trends will become ascendant politically, too, and those fighting them will lose out. There will be an opportunity for a new reform politics that takes up this great task.

The starting points, however, are the revolutions that are creating an economically ascendant America.

AMERICA'S ENERGY REVOLUTION

"What's happening with unconventional natural gas," John Deutch declared from his vantage point as deputy defense secretary, undersecretary of energy, and head of the CIA, "is the biggest energy story that's happened in the forty-plus years that I've been watching energy development in this country."[1]

North American gas production from shale jumped 51 percent starting from the breakthrough year of 2007 through 2012. That was so stunning because the whole energy community was poised to address America's declining reserves of natural gas. The flooding of the market produced an unexpected two-thirds drop in price for natural gas, getting everyone's attention and requiring wholly new calculations about home heating, electric utilities, and the new cost advantages of locating manufacturing in the United States. By 2013, shale gas production accounted for 40 percent of total natural gas production, surpassing gas well production for the first time to become the largest source of natural gas in the country.[2]

In addition, U.S. oil reserves rose 80 percent between 2008 and 2014, thanks in part to the oil from shale, sending the country's proven oil reserves to "one of the highest levels ever reported in records that go back to the nineteenth century," according to *The Financial Times*. The per-barrel price of crude oil plummeted from $107 in mid-June to $59.30 in mid-December of 2014; and consumers saw the cost of gas at the pump return to 2010 levels—an average $2.63 a gallon. These developments represent a huge transfer of wealth and gain for the U.S. economy, companies, and consumers.[3]

And when the Organization of the Petroleum Exporting Countries (OPEC) reacted to the collapse in the oil price with a scramble for market share rather than reduced supply, it brought the geopolitical consequences of America's energy revolution home to Vladimir Putin, Iran, and the Chavista leaders in Venezuela—countries that are struggling financially and rely on high oil prices.[4]

During the Great Recession and meager recovery, the United States was increasing oil production by 24 percent and natural gas by 19 percent, leading two economists to sheepishly entitle their presentation "America's Emerging Growth Story." New fuel-efficiency regulations on cars and trucks produced a plummeting demand for oil, and so, too, did the introduction of biofuels and renewables. America is heading toward energy independence and is projected to become a net exporter of natural gas by 2020. At the same time, America's release of greenhouse gases is plummeting. Who knew?[5]

The success of hydraulic fracturing and horizontal drilling techniques drove this most dramatic change. It says something about why innovations get adopted in the United States and how America's swings in partisan control nationally and in the states can sometimes be functional, not destructive.

What drove the search for a breakthrough was the conviction of the pioneering petroleum engineers that oil and gas were trapped in the vast layers of shale across much of the United States and could be captured. Michael Levi describes the geology at the heart of the revolution: "About four hundred million years ago, mud and organic matter settled around bottoms of large water basins covering much of what is today the United States. The thin layers of material from plants and animals, together with silt and mud, added up. Over millions of years, the resulting pressure formed the sedimentary rock known as shale. Trapped in the rock, the organic material turned into chains of carbon and hydrogen atoms—oil and gas—and began to turn the shale black."[6]

There were many failed efforts to access these deposits in the early nineteenth century and after World War II. In the mid-twentieth century, Halliburton obtained an exclusive license on the hydraulic fracturing method, which shoots water, chemicals, and other materials deep underground to break apart rock and release gas. During the 1980s a French firm, Elf Aquitaine, working in southwestern France and off the Italian coast, successfully used a new drilling method, drilling down before making a ninety-degree turn to drill horizontally for a mile or more.[7]

But it took both of these techniques, decades of innovation, and unyielding commitment to develop a commercially viable fracking technique. Starting in the early 1980s, George P. Mitchell, a Greek immigrant and Texas entrepreneur for whom "natural gas was virtually a cause," worked three decades and through many failed attempts to get the huge Barnett shale deposit around the Dallas–Fort Worth area to release its potential. His breakthrough method employed a combination of new 3-D seismic readings, the development of the light-sand fracking (LSF) technique, and horizontal drilling. Most thought Mitchell's efforts had failed until 2001, when observers began to witness a surge of natural gas supply from the Barnett shale. The investors followed.[8]

In 2000, 1 percent of U.S. natural gas came from shale. Then the "shale gale" occurred. By 2011, shale was 25 percent of the national natural gas supply, and within a couple of decades it could be 50 percent.[9]

The shale industry boom is already producing a surge in employment in localities across the country. It employed about 150,000 people in 2010, but by 2020, it will add up to $150 billion to the U.S. economy and employ 250,000.[10]

The employment benefits of these game-changing advances extend to manufacturing, construction, and transportation. McKinsey Global Institute estimates that the increase in manufacturing in industries that rely on natural gas will account for $55 billion to $85 billion of the rise in annual GDP. Petrochemical producers are expanding use of its by-products to produce plastics and petrochemicals; this could add 400,000 jobs. When you include increasing demand in construction, trade and transportation, and professional services, McKinsey estimates the expanded GDP at 2 to 4 percent points and 1.7 million permanent jobs by 2020.[11]

But reaching the full potential of the energy revolution will require winning public support as it disrupts communities across the country. That means new regulations at the state and national levels to protect groundwater supplies and minimize the release of gases that worsen the global-warming problem. Former petroleum engineer and secretary of the interior Sally Jewell insists fracking "can be done safely and responsibly" though it "depends a lot on factors like well bore integrity and if you have a good cement job." Tougher controls are necessary to keep up with the advances in the industry. Many states have already combined continued production with stricter regulation, including Colorado, Pennsylvania, Ohio, North Dakota, and North Carolina. Some eastern states, like New York and Maryland, have imposed moratoriums while assessing the public health risks and potential threat to drinking water supplies and vital habitat and fisheries.[12]

At the national level, the Department of the Interior has proposed new national rules for fracking that will require proper well integrity and water management to prevent groundwater contamination. The American Petroleum Institute has fought against any federal regulations, and Republican congressmen from the traditional oil states have insisted they are unnecessary. Oil industry lawyers have partnered with Republican state attorneys general to sue the Environmental Protection Agency (EPA) and the Bureau of Land Management.

For its part, the public largely trusts these regulators to get these issues right and believe that they, not the U.S. Congress, should set new pollution standards. Huge majorities of the public say cleaner air is a higher priority than reducing regulations on business and support a new EPA rule that would require the oil and gas industry to reduce methane emissions by 50 percent by 2020.[13]

Shale gas's growing supply, falling prices, and lower carbon emissions have disrupted the economics of America's main source of energy, coal. Plans for 166 new coal plants were dropped over the past decade and almost half of the country's 362 coal-fired plants have been retired. Many have been converted to gas. The economics of new nuclear power plants have also been disrupted, and solar and wind are forced to compete at a lower price point.[14]

Why was George Mitchell able to continue his trial-and-error methods to shatter the shale rock and release the gas for three decades without making a profit? As a start, certain oil and mining states, such as Texas, Pennsylvania, Ohio, and North Dakota, were more relaxed about the environmental risks; and the U.S. market for natural gas is fairly open. It could not have happened, however, without Section 29 of the Windfall Profits Tax Act, enacted in 1980, which granted a federal tax production credit for drilling for unconventional natural gas. The U.S. Congress and President Jimmy Carter decided to pick winners and losers in the economy because producing this new energy was in the national interest. The expansion of renewable fuels was only possible because of the nonconventional fuels tax credit and laws passed in 2003 that extended support for unconventional natural gas and alternative fuels.[15]

The other big parts of the energy story that strengthen the future economy also begin with government.

When the Democrats swept to control of the Congress in 2006, the House Democrats passed what would become the Energy Independence and Security Act (EISA) in their first hundred hours. Signed into law by President George W. Bush in 2007, the law raised the fuel-economy standard by 40 percent. Auto companies would be required to reach 35 miles per gallon on average by 2020. It created new incentives and supported research for electric vehicles and batteries, increased efficiency requirements for appliances and lightbulbs, and extended weatherization funding to make residential buildings more energy efficient. The law also expanded the renewable fuels program and the volume of advanced biofuels from nine billion gallons in 2008 to thirty-six billion gallons in 2012. The oil industry fought against these changes, though they successfully protected their own subsidies from the Democrats who sought to demonize them.[16]

After the government bailed out and rebuilt GM and Chrysler, President Obama used his leverage to get a historic agreement with the auto industry that required they meet the 35 mpg fuel-economy target by 2016. In 2011, the agreement was extended to cars and light trucks for the first time, requiring they reach 54.5 miles per gallon on average by 2025. This is a new era for cars, spurring industry innovation on a large scale.[17]

Cars and trucks are responsible for the bulk of U.S. oil consumption, and between 2007 and 2011 that consumption fell 10 percent. The recession played a big part, but that does not account for the entire decline. The fuel economy of American cars rose 15 percent in five years, in part as a response to changing consumer preferences in the face of high gas prices, but even more as a response to a federal government pushing for greater efficiency. Electric cars are also an emerging part of the auto mix. In 2011, one in every twenty-five cars sold was an electric hybrid, up from one in every two hundred in 2004. This dramatic change was produced by a government that moved the goalposts and an auto industry that accepted the new norms and ultimately welcomed the challenge to innovate.[18]

The elites, including myself, would have preferred to obtain these outcomes with a carbon tax or higher gas taxes and allow the market to reduce consumption, but the public was opposed to that approach, preferring regulation, standards, and quotas. In national polls, the public showed even greater support for an energy agenda that required higher auto fuel-efficiency standards, increased investment in solar, wind, and hydrogen technology, and alternative fuel sources for cars.[19]

Well, the voters got their way, with pretty dramatic consequences.

The American Recovery and Reinvestment Act, passed in Obama's first month, included $90 billion in investments and incentives for promoting clean energy in the country. Conservatives understandably jumped on the bankruptcy of Solyndra and Abound Solar leading up to the 2012 elections, but their critique ignores the scale and sustainability of the new industry these government funds make possible. The dramatic drop in natural-gas prices has made the economic equation more difficult for renewables, but the cost of solar panels has been falling, too. The turning-point year was 2014. The cost of producing electricity from wind and solar had dropped so much by that point that it cost less than power generation from coal or natural gas in some parts of the country. The federal and state governments continue to offer a mix of tax credits and grants for wind-farm developers and for deploying solar panels, despite resistance by Republicans in Congress. More than half of the states have passed mandatory renewable portfolio or electricity standards (RPSs or RESs), and eight have passed voluntary ones. Oregon will require that 25 percent of the state's power come from renewable sources by 2025, but New York has gone further, requiring 29 percent by 2015.[20]

California has led the way, not surprisingly. More than a decade ago, it established a 20 percent statewide renewable standard for retail sales, a goal the state met. It has moved the standard to 33 percent by 2020. Perhaps most importantly, Governor Jerry Brown issued an executive order to accelerate the viability of zero-emission large cars and light-duty trucks. The governor required that automakers sell 1.5 million zero-emission cars to consumers by 2025 and that state departments raise their zero-emission vehicle purchases to 25 percent by 2020. This order was challenged by the auto companies and the oil industry, but the state standards were upheld.[21]

As a result, California is home to 26 of the 122 companies in the Bloomberg

Americas Clean Technology Index, and California-based clean technology companies forecast greater returns because of their commitment to R & D.[22]

Renewable energy is also an appreciable part of the energy mix now, and only because the government said it should be. Leading into the elections of 2006 and 2008, Democracy Corps polls repeatedly showed voters wanting to vote for a member of Congress who "says the best way to renew our economy in the long run is to make a real investment in a new American renewable energy industry so we can create millions of good jobs that can never be outsourced while lowering the cost of energy for American families and businesses alike."[23]

As we can see, the voters' priorities produced real results.

The same is true for coal—the source of energy that the public is most doubtful about. The Obama administration's Environmental Protection Agency is requiring new and existing coal-fired plants to meet stringent requirements on greenhouse gas emission. This will likely raise the costs of electricity from coal-fired plants, though projected natural gas prices are a bigger factor when it comes to marginalizing coal in America's energy mix. "As we look out over the next two decades," the president of Duke Energy observed, "we do not plan to build another coal plant" because shale gas "is proving to be the real deal." The proposed regulations were nearly unimportant.[24]

Conservative opponents say the government is waging "a war on coal," and Republican Senate leader Mitch McConnell vowed "to go to war with [the president] over coal." His U.S. Senate office worked arm in arm with the largest coal companies to rally Republican state leaders to refuse to submit any plan to cut coal-fired power plant emissions, as required by the EPA. But the politics has already turned against coal and in favor of sustainability, which is an ascendant value in the corporate world and among the new generations. It is hard to imagine government not continuing to evolve the rules in the ways that the needed revolution on climate change requires.[25]

What has happened with natural gas, auto efficiency, and renewable energy has dramatically changed America's energy position, reducing its dependence on Middle East oil and its exposure to political and economic shocks. A few years ago, half of American oil was imported, but that figure has fallen to 37 percent and is projected to fall to 25 percent in 2016. The United States will be effectively energy independent in the next couple of years, with growing pressure for it to become an energy exporter. The reduced trade deficit alone will add to the growth of the U.S. economy, reinforced by the inward investment from companies now viewing America as one of the most competitive places for manufacturing. It has also produced, according to Michael Levi, a 37 percent reduction in emissions from carbon dioxide. We hardly know all of the ways this will prove beneficial to the country.[26]

This energy revolution was deeply affected by political decisions, and they will continue to shape our energy future. When it comes to energy, we are a country that picks winners and losers. It is easy to imagine that this debate between old and new energy could have resulted in the usual political dysfunction, but instead we have ended up with an "all of the above" approach, except for coal. How did we get there? Part of it is America's greater trust of private enterprise and entrepreneurs, romance with drilling and hitting the big well, and identification with technology and support for innovation. But the revolution only happened because different kinds of politics dominated different states and the nation at different times.

Republican pro-oil and pro-mining states from Texas and Louisiana to West Virginia and North Dakota are more willing to risk environmental damage and use a light regulatory hand. They fought to keep oil industry tax breaks and subsidies. Even after 300,000 West Virginia residents lost drinkable water because chemicals used to clean coal leaked from old and unregulated storage tanks into the Elk River, U.S. senator Joe Manchin, from West Virginia, observed, "Coal and chemicals inevitably bring risk—but that doesn't mean they should be shut down. Cicero says, 'To err is human.' But you're going to stop living because you're afraid of making a mistake?"[27]

But other states acted to shape our energy choices through regulation. California led with a regulation that requires better fuel efficiency for automobiles and demands the production and purchase of zero-emission vehicles. More than half of our states require that state utilities draw a growing percentage of their energy from renewable energy sources. These states use government to encourage clean energy development and to help create markets for clean vehicles and other technologies.

At the national level, the U.S. government moved urgently to find domestic courses to decrease dependency on foreign oil when faced with the rise of OPEC and oil price shocks. The federal government provided tax credits that made possible the two-decade-long pursuit of natural gas trapped in shale. The Democratic takeover of Congress in 2006 and the election of President Obama produced dramatically higher fuel-efficiency standards, expanded the renewable fuel standard, and supported renewable sources of energy.

That pluralism of political control and culture combined to produce our energy revolution. It will be hard to replicate. We are lucky that increased natural gas use also happens to be lowering carbon emissions.

AMERICA'S IMMIGRATION REVOLUTION

Immigration is the second most important reason America will be ascendant and the doomsayers proved wrong. Immigration is central to our character and identity, as we shall see in the next chapter, but it is also a key to America's economic vitality, competitiveness, and growth.

Since 1990 the world has watched a massive increase in global migration; the number of migrants rose from 154 million to 232 million in 2013.

Amazingly, one in five of these migrants lives in the United States. The number of immigrants in the United States doubled from 23 million to 46 million, and America is the number one destination for migrants from a quarter of the world. No other country has anywhere near that number of foreign-born people making a life inside its borders.[28]

America's largest metropolitan areas and cities are being shaped by this accelerating wave of immigration. More than three million, roughly 37 percent, of New York City residents were born outside of the United States, and more than one-third of those residents have arrived since 2000. The foreign-born make up nearly 40 percent of the residents in Los Angeles and more than a third in San Francisco. They count for almost 60 percent of Miami's residents and almost 30 percent of Houston's.[29]

Look at New York City. It tells the story of generations of young immigrants, many uneducated and on their own, who came here and worked in restaurants or hotels, received a green card, and moved many family members here on family-related visas; some won asylum. The city is now home to 350,200 Chinese, just behind the city's largest immigrant group, the 380,000-person-strong Dominican population. But it is the Mexican population that has surged the most in the past decade, rising by 52 percent, to 186,000 people, moving them to third ahead of the Guyanese and Jamaicans. Rounding out the top ten are immigrants born in Ecuador, Haiti, Trinidad and Tobago, India, and Russia. Queens is nearly half foreign-born, and 37 percent, just under 1 million, of Brooklyn's residents are, too.[30]

The suburbs are also being reshaped by immigration, as many migrants skip the normal path of starting in the inner city. The Washington, D.C., suburbs of Fairfax and Arlington are one-quarter foreign-born. And then look at Gwinnett County, outside of Atlanta. In 1990, it was 90 percent white and home to only 8,470 Hispanics and 18,000 blacks, legacies of the area's cotton-growing past. That was before the county was reshaped by massive construction of suburban subdivisions and shopping centers. The Hispanic population started to grow thanks to the economic boom and construction associated with the 1994 Olympic Games, and African Americans began gravitating to the suburbs, too. Then the world descended on Gwinnett, attracting immigrants from India, Vietnam, Korea, sub-Saharan Africa, and post-Soviet East European countries. By 2010, Gwinnett was home to 456,167 more residents, and the white Anglo residents fell to 49.43 percent of the population.[31]

The new immigrants joined the growing diversity found in America's metropolitan centers. Our cities are increasingly shaped by this conglomeration of African Americans, Hispanics, Chinese, Indians, Asians, and other immigrants, documented or not.

While the national political debate is consumed with the undocumented and growing Hispanic minority, the economy is being reengineered by immigration. As we shall see, their addition to service and high-skill sectors is the most vibrant part of the economy. The Silicon Valley start-up world is a great mix of Indian, Chinese, British, Japanese, Canadian, Russian, German, French, and Israeli immigrants. Half of Silicon Valley's engineers are foreign-born, and by one estimate 44 percent of the valley's high-tech start-ups were founded by someone born abroad. Almost one-quarter of all new engineering and tech companies founded in this country between 2006 and 2012 had at least one owner born abroad. During that period, immigrant-founded companies in the United States produced $63 billion in sales and employed 560,000 people.[32]

If one is looking for a measure of where the future lies, consider that our universities have given more than 200,000 PhDs to foreign students over the past two decades, and 70 percent of those students remained in the United States after graduation, including 92 percent of the Chinese graduates and 81 percent of the Indian graduates. Even in the absence of immigration reform, all players seem to be conspiring to ensure America has a large and growing infusion of the world's most educated, which has implications for America's future growth. By the way, one-quarter of American recipients of the Nobel Prize were immigrants.[33]

As a consequence of immigration and even more so the higher birthrate of the new immigrant populations, America has a large young population and is getting older at a much slower pace than Europe, Japan, and China. Younger populations participate more fully in the economy and pay taxes, while aging ones work less and demand more from government social, health care, and pension programs. The great reluctance to entertain foreign immigration has contributed to the stagnation, lack of innovation, and slower growth in Japan.[34]

Western Europe is coping with very modest economic growth, declining birthrates, and constrained immigration that is putting their welfare states at risk. Germany has allowed increased migration in recent years, but the birth deficit is growing rapidly. In 2008 seniors made up 20 percent of the German population, though it will rise to 34 percent by 2060. In France, seniors will make up 30.6 percent of the population in 2035.[35]

The Chinese government is hardly generous with its pensioners, but the growing "specter of elderly pensioners" could threaten the Communist regime's bargain with the public. In 2011 it had three workers for every pensioner—and that ratio will shift to two to one in 2015 and in thirty years every worker will be supporting two pensioners. By 2025, China will be home to nearly one-fourth of the world's seniors.[36]

At the same time, the United States' over-sixty-five population is also growing, but at a much slower pace. Seniors made up 13.4 percent of the U.S. population in 2012 and will count for 19.3 percent in 2030 with the full retirement of the baby boomers, and reach only 20.2 percent by 2050. Between 2030 and 2050 that proportion will remain practically unchanged because of the generations of younger immigrants in this country. China and Europe face great challenges as the number of seniors dependent on government approaches the number of those working, but because of immigration, America's social contract is much more sustainable.[37]

Growing American immigration builds on an immigrant tradition and is strengthening the U.S. economy and global position. The most highly skilled and educated students, professionals, and entrepreneurs are flocking to the country from all over the world along with those driven individuals trying to make a better life. They come here legally and illegally and contribute to our economy as consumers, employees, and employers.

The United States will some year soon enact a transformative law that formalizes and builds on the vast changes immigration is bringing. All of civil society has joined in to support the change, including the National Council of La Raza, the U.S. Chamber of Commerce, the AFL-CIO and SEIU, the American Farm Bureau, numerous faith groups, and Mark Zuckerberg and his high-tech coalition. It will not happen while the Republican Party, dominated by the anti-immigrant and anti-immigration Evangelical and Tea Party base, controls Congress. It is a near certainty though that the next president will mobilize after taking office to pass comprehensive reform, and the new president will have the strong support of an exasperated business community and perhaps the Republican establishment, too.

The U.S. Senate first passed in 2013 the Border Security, Economic Opportunity, and Immigration Modernization Act by a 68 to 32 vote, a bipartisan majority. If enacted, the legislation would transform America's immigration system. CBO estimates it would expand the population by 10 million people in ten years and 16 million by 2033. It would allow the roughly 11.7 million undocumented residents to gain legal status and place them onto a path to citizenship after ten years. The "DREAMers" would obtain citizenship on an accelerated basis. It would remove country-specific visa caps, a legacy of a more racist past, which limited applications from countries such as China and India. It would remove limits on family-based visas for spouses and minor children, immediately clearing up the backlog of family visas and impacting future immigration. The Senate bill would create new guest-worker visas for low-skilled workers in industries such as construction and hospitality. Additionally, agricultural workers that meet certain requirements could be eligible for registered provisional immigrant status within five years.[38]

Green card limits would be lifted for the highly skilled and exceptionally talented, including researchers, professors, artists, executives, athletes, and those graduates with advanced degrees in science, technology, engineering, and mathematics (STEM) from U.S. universities. The bill would introduce a point-based merit visa system that takes into account skills, employment history, and educational credentials to grant visas to between 150,000 and 250,000 immigrants a year, depending on the numbers of applicants and the U.S. unemployment rate. The H-1B visa program would be reformed, the cap for high-skilled workers substantially raised, and the exemptions for advanced STEM degrees increased. Finally, a start-up visa would become available to entrepreneurs abroad that wish to start a company in the United States.[39]

What would these changes mean for the U.S. economy? A lot, according to the authoritative estimate of the nonpartisan Congressional Budget Office. By expanding the U.S. population by 4 percent, granting legal status to the undocumented, and increasing the number of skilled and unskilled workers, this overhaul would also increase America's real GDP by 3.3 percent by 2023 and 5.4 percent by 2033.[40]

Immigration has been a flash point because of the presumption that new immigrants compete with citizens for employment and public services and impact wages. The CBO studied these questions and concluded that the downside risks were minimal. Compared to projections under current law, the bill would cause the unemployment rate to go up just 0.1 percent between now and 2020, and there would be no effect after that. Overall, the effect on wages is truly minimal. On average, wages would be lower by 0.1 percent until 2023 and then higher by 0.5 percent per person by 2033. The big winner would be the formerly undocumented workers, whose pay would increase by 12 percent.[41]

Moreover, rather than reducing the resources of the government, the newly legal immigrants would participate in the labor force at a higher rate and pay more taxes. According to the CBO, the new tax revenue would offset the extra costs for border protection required by the law in the first decade and in the next, reducing the deficit by $300 billion.[42]

The immigration revolution today, like the one that shaped America from the outset, will renew, grow, and strengthen the U.S. economy and society in more ways than we can imagine.

THE INNOVATION REVOLUTION

Countries that commit to promoting learning and education, science, and basic research will be home to tomorrow's leading industries. That will include the countries that commit an ever larger portion of their military budget to supporting technology and advanced engineering, the countries that encourage people to think creatively and seek innovative solutions, and those that are open enough to welcome new professions and new industries.

Those commitments are the reason why America came to lead in high-tech, aerospace, and the creative industries. And that is why America continues to lead the world in investments in human capital and R & D and why it is home to great research universities that promote the most advanced research. In a globally competitive age where human capital and the knowledge economy are ascendant, who do you think is leading the advancement of big data?

Consider where America starts: it has increased its R & D spending by

5 percent a year in real terms for sixty years. That has slowed for the past few years because of the economic crash and Republican efforts to cut federal research spending and support for state universities; nonetheless, it reached $465 billion in 2014. And while the European Union countries and China have upped their research game significantly, only by combining all of their efforts do you get ahead of the United States.[43]

U.S. spending on public education as a percent of our total economy has risen steadily to 7 percent—that is more than double the share of GDP spent in China or India. On a per capita basis, the United States is just behind Luxembourg, Switzerland, and Norway among the OECD countries.[44]

To be sure, America must raise its investment in public education and teachers and rally around bold reforms that demonstrably raise skill levels, allocate education resources more equitably, and narrow the gap between the privileged and the poorest. I take seriously the comparisons of U.S. students on key tests with students in South Korea, Finland, and Shanghai. There is no way to address some of America's biggest contradictions unless it addresses education in a very different way, which I discuss in chapter 12.

But we should also remember the "Johnny can't read" campaigns of the 1950s, which hardly portended a period of American decline. America never performed well on international tests in the 1960s, 1970s, and 1980s, Fareed Zakaria wrote in *In Defense of a Liberal Education*, yet somehow America ended up producing college graduates who furthered America's competitiveness.

America is home to virtually all of the top research universities at the center of the knowledge economy that promote the research advances and innovations at the heart of our growing metropolitan centers and that fuel the global migration of talent to the United States. In one respected rating of global universities, only Cambridge and Oxford make it in the top ten, followed by the Swiss Federal Institute of Technology in Zurich and the University College of London, in the nineteenth and twentieth positions, respectively. All the rest of the top twenty are in America.[45]

America's strength lies in its top universities serving as advanced research institutions, not as institutions educating a large number of graduates who excel in their learning. If you look at all Americans with only bachelor's degrees, they score below average on international tests. America's top universities are very clear in their central purpose, and on that they are unchallenged.[46]

American academics dominate as authors of the top-cited articles in science and engineering, as holders of patents registered in the United States, the European Union, and Japan, and as holders of patents in biotechnology. Collectively the West owns 85 percent of triadic patents, while China barely owns 1 percent.[47]

America's research universities are part of "a triangular relationship among government, industry, and academia," characterized by Walter Isaacson as "one of the significant innovations that helped produce the technological

Stanley B. Greenberg

Academic ranking of world universities, 2014

1. Harvard University
2. Stanford University
3. Massachusetts Institute of Technology (MIT)
4. University of California, Berkeley
5. University of Cambridge
6. Princeton University
7. California Institute of Technology
8. Columbia University
9. University of Chicago
9. University of Oxford
11. Yale University
12. University of California, Los Angeles
13. Cornell University
14. University of California, San Diego
15. University of Washington
16. University of Pennsylvania
17. The Johns Hopkins University
18. University of California, San Francisco
19. Swiss Federal Institute of Technology, Zurich
20. University College, London

"Academic Ranking of World Universities," Institute of Higher Education, *Shanghai Jiao Tong University*, 2013.

revolution of the late twentieth century." The U.S. military has played a larger-than-life role in promoting basic science and technology, just as war drove the Greeks to invent the catapult and Cesare Borgia to exploit the inventions of Leonardo da Vinci, his military engineer. America's military, for its part, led the advance of computers, atomic power, radar, and the Internet.[48]

With the Second World War looming in Europe, the U.S. Army promoted electrical engineering at universities and supported the development of machines that could advance computational power to make artillery more accurate, break enemy codes, and calculate the force of nuclear fission. The best scientists were recruited for the Manhattan Project, which developed the atomic bomb, and for AT&T's research facility, Bell Labs, which took on a huge number of projects for the military.

The Defense Department, the National Science Foundation, and the National Aeronautics and Space Administration (NASA) funded the surge in basic research through the 1980s that centered on Harvard, MIT, Princeton, and Stanford. With defense contractors setting up to meet the Soviet challenge in space and Stanford University's dean of engineering setting up a new industrial park, Silicon Valley became ground zero for the new companies of the computer and Internet age.[49]

The commitment to R & D, education, and university research is already shaping the emerging successful and globally competitive sectors in the U.S. economy.

America's high-tech sector is vibrant and continuously evolving, and will undoubtedly produce disruptive new technologies and new ways of organizing our lives. The Silicon Valley model remains hard to replicate as it grows in importance. The proximate universities and incubator labs continue to attract great scientific talent and research funds. There is even more start-up money and would-be entrepreneurs reinvesting there, combined with patience and disdain for short-term thinking. The ethos is open, transparent, experimental, mobile, and accessible, without many class barriers; indeed, it is irreverent and bohemian. While some of the biggest global companies are based in the vicinity, there is a conviction that one can produce groundbreaking, enriching change. That spirit is refreshed by the international character of today's Silicon Valley.[50]

Some of the biggest gains in productivity and business competitiveness in the future will come from big data and advanced analytics. We are just beginning to see the scope of what is being created in economic transactions, product design, medical records, legal research, government services, and social media. Who do we think is in the best position to take advantage of those changes? According to McKinsey Global Institute, "the United States owns a disproportionate share of the world's data assets . . . and its companies, entrepreneurs, and universities are leading the development of this technology." The United States has one-third of the world's data, and new analytics could drive up productivity in retail, health care, and government—industries which have not shared the productivity gains experienced by other sectors.[51]

Big data is the future, though who would have thought that an old manufacturing sector, the U.S. auto industry, would emerge profitable, competitive globally, and innovative? Headlines in business journals tell the story: "New Chapter for Detroit Auto Makers"; "Detroit's Plan: Export Cars, Import Chinese Investment." A revived U.S. industry is now back to prerecession levels of production, and amazingly, plants are pushing to 100 percent of capacity to meet projected sales of seventeen million vehicles a year by 2016.[52]

The American auto industry is part of America's innovative future because the government rescued, restructured, and renewed the industry. It forced successive and sometimes dramatic increases in fuel efficiency, including recently requiring the shift to zero-emission vehicles. The higher standards moved the industry to innovate and to produce much more efficient cars that are able to compete in the United States and globally. With lower energy costs and "competitive wages," the auto industry has joined other U.S. manufacturers that are on the move.

With manufacturing employment barely increasing, manufacturing is increasing its contribution to the economy and American exports are up. America is becoming one of the cheapest and most productive places for manufacturing in the developed world, with costs 8 to 18 percent less than in Japan, Germany, France, Italy, and Great Britain by 2015. The starting point, cited by the heads of car and petrochemical companies alike, is the very real decline in energy costs. Industrial electricity prices in Europe, according to a European Commission report, are twice those in the United States.[53]

These shifts have come with a high price tag for the workers in the auto industry and manufacturing, a price that will have to be addressed if America's economic gains are to be sustained. The scale of manufacturing employment will never get back to earlier levels, and the shift of manufacturing to the southern states, where the political and business classes are hostile to labor unions, has accelerated the downward trend in wages. Production wages rose less than 4 percent between 2005 and 2010.[54]

Labor costs are now inviting more onshoring and expansion in the United States. Thanks to heavy capital investment, computerization, and robotics, the United States has seen continued productivity gains, which means that labor makes up a smaller and smaller share of production costs. Plus, America's relatively open immigration policies and research universities often allow access to what may be the right mix of skills needed to drive innovation and fill both skilled and production positions.[55]

"The markets generally seem to be doing quite well in the United States, raw materials are plentiful, energy is cheap, skills are great," one prominent British industrialist notes. A few years ago, "people were shutting things down" in America "because it wasn't competitive. Now it's become immensely competitive." Large manufacturing companies such as General Electric, Caterpillar, John Deere, Siemens, United Technologies, and Mitsubishi must agree, because they have all announced plans to expand manufacturing operations in the United States.[56]

Sustained military spending on R & D and advanced aerospace engineering along with low energy and manufacturing costs will assure that the American aerospace industry will be ascendant and the dominant exporter, even if it shares the global market with Airbus and Chinese and Brazilian companies. While defense spending is trending downward, the United States will significantly outspend the rest of the world. The United States spent $582.4 billion on the military in 2014—roughly the amount of the next twelve largest foreign military budgets combined, or 44 percent of what the whole world is spending—and will spend $585 billion in 2015. American defense companies are ramping up to respond to increased military spending in the Middle East and Asia.[57]

That will drive American innovation through R & D and adoption of technology. Chicago-based Boeing has restructured and taken advantage of all these trends to expand its domestic production of the 787 Dreamliner in North Charleston, South Carolina, and Everett, Washington; the Next Generation 737 in Renton, Washington; and its operations across the board in Southern California.[58]

Former chief of the Federal Reserve Paul Volcker doubted all the innovation and technology in the banking sector produced anything of value for the U.S. economy or significantly improved productivity in markets. He famously said that the only financial innovation he could think of that has improved society is the ATM, and he is particularly down on new products such as credit-default swaps and collateralized debt obligations. The jury is out on whether America's more regulated and concentrated financial sector makes America's economy stronger and less prone to crisis.

The jury has already reported, however, on whether this New York City–centered industry is still leading globally.

The United States undoubtedly has the deepest and most sophisticated capital markets in the world. Foreign capital still pours into the United States at higher levels than anywhere else because America remains the safest place to invest. American banks are better capitalized and have less exposure to risky assets than their foreign counterparts. Though the postcrisis recovery in the United States has been lackluster, the United States had a measurably better and more stable recovery than Japan and continental Europe, which have less developed and less indispensable capital markets.

Hollywood and New York are home to the entertainment, theater, movie, television, and recording industries, and these too are key to imagining the future. The entertainment industry added $500 billion to the U.S. economy in 2012 and accounts for nearly 30 percent of the $2 trillion in global entrainment revenue. Led by Hollywood movies, video services, advertising, and cable TV production, the industry is larger than even the U.S. tourism industry. The entertainment industry employs 1.9 million people, and 310,000 of these employees work in Hollywood and the video industry alone—and the industry is growing 3.4 percent a year. The United States will continue to dominate the global entertainment market thanks to new streaming services such as Netflix and Hulu, which will create more than $17 billion by 2017.[59]

American movies took in $25 billion of the $36 billion in worldwide box-office ticket sales outside the United States in 2013. That lead is being slowly eroded. Over a decade, English-language films' share of the market fell 10 points, to 63 percent, and U.S.-based film producers' share dropped 6 points, to 47 percent. Yet despite a flood of action films from Hong Kong and pressure from the Chinese government to screen them, U.S. films are shown on about 40 percent of China's screens, and films such as *Interstellar* still make a strong run there.[60]

Hollywood's global position remains impressive, and the entertainment industry is a major U.S. exporter. U.S. trade negotiators, as a result, now seem more intent on protecting intellectual property than on opening up markets for U.S. manufacturers. That is fairly revealing about how America's national political leaders view the innovative entertainment industry and its role in America's economic future.[61]

THE METROPOLITAN AND MILLENNIAL REVOLUTIONS[62]

"A metropolitan revolution is stirring," Bruce Katz and Jennifer Bradley write, because America's cities and metropolitan areas are now "the engines of economic prosperity and social transformation." That aligns with studies by the McKinsey Global Institute which focus on the cities, not nations or states, as the real global building blocks because of "their economic size, population density, political dominance and innovative edge." And what is transformative and exceptional is the return to urbanism; the clustering of innovative firms, universities, and research institutions; and the influx of immigrants, the younger generations, and the best-educated, producing a rich racial and ethnic tableau. The radical changes in the family, lifestyle, and culture feed on each other to promote innovation, attract the most ambitious and talented, and drive up America's economic growth. The metropolitan revolution is host to dynamics that enhance America's economic prospects and allow America's multiculturalism to strengthen the country.[63]

The metropolitan revolution is working in part because mayors are working—indeed, they seem almost empowered by the example of national political dysfunction on display in Washington.

America's growing concentration in cities makes them increasingly "the center of gravity" of the economy and a major factor in America's leading the world in per capita GDP. A striking 80 percent of Americans live in large cities, compared to 60 percent in Europe; 85 percent of our country's GDP is produced in large cities, compared to 65 percent in Western Europe. McKinsey Global Institute estimates that three-quarters of America's lead over Western Europe is explained by the growing role of its large cities.[64]

The United States' two global megacities, New York and Los Angeles, will remain among the top cities in the world by the size of their economies. Chicago, the third-largest American city by population, is first in the country and second in the world in direct foreign investment and will also compete globally.[65]

But what really sets America apart, according to McKinsey, is what they call the "middleweight cities"—metropolitan areas with populations over 150,000, excluding the megacities. America has 257 of these smaller, more dynamic cities, and they account for 70 percent of its economy. Compare this to the 180 middleweight cities in Europe that generate a little over 50 percent of Europe's GDP. The middleweight cities with rising incomes and populations over the past decades include cities such as San Jose, Boston, Portland, Raleigh, Austin, Phoenix, Pittsburgh, Philadelphia, Minneapolis, Miami, Orlando, and Charlotte.[66]

A rich combination of ingredients is transforming these cities and raising their economic importance—clusters of high-tech companies and defense contractors, advanced research institutions and prominent universities, growing immigrant communities and Millennials looking for a higher quality of life, and new urbanism. The high-tech industries in Silicon Valley and Palo Alto and at Stanford and Berkeley, great research universities that attract global talent, along with magnificent environs, make San Jose and the San Francisco Bay Area centers of growth. Advanced manufacturing at Boeing, high-tech giants such as Microsoft and Amazon, the University of Washington campus, and the high quality of life around Puget Sound combine to make Seattle one of the fastest-growing cities. The concentrated Asian communities in San Francisco and Seattle have contributed to their integration into global trade.

The Washington, D.C., metropolitan area is one of the richest in the country. It is home to the federal government, prominent research institutions such as the National Institutes of Health, numerous universities, large defense and telecommunications companies, NGOs and nonprofits, and the professional services associated with politics and governing. Though who knew that Washington would top *Forbes*'s list of America's coolest cities in 2014? It got to the top because of its museums and high culture, and also because of the concentration of bars and local nonchain restaurants and farmers' markets. The city is racially and ethnically diverse and so connected that there is a good chance a resident will meet someone of a different race. Millennials are 30 percent of metropolitan areas' population and there is a growing influx of educated, younger, and innovative workers, according to *Forbes*.[67]

Research universities along with many of the 4,500 American colleges and junior colleges find ways to partner and create clusters of innovation in places such as the Research Triangle Park near Raleigh and Durham, or the Cambridge University Park around MIT, or in Austin, Texas.[68]

Some cities, such as Dallas, Atlanta, and Salt Lake City, have made the most of their affordability; others, such as Portland, Oregon, have stressed their quality of life; in Denver and Boulder, their high quality of life combined with their major research universities and diversity.

And while Seattle demolished Denver, 43–8, in Super Bowl XLVIII, *The Wall Street Journal* posed a more important challenge: Which city is more attractive to people looking for a job? According to the job search Web site Simply Hired, the unemployment rate is comparably low in both cities and job seekers in New York, Chicago, and Los Angeles give them comparable attention. Seattle struggles more because it experiences only 71 sunny days a year, compared to Denver, where the sun shines for 115 days. Despite that handicap, Simply Hired gives the edge to Seattle because the average salary is $65,000, though those job seekers are probably looking over their shoulder at the $239,000 average price for a home in the Denver area.[69]

Miami has become a magnet for new immigrants from Colombia and Honduras in Central America, from Peru in South America, and from the Dominican Republic and Haiti in the Caribbean. Anglos are now just 15 percent of the population. Miami is also being shaped by the most affluent families from Venezuela, Brazil, and Argentina who are buying up properties for their holidays and shopping trips. Miami has become the corporate home for Latin American companies, and it is home to Miami International Airport, the largest airline hub for Latin American flights to the United States. The cranes of the building boom dominate the skyline, with the old, declining city a fading memory. The city elite was once dominated by the Cuban upper classes who came in traumatic waves after the Cuban Revolution, but the younger generations of leaders are more ethnically diverse and focused on America and Miami.[70]

When Brazil hosted the World Cup in the summer of 2014, Miami hosted the Colombian, Brazilian, and Argentinian car caravans blasting samba music, with fans rooting in their national soccer jerseys. However, "it was less a commentary on soccer," Lizette Alvarez wrote in *The New York Times,* "than a tableau vivant of the new Miami," one that "is increasingly turbocharged by a surge of well-educated, well-off South Americans in the last decade."[71]

So the dynamism and growth of the inner cities is challenging the traditional path to the American Dream, including America's unique attachment to the suburbs, homeownership, and owning a car. Each wave of new Americans over the past century made their way from the inner cities to seek opportunity elsewhere in the country. After World War II, the new middle class bought homes and cars and moved out to Levittown-like suburban developments, followed by the strip malls along the crowded four-lane highways and then by big enclosed malls, and followed inexorably by the move to the exurbs at the outer limits of the metropolitan areas. With the delayed breakdown of racial barriers, African Americans in the past decade have been moving in large numbers to the suburbs of Washington, Atlanta, and Chicago. Apparently they did not get the memo. Most other Americans have dramatically reversed course during the past decade and started moving back into the cities seeking an urban environment. The Millennial generation has abruptly changed where and how they want to live, and employers are following them. In recent years, companies have created more jobs in the city center than in the suburbs.[72]

The deindustrialization and stunning drops in crime rates in the cities a few decades ago contributed to what Alan Ehrenhalt calls "the great inversion," and what Leigh Gallagher describes as "a powerful tectonic shift." America's cities are increasingly the center for a mobile, broad, and growing population of people working in services, small businesses, technical and professional occupations, the most highly skilled, and the entrepreneurs—who are passing over the suburbs and opting for inner cities. As a result, public transport and walkable communities are increasingly important. Companies are finding that their employees want to live in urban areas and close to work. Now, two hundred of the Fortune 500 companies are head-quartered in the fifty largest American cities.[73]

For every decade since the advent of the automobile, building in the suburbs exceeded construction in the inner cities. In 2011, that was reversed. People are not buying single-family homes in the suburbs, but rather looking for more density, smaller homes, rentals in multifamily buildings, and proximity to public transportation. So when the housing bubble burst in 2007, housing prices and values crashed in the suburbs, though not in the cities. In the aftermath, poverty increased in the suburbs at twice the rate of the cities. This is not the America we once knew.[74]

The revolution in the cities is also a revolution in the family. Driving the inversion more than anything else are the profound changes taking place in marriage, child-rearing, and women.

Household size is declining. There are fewer children, young people are delaying marriage, and fewer people are getting married, period. Indeed, barely half of American adults are married, and among those under thirty years of age that drops to a mere 20 percent. In 1960, 60 percent of that age group was married. The scale of the changes at home becomes even more real when you consider that in some cities, 40 percent of the households include only a single person. Within a decade, single-person households will equal the number of households made up of families.[75]

The Millennials are in the vanguard of all these transformative changes. Born between 1981 and 1997, their numbers reached 75 million in 2015, now equal in size to the baby boomers. And the Millennials have chosen their own unique path. To start, they have opted out of the traditional American suburban lifestyle. More than three-quarters of Millennials want to live in an urban area, and a majority eschew interest even in a car. In 1980, two-thirds of seventeen-year-olds had a driver's license, but that has dropped now to less than half. People are acting on these views and moving to be in greater proximity to retail shops, restaurants, street life, and public transportation. Of those living within a mile of work, 40 percent walked or biked there. Who would have thought that divvy bikes would be one of Mayor Rahm Emanuel's big accomplishments in Chicago or Mayor Michael Bloomberg's in New York City?[76]

The Millennials armed with four-year-college or postgraduate degrees are highly mobile and moving in stunning numbers across state lines and into cities. Two-thirds of college-educated Millennials already live in the fifty-one largest cities and are moving into the close-in neighborhoods.[77]

You get a sense of the change when you read Mark Oppenheimer's fascinating *New York Times Magazine* account of our urban public spaces. In it he describes the differences between videos shot in 1975 by famed sociologist William H. Whyte and videos shot three decades later for Rutgers professor Keith Hampton. Both captured the same four public spaces: Bryant Park behind New York's main public library, the steps of the Metropolitan Museum of Art on Fifth Avenue, Chestnut Street in Philadelphia, and Downtown Crossing in Boston. Professor Hampton reports there are more people using the spaces as meeting places, and above all, more women in these public spaces. The number of women increased by 33 percent on the Met stairs and by 18 percent in Bryant Park. Public spaces are coming to reflect the changing demographics and culture of America's cities.[78]

These videos give you a visual sense of the change in public spaces, but that space is part of an appetite for urbanism, the change in families and immigration, and the clustering of institutions, assets, and talent that are changing our way of life but also making America more economically vibrant.

THE HEALTH CARE REVOLUTION AND THE DEFICIT

The national debt and the federal deficit are at the heart of the declinist judgment about America's bleak future—what allows China to hold the United States on a tight leash. A big swath of the political class—from Alan Simpson and Erskine Bowles to the editorial writers of *The Washington Post* and *The Wall Street Journal* to presidential hopefuls Ted Cruz and Marco Rubio and former House Budget Committee chair Paul Ryan—says the biggest problem facing the country is the growing deficit, driven above all by unsustainable entitlement spending. Today "we face the threat of a debt crisis," Ryan states at the outset of the 2014 Budget Committee report. "Without reform, entitlement programs will overwhelm all other items in the federal budget. And the resulting national debt will overwhelm our economy."[79]

The point of all their focus on the "debt crisis" is unashamedly to justify cuts to Medicare, Social Security, and Medicaid.

The United States also faced lectures from Eurozone bankers committed to austerity and from the International Monetary Fund when its budget deficit hit $1.4 trillion and exceeded 10 percent of the GDP at the height of the Great Recession.

So what has happened since?

America's deficit spending has been slashed in half, to $680 billion in 2013, and it fell to $514 billion in 2014. That is about 3 percent of the GDP, which is considered a sustainable level by economists. "Oh, by the way," Paul Krugman uncharitably observed in May 2013, "it is now 26 months since Bowles and Simpson predicted a U.S. fiscal crisis within two years."[80]

What reduced the anticipated deficits was a decision to raise taxes, first on those earning more than $450,000 and then by eliminating the payroll tax paid by ordinary workers. A faster-growing economy with lower unemployment reduced outlays for unemployment benefits while increasing tax revenues. A very ugly, ongoing congressional impasse has slowed the growth of discretionary spending. And guess what? The deficit has contracted significantly because of an unexpected slowdown in rising health care costs. The last has huge implications for the whole "deficit crisis" narrative and the future strength of the American economy.

Freed from the shrill urgency of the financial crash that produced surging deficits and legitimated austerity policies, what is the real level of risk ahead? Social Security is not and never was in crisis. Just as happened under President Reagan, a bipartisan commission can and will make proposals to secure the program well into the future. Any future plan will include the most popular solution: lifting the Social Security payroll cap so higher salaries get taxed as well.[81]

Medicare and Medicaid, the government's main health care programs for seniors and the poor, are genuinely at risk because the long-term and inexorable rise of health care costs could put the programs in fiscal jeopardy by 2030. Understand that the "entitlement reforms" proposed by the bipartisan commissions and Republican balanced budget plans reduce the risk by simply cutting benefits. They get health care spending off the government's books by offloading it onto the poor and seniors.

The bloated, inefficient U.S. health care system doubled as a proportion of the total economy over the past three decades without producing better health or raising life expectancy, yet few of these reforms squeezed costs out of the health care industrial complex.

Something revolutionary may be happening with health care costs though—and that has big implications for America's projected debt, public health programs, real incomes, labor costs, and American competitiveness. What could be going on in health care could be as revolutionary as what is happening with energy, immigration, in metropolitan areas, and the Millennials.

The expected deficit reduction from the Affordable Care Act for its first decade between 2013 and 2022 will reach $109 billion, and the deficit savings will increase over time. Since the Affordable Care Act was enacted, the Congressional Budget Office reduced its projections for Medicare spending in the law's second decade by $1.6 trillion. The Trustees of the Medicare program note the amazing fact that it is spending *less* money for each beneficiary than a year ago because health costs fell. They projected that in 2015 it will be

Extraordinarily high U.S. health care spending does not produce greater life expectancy

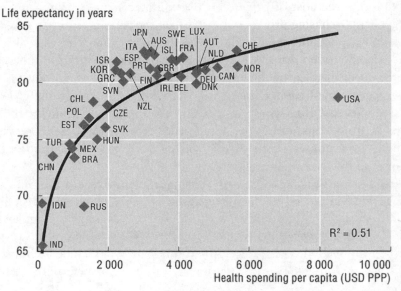

Life expectancy in years

"Society at a Glance 2014: OECD Social Indicators," Organization for Economic Co-operation and Development, Figure 6.3, March 18, 2014, p. 123.

spending less on hospital care than it spent in 2008, which prompted Human Services secretary Sylvia Mathews Burwell to repeat, "that is a growth rate of zero percent."[82]

The cut in Medicare spending is comparable in scale to eliminating the tax deduction for charitable giving, converting Medicaid into a block grant, or cutting military spending by 15 percent—the kind of bold proposals the bipartisan commissions entertained.[83]

In 2011 and 2012, health care spending as a portion of the economy fell for the first time since the managed care squeeze in the late 1990s. In the 1970s health care spending increased 10.6 percent a year and rose to 13.1 percent in the 1980s. In the past decade, during the years before the financial crisis, the annual increase in health care spending fluctuated between 6.3 and 9.7 percent a year. In the years since the enactment of the Affordable Care Act, however, health care costs rose by less than 4 percent a year.[84]

In 2013, the White House Council of Economic Advisers reported that between 2010 and 2013, per capita health expenditures rose only 1.3 percent, the slowest rate ever recorded. That is the fifth straight year of surprisingly cooled health care inflation. Per capita, there was no change in Medicare expenditures; Medicaid expenditures decreased by 0.5 percent despite increasing enrollment, and private insurance costs increased only 1.6 percent. In addition, health care price inflation rose only 1 percent during that period, the lowest rate in thirty years.[85]

And with the cost of private insurance notably moderating, the federal budget for purchasing private insurance over the coming decade has been cut by another $419 billion.[86]

As one considers America's ability to address its long-term deficits, it is worth staring at the growing gap between the Congressional Budget Office's 2009 projection of federal health care spending and what its revised picture looks like today. It tells you, first, to be cautious about some of the most alarmist projections, and second, that health care spending can be restrained fairly dramatically.

Federal health spending projections down significantly over the past 5 years

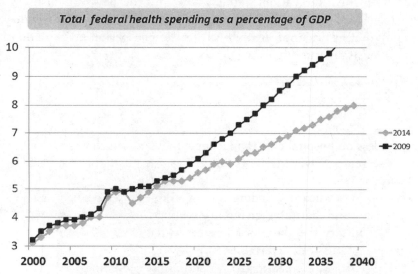

Total federal health spending as a percentage of GDP

"The Long-Term Budget Outlook," Congressional Budget Office, Supplement Tables, Figure 1-1, June 2009; "The Long-Term Budget Outlook," Congressional Budget Office, Supplement Tables, Figure B-3, July 2014; Louise Sheiner and Brendan M. Mochoruk, "Health Spending 25 Years Out," *Brookings Institution*, July 15, 2014.

The debate is ongoing about whether these are one-time reductions from the recession and whether changes in health care and costs will begin to grow again, as was the case with the managed-care programs of the 1990s, or whether there are new dynamics, transparency, competition, and accountability that are shifting the cost curve. It is possible that the Affordable Care Act has created a public debate on health care outcomes and a possibly grim electoral accountability if you do not shift the curve. In his new book, Zeke Emanuel argues that big structural changes are producing long-term reductions in health spending and could produce more.[87]

We also know that the accelerating immigration of diverse young people is also stabilizing our aging population, keeping our seniors at about 20 percent of the population up to 2050. If something like comprehensive immigration reform passes, the deficit will be reduced further by $300 billion in the second decade after enactment and is almost certain to be further reduced in later ones. If the Congressional Budget Office is right, large-scale immigration reform and "Obamacare"—hated by conservatives—will work to reduce the deficit and our supposed dependency on the Chinese. They will contribute to America's economic ascent.

All of these things may free us from the obsession with the deficit as the principal national challenge before the country. That produces a constricted national debate, and almost certainly a continued pessimism about the country's future. What should be apparent by now is that America is a dynamic and diverse country that is uniquely positioned to take advantage of new developments in energy, innovation, immigration, and the new urbanism. As we know from reading Thomas Piketty's *Capital in the Twenty-first Century*, an economy that grows appreciably over a sustained period gives a country a lot more pleasant and interesting choices.

3 AMERICA'S CULTURAL EXCEPTIONALISM

Most of those betting on America focus on its economic dynamism and how many times the United States has proved the doomsayers wrong, though one should not underestimate its cultural dynamism, too. America is racially blended, immigrant, multinational, multilingual, and religiously pluralistic, and that is becoming more and more central to our national identity. The country's diversity and multiculturalism are not just demographic facts or history but things heralded and honored and integral to our ascendant values. America is forging a unified identity out of its vast differences.

Through the centuries, writers described America as a "melting pot" or as "one universal nation," though those claims were always incomplete or aspirational until recently. Today, institutions in civil society, major companies, and the most prominent national leaders are embracing the country's multiculturalism. And those who identify with America's growing diversity are politically ascendant, while those struggling against it are being marginalized.

Unfortunately, America's route to multiculturalism is not a particularly helpful guide for other countries now. It took two centuries of racial, religious, and ethnic conflict, an entrenched system of slavery, a civil war that killed more than half a million, waves of unrestricted immigration that produced a racist, anti-Catholic, and anti-Semitic reaction, and a great dialectical struggle to forge a new American unity out of that history. But that identity and culture are very tangible now and part of why America may be newly exceptional.

Racial "minorities" are now 37 percent of the population, 43 percent of the Millennials, and will form more than 50 percent of the country in 2042. A majority of births are nonwhite now. You get a fuller sense of the demographic and cultural changes when you consider that one in ten marriages and 15 percent of all new marriages in the United States are interracial.[1]

America has an extraordinary immigrant history. Immigration was largely unregulated during our first century as a republic, creating our diverse ethnic communities. That was matched by the transformations of the post–civil rights period, when America opened up to Latin Americans and Asians and welcomed skilled professionals, engineers, and scientists from all over the world. Today the people in our most populous and dynamic cities are almost 40 percent foreign-born.[2]

Religion is a continuing part of America's diversity, multiculturalism, and dynamism. The prohibition against an established state religion was affirmed in the Constitution, allowing a vast number of denominations to flourish in America, and they multiplied by fissures, new sects, and new immigration from scores of countries. With congregations the dominant way people of faith organized themselves in communities, America sustained an unprecedented level of religious identification and practice compared to the rest of the developed world. That is eroding, to be sure, but more than three-quarters of Americans still identify with a denomination and nearly 40 percent still participate in a congregation weekly.[3]

America's national leaders increasingly recognize and embrace this inexorable diversity, and that makes America exceptional. Growing demographic and cultural diversity is contested in virtually every other country on earth, except perhaps Brazil and Canada.

When Bill Clinton became president, he was determined to produce a government that "looked like America" and strived for unity, despite unfinished racially charged political debates over welfare and affirmative action. He kept his eye on the goal, declaring in his inaugural address at the outset of his second term: "For any one of us to succeed, we must succeed as one America." In the final years of his second term, he opposed the anti-immigration initiatives that were then red-hot in the country, and he reaffirmed the need "to build one America at home." President Clinton self-consciously spoke to America's emerging character and challenged us "to make strength of our diversity so that the other nations can be inspired to overcome their own ethnic and religious tensions." Clinton called on America to find unity in diversity, and America did, electing Barack Obama twice.[4]

Just think how exceptional is that call.

Canada has a unique immigrant story of its own to tell. It has a long tradition of recruiting and welcoming immigrants as part of "nation building" and a long tradition of accepting refugees. More than one-fifth of its population is foreign-born and one-fifth identifies as a member of a visible minority population. In the most recent period of large-scale global migration, it has accepted more than a quarter of a million new immigrants every year since 2006. They use a merit point system at the national level, and provinces can directly recruit immigrants as well. Canada codified a national multiculturalism policy in 1988 that celebrates multiculturalism as fundamental to the national heritage, guarantees equal treatment, and recognizes the rights and cultures of minorities. It should not be surprising, then, that two-thirds of Canadians say immigration is a positive feature of their country and that political parties actively appeal to immigrant voters. While voters disapprove of the undocumented living there illegally, there are no anti-immigrant parties competing in their elections.[5]

Brazil has a story to tell, too. It is home to the largest population in the

Americas of those descendant from Africa, a legacy of a brutal slave trade system that brought one-fifth of the whole slave trade through the market in Rio de Janeiro. They worked on Brazil's plantations until 1888, when Brazil became the last country in the Americas to outlaw slavery. In the late nineteenth and early twentieth centuries, a diverse European migration from Portugal, Italy, Spain, Germany, and Ukraine and later from Japan, Syria, and Russia took up work in agriculture and in the industrializing cities. Ultimately, Brazil would promote racial integration, and it stands out as the country with the highest rate of interracial marriage in the world. That has produced an extraordinary racial blending so that 43 percent of the population is *parda,* a mixture of Europeans, blacks, and indigenous peoples. When Brazil adopted a new constitution in 1980, it declared all men and women equal and made acts of racism a crime, without the right to bail.[6]

By contrast, the major and rising powers in Asia—Japan, China, and South Korea—will not allow foreign immigrants, full stop, except as contract laborers with no citizenship rights. With low birthrates and aging populations, these countries are willing to pay a high economic price to avoid the challenges of diversity. To maintain national homogeneity, they are now trying to push more women to enter the labor force, as Japanese prime minister Shinzo Abe told world leaders at Davos in 2014: "Enhancing opportunities for women to work and to be active in society is no longer a matter of choice for Japan. It is instead a matter of the greatest urgency."[7]

Across the Arab states, civil wars rage among Sunnis and Shi'ites and Islamists, and the more secular and autocratic regimes are no longer able to keep order or demand legitimacy in this pluralistic region. The Alawite, Shi'ite-allied regime in Syria has held on to power by leading the slaughter of nearly 200,000 mostly Sunni civilians and forcing millions to leave their homes by the summer of 2014. That pales before ISIS's attempt to spread a bloody war between Sunnis and Shi'ites and spread the bloody battlefield from Syria and Iraq to Tunisia, Kuwait, and the Gulf countries, while targeting Britons, French, and Americans where they can.[8]

The Christian-Muslim fault line is no less violent and bloody across Nigeria to Sudan and to Eritrea beyond that. Choose a country at any given moment. In the Central African Republic, Christian vigilantes armed with machetes have killed scores of the Muslim minorities, and tens of thousands have fled to neighboring countries. In 2002, Eritrea banned practicing "unregistered" religions (anything other than Sunni Islam, Eritrean Orthodoxy, Roman Catholicism, and Evangelical Lutheranism). Thousands of Christians have been imprisoned indefinitely and hundreds of thousands have fled the brutal persecution and sought refuge in other countries. The Christian communities in northern Iraq have fled the country as the Islamic State of Iraq and the Levant (ISIL) took control and demanded they convert to Islam. ISIS fighters obliterated ancient religious sites because of the evident idolatry that offended Allah, and they may have slaughtered thousands of mostly Shi'ite Iraqi soldiers.[9]

And the Islamic extremist group Boko Haram got the world's attention when it kidnapped more than two hundred Muslim schoolgirls, but its determined battle to achieve an Islamic government starts with a war on Christians, as well as Muslims who do not share its vision, and it had killed more than eight thousand people by 2014.[10]

Israel is one of the few countries in the world to formally embrace a diaspora that is racially, nationally, and culturally diverse. Yet today, half of its primary school students are Israeli Arabs or come from ultra-Orthodox families, and the political battles playing out around these groups bring home the implications for a multicultural and diverse Israel where civic equality is also supposed to rule. The ultra-Orthodox consider religious study a greater calling than the Israeli Defense Forces, and they vigorously protest a "sharing of the burden bill" that passed the Knesset and a High Court of Justice injunction that cuts off government funding for draft-dodging yeshiva students. The ultra-Orthodox chief rabbis profusely attack the new law and the High Court as secular, antireligious, and illegitimate. Israel is "the only country in the world," according to one Orthodox elected leader, where "a person who studies the Torah is accused of committing a crime."[11]

With respect to the Israeli Arab students, the government endorsed a bill requiring schools to "educate toward strengthening the value of the State of Israel as the Jewish nation-state." These changes align the school curriculum with what the right-wing parties demand as a precondition in negotiations with the Palestinians and their proposed changes to Israel's basic law, its constitution. With Arabic potentially diminished as an official language and Jewish citizens given a higher legal status, Israeli Arabs joined the widespread protests and political turmoil that followed.[12]

Prime Minister Benjamin Netanyahu was able to win election when he rallied and mobilized the Jewish nationalist and religious voting blocs. He promised them no Palestinian state and expanded Jewish settlements in the Palestinian territories, and he warned that Israeli Arabs were voting in large numbers to elect a left-wing government. With those incendiary remarks still reverberating, Israel's president called for considered gestures to bring Jewish-Arab understanding, though he warned ominously that Israel was forming into "tribes" and needed to find a new national identity.

In Europe, the growing racial and religious diversity and number of foreign-born have hardly moved countries to develop an accommodative framework. And the January 2015 terrorist attack by French Muslims linked to Islamist groups in Yemen and Syria only confirmed people's starting presumption against multiculturalism.[13]

The only way the old Yugoslavia could survive without religious war and ethnic slaughter, nearly all parties agreed, was by separating the country along ethnic and historical lines into Bosnia and Herzegovina, Croatia, Kosovo, Macedonia, Montenegro, Serbia, and Slovenia. Despite the "Velvet Revolution" that liberated Czechoslovakia from Soviet rule, linguistic differences quickly proved irresistible, and the Czech Republic and Slovakia took different paths. President Vladimir Putin is resistant to such a solution in the Russian Federation and is battling to suppress Islamist resistance in Chechnya and Dagestan. In neighboring Ukraine, Russian-backed paramilitary forces have fought to keep the Russian-speaking eastern part of the country on a separate trajectory from the European-oriented center of the country. In the Crimea region, Russia backed the ethnic Russian majority's desire to be severed from Ukraine, and people voted in a referendum to join the Russian Federation, which stations its Black Sea fleet at Sevastopol.[14]

The Scottish National Party (SNP) shocked everyone when their "yes" campaign nearly won the referendum to separate from the United Kingdom, and then proceeded to sweep nearly all of Scotland's parliamentary seats the next year. And when Scotland won increased autonomy and powers, major parties began advocating an English parliament for English laws, too. The Spanish government blocked a similar referendum in Catalonia that likely would have prevailed, frustrating the proindependence plurality in the Catalan parliament.[15]

Immigration is now the big disruptive issue in virtually every European country.[16]

In Britain, where the foreign-born population has almost doubled in the past decade, to 11.4 percent, a majority say immigration is "bad for Britain, because immigrants take jobs and push down wages"; just a third think it is good on balance for the country. The proportion of the public in Britain saying religious and ethnic hatred is the greatest threat to the country (39 percent) rivals the level of concern expressed in the Palestinian territories and Nigeria.[17]

That is hardly surprising given the tone of newspaper coverage of the immigration issues. When *The Times* of London reported that 193,000 foreign-born residents mostly from former British Commonwealth countries had become citizens, it ran the story under a banner headline across the whole top of the front page, "The Great UK Passport Giveaway." The story made no mention of poignant ceremonies at government offices where people proudly recite an oath of allegiance and family and officials hug and congratulate them for assuming the responsibilities of citizenship, as happens every day in the United States.[18]

The British government under Prime Minister David Cameron attempted to cap the number of non-E.U. citizens and government vans canvassed immigrant areas with posters worded "Go Home or Face Arrest" to discourage Romanian and Bulgarian immigration. In 2011, Cameron declared the "doctrine of state multiculturalism" a failure and warned that Islamic extremists were graduating from British universities and becoming terrorists because multiculturalism "encouraged different cultures to live separate lives" and made it "hard to identify with Britain" because it "allowed the weakening of [Britain's] collective identity." To show he was dead serious about what was happening to Britain going into the 2015 general elections, Cameron announced he would negotiate with other E.U. leaders to establish a four-year waiting period before their nationals could get in-work benefits or access to social housing, a right to deport immigrants who have not found work after six months, and a much longer waiting period before job seekers from new E.U. entrants such as Turkey may come to Britain. And as the ultimate leverage, he committed to hold an in-or-out referendum in 2017 on Britain's membership in the European Union if the Conservative Party forms the next government.[19]

Even before Islamist French Muslim terrorists slaughtered ten journalists and cartoonists at *Charlie Hebdo* and five Jews at a kosher supermarket, two-thirds of the French public believed there were too many immigrants in the country and almost 60 percent believed immigrants make little effort to integrate into French society. Just think about that poll question. It assumes that immigrants are obligated and judged by their degree of integration into a unified and static French identity.[20]

The French courts have upheld a 2004 prohibition against conspicuous religious symbols in schools that are meant to be secular and a 2011 prohibition against covering one's face in public. By these laws, France has effectively banned the wearing of the niqab in public and head scarves in schools. The French public overwhelmingly supports these laws and argues that they protect human rights and the secularism needed for religious liberty.[21]

Revulsion at the Islamist terrorist attack of January 2015 brought 3.6 million people to march in protest in Paris and cities across France. In a sign of unity, Jewish, Muslim, and Catholic leaders including Benjamin Netanyahu and Mahmoud Abbas were featured prominently in the front rows of the marchers. The leaders of the French government called for national unity and for reaffirming the values of liberty and the Republic. They vowed to protect the Muslim and Jewish communities, yet you did not hear any openness to multiculturalism or any new model for dealing with France's diversity. In fact, you did not hear from Marine Le Pen at all, because the National Front leaders were not invited to join the march, though she did urge government surveillance of French mosques.[22]

The European public's reaction against immigration and the elite's failure to defend national identities got fully expressed in the 2014 elections for the European Parliament. The populist, anti-immigration, Eurosceptic bloc in the parliament grew by two-thirds, led by Marine Le Pen's National Front (FN), which took a quarter of the vote and topped the polls in France for the first time. It joins the U.K. Independence Party, which finished first in Britain. Austria's Freedom Party won 21 percent of the vote, and Greece's Golden Dawn, with its prominent display of Nazi salutes, won 10 percent.[23]

But these anti-immigrant and nationalist parties are also a growing force in national politics, and they are shattering the electoral coalitions of both the established center-left and center-right parties. Austria was formally ostracized when the anti-Muslim and anti-immigration Freedom Party won 27 percent of the vote in 1999 under Jörg Haider and joined the government, though the FPO now regularly gets a fifth of the vote in national elections. The Progress Party in Norway won about 23 percent of the vote in 2009, and the far-right Sweden Democrats doubled their support to 12.9 percent in 2014. Both have forced a national debate over welfare benefits for immigrants and the impact of immigration on national identity.[24]

The U.K. Independence Party won its first parliamentary seats in by-elections in 2014, and while it won only one seat in the 2015 general election, it quadrupled its support nationally, getting 13 percent of the vote. UKIP leader Nigel Farage told his party delegates that "in scores of our cities and market towns, this country in a short space of time has frankly become unrecognizable." Farage declared, "Whether it is the impact on local schools and hospitals, whether it is the fact in many parts of England you don't hear English spoken anymore. This is not the kind of community we want to leave to our children and grandchildren." That disdain for immigration and the E.U. as well as the condescension of the cosmopolitan and political elites have allowed the UKIP to build deepening support among disaffected working-class and older voters determined to affirm traditional British values.[25]

The quandary facing the established parties played out vividly in the third season of *Borgen*, the top-rated TV series in Denmark and Britain, which follows the fictionalized first female prime minister. She is forced to form her own party because she is outraged that all the mainstream parties have catered to the anti-immigration Freedom Party, starting with their support for a new proposal to deport immigrants found guilty of a misdemeanor. Then, real life took over. In 2015, the Danish People's Party surprised the pollsters, finished as the second largest party and ensured a new right-wing government would act to address the influx of immigrants. The center is not holding in real life and in this fictionalized television world, and it is the nationalist, anti-immigration, anti-elite parties that are setting the agenda.

What is missing in the European countries is a broadly accepted framework that sets rules for governing immigration and integration and that accepts the new diversity as part of country's character. Clinton's "diversity is our strength" formula seemed like a pretty innocent way to organize a country in light of the big disruptions produced by ongoing globalization, yet his approach is winning out and working. In any case, it is the hand America has been dealt.

THE NEW IMMIGRANT COUNTRY

When fashioning the U.S. Constitution and justifying our form of government, the author of *Federalist Paper, No. 2* wrote:

Providence has been pleased to give this one connected country to one united people—a people descended from the same ancestors, speaking the same language, professing the same religion, attached to the same principles of government, very similar in their manners and customs.

He gave voice to an assumption ascendant then and to this day in Europe, the Middle East, and Asia about what is necessary for a country to be stable, united, governable, and capable of making progress for its own citizenry. Our founders solved the inconvenient problems of Native Americans, slaves, and women by excluding them constitutionally from full personhood, citizenship, or enfranchisement, as was the norm in that era. The first Federalist administration after George Washington passed the Alien Acts, which gave the president the power to expel foreigners and extended the residency requirement for citizenship from five to fourteen years.[26]

That incipient nativism was stifled once the Jeffersonian Democrats won the 1800 election. They repealed these laws and opened the country. Amazingly, for the first four decades of the nineteenth century, there were no new national laws regulating immigration.[27]

From the beginning, the economic and political elites and the public intellectuals constructed an intellectual framework that highlighted America as a welcoming nation for people from different traditions, histories, and battles. The revolutionary ideals in the Declaration of Independence and the dominant Protestantism did presume an essential equality and that different people would come to live in unity. The Jeffersonian Democrats generally supported the liberal revolutions across Europe, and Latin America welcomed their refugees. Between the 1850s and the end of the nineteenth century, German immigrants, many of whom went to the Midwest, were the largest immigrant group, followed by British, Irish, Scandinavians, and French Canadians. They were opposed to slavery, and almost one-half million foreign-born men served in the Union Army. There was brief rioting among the Irish working class of New York in opposition to the draft, but for the most part the shared experience of the Civil War subsumed immigrant distinctions under a common nationalism.[28]

The commercial and business classes promoted immigration and brought a rising number of laborers to the cities, railroads, interior land grants, mines, and manufacturing jobs from Pennsylvania to the Rockies. From 1870 until 1920, one-third of the employees in manufacturing were immigrants. The New England factories and the agents of different states actively recruited workers in Europe and French Canada and promoted it as central to American prosperity. The opening up of America and the expanding immigration went hand in hand with the invention of the steam engine that made the Industrial Revolution transforming and catapulted America to its economic ascendant position.[29]

America's leaders mostly accepted that different peoples would assimilate and become part of America's nationalism. Indeed, Radical Republicans began to argue before the Civil War, and certainly with Emancipation, that African Americans and the former slaves could have freedom and live in harmony and unity. The post–Civil War Republican Party pledged to encourage immigration. The democratic and Christian traditions created a framework for, in John Highan's words, "an inclusive nationality, at once diverse and homogeneous, ever improving as it assimilated many types of men into a unified superior people."[30]

Liberal enlightened opinion, from Ralph Waldo Emerson to Herman Melville and Oliver Wendell Holmes, described America as a unique country. Holmes labeled Americans as "the Romans of the modern world"—"the great assimilating people." And Melville: "We are the heirs of all time, and with all nations we divide our inheritance. On this Western Hemisphere all tribes and peoples are forming into one federated whole; and there is a future which shall see the estranged children of Adam restored as to the old hearthstone in [an American] Eden."[31]

Even Darwin and social Darwinists wrote about an America that received the most ambitious of those from Europe and created a melting pot that was producing a higher order of man. Fredrick Jackson Turner wrote of immigrants reaching the Mississippi Valley: "In this crucible of the frontier the immigrants were Americanized, liberated, and fused into a mixed race, English in neither nationality nor characteristics."[32]

That was a lot more romantic than the teeming tenements that immigrants occupied in most of America's cities. The muckrakers famously focused on what was really happening in the slaughterhouses and factories and tenements of Chicago and New York where immigrants lived and worked. "Life here means the hardest kind of work almost from the cradle." Jacob A. Riis described "Jewtown" on the Lower East Side, where there were 330,000 Jews per square mile, almost double the crowding of London at its worst. Every foot, alley, and child was crowded and dirty. But it was worse still, says Riis, for "the Italian [who] comes in at the bottom." They were the preferred tenants because they were, according to Riis, "content to live in a pig-sty and [submit] to robbery at the hands of the rent-collector without murmur." And while it was well known for all the immigrants that there was some level below which a man's wages could not fall, "woman's wages have no limit, since the paths of shame are always open to her."[33]

Yet these immigrants had only recently fled the potato famine in Ireland, the deep poverty of southern Italy, and the anti-Semitic pogroms in Galicia, the mandated region for Jewish settlement in Imperial Russia. America began as a refuge for people who fled oppression in Europe and sought freedom here, as Tom Paine wrote at the time of the Revolution. More than a century later, Emma Lazarus penned a poem to raise funds for erecting the base of the Statue of Liberty, a gift from the French: "Give me your tired, your poor, Your huddled masses yearning to breathe free, The wretched refuse of your teeming shore, Send these, the homeless, tempest-tost to me, I lift my lamp beside the golden door!"[34]

But the waves of immigration produced waves of opposition that would ultimately taper off the free flow of immigrants after World War I. Indeed, the growing resentment and organization against immigration would keep the Statue of Liberty dedication speeches focused on promoting liberty more than opening America's doors to refugees. The growing opposition of Evangelical Protestants, white southerners, and northern reformers was increasingly being heard.[35]

Anti-Irish, anti-Catholic sentiment was first to break through in strong nativist form. The Irish had made their way into the eastern cities working as common laborers and in the new industries. But with Catholicism dominant in the surrounding Spanish and French territories, this influx looked especially threatening to some. Emerging critics worried that the authoritarian Church and papacy were incompatible with American liberty. They spoke of a Catholic Church with "separate organization, unknown to the laws," and not acting "as a portion of the great American family of freemen."[36]

In the 1850s, the anti-immigration societies formed the American Party. It was consumed with Irish immigration, the rising power of the Catholic Church, and the flock of new Catholic voters available to the urban machines. With 427,000 immigrants arriving in 1854, and nearly one-quarter of them Irish, the "nativist" candidates won six governorships the next year. With little evidence of the welcoming tone in Emma Lazarus's poem, the American Party warned that the "almshouses of Europe" are being "emptied upon our coast," transporting "the feeble, the imbecile, the idle and intractable." Sooner than you can imagine, it claimed, "the natives of the soil [will be] a minority in their own land!"[37]

More than anything, the anti-immigrant forces feared the electoral power of new immigrants. *The Philadelphia Inquirer* cautioned that many "get no farther than New York" before they "take out naturalization papers" and "sell themselves to Tammany." Henry George wrote of the British government paying to empty ports on the western coast of Ireland and "dumping them on the wharves of New York and Boston."[38]

A couple of decades later, the American Protective Association won some Republican political support when it attacked that "un-American ecclesiastical institution," boycotted Catholic merchants, and pledged never to vote for a Catholic. They fabricated a document entitled "Instructions to Catholics" that was supposedly circulated by papal agents. "In order to find employment for the many thousands of the faithful who are coming daily to swell the ranks of our catholic army, which will in due time possess this land," it stated, without much subtlety, "we must secure control of every enterprise requiring labor" and "remove or crowd out the American heretics who are now employed."[39]

That deep Protestant hostility to the Catholic Church would survive a century—forcing John F. Kennedy, late in the 1960 campaign, to address the Protestant ministers of the Greater Houston Ministerial Association, telling them: "But because I am a Catholic, and no Catholic has ever been elected president, the real issues in this campaign have been obscured—perhaps deliberately." So he restated, to be clear: "I believe in an America where the separation of church and state is absolute." That means, "I do not speak for my church on public matters, and the church does not speak for me."[40]

The expanded federal role to control and limit immigration came piecemeal and was contested every step of the way. It took four decades before America's unique history with global migration was sharply curtailed. The deep recessions of the 1870s and 1880s were impetuses for the first laws in this spirit. The Immigration Act of 1882 made authority over immigration a federal responsibility and refused entry to those likely to become public charges. In addition, the Chinese Exclusion Act of 1882 placed a ten-year moratorium on Chinese immigration, reflecting the virulent attitudes toward Chinese labor, even among the new Irish immigrants. The 1891 Immigration Act went further, confirming the federal control over immigration, commanding the deportation of illegal immigrants and those who became a public charge within one year of their arrival, and making steamship companies responsible for returning rejected immigrants.[41]

The assassination of President McKinley by an anarchist of foreign extraction in 1901 provided fodder for those seeking to restrict immigration. The Congress passed laws allowing for the deportation of foreign anarchists and extending the period to three years when an immigrant could be deported for becoming a public charge. And, alert to the political advantage Democrats were gaining with the immigrant population, the Naturalization Act of 1906 barred the distribution of immigration papers on the eve of an election.[42]

The opponents of immigration battled to impose a head tax on each new immigrant and to require that they take literacy tests in their native language. The proponents of these restrictions now included the American Federation of Labor, some civic reformers, and nearly every southern U.S. senator. By the turn of the century, major sections of the Republican Party allied with the anti-immigrant movements and led the battle for further immigration restrictions. Senators such as Henry Cabot Lodge lent legitimacy to the idea that Anglo-Saxon stock was in jeopardy and the country was at risk of being overrun.[43]

After such ferment, what is most striking in this account was the inability of the anti-immigration forces to pass into law anything more substantial. Serious restrictions were lost or blocked in the Congress or vetoed by successive presidents. The Republican Party and the labor unions were both divided on the issue, and big commercial interests continued to believe America's industrial miracle needed the fuel of continued influxes of immigrant labor.[44]

Most important, the immigrant communities fought back. The 1.5 million members of the German-American Alliance rallied with the Ancient Order of Hibernians and the Irish bosses in the Democratic Party to oppose further immigration restrictions. The rapidly assimilating Jewish community lobbied against rigid quotas and anti-Semitic attacks. President Teddy Roosevelt tried to assuage those concerns, and during the historic three-party election in 1912 all three presidential candidates worked to win support in the immigrant communities.[45]

The end of World War I, however, brought a wave of isolationism that would keep America out of the League of Nations and end America's open door to immigration as we know it.

As the country slipped into recession, the upheaval in Europe sent massive numbers of immigrants to the United States. By one estimate, 119,000 Jews arrived in the one-year period between 1920 and 1921—including some of my family—to escape persecution in Eastern Europe. American consuls in Europe described the Jews as "unassimilable" and "filthy, un-American and often dangerous in their habits." The Communist revolution in Russia and a surge of union-organized strikes in the United States elevated the worries about what would happen here. Exploiting that red scare, Attorney General A. Mitchell Palmer launched raids first in eleven and then thirty-three cities to expel hundreds of Russian immigrants and Communists.[46]

This time the revulsion with the new Jewish immigration, the eugenicists' urgent insistence that America's Anglo racial mix was at risk, and the victory of the Ku Klux Klan in the Democratic South produced a rising demand for "100 percent Americanism."

In 1921, the anti-immigrant forces elected Republican president Warren G. Harding, who called Congress into special session to pass a two-year delay on new immigration, with a singular exception for immediate family reunification. In 1924 the tide was stronger, and President Calvin Coolidge signed the Johnson-Reed Act into law. The House Committee described the purpose of the law as an effort to "maintain the racial preponderance" of the country. The law restricted immigration to 287,000 people a year, barred Japanese and Chinese immigrants altogether, and most importantly, commanded that all future immigration reflect the national origins of the United States beginning in 1929.[47]

These restrictive laws would govern America's ethnic and racial character over the next four decades, though not always as intended by those trying to protect America's Anglo-Saxon character.

Despite the restrictions on immigration, the 1920s was a period of dizzying economic growth, and businesses figured out new ways to carry on that would further America's growing diversity. The black population had remained in the cotton and tobacco sharecropping areas of the South in the half century following emancipation from slavery. Before World War I, nine out of ten blacks still resided in the former slave states. But between 1910 and 1930, a million blacks moved north en masse. They left Alabama and Mississippi first, and after the war, they began to flee the eastern states of Virginia, South Carolina, and Georgia. They moved along rail lines and where relatives preceded them, pausing in border cities such as Baltimore, and arrived in large numbers in Philadelphia, New York, Chicago, and Detroit.[48]

For the black sharecroppers, the South never offered much more than subsistence and political repression, though it was the spread of the boll weevil that created depression-like conditions in the Deep South. Labor agents recruited workers, and black city papers with job listings, such as *The Chicago Defender*, were widely circulated in the rural areas, taunting: "Have they stopped their Jim Crow cars? Can you buy a Pullman sleeper where you wish? Will they give you a square deal in court yet?" Blacks coming to the North found themselves at the bottom of the totem pole and crowded into neighborhoods with the worst conditions.[49]

Businesses also began to recruit Mexican labor in larger numbers to work on the railroads, in mines, and in other industries: 750,000 Mexicans came here legally by 1929. The Spanish-speaking were already part of America's ethnic mix. The Mexican-American War and America's westward expansion in the late nineteenth century brought almost half of the territory that had been Mexico into the United States, as well as many Mexican migrants and nationals, concentrated mostly in Texas and New Mexico.[50]

The Central Mesa of Mexico was dominated by haciendas that were consolidating the land and deepening the servitude of peasants who faced rising debt. But the bloody Mexican Revolution of 1910 and protracted upheaval would free six million from serfdom; 650,000 legally migrated to the United States by the end of the twenties. Many worked in the fields, but a growing number lived and worked in cities such as Los Angeles.[51]

That influx was suspended with the advent of the Depression, and almost a half million Mexican immigrants were expelled from the United States. The same would happen during the Korean War, when "Operation Wetback" deported one million Mexicans without working papers.[52]

After World War II, the tide of Mexican immigration became unstoppable. The Bracero Program, which gave visas to Mexican workers to work mostly in farm labor, allowed almost half a million Mexican workers into the country by the mid-1950s, and Mexico, exempted from the immigration quotas, sent about 50,000 new immigrants to the United States a year legally by 1963. Latinos were working in farming areas in California and Texas and moving to border cities such as El Paso, San Antonio, and Los Angeles. Other Latino immigrants came from Cuba and Puerto Rico and went to Miami and New York City.[53]

Black migration also stalled during the Depression, but in the two decades beginning with World War II, three million blacks fled the South for war-boom cities of the North and West Coast states such as California in one of the most massive labor migrations in the country's history. The mass migration leveled off in the mid-1960s, and when it was done, as many blacks lived outside the South as in it, and 70 percent lived in cities. It was a massive and sudden upheaval, perhaps as big as the flight from the potato famine in Ireland or from poverty in the south of Italy. These migrants quickly settled in segregated black neighborhoods where the churches, fraternal orders, and Democratic Party would play important roles, as with previous immigrant communities.[54]

Nathan Glazer and Daniel Patrick Moynihan, in *Beyond the Melting Pot,* described New York City as "a merchant metropolis with an extraordinarily heterogeneous population." The cities in fact looked less like a "melting pot" and more like a checkerboard of culturally distinct and separate lower-income, poor, and working-class communities that tried to find stability in their own mutual aid societies, churches, schools, businesses, foods, and traditions. As with the waves of immigration before, those from the poorest rural areas faced the opposition of the more established locals, whose control of city hall and the local Democratic Party reinforced the segregation and hierarchy. The blacks and Hispanics put pressure on the Poles, Jews, Italians, and Irish who had come to dominate different neighborhoods and caused some to join the white flight to the suburbs. Racism played a big role in shaping the black urban ghettos, the locations and conditions of public housing, and discriminatory rental and housing practices.[55]

The 1950s and 1960s were a period of rapid economic growth and mobility, though it was politically disruptive and produced violent resistance, riots, and simmering race relations in cities across the country.

When Lyndon Johnson signed the Civil Rights Act, he observed to his closest advisers, "we just delivered the South to the Republican Party for a long time to come." That came to pass, but so did a change of attitudes that is central to this whole story of American exceptionalism. Public opposition to racial discrimination in voting, public accommodations, housing, employment, and even marriage grew steadily over the three decades from the mid-1960s to the mid-1990s.[56]

While Lyndon Johnson will properly be remembered for the Civil Rights Act, the Voting Rights Act, Medicare, and the War on Poverty, his passing the Immigration and Nationality Act of 1965 was just as transformative. It opened a new chapter of immigration that changed the character of the country and made possible the economic and cultural changes described in this book. One in five global immigrants would not be living in the United States, and half of our most talented engineers would not be living in Silicon Valley but for that 1965 law.

For four decades, immigration had been capped at 150,000 a year. The immigrant composition was based on a country-of-origin formula that unsubtly meant that 70 percent of the new immigrants came from three countries—the United Kingdom, Ireland, and Germany—and the remainder from Italy, Greece, Portugal, and Poland. Under the 1965 immigration law, by contrast, the ability to immigrate to the United States was based on family reunification and needed job skills, with special visas for professionals, scientists, and artists of exceptional ability. President Johnson assured the country that this was a way to maintain control, but the new law immediately doubled the number of legal immigrants and eventually tripled it. Barely six million immigrants had been admitted in the three decades prior to the 1965 reform, but eighteen million entered in the three decades after its passage.[57]

What was tectonic about the shift was the global reach and diversity of those who would come to America. Four in every five of the new immigrants would come from Asia or Latin America—and in almost equal proportion. Just about 10 percent of immigrants in the following decades would come from Europe. The die was cast.[58]

President Johnson signed the new law at Liberty Island in sight of the Statue of Liberty, and his speech reflected a renewed consciousness about a multicultural America that was "built by a nation of strangers." "From a hundred different places or more they have poured forth into an empty land, joining and blending in one mighty and irresistible tide." Diversity, he declared, would unite and strengthen America.[59]

And once the new policy reopened the gates, human inventiveness and resolve would have its way in America's coloration. That was most evident in the case of Mexicans. The new immigration law virtually ended the Bracero Program; guest-worker permits fell from 400,000 in 1959 to 1,725 in 1979, and resident visas declined to 20,000. Demand for Mexican workers, however, was still high and produced the wave of undocumented "illegal" immigrants that has become central to the U.S. political debate. Border arrests climbed from 55,000 in 1965 to 1.7 million in 1986.[60]

While Ronald Reagan was a staunch opponent of the Civil Rights Act, the War on Poverty, and affirmative action, he was more a traditional Californian when it came to immigration. He would play a major role in promoting the cultural changes that had been unleashed. In 1986, Reagan embraced amnesty for three million illegal immigrants living in the country. Following Lyndon Johnson's example, he signed the Immigration Reform and Control Act at the Statue of Liberty, observing: "We have a statue in New York Harbor . . . of a woman holding a torch of welcome to those who enter our country to become Americans. . . . She represents our open door. All of the immigrants who came to us brought their own music, literature, customs, and ideas. . . . In fact, what they brought to America became American. And this diversity has more than enriched us; it has literally shaped us."[61]

The new law traded amnesty for increased border security, as demanded by the law's opponents, though that only increased the number of undocumented workers who stayed in the country and encouraged many to move to metropolitan areas away from the traditional border states. Historically, many of the immigrants to the United States chose to return to their home countries. Between 1900 and 1924, when immigration to the United States was quite open, for example, about 40 percent of immigrants returned to their home country. In 1980, right before the passage of Ronald Reagan's Immigration Reform and Control Act, 46 percent of undocumented Mexicans returned home within twelve months. With the enhanced border security in place, however, many of the undocumented immigrants chose not to risk returning. By 2007, only 7 percent of undocumented immigrants were returning to their home country. Not surprisingly, the Hispanic community began to ask, with increasing insistence, how the growing undocumented population could gain legal status.[62]

That history has colored America, so that Hispanics are nearly one in five in the population and will likely be one in ten of those who vote in 2016.[63]

The Republican Party has led a two-decade-long battle since 1994 to get control of illegal immigration, focusing heavily on the growing unlawful and permanent Hispanic population. Governor Pete Wilson of California led the party's anti-immigration effort by backing passage of Proposition 187, which barred illegal immigrants from using public services, including education and health care, and required all state and local officials to report illegals to law enforcement. It passed handily, with 59 percent of the vote, though federal courts ultimately declared the referendum unconstitutional and kept the law from ever being implemented. Whether to bar illegal immigrants from getting driver's licenses became the next hot issue in California and New York.[64]

It was Governor Jan Brewer of Arizona who picked up the torch and led the Republican Party into the closing years of this battle, signing S.B. 1070 into law during the summer of 2010. The law required state law enforcement officials in the process of carrying out their duties to detain suspects if there was reasonable suspicion that they were illegal immigrants. The law imposed penalties on those sheltering, hiring, or transporting "unregistered aliens," and the stated intent was to achieve "attrition through enforcement." Arizona's passage of the toughest immigration law in the country gave Republican-controlled states the mandate to act. Georgia, Indiana, South Carolina, and Alabama passed laws based on the Arizona model, and all but seven states passed anti-immigration measures that same year. But in the summer of 2012, the Supreme Court overturned the Arizona law as an infringement of federal constitutional prerogatives regarding immigration.[65]

Mitt Romney ran for president as the toughest Republican on immigration, attacking his weak-kneed opponents who allowed the undocumented to avail themselves of in-state tuition prices at state universities. He promised unwavering policies that would lead the undocumented to "self-deport"— very much reflecting the most extreme anti-immigration posture of the Republican Party. Democrats swept the Hispanic vote on Election Day.

The Republican Party's official postmortem said, "If Hispanic Americans perceive that a GOP nominee or candidate does not want them in the United States (i.e., self-deportation), they will not pay attention to our next sentence. It does not matter what we say about education, jobs or the economy," and "among the steps Republicans take in the Hispanic community and beyond we must embrace and champion comprehensive immigration reform. If we do not, our Party's appeal will continue to shrink to its core constituencies only."[66]

In 1964, the Democratic Party and the Republican Party traded the support of black voters for white voters in the South and the suburban North. This time, the Republican Party traded in Hispanics, Asians, and new immigrant voters—Democrats now win close to 70 percent of these votes—and the GOP got the Tea Party in return.

The politics of immigration today take place within a normative and material posture acknowledging that immigrants and immigration contribute to and are good for the country. A huge 80 percent majority of Americans favors granting legal status and an eventual pathway to citizenship for the more than 11.7 million immigrants not here legally.[67]

All lines rise for "fix our broken immigration system" with sharper rise among Democrats

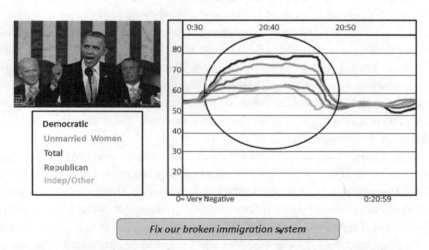

Dial testing focus groups among 44 swing voters in Denver, Colorado, conducted by Greenberg Quinlan Rosner Research for Democracy Corps and Women's Voices Women Vote Action Fund, January 28, 2014.

During President Obama's 2014 State of the Union address, the president's statement that it is time to "fix our broken immigration system" earned him support rather than cost him in dial-meter research conducted by Democracy Corps. As you can see in the overlay of lines that represents the minute-by-minute reaction of voters, everyone dialed up, regardless of party.[68]

Republicans are still thinking more about borders than legalization and inviting new immigrants, though they could only stall the president when he issued an executive order that allowed five million of twelve million currently undocumented immigrants to remain in America and made them eligible for legal status. The president made clear his purpose and underlying values: "When people come here to fulfill their dreams—to study, invent, contribute to our culture—they make our country a more attractive place for businesses to locate and create jobs for everybody."[69]

When Obama spoke at the Democratic National Convention a decade earlier, the then Senate candidate reflected on his kaleidoscopic biography:

> My father was a foreign student, born and raised in a small village
> in Kenya. He grew up herding goats, went to school in a tin-roofed
> shack. His father, my grandfather, was a cook, a domestic servant
> to the British. But my grandfather had larger dreams for his son.
> Through hard work and perseverance my father got a scholarship to
> study in a magical place, America, that shone as a beacon of freedom
> and opportunity to so many who had come before him. . . . And I
> stand here today grateful for the diversity of my heritage . . . knowing
> that my story is part of the larger American story.[70]

AMERICA'S RELIGIOUS PLURALISM

America is a religious country to be sure, though that is not why it is exceptional. America is religiously pluralistic, with a vast churn across untold types of Protestants alongside ethnically diverse Catholics, Muslims, Mormons, and myriad types of Jewish congregations. Americans experience their faith in congregations that make religion more important for them, yet the dominant faiths are mostly nonjudgmental and tolerant. That combination, in turn, allows for more religious diversity and denominational mobility and less enduring sectarian conflict.

More than three-quarters of Americans have a religious preference, and almost 60 percent say religion is very important to them. More than 90 percent of Americans believe God or a Universal Spirit exists, and more than two-thirds are absolutely sure of it; a striking 60 percent believe that there is a heaven. People use religion actively as a personal guide. Nearly 40 percent attend services at least once a week and have a place of worship, and a third turn to scripture almost every week.[71]

That level of religious attendance puts America on a par with Iran, though the United States' level of observance is modest compared to India, strong Catholic countries such as Poland and Brazil, and Muslim nations such as Egypt, Indonesia, and Jordan.[72]

America is exceptional, however, in comparison with Western Europe and nearly all the other major economic powers. In Britain, a sizable majority say they never pray, compared to the United States, where less than a fifth never turn to God for help. Just a quarter in Germany and a fifth in Britain say their religion is important to them. And leading the secular disengagement are the oldest Catholic countries, Italy and France, where just 9 and 4 percent, respectively, are active in a religious organization. The great cathedrals of Europe are still standing, though they are virtually empty.[73]

Church attendance is relatively low in China and very low in Russia, each with their Communist history and continued government restrictions on the exercise of religion. While Orthodox Catholic affiliation in Russia has more than doubled in the past two decades, to 72 percent, barely 7 percent attend services at least once a month. Religious service attendance in Japan is almost as low, at roughly 3 percent, with a majority of Japanese claiming no religion and 41 percent identifying as Buddhists.[74]

Though religious observance is also on the decline in the United States, it is nonetheless striking that 37 percent report attending religious services at least once every week and, even more meaningfully, 40 percent describe themselves as being an active member of a church or other religious organization. This dominates all other types of civic organization in American life. The number of people who reported participating in leisure activities—including hobbies, music, arts, and sports—in the past year falls well below the 62 percent of people who reported going to a regular place of worship in the past year. School, youth, and parent support groups are important to Americans, but only half as many attend those as participate at church. Participation in professional groups, trade associations, self-help groups, and service and fraternal organizations is much lower, with involvement in neighborhood, ethnic, or political associations at the very bottom. It is the church congregations that continue to play the local community role.[75]

Religious practice in congregations is uniquely American and deeply connected to the country's Protestant heritage and frontier history. Americans do not just prefer or identify with a denomination. They join a congregation with a finite membership. The congregation is a social space where people can share their faith, play roles at the church, celebrate holidays with others, educate and counsel young people and families, and have a social hall to host community events. Robert Putnam and David Campbell call this "congregationalization"—and all American faiths have moved toward it. Mosques and Hindu temples operate differently in America compared to elsewhere in the world, where imams and priests have more limited functions.[76]

America has also nurtured a mad number of religious denominations. Many emerged out of fluid beliefs, schisms, and mergers, some are new faiths founded in America, and still more came with diverse immigration, historically and contemporaneously. Mainline Protestantism encompasses vast numbers and types of Lutherans, Presbyterians, Methodists, Baptists, and Pentecostals. Modern Jewry includes the major Reform, Conservative, and Orthodox movements, as well as the Reconstructionists. The Orthodox movement also captures the various Hasidic traditions and Haredi rabbis with sect-like followings among the ultra-Orthodox in Brooklyn. Many Christian churches and megachurches are not grounded in any specific denomination. The black Protestant churches have their own distinct histories and traditions. And the Sunni and Shi'ite are distinct denominations, not surprisingly with their own mosques.

This is exactly what Thomas Jefferson aimed to achieve by the inclusion of the First Amendment: "Congress [will not endorse or establish] religion." While the First Amendment does not bar the establishment of state religion, all state subsidies to support denominations ended by the early 1800s and "nonestablishment" has remained the rule. The new states of the New World were mostly Protestant: Puritans who were looking for freedom from religious persecution, Anglicans aligned with the Church of England, and re-formed faiths in the Calvinist tradition. While Europe spent a good century contesting the relationship of state and religion, the United States disestab-lished its churches and promoted religious freedom from the beginning, even as America grew more religiously diverse. That is why America's religious pluralism and greater involvement through congregations have, amazingly, endured.[77]

We should remember that the nativist reaction against the waves of immigration also included hostility to certain faiths, particularly toward the Catholic Church, as the papacy was presumed to exercise a foreign and authoritarian control incompatible with American liberties. John Kennedy, as we discussed earlier, had to assure the Protestant South that "I do not speak for my church on public matters, and the church does not speak for me." Mormons faced enmity and discrimination. Jews were subjected to virulent persecution and quotas that limited access to universities, clubs, neighbor-hoods, and corporate boards.

In the post-9/11 world, Muslims have not been embraced, and close to half of all American Muslims say they face a lot of discrimination here, and opposition to building mosques still has the potential to be politically explo-sive. Hostility to Islam figured prominently in many Christian conservatives' rejection of Barack Obama, whose middle name is Hussein.[78]

But with secular culture so intrusive, the religiously faithful are very conscious of America's religious diversity and for the most part are mutually supportive of other faiths. It helps that the observant look to a more loving than judgmental God and are more likely to believe in heaven than hell. Across all denominations, large majorities believe someone not of their own faith can go to heaven and receive God's grace. More than 80 percent of Mormons, Catholics, and mainline Protestants believe that about non-Christians, as do about six in ten black Protestants and Evangelical Protestants.[79]

As Putnam and Campbell point out, "Americans' God is more avuncular than angry, and it turns out that this sort of everyday theology has real implications for the ways in which Americans get along with one another." The authors provide readers with a scorecard: "Almost everyone likes mainline Protestants and Jews"; "almost everyone likes Catholics more than Catholics like everyone else"; "Mormons like everyone else, while almost everyone [except Jews] dislikes Mormons"; "Evangelicals like almost everyone else more than they are liked in return"; "Catholics and evangelicals rate each other warmly," with no sign of our earlier religious wars; but "almost everyone dislikes Muslims and Buddhists more than any other group."[80]

While Muslims are victims of America's new religious polarization, they still do much better economically in the United States than in Europe. And while one-third of Americans say they would be bothered if a large mosque like the one proposed at "ground zero" in Manhattan was built in their area, two-thirds of Americans say they have no problem with it.[81]

America's religious pluralism is being sustained and renewed by the forces driving the country's immigrant and racial diversity. The growing Hispanic community reflects the religious diversity of the Americas, and each evolution of America's black community continues a commitment to black churches. Immigration from Asia and Muslim countries also adds to the mix, underscoring how much religious observance and new congregations are part of the modern American landscape, not just hangovers from past periods.

The African American Protestant churches offer a mixture of evangelism, social gospel, and black identity, with a long history of protecting and guiding their parishioners in a racially segregated world. About 8 percent of all Americans belong to an African American Protestant church, and attendance has been rising; indeed, attendance is trending upward among the blacks with a four-year college education—the reverse of trends for other denominations. African American Protestants are more likely than mainline Protestants and Evangelicals to say religion is important to their daily life and to their identity. They are more likely to attend church weekly and to read scripture literally. They are also more likely to pray daily, say grace daily, talk about religion daily, and read scripture daily.[82]

The African American Protestant church is the ultimate congregation, community center, and venue for politics as well. For their parishioners, the church is part of a racial and political identity with a history of providing institutional support to the black community that extends from the abolitionist movement through the civil rights era and today. African American

Protestants stand out among other religious groups as the most likely to make political decisions based on religion. And virtually no blacks voted for John McCain in 2008 or Mitt Romney in 2012.[83]

Hispanics are similarly religious and are helping to sustain religious observance in the United States. About 20 percent of Hispanics belong to Evangelical churches, similar to the proportion in Latin America. But two-thirds are Catholic, and that is changing the face of the Church in this country, just as the waves of Irish, Italian, and East European Catholics did when they dominated immigration to the United States. Today, more than a third of American Catholics are Hispanic, and that climbs to nearly 60 percent among those under age thirty-five. They are more observant and value religion more than non-Hispanic Catholics. They hold more traditional views on issues such as abortion and gay marriage while sharing blacks' views on government, including aid to the poor and narrowing the gap between rich and poor.[84]

The church has a special importance in the growing number of Hispanic neighborhoods. Many of their parishes are almost entirely Hispanic and provide a space that nurtures shared traditions and a sense of belonging. The clergy in Hispanic communities have also become strong advocates for undocumented immigrants and immigration reform.

So this diverse, dynamic religious landscape plays an enduring role in America, despite the very real secularizing trends in the country.

But for all of its continued and unique importance, there are vast, long-term changes taking place that are dramatically changing the role of religion in politics and fueling the country's political polarization. The slow, long-term decline in church attendance obscures dramatic and polarized generational and denominational shifts that are unfolding. Putnam and Campbell describe these shifts as "seismic societal shocks."[85]

The first shift is the rising number of people with no religion. Starting in the 1990s, the number of Americans who no longer attended church rose steeply from about 13 percent to more than 20 percent by 2010. We saw similar trends among those with no affiliation, climbing from about 7 percent and approaching 20 percent during the same period. The secular "none's" now exceed the number of mainline Protestants and are only outnumbered by Catholics and Evangelical Protestants.[86]

The second set of big shifts is generational and begins with the baby boomers, though the Millennials have the last word. The baby boomers lived the tumult of Vietnam, civil rights, changing gender roles, and the sexual revolution. They emerged more open to premarital sex than their parents and upcoming generations. More than 80 percent of baby boomers came to believe that premarital sex is acceptable, which turns the traditional value judgment at the heart of marriage and gender roles upside down. Their elder generations believed premarital sex was unacceptable with equal conviction and unanimity. But the baby boom was the largest generation, and its views on sex and marriage and skepticism about big, traditional institutions led it to pull back from organized religion. Between 1952 and 1978, the proportion of baby boomers saying religion is important to them fell from 75 to 52 percent. They became less observant than any other generation, and they have not returned as they have aged.[87]

The baby boom generation's marked shift produced a counterreformation in the generation behind it, which became more observant and more traditional on the disruptive issues of the 1960s. That generation identified more with the conservative Evangelical churches. This anti–baby boom generation gave religious conservatives the most support when they mobilized to forcefully defend traditional values from the cultural trends in the 1980s and 1990s.

But the shifts in the Millennial generation are of a whole different order. Church attendance has been dropping sharply with adolescents since the late 1990s, producing a generation where a stunning three in ten have no religious affiliation. In the mid-1980s, many young people were gravitating to the Evangelical churches in greater numbers than those who gave up on religion; but since 2000, the seculars widely outnumber Evangelicals among the Millennials— and the gap grows wider still with those under thirty. Today, 36 percent of adults under thirty are seculars while just 20 percent are Evangelical.[88]

And the third big shift forming Putnam and Campbell's "seismic societal shocks" is the deepening, polarized, and politicized reaction to the secularizing trends in the country. Over the past two decades, as church attendance plummeted among both non-Hispanic Catholics and mainline Protestants, the Evangelical churches gained more adherents and Evangelicals became more observant. And on matters of sexuality, there is a widening gap between them and the rest of the country. Through the 1990s, just 20 percent of non-Evangelicals judged premarital sex as always wrong, but Evangelicals grew more opposed over the decade.

The judgment that homosexuality is always wrong is a core belief among Evangelicals, and about 80 percent continued to be opposed through the first decade of the new millennium. Meanwhile, opposition in the rest of the country fell to just 45 percent. As same-sex marriage gained legal standing in more parts of the country and the Supreme Court's decision granting constitutional equality to gay unions paved the way for even more disruptive changes, almost seven in ten white Evangelicals remained strongly opposed to it. A 60 percent majority of the country and rising now favors recognizing same-sex marriage, up from about 30 percent a decade ago, and support has even surged among black Protestants, rising from 32 to 43 percent in one year. But among white Evangelicals support reached only 23 percent in 2014, though that reached 27 percent in 2015.[89]

In 2004, after the Massachusetts Supreme Court ruled to legalize same-sex marriage, only religiously unaffiliated and Jewish voters supported the change—and John Kerry paid a considerable price. But today, three-quarters of the unaffiliated and even more Jews support same-sex marriage, and they are joined by 62 percent of white mainline Protestants, 58 percent of white non-Hispanic Catholics, and 56 percent of Hispanic Catholics. Support for gay marriage is the emerging norm among many religious denominations, and that says a lot about America's religious pluralism and multiculturalism.[90]

Sometimes it is hard to see past the intensifying polarization and remember that this is a country where 40 percent still attend religious services each week and where religious pluralism and tolerance are very much alive.

BLACK AND WHITE?

America's "black and white" story has many chapters: a violent history of slavery; a civil war to achieve emancipation; a century of racial domination and legal segregation and disenfranchisement; periods of abolitionist opposition and struggle for civil rights, culminating in the Civil Rights and Voting Rights laws; antipoverty organizations and urban riots; affirmative action; and national protests demanding police reform after police killed unarmed blacks in Ferguson, Missouri, Staten Island, New York, and Baltimore, Maryland.

Mexican, Chinese, and Japanese Americans each have their own racial history, too. Nonetheless, America is undoubtedly in a new chapter of that history today. Consider this fact about the new America: a record 10 percent of couples told America's census takers in 2010 that their marriages are interracial—up from 7.4 percent in 2000. How annoying these spouses and their multiracial children must be for the census takers or pollsters trying to fit Americans into neat categories.[91]

The proportion of newlyweds that entered mixed-race marriages doubled, from 6.7 percent in 1980 to 15.1 percent in 2010. Among newlyweds, a stunning 17 percent of African Americans, 26 percent of Hispanics, and 28 percent of Asian Americans married someone of a different race. About a quarter of newly married African American men, a quarter of all Hispanics, and more than a third of Asian women formed interracial households. In big metropolitan areas such as San Antonio and Los Angeles, one-third of third- and fourth-generation Mexican Americans "married out."[92]

The proportion of Americans who are multiracial Americans is growing at triple the rate of the whole country and reached 6.9 percent of the population in 2015, according to a special Pew survey. Most Americans with a mixed-race background said they faced racial discrimination at various points, yet three in five "felt proud to have a multiracial background." That background, they reported, came with more "advantages" than "disadvantages."

Given America's history of excluding, segregating, and discriminating against blacks, Latinos, and Asians, not to mention Muslims today and Jews, Italians, and Poles in the past, one in ten is both remarkable and revealing of the plate-shifting social transformations that are changing the country before our eyes.

President Barack Obama is the living embodiment of this trend—the

American melting pot incarnate—as he noted during his address on the long-since-forgotten Rev. Jeremiah Wright controversy. "I have brothers, sisters, nieces, nephews, uncles and cousins, of every race and every hue, scattered across three continents," he said, "and for as long as I live, I will never forget that in no other country on Earth is my story even possible."[93]

The often racially charged opposition of white conservatives to America's first multicultural president is due less to his own mixed heritage and more to what he represents: the big demographic and cultural wave that threatens to swamp so many certitudes.

Three-quarters of New Yorkers voted to elect Bill de Blasio as mayor of New York City after he and his multiracial family attacked the NYPD's "stop and frisk" policy as racial profiling and spoke of a "tale of two cities." De Blasio is the grandson of Italian immigrants from Naples and Grassano on his mother's side and German immigrants on his father's. His wife is the granddaughter of Bajan immigrants. Their sixteen-year-old son, Dante, famously sported a hard-to-miss Afro when he delivered de Blasio's message in the first television ad of the campaign, which self-consciously embraced the multicultural identity of his family and the city. "We will succeed as One City," the new mayor declared in his inaugural speech, "a city of five boroughs—all created equal. Black, white, Latino, Asian, gay, straight, old, young, rich, middle class, and poor."[94]

The police union and many police officers expressed their frustration by turning their back on Mayor de Blasio at funerals for the two policemen shot by a deranged black gunman who said he was avenging the deaths at the hands of the police of Eric Garner in New York City and Michael Brown in Ferguson, Missouri. But even this tragedy shows a very different America. The two policemen assassinated by this gunman were Hispanic and Chinese American and part of a police force that came from fifty different countries and spoke sixty-four languages. "I believe that this great police force of this incredibly diverse city can and will show the nation how to bridge any divide," Vice President Joe Biden observed, reflecting the mayor's strong call for unity.[95]

President Obama's and Mayor de Blasio's stories were made possible by three big dynamics, without which these households would not exist or be growing in such numbers: the first is the rapidly growing diversity of the country and the electorate over the past two decades; the second is the prohibition of racial discrimination and promotion of legal equality before this recent influx began; and the third is the increased tolerance and acceptance of other races and racial diversity.

1. Diversity

It is hard to overstate the pace of growing diversity in the country over the past two decades, concentrated among younger populations, particularly the Millennials. The black, Hispanic, and Asian portion of the presidential electorate grew inexorably from 16 percent in 1996 to 18 percent in 2000, 21 percent in 2004, and 24 percent in 2008, reaching 26 percent in 2012. The rise was driven by above-average turnout of African Americans, a growing Hispanic population, and accelerating Asian immigration. Between 1990 and 2010, the white portion of the population dropped from 80 percent to 72 percent; in the electorate, the white share fell from 87 percent in 1992 to 74 percent in 2012.[96]

Among voters under age thirty, the white proportion has fallen even faster to 58 percent and is expected to shrink to 56 percent by 2020. Racial minorities will form the majority very soon in key swing states such as Florida, Georgia, and Nevada. It is no longer immigration driving this demographic swing, but higher birthrates: in 2011, the Census Bureau reported that nonwhite births outnumbered white births in the United States for the first time.[97]

2. Formal racial equality

But racial diversity alone does not produce the necessary and sufficient conditions for the Obamas and de Blasios. America had plenty of racial diversity in past eras, particularly in the South and Southwest. For most of the twentieth century in the pre–civil rights South, blacks were more than a quarter of the population. Hispanics comprised 20 percent of the Southwest after 1900 (a number up to 30 percent today). But despite sizable minority populations in the South and Southwest, the doctrine of white racial supremacy was the norm, discrimination and segregation were commonplace, and interracial marriage was illegal. It takes other ingredients.[98]

Prior to this new period of growing diversity, the country created a legal framework for ensuring racial equality, building on the Fourteenth Amendment's prohibition: no *state* shall "deprive any person of life, liberty, or property, without due process of law; nor deny to any person within its jurisdiction the equal protection of the laws." The Civil Rights Act of 1964 prohibited public and private facilities and employers from discriminating on the basis of race, color, religion, or national origin. In addition, Congress passed the Voting Rights Act of 1965, the Fair Housing Act of 1968, the Equal Credit Opportunity Act of 1974, and the Immigration Reform and Control Act of 1986, which made it illegal for employers to discriminate on the basis of citizenship or national origin. The U.S. Supreme Court struck down state anti-miscegenation laws in *Loving v. Virginia* in 1967.

Racial integration and affirmative action were deeply contested leading up to this period of growing diversity, but the legal framework and racial equality eventually became the norm.

3. Attitudinal and cultural changes

The demographic and cultural changes that transformed American families were ultimately produced by a change in attitudes. America had a long history of overcoming ethnic exclusivity and accepting ethnic diversity and multiculturalism, but moving beyond our racial differences was a much longer and more violent challenge. There is little doubt today that America has become more tolerant and accepting of racial diversity and has embraced it as part of the American character.

The country had passed numerous measures to bar discrimination, and those produced changes in behavior and attitudes. But acceptance of interracial marriage became the threshold for real racial acceptance and equality. It was not until 1968, a half year after the antimiscegenation laws were ruled unconstitutional, that we saw the first mainstream portrayal of a mixed-race couple in the movie *Guess Who's Coming to Dinner?* It is not very dissimilar from gay marriage today, where marriage meant the change was real, just, and unstoppable.

Only recently, in fact, have Americans embraced interracial marriage in overwhelming numbers. Overall approval went up slowly during the civil rights era and stalled short of a majority in the 1980s before it began to climb again in 1997; today, approval is at an all-time high of 87 percent. White approval also jumped in 1997 and now stands at 84 percent.[99]

Some Americans were simply coming to terms with the inexorable march of demography, but some, like the young, were coming to view interracial marriage as a positive thing, something that shows we are a better society. More than 60 percent of those under age thirty and almost half of those under fifty believe that more interracial marriages has been a change for the better, while only 5 percent say it has made things worse. Contrast that with older and more conservative Americans: just a quarter of seniors and a third of conservatives look at interracial marriages and say this makes us a better America. Barely a majority of those over fifty and just over a third of seniors tell pollsters it would be okay if a member of their own family married someone of a different race.[100]

Millennials—those born between 1980 and 1995—will make up well over a third of eligible voters in 2016 and will count for four in ten eligible voters in 2020. There is every reason to believe that the younger generation behind them shares their same outlook with a vengeance. For many young people, tolerance is a point of pride: they embrace intermarriage and racial diversity as part of their consciousness, in contrast to their perception of the views of older people. A plurality of Americans agrees that younger people have better attitudes toward other races and groups than do older people.[101]

Accelerating diversity, legal equality, reduced barriers, and, most important, changes in attitudes and dominant values that allow for the greater frequency of interracial households are changing the country well beyond the institution of marriage.

With 111.5 million people watching "America's game," Coca-Cola aired a sixty-second Super Bowl commercial. It began with a classic American archetype—a cowboy, riding out of a forest and looking out on a remote lake—but went on to capture the rest of the faces of America today. It showed, for the first time in a Super Bowl ad, two dads skating with their young daughter. It displayed the vast racial and ethnic diversity of the millions watching—Jews wearing skullcaps, Arab Americans in head scarves, African American kids break dancing, Mexican Americans at a movie, and a Native American grandmother with her grandchildren. America's unofficial anthem, "America the Beautiful," played in the background, and the lyrics rang out in English, but then in Spanish, Tagalog, Hebrew, Hindi, Keres, and Senegalese French. In an official statement, the president of Coca-Cola North America said, "We hope the ad gets people talking and thinking about what it means to be proud to be an American."[102]

Well, it sure did! Conservative critics took to Twitter to condemn Coke's choice to use languages other than English. The hashtag #BoycottCoke became a globally trending topic, with some expressing their frustrations, though more condemned or made fun of the conservative backlash. Surprising no one, Rush Limbaugh conjured up an entire conspiracy where the Republican leaders in Congress had aired the ad to drum up support for the immigration reform plan opposed by Limbaugh.

But the conservative discomfort is less interesting than Coke's decision to double down on the ad, announcing they would run it during the Olympics as well. Corporate America is on board with this rapidly changing America, and brands such as Coke are proudly aligning themselves with this multicultural nation on the world stage.

This just underscores how President Bill Clinton's formulation about unity from diversity has become the common sense of our times and the ascendant framework for our society and politics. We have come a long way from the old Europe and even the old America.

Part II

AMERICA'S DEEPEST PROBLEMS

4 CONTRADICTIONS OF THE NEW ECONOMY

The president of the United States believes America's economy is ascendant and exceptional. For a considerable time, he has tried to educate the American people about the transformative economic changes leading "business leaders around the world" to declare that "China is no longer the world's number one place to invest; America is." The United States "is closer to energy independence than we've been in decades" and "is better-positioned for the twenty-first century than any other nation on Earth."[1]

His confidence makes me believe he peeked at an early draft of this book. He piles on the evidence in almost every speech. America is producing "more oil here in the United States than we buy from abroad"; our "high school graduation rate is a record high"; "more young people are earning college degrees than ever before"; and "the deficit is coming down to boot, been cut more than half."[2]

The American people, on the other hand, could not have been more unenthusiastic in their reactions to this account of America's position and future glory. Democracy Corps captured their reactions to the president's portrayal of America's economic situation in his 2014 State of the Union address. We observed fifty voters who turned their dial meters up or down in reaction to his words, and while they rallied appropriately to America beating China, their lines headed down when the president turned to the future.

That is the rub. Except for a five-year interlude in the late 1990s, the majority of Americans have been critical of America's economy and successive presidents' economic stewardship for the past thirty years. The Clinton interlude was the one period of very low unemployment, a rising median income, a falling poverty rate, moderated inequality, and budget surplus. Ordinary citizens are very focused on what is happening to the average American and to their own families. The almost three-decade-long stagnation for those in the middle is the dominant thread in people's consciousness. That is the starting point and why such negativity of spirit is the not-so-new normal.[3]

The focus on the pessimism alone, however, understates the scope of people's new economic consciousness. Almost never getting a raise was already a given, but then came the consolidation of manufacturing and the advent of outsourcing and new technologies that all spelled fewer American

Lines flat or fall for "better positioned for 21st century"

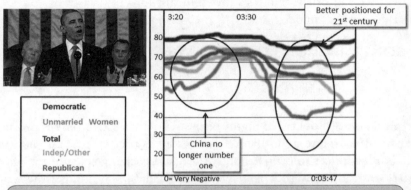

Dial testing focus groups among 44 swing voters in Denver, Colorado, conducted by Greenberg Quinlan Rosner Research for Democracy Corps and Women's Voices Women Vote Action Fund, January 28, 2014.

jobs. Americans were working more hours and jobs were now paying less and offering fewer benefits. They recalled when the floor fell out from under the economy and their leveraged families lost their jobs and the equity in their homes. They watched when the government only rushed to rescue the banks and the auto industry. They watched failed CEOs receive taxpayer-funded bailouts and then take millions in bonuses, and the super-rich with their Super PACs kept winning even more influence in Washington.

The ascendant economic trends in the country are very important, but ordinary Americans live the contradictions. Their experience with this new economic reality sets the stage for a new economic consciousness.

THE ECONOMIC REALITY

Consider how the households at the midpoint of the income scale are faring. The median household income, $51,017, is just $2,497 more than it was in 1979—that is a cumulative increase of just 5.1 percent over a span of more than thirty years. After reaching a high point in 1999, the median income has fallen 9 percent. It fell steadily leading up to and during the financial crisis and recession, and has not rebounded since. Today, a large majority says their family's income is falling behind the cost of living, including 56 percent of the sizable bloc of Americans earning between $30,000 and $75,000 a year. The bottom 40 percent of the population is spending nearly 40 percent of its income on housing alone.[4]

The median income continued to slope downward because those who became unemployed during the crisis and then found a new job took an average $610 cut in monthly salary and benefits, 17 percent below their compensation before the crisis. That sizable and abrupt cut, we shall see, deeply impacted people's understanding of the new jobs created in this economy.[5]

"Put simply, the recession took middle-class jobs, and the recovery has replaced them with low-income ones," *The New York Times*'s Annie Lowrey concludes. The data bears this out. The Federal Reserve Bank of Atlanta estimates that almost half of the jobs gained during the recovery were low-wage jobs.[6]

Two of the sectors that saw the largest employment gains during the "recovery" were leisure and hospitality (mostly in restaurants) and education and health services (mostly nursing aides and technicians), not the highest-paying sectors. The employment growth in business and professional services jobs was the largest, though this came mostly from new secretaries and temporary workers, not architects, accountants, and lawyers.[7]

Automation and robotics are now taking a real toll, and now even the economic profession has moved to a new judgment about this new economy. A full three-quarters of the leading economists surveyed by the University of Chicago thought automation in the past had not eroded employment. It had created new occupations in its wake. But when asked about the last few years, a third said automation was the main reason median wages had fallen and fully 29 percent were not sure. Economist Lawrence Summers concluded that automation does not always create jobs, and "This is something that's emerging before us right now."[8]

American manufacturing is in a kind of renaissance as it recovers as a proportion of the overall economy, though with manufacturing transformed, it has regained only 568,000 of the 6 million jobs lost between 2000 and 2009—and they are paying much less. The new hires and new UAW members in Michigan now earn between $16 and $19 an hour. The starting pay for the new GE jobs in Louisville is even lower, at $13.50 an hour, and the new Volkswagen jobs in Chattanooga pay just a dollar more—less than half of what it costs to employ autoworkers in Germany. Even at that level of pay, economists estimate that a quarter of American jobs can be offshored, which puts employers under further pressure to keep wages low.[9]

Moreover, the leading and admired companies of the new high-tech age, such as Apple, Google, and Amazon, just do not employ as many people in the United States in comparison to the major industries of the past. As Harold Myerson notes, the biggest employers here today are all low-wage retailers, while in the 1960s, it was GM, AT&T, and Ford.[10]

Those developments split the economy "into both very stagnant sectors and some very dynamic sectors." People see the writing on the wall and are aligning their skills accordingly, such that "ever more people are starting to fall on one side of the divide or the other."[11]

During the rest of this decade, job growth will continue to come heavily in the service sector and low-wage occupations. The occupations expected to grow the most are those of registered nurses, postsecondary teachers, truck drivers, customer service professionals, office clerks, laborers and movers, retail sales clerks, home health aides, personal care aides, and fast-food workers. The average yearly wage for these job categories—$32,386—is dramatically below the median income.[12]

People are not deluded when they describe the jobs of the new economy as minimum-wage jobs. The minimum-wage labor force more than doubled between 2007 and 2012, growing from 1.7 million workers to 3.6 million workers. These are not the jobs filled by teenagers on a pathway to a lifetime of work, as described in the conservative portrait. Four in ten minimum-wage workers have some college education or a four-year degree; only one in seven is a teenager. Worse still, the minimum wage, which Republicans refuse to raise, is only 38 percent of the national median wage, putting America's minimum-wage workers at the low end among OECD countries, on a par with Estonia, the Czech Republic, and Japan, and dramatically below mainstream Europe. In Britain, the last Labour government introduced legislation raising the minimum wage, and now minimum-wage workers make nearly half the median wage.[13]

The service sector jobs that account for most of the job growth in America do not offer appreciably more pay and therefore are hardly a reason for a person to pack up and move to another city, which is a major reason why Americans have become more averse to moving to another state or metropolitan area.[14]

In addition, many Americans—indeed, 27 million—are working part-time. More than a quarter of part-timers would prefer to work full-time. During the summer of 2014 the number of involuntary part-time workers reached 7.5 million, a figure that stood at 4.4 million seven years earlier. However, most prefer to work part-time as they balance the demands of work and family or juggle multiple jobs to get to the level of income they need.[15]

This decline in full-time, permanent employment is related to a larger transformation away from direct, centralized employment toward a "free agent" economy. According to Carl Camden, the CEO of Kelly Services, two in five American workers "were working as free agents, independent contractors, freelancers . . . temporary employees, self-employed professionals, [or in] small businesses of one or two" in 2014, a trend that "has been moving up steadily by 1 or 2 percent a year." Tyler Cowen labels this accelerating change in the nature of employment the "freelancing explosion," though *The American Prospect*'s editor Robert Kuttner labels it, more skeptically, "the TaskRabbit Economy."[16]

All these changes in the new economy leave the labor movement greatly weakened and unable to push up wages in the workplace and to press government to make things better for working people. As a result, the unionized proportion of the labor force dropped from 20.1 percent in 1983, the first year the Bureau of Labor Statistics began collecting such data, to 12.4 percent before the financial crash. On top of that, unions took a big hit during the recession and recovery years when state governments slashed public employment and limited union bargaining rights. Union membership stood at only 11.3 percent by 2014.[17]

Ronald Reagan gave business the moral and legal support to actively fight unions when he fired and decertified the striking air traffic controllers' union. As a result, America's largest retailers made opposition to unions central to their identity and business strategy. The southern political and business leaders in particular decried any potential breach. Republican state lawmakers, Senator Bob Corker, and outside activists such as Grover Norquist mobilized to defeat Volkswagen's momentary openness to union representation, going so far as to threaten to withhold tax incentives for the plant's expansion should the workers choose UAW representation.

Wal-Mart exported that southern employment model during its rapid countrywide expansion. As the largest private-sector employer with 1.3 million workers in the United States, it has had major influence on wages in the U.S. job market and has blocked union inroads. Managers are directed to keep labor costs below the norm for the retail industry, and the company presses for the lowest costs throughout its supply chain. When Wal-Mart locates in a county, it demonstrably produces lower wages across *all* employers over the longer term.[18]

With big companies pressing for the lowest possible payroll expenses and unions significantly weakened, workers have not been able to leverage their rising productivity into wage gains.

The full employment and high growth coming out of World War II—propelled further by rapid urbanization, government spending on education and infrastructure, new immigration, and high upper-income tax rates—produced a broadly shared prosperity for three decades. By contrast, America of the twenty-first century leads the advanced world in inequality, and according to major indicators, it has returned to levels of inequality unseen since the 1920s. Thirty years ago, the top 1 percent earned just 12 percent of the nation's income. But in the five years before the financial crisis, the top 1 percent took 65 percent of the total national income gain, and in the years after the recession they took *virtually all* of it (95 percent). The focus now is on the super-rich .01 percent because they took 90 percent of the income gains all on their own.[19]

Sitting atop the global economy are sixteen hundred billionaires. The number of billionaires has multiplied elevenfold since *Forbes* first compiled

U.S. worker productivity outpaces earnings

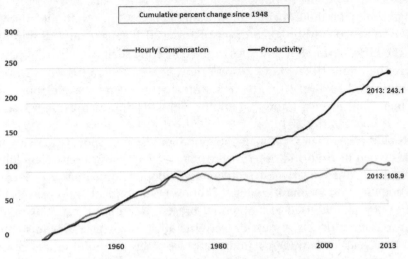

EPI analysis of Bureau of Economic Analysis and Bureau of Labor Statistics data.

its list in 1987. While the growth of their total worth fell briefly during the financial crisis, it has mercifully recovered at an accelerated pace. Billionaire status no longer even guarantees you a spot on *Forbes*'s list of the four hundred richest Americans.[20]

In *Capital in the Twenty-first Century*, Thomas Piketty argues that America and Europe are returning to a Gilded Age of inequality because income from capital (i.e., dividends, corporate profits, property sales, and rents) is rising above income from wages. Between 2000 and 2013, labor's share of national business income—meaning wages, salaries, and benefits—fell from 63 percent to 57 percent, three times what it decreased between 1947 and the turn of the century.[21]

According to Robert Samuelson, the shift of roughly $750 billion from labor to capital leaves the economy with a lot of investment potential, though not much expendable income for consumer spending. It is no surprise then that stores that serve Middle America, such as Olive Garden, Red Lobster, Loehmann's, and Sears, are in "dire straits," says Nelson Schwartz of *The New York Times*. JCPenney is closing thirty-three stores and is laying off 2,000 employees, and its shares have lost half of their value since 2009. But in a sign of our times, shares of Dollar Tree and Family Dollar Stores have doubled, and so have shares of high-end retailer Nordstrom—stores that serve an increasingly polarized economy.[22]

When return on capital is greater than the rate of economic growth—and the falling population rates in most developed and emerging economies are added in—you have a recipe for surging inequality and, ultimately, an economy dominated by inherited wealth. What Piketty establishes irrefutably, Paul Krugman writes, is that "talk of a second Gilded Age, which might have seemed like hyperbole, was nothing of the kind," and "incomes of the now famous 'one percent,' and of even narrower groups, are actually the big story in rising inequality."[23]

Piketty goes further, saying that those with inherited wealth will come to dominate those who earned it. His central conclusion is that Europe and America are returning to a "patrimonial capitalism" where "the commanding heights of the economy are controlled not by talented individuals but by family dynasties." That is not yet the American story, however.[24]

Piketty, who is fully immersed in American TV and literature, must have watched the 1944 classic *Mrs. Parkington*. The film depicts a very wealthy entrepreneur who makes his money in the West and returns to New York City, where the best "old money" families boycott a dinner for his wife at his new Fifth Avenue home. He maintains a list of "all those stupid, stingy little people" who "haven't got brains enough to make money of their own. They can only inherit it" and seeks to wreak havoc on them for "trying to ruin this country. This great, blasted, wonderful country" by "trying to make it into a closed corporation."[25]

But America's 1 percent story is exceptional: propelled by earned income and CEOs. American inequality "is quantitatively as extreme as in old Europe in the first decade of the twentieth century," Piketty acknowledges, though "the structure of that inequality is rather clearly different." Two-thirds of their wealth is from income, not capital accumulation. Today's economic titans are the CEOs and senior executives "earning" their "supersalaries," not rentiers living off inherited wealth and capital gains. In other words, our inequality is driven more by people like Mr. Parkington than the wealthy inheritors he so despised.[26]

The wages of the American 1 percent are up 165 percent since the early 1970s, and that rises to 362 percent for the wages of the top 0.1 percent. The ratio between the compensation of the average worker and the CEOs of the top 350 American firms (ranked by sales) began to surge in the mid-1990s, interrupted dramatically by bursting bubbles, though headed to an unimaginable gap. The ratio in 2013 was 295.9 to 1.[27]

While the average worker has yet to receive a raise, the pay of CEOs of the top firms increased 21.7 percent between 2010, when the recession had ended for companies, and 2013. The CEOs of the two hundred largest U.S. firms received a median pay package of $15.1 million, up 16 percent from 2011. "In other words," Gretchen Morgenstern writes, "it's still good to be king."[28]

In the period between 1940 and 1970, the average American CEO earned under $1 million. But changes in corporate governance and tax rates in the

CEO-to-worker compensation ratio, 1965–2013

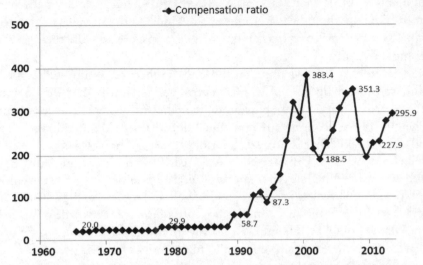

◆ Compensation ratio

Lawrence Mishel and Alyssa Davis, "CEO Pay Continues to Rise as Typical Workers Are Paid Less," *Economic Policy Institute*, June 12, 2014. Authors' analysis of data from Compustat's ExecuComp database, Current Employment Statistics program, and the Bureau of Economic Analysis NIPA tables. CEO annual compensation is computed using the "options realized" compensation series, which includes salary, bonus, restricted stock gains, options exercised, and long-term incentive payouts for CEOs at the top 350 U.S. firms ranked by sales.

1980s and 1990s produced an unseemly race to the top. It multiplied CEO compensation fifteenfold, accompanied by surging pay in C-suites and on corporate boards.

The Financialization Project of the Roosevelt Institute shows how the "shareholder revolution" allowed shareholders to defeat all other stakeholders and put "shareholder value" on a pedestal. When the top income tax rates were slashed and CEO compensation was linked to stock performance and capital gains were taxed at a lower rate than ordinary income, corporations made different choices: they now use their internal funds to boost executive pay or buy back stocks and put off raising wages or investing in their own companies. Having available credit no longer leads companies to invest, produce things, or hire people.[29]

Thus, the defining economic challenge in the United States is the stunning escalation of the compensation awarded to the CEOs of the country's largest companies and the stubborn stagnation in the wages and salaries of their employees, not inherited wealth and capital accumulation. And as we shall see, the growing disparity and changes in corporate America are very visible to ordinary citizens.

The income gap is most vivid in America's metropolitan centers, which attract the super-rich, top earners, and professionals, as well as new immigrants and those drawn to the expanding service economy. While these cities are the center of our economic and cultural dynamism, they are also ground zero for the country's growing income inequality. The city of Atlanta has the largest gap between the top 5 percent and the lowest quintile of income earners. Boston, Miami, Washington, D.C., San Francisco, New York, Chicago, Cleveland, Detroit, and Dallas round out the list of the top ten most unequal American cities.[30]

The inequality story is allowed to play out remarkably undisturbed by the infusion of new people into the upper class. The rate of intergenerational income mobility in the United States looks very much like the old Europe of France, Italy, and the United Kingdom. Despite growing inequality, the probability that a child born in the bottom quintile will reach the top fifth of the income scale has not worsened over the past three decades and a child had an 8.4 percent chance of making it in 1971 and a 9 percent chance in 1986 of making it. Nonetheless, the pathetic pace of people up the ladder of opportunity and the growing gap between the rungs clashes with America's presumptions about how this country is exceptional.[31]

It also makes itself felt in the real bottom line: how long you live.

Change in average additional life expectancy (in years) at age 55, by income, between cohorts born in 1920 and 1940.

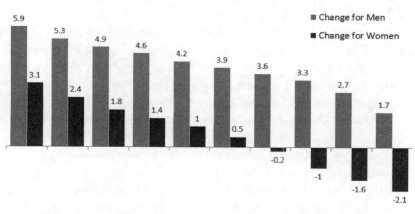

Derek Thompson, "Get Rich, Live Longer: The Ultimate Consequence of Income Inequality," *The Atlantic*, April 18, 2014. Data from Barry Bosworth, Brookings Institution, WSJ.com.

Men in the top 10 percent of income earners can expect to live six years longer than a man of similar means twenty years ago, but men in the bottom 10 percent will live only 1.7 years longer. Women in the top 10 percent can expect to live past ninety years old, three years longer than they did two decades ago. And here is the truly depressing news: women falling in the bottom 40 percent of income earners are now living shorter lives by as much as two years.[32]

The scale and consequences of American inequality, Joseph Stiglitz writes persuasively, "didn't just happen"; "it was created." While "economic laws are universal," America's "growing inequality—especially the amounts seized by the upper 1 percent—is a distinctly American "achievement."[33]

Under Franklin Roosevelt and the New Deal regime, the United States went much farther than Europe to establish the progressive taxation that Piketty prescribes. The top marginal tax rate fluctuated between 70 and 94 percent from the mid-1930s until 1981. But Ronald Reagan won a mandate for across-the-board tax cuts, and his tax reform cut the top tax rate to 50 percent in 1982, 38.5 percent in 1987, and all the way down to 28 percent in 1988. The decrease in the top tax rate has proven to be "perfectly correlated" with the increase in the top earners' proportion of the national income. Before the 1980s, there was little financial incentive for a CEO to press for higher pay but the dramatic drop in top rates "totally transformed the way executive salaries are determined." "Executives went to considerable lengths to persuade other interested parties (as in, the compensation committees that the executive often appoints) to grant them substantial raises."[34]

America's conservative-led governments slashed taxes on corporations and taxes on inheritance. In the mid-1950s, corporate income tax contributed almost one-third of federal tax revenue, but accounting and policy changes such as offshoring brought it down to less than 10 percent by 2013. During the 1950s through the 1970s, the statutory tax rate was roughly 50 percent; then Ronald Reagan dropped it dramatically to 34 percent in 1988. The *effective* rate for profitable companies is now 17 percent, down from about 30 percent in 1980, and well below the OECD average. The inheritance tax was 77 percent from 1941 through the post–World War II period until 1976 and has gradually declined over the past three decades, settling at 40 percent in 2014.[35]

Obviously, politics is very integral to how this new economy works. And as in other areas of American life, "following the money" will give you your best clues to what is happening. The campaigns for president and the U.S. Congress cost $6.3 billion in 2012, with a growing proportion spent by tax-exempt organizations that do not disclose their donors and by independent Super PACs, now the vehicles of choice for corporations and America's billionaires. Four-fifths of that outside money went to Republican-aligned conservative groups that in turn have backed Supreme Court decisions giving corporations a right to free speech—in particular, the "right to devote one's resources to whatever cause one supports." A decade ago, the Republican Party supported full disclosure of contributions and opposed the "soft money" that allowed special interest groups to influence elections. With increasing dependence on large undisclosed donations, the Republican Party now officially opposes any contribution limits and any disclosure rules.[36]

For better or worse, that money in politics is an integral part of the new economy.

THE NEW ECONOMIC CONSCIOUSNESS

These transformative economic changes are all too real for ordinary people, and they have forged a new economic consciousness to cope with them. They believe this new economy is governed by six principles.

The first is the most important, and nearly everything follows from it: jobs in the new economy don't pay enough to live on. All of the economists' data and accounts of long-term trends boil down to this simple reality. People are on the edge financially as they cope with stagnant wages, pay cuts, and the lack of middle-class jobs that pay well, and it means people will put together multiple jobs and come up with new strategies to get by.

The second principle says we live with an endemic cost-of-living crisis. Because people are right on the edge financially, they are consumed with the rising cost of everything. Top of mind are the costs of child care and student debt—expenses that can't be avoided but are just inexplicably high and can send them into economic ruin.

The third principle says that hardworking people in this new economy can aspire to a "more comfortable life," but not the middle-class dreams or Horatio Alger–style success, as in previous generations. People are very aware that the goalposts have been moved for their generation, and they are still determined to score. But scoring in this new economy has been recalibrated.

The fourth new principle says to pay attention to the growing number of people working independently as service providers, consultants, freelancers, and in their own small business, because that may be their ticket out. These new forms of self-employment provide many with added income to supplement their insufficient pay from today's full- or part-time jobs. They also potentially grant greater autonomy and an opportunity to escape the constraints of this new economy.

Fifth, while people accept that they are now globally connected, they think globalization makes the economy more complicated and the job market more competitive, and hurts the little guy. Globalization only excites the big winners.

And sixth, big businesses and CEOs are the big winners in this new economy, and they are the villains of the piece. They broke the social compact with their employees and their country and enriched themselves. They use their money and influence with government to tilt the economy to work for them.

Principle One: Jobs don't pay enough to live on

For the overwhelming majority of Americans, the core problem of the new economy is that jobs simply do not pay enough to live on. The new jobs and what they pay, or rather what they don't, concentrate the mind. They think America's ascendant trends are producing a fundamentally restructured economy with low-wage jobs at the center. How you cope with that low-wage reality determines how you survive and what kind of future is possible.

After the most successful year of job creation since the late 1990s and with employment levels back to precrisis levels, median income has barely budged. The dichotomy is perfectly illustrated by the change in people's feelings about the macro-economy and their own personal economic situation. While people's feelings about the state of the American economy have improved almost threefold between late 2008 and late 2014, their feelings about their personal finances are unchanged.[37]

Positive feelings about the macro-economy have improved, but no change in feelings about personal finances

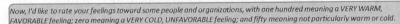

Now, I'd like to rate your feelings toward some people and organizations, with one hundred meaning a VERY WARM, FAVORABLE feeling; zero meaning a VERY COLD, UNFAVORABLE feeling; and fifty meaning not particularly warm or cold.

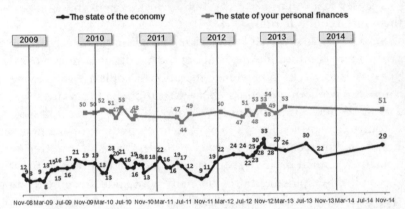

National Survey of 950 2012 voters conducted by Democracy Corps for the Roosevelt Institute, October 16–21, 2014.

The ordinary citizen has lived with these structural changes for a long time, but the elites and national leaders viewed the job situation through the lens of the so-called building recovery. In the years after the financial crisis, few things have enraged people in our focus groups more than simply reading a positive government jobs report. One moderator was almost attacked after reading a news report on the jobs gained in one month during the recovery. Voters in Ohio and Denver talked over each other as they disputed and qualified the news, rushing to dispel the conventional wisdom about the recovering economy.[38]

> [They] keep saying they created 225,000 jobs—and what is the job doing?
> I mean, you can work for McDonald's for $9 an hour to $11 an hour.
> (non-college-educated man, Ohio)

Yeah, you can always sway numbers. (non-college-educated man, Ohio)

What kind of jobs are they? (non-college-educated man, Ohio)

Exactly, and who got those jobs? I mean, who got those jobs? (non-college-educated man, Ohio)

What was the average salary of those jobs. . . . That would be my first question. (non-college-educated woman, Ohio)

Where are these jobs? (non-college-educated woman, Ohio)

What types of jobs? (non-college-educated woman, Ohio)

Are they part-time? (non-college-educated woman, Colorado)

Yeah, fast-food jobs? (non-college-educated woman, Ohio)

Are these jobs that people can live on? Or are they jobs you take because you have to? (non-college-educated woman, Colorado)

What kind of jobs? (non-college-educated woman, Colorado)

Or there's 2 million applying for the 240,000. (non-college-educated woman, Colorado)

Democracy Corps tracked aspects of people's personal economic experiences during the recovery and found that people continued to report stubbornly

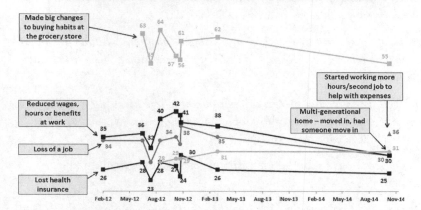

Micro-economic indicators show ongoing personal struggle

I'm going to read you a list of economic experiences some people have recently had. For each one, please tell me if you have directly experienced this in the last year, if your family has directly experienced this in the last year, or if someone you know well, like a friend, neighbor or co-worker, has experienced this or if no one you know well has experienced it.

*Data reflects the total of those who have felt a personal impact or an impact on someone in their family.

From Democracy Corps surveys from February 2012 to present. Data reflects the total of those who have felt a personal impact or an impact on someone in their family.

reduced wages and benefits, the loss of health insurance, struggles with prices at the grocery store, or needing to move in with a partner or into a multigenerational home. The results in the fall of 2014 looked painfully similar to those from early 2012.[39]

These findings are corroborated by Pew, which also reports on the continued difficulty of paying for medical care, rent, and mortgages. With that unchanging reality, the adjustments people are making look increasingly like long-term strategies and enduring struggles, not short-term reactions to a crisis.[40]

What was once the story of the aftermath of the financial crisis is now the story of every focus group we conduct, whether it is with the college-educated, new graduates, people living in the growing metropolitan centers, unmarried women, or working-class people without college degrees. They recall the "career jobs" that paid enough to live on, but now they are piecing together a bunch of "disposable jobs," often part-time jobs that pay much less.

The lower-income jobs, those grew exponentially . . . a lot of them in the mid-range, you know, where most middle-class people are, those really kind of stayed static in the last years. I'm actually looking for a job right now. There are lots of jobs out there in housekeeping, things like that. (young college-educated woman, Florida)

I always wonder how many of those jobs created are because of like what I talked about earlier where places are having two part-time workers versus one full-time worker. I think a lot of it is service industry jobs or part-time jobs. (non-college-educated woman, Ohio)

My mom works for Wal-Mart and she has to work on the night because the only position that they offer as full-time is the overnight . . . but that doesn't mean that it's full-time and offering benefits and everything else that people need. (young college-educated woman, Florida)

[I have] a job working overtime, my husband [has] one full-time job and a part-time job . . . and we are still just scraping by. (non-college-educated woman, Ohio)

It's getting better, but there was a hard point where I was out of work for six months, and I had to work five jobs, ten full shifts a week just to try and get back. (college-educated man, Ohio)

Temp work has become a lot more prevalent. (college-educated man, Oregon)

Last week at my part-time job I worked thirty hours and made $180. That's where a lot of people are at with being underemployed. (some-college-educated woman, Oregon)

That leaves them consumed with the cost of living. "It's very depressing" (non-college-educated woman, Ohio). "The cost of food is going up but raises aren't happening in the workplace so it's going to be really hard for people to afford food" (non-college-educated woman, Ohio).

They respond to the challenges with much more bargain hunting and some "extreme couponing" (non-college-educated woman, Ohio). They also engage in more bartering or share with their friends and neighbors to avoid large expenses.

I know with my girlfriends and I, we trade clothes like between our kids. I mean, I haven't bought clothes for my children in a long time. (non-college-educated woman, Ohio)

Our neighbors are all doing the same, we're . . . not buying extra stuff that we don't need. We borrow each other's lawnmower. . . . We help each other out. (non-college-educated woman, Ohio)

I've noticed there's this subeconomy of people who find a way to get the things that they need without having to make a lot of money. . . . I call it the Bartertown, like Mad Max. I don't have a lot of money; I trade for haircuts, I trade for my car getting fixed, my care of my animals. (college-educated woman, Oregon)

They are also making enormous changes in their living arrangements, including moving in with or taking in family members. Today, one in five Americans lives in a multigenerational household—and that number has doubled since 1980. During the recession, some young people moved back in with their parents and some parents moved in with their adult children, but five years later this is looking like a more enduring strategy for dealing with low wages and underemployment. Immigrant families and the financially pressed Millennials marrying five years later are the most likely to live in multigenerational homes. One Florida woman described her experience: "I moved my mom in with me last month. I am currently supporting my mom; her factory shut down and she was on unemployment" (college-educated woman, Florida).

In discussions with unmarried working-class women in Wisconsin, the younger women were more apt to say that they are "comfortable" but then qualified that definition by explaining that means they are just able to make ends meet or staying afloat with help from family or public assistance such as food stamps. One of the young women described "comfortable" as "I live check to check" (non-college-educated woman, Wisconsin). It was much tougher for the older unmarried women in the groups. One said she was "hoping for more but broker than poverty"; another reflected it "gets worse as the years go by"; another admitted, "I don't have any money" (non-college-educated unmarried woman, Wisconsin).

When the moderator mentioned the "recovery" to the older women, they erupted in laughter. When told that laughter was difficult to transcribe, one woman narrated, "Everybody's laughing really loud," and then she summed up her experience with the new economy for the elites:

> *I was working two jobs, working fifty to sixty hours and not even making what I made when I was eighteen years old . . . and that was fourteen years ago. It took me until now to finally find a job that is close to what I was making. I was working retail, and in retail they do give you nothing.*
> (non-college-educated unmarried woman, Wisconsin)

She isn't the only one zooming in on that inescapable equation:

> *You're still making the same salary when you get a job that you made ten years ago, but you can't even pay your bills. You're drowning. You're drowning.* (non-college-educated unmarried woman, Wisconsin)

> *You have to work twice as hard to make half as much as you used to.* (Hispanic man, Florida)

> *Back six years ago, 2006, 2005, you know, I was making double the income that I'm making now, you know, and every year, I just see a decline.* (Hispanic man, Florida)

That means being forced to make impossible trade-offs: "After we pay our bills we make sure that our children eat, but there's times my husband and I can't afford it and we eat peanut butter, potatoes, or rice. We make sure our children are eating four food groups, but we can't" (non-college-educated woman, Ohio).

Even those in "career jobs" feel the squeeze. One former payday loan employee observed the pressure of lower wages through the types of customers frequenting the store: "Watching as the economy got worse, the clientele that we had through the door started as people that just wanted extra money to go have fun and ended up as people that were teachers and worked for the IRS and had good-paying jobs but just weren't getting enough money" (college-educated man, Texas).

So what about the better-educated Americans who are better placed to adjust to the new economy? In the early summer of 2014, Greenberg Quinlan Rosner and North Star Opinion conducted extensive online focus groups for the Markle Foundation among those with some college education, a four-year college degree, or an advanced degree, as well as in-person focus groups with those with a four-year or postgraduate degree in the growing metropolitan centers of Portland, Oregon, and Austin. And guess what? Even though they are a step back from the edge, it is clear by their shared frustrations that they work in the same economy and live in the same America.[41]

The better-educated begin with a more stable foundation and bring more skills and capital to the challenges of the new economy. But most of them are focused on the same negative equation as those without a degree.

I'm doing okay but constantly find myself living paycheck to paycheck. (college-educated man, online)

Huh! Well, I'm doing okay. I have not lost my job. However, I think wages are stagnant and it is difficult to meet all expenses. (postgraduate-educated man, online)

Jobs pay less compared to inflation. (college-educated man, online)

Prices are going up on everything . . . yet we still earn what we earn. (some-college-educated man, online)

My experience with the economy can be stated as okay. I am happy to be employed. That is going right for me. I am happy to be married as well. I just feel that the workforce isn't exactly where it should be and companies aren't paying the salaries they should and sometimes I feel unappreciated. (college-educated man, online)

Everyone in the household has a job but raises are far and few between. It is hard to make ends meet and I am always watching my money. There is no discretionary money to use. Very hard to save anything except in 401k. (college-educated woman, online)

My wife and I still have jobs, unlike some of our friends. We have not gotten raises in about three years or more. Our expenses still go up and so has our credit card debt. (college-educated man, online)

It seems like it's about the same amount for the last five years. I don't feel like I'm making any gains. Perhaps, maybe at an inflation rate 0 to 1 percent, but from an income standpoint that's how I perceive my own condition. (college-educated man, Oregon)

Things are tight right now and have been for about the last two years— grocery prices are higher, gas prices are higher, insurances (car+health) have risen in cost. It seems like the price of everything is rising lately—and quickly and noticeably. (postgraduate-educated man, online)

Salaries for me personally and in general do not seem to be keeping up with inflation, with the rapidly rising costs of food, gas, and stuff. (postgraduate-educated man, online)

I am currently earning a reasonable amount, but the cost of items does add up. My family bargain-shops more than we use to. (college-educated woman, online)

Some of them lost businesses, houses, and jobs during the financial crisis and Great Recession and are getting back on a stable footing, though they are still conscious that they are living at a somewhat diminished level.

> *I am an architectural interior designer. When the housing market died so did my business. Being older it has been hard to find a job. My income has really dropped. I am doing other work, but it is just a job.* (college-educated woman, online)

> *My spouse lost his job at the end of 2013 and he only recently got a new position. Unfortunately, this job pays only about half of what he was receiving before. Needless to say, the economy and its personal effect has been difficult for us. On the other hand, we feel fortunate that he has a new position and that it comes with health benefits!* (college-educated woman, online)

> *I am doing well based on years of saving but it would have been better if the economy allowed my investments to do better. My husband had to take a job making less money for a while. It's a good thing we did so much saving over the years.* (postgraduate-educated woman, online)

> *We walked away from a home we were buying in 2010 because the lender would not work with us. We have been living in an apartment. My husband has been underemployed for over two years. Hard times have brought our family close together. I have been steadily working. I feel hopeful about our future.* (college-educated woman, online)

Equally striking are the efforts these people are also making to adapt to the new economy—to what they spend, how they live, what further education they seek, and what businesses they seek to create. The recent college graduates prepared themselves for the new economy. There is more than a little sense of entitlement to a certain type of job and level of income, and none of them are forced to decide whether their children will get four food groups each day, a choice described by one of the non-college-educated women above. The jobs available do not come close to getting them on a path that would make them confident, however, and they are adapting like everyone else.

> *I'm doing pretty well. I just graduated from college with my master's degree in chemical engineering and have been looking for a job. Currently I have a temporary job as it is pretty hard to find a permanent position. Therefore, I'm also trying to start my own company in biosensing, which is challenging. So I have a job, which is pretty good. I'm twenty-four and not making at least six figures so I would consider that not going right.* (postcollege-educated man, online)

As a recent college graduate, I am quite sensitive to the current economic situation. I am currently unemployed and have quite a bit of debt to pay off. So my decisions on spending money are usually not to spend much money, which I know won't stimulate the economy. (college-educated man, online)

It seems people are now in a never-ending search for better jobs that pay enough. A majority nationally said they or a family member started looking for a better-paying job in 2014, though even those with a college education are having a difficult time finding one. That reflects the lower-paid jobs that dominate the new economy.[42]

Principle Two: People face an endemic cost-of-living crisis

People are coping with stagnant or falling wages, and that makes them acutely conscious of rising prices, even though economists tell us inflation is tame and prices are barely rising. In Democracy Corps's poll for the Roosevelt Institute in late 2014, 55 percent of people said their family had to make big changes to their habits at the grocery store to deal with rising prices, and more than a third said they took on a second job or worked extra hours to keep up with expenses.[43]

For the college-educated participants in the online focus groups, this was top of mind when asked about their understanding and experience with the "new economy" and how the nature of the economy has changed.

INFLATION!!!! (college-educated man, online)

Inflation inflation and more inflation. (some-college-educated man, online)

Jobs pay less compared to inflation. (college-educated man, online)

We have to pay more with less income. (some-college-educated woman, online)

Capturing the essence of their struggles with wage stagnation and the feeling of inflation, one man used the sobriquet "stagflation" (some-college-educated man, online).

They know that struggling this seriously with everyday items is not what it should feel like to be in the middle class.

Whatever happened to middle class???? (college-educated man, online)

New economy=being forced to live much more modestly. (postgraduate-educated man, online)

We struggle more. (college-educated woman, online)

Everyone is hurting. (some-college-educated man, online)

The new economy to me means that the rich rule. (college-educated woman, online)

Rich keep getting richer. (college-educated man, online)

Larger spread between well off and the poor. (some-college-educated man, online)

The long-term stagnation of income in the country has led both working-class and middle-class Americans to believe that there is a cost-of-living crisis. "Everything keeps getting more and more expensive and cost of living is increasing but wages are not" (college-educated woman, online). That weighs down on even the better-off, as reflected in these responses from post-high-school-educated online:

I think everything is just so much more expensive and such higher expectations. (college-educated woman, online)

It is harder to live now because the prices are so high. People are not able to save enough for retirement. (college-educated woman, online)

[Health care] deductions and copays, high prices on every product in the market especially grocery items. (college-educated woman, online)

It is a more higher-priced economy, where everything is more expensive and the government takes more and more. (some-college-educated woman, online)

Higher gas prices. Foreclosures. It's the new norm. (college-educated woman, online)

Almost everyone is "living smaller" than their parents (college-educated woman, online). For past generations, ordinary expenses were not such a burden.

My parents were able to pay less for the things they bought. (some-college-educated woman, online)

Cost of living was less back then. (some-college-educated woman, online)

I think that families have to spend much more than my parents did just for the essentials and some wants. (college-educated man, online)

Gas was so cheap. (postgraduate-educated woman, online)

Plus, college was a lot less costly. (some-college-educated woman, online)

People have student debt today. My parents didn't have student debt.
(postgraduate-educated man, online)

They bought a home when they were very young and I have spent most of my life in an apartment. Everything costs so much more now and you can't live a simple life anymore. (college-educated woman, online)

Another thing that has changed since their parents' day is the rise of the two-income household and women in the workplace. Two-thirds of married mothers now work outside the home, compared to just 37 percent in 1968, and four in ten women are the primary breadwinners in their households. That is a perfect recipe for a surge in women talking up front in focus groups about the impossible and irrational costs of child care—a necessary expense for most families trapped by the new economy.[44]

Those women who are married, who have middle-class incomes, and with close extended families are better able to cope with child care, but do not raise the subject without expecting a fight about affordability. Nearly every newspaper article about child care begins with how "startlingly costly" it can be even for middle-class and two-salary couples, quoting parents who describe "the shock of day care costs." The $25,000 to $30,000 a year cost in a state such as New York really can take up to 30 percent of your income. In thirty-one states the cost of day care exceeds the cost of college tuition.[45]

This is the front line in the cost-of-living crisis, where the bill can be more than your mortgage payment. You feel how painfully disruptive child care costs can be for working-class women without college degrees.

I have two kids and . . . they have to go to child care because I have to work full-time just so that I can afford to feed them . . . in the summers I pay like $1,500 dollars a month for child care for two kids . . . I mean, it's more than my mortgage payment. (non-college-educated woman, Ohio)

We are just scraping by but child care continues to go up . . . [and] I have to have extended care because of my working hours. (non-college-educated woman, Ohio)

Raises aren't happening [but] child care continues to go up. Nobody's going to be able to do anything. (non-college-educated woman, Ohio)

My main consideration was for child care. I mean, it's just outrageous. (non-college-educated woman, Ohio)

People feel powerless in the struggle with the unimaginable price for something that is close to a necessity for working people but whose jobs don't pay enough to live on. This is such a dilemma that many wonder whether they are just treading water:

> [M]y husband and I are both midlevel managers but we both work full-time. We have three little kids at home and child care is ridiculous . . . when [my parents] can't watch my kids before they go to school that will be a decision where we're like, "Is it really worth working if you can't have reduced child care? That's almost your income for three kids." That's a challenge. (college-educated woman, Oregon)

> [If] I get a job right now that I am qualified for, I will basically make enough just to pay for the day care, so that's pointless. (non-college-educated unmarried woman)

> I can't not do it because the money that I still bring in pays for electricity and food and so it's, I mean, it's just a complete vicious circle. But at the same time, I mean, I don't have any more to give so I don't know what to do. (non-college-educated woman, Ohio)

Another woman was getting help from the state, "so [she wasn't] paying for all of day care," but when she got a raise she went $5 over the eligibility limit and then faced a $1,000 bill each month. She summed that up: "Either if you're wealthy you're okay. If you're poor, you get help, but if you're working you are pretty much screwed" (non-college-educated unmarried woman, Wisconsin).

The cost of college and student debt are right up there with day care on the list of those expenses that are massive financial burdens but increasingly necessary. Student debt has exploded to more than $1 trillion in the past decade, rising $338 billion between 2008 and 2013 alone to become the lion's share of the $3 trillion in consumer credit. Student debt has gone past auto and credit card debt and weighs down on graduates and families. Moreover, while delinquency rates on other kinds of debt have fallen over the past few years, the number of student loans that are delinquent for more than ninety days surged from roughly 7.5 percent in 2008 to almost 12 percent in 2013.[46]

At the same time, people feel a college education is increasingly necessary to get a job that pays well. So it should not be surprising that student debt and college affordability produce animated discussions in this world of debilitating costs. Many raise questions about whether college is worth it, and the debt burden may be putting the training people need out of reach. For many of the Millennials we talk to in groups, this is their central economic worry. The participants in our groups in Orlando, Florida, went right to the word "crisis."

We have a student loan crisis basically where you're getting into so much debt to get that degree, to get that better job, that that is becoming cyclical where you are working just to pay off your student loans so it's almost, it's a double-edged sword. (Hispanic man, Florida)

When you come out of school you're $50,000 or $100,000 in debt. You're lucky if you're making, you know, $30,000 or $40,000 a year. That's paying your bills. That's paying your rent. You're not paying off your debt so you're never getting ahead. (college-educated woman, Florida

People coming out of college are getting off on the wrong foot. My husband has $58,000 worth of student loans and isn't making even close to what he needs to be making to pay it off. They're saying that you need all this education to get these jobs to make more money but yet you come out of college with all this debt and you can't ever catch up. college-educated woman, Florida)

Many work jobs outside their degree, live with their parents, or make other strategic sacrifices so they can afford to pay off their loans.

I have plenty of student loans that I'm paying. I have a degree. I'm working as a bartender not by choice; not saying I love it but I make more money doing that than any position I could get in my degree so I pay my student loans as a bartender. (college-educated woman, Florida)

I live with my parents, rent free, so that I can focus on paying back my student loans. (postgraduate-educated woman, Ohio)

One woman battling cancer was going to have to go off disability and return to work sick because, as she said, "I'm looking at $40,000 in student tuition loans that I have to pay back. Unless I can win the lottery, or find a sugar daddy" (college-educated woman, Oregon).

Their near-breathless reactions to the cost of child care and the scale of student debt takes place in the context of an endemic cost-of-living crisis created by the jobs that don't pay enough to live on and with the price of everything going up. In its fall 2014 survey for the Roosevelt Institute, Democracy Corps asked people which three problems are the most important for the country to address. People zeroed in on the plain fact that jobs don't pay enough to live on, what they make cannot possibly cover child care expenses or student debt, and working women don't make as much as their male coworkers.[47]

Those perceptions of rising prices across the board and the inability to earn enough to pay them set the stage for deep worries about big, sudden

Jobs that don't pay enough at the center of economic consciousness

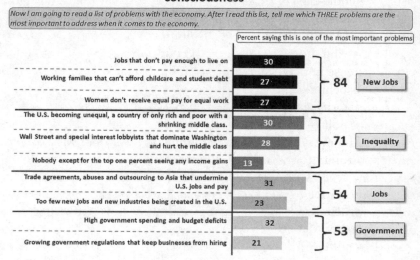

Now I am going to read a list of problems with the economy. After I read this list, tell me which THREE problems are the most important to address when it comes to the economy.

Percent saying this is one of the most important problems

Jobs that don't pay enough to live on	30	New Jobs (84)
Working families that can't afford childcare and student debt	27	
Women don't receive equal pay for equal work	27	
The U.S. becoming unequal, a country of only rich and poor with a shrinking middle class.	30	Inequality (71)
Wall Street and special interest lobbyists that dominate Washington and hurt the middle class	28	
Nobody except for the top one percent seeing any income gains	13	
Trade agreements, abuses and outsourcing to Asia that undermine U.S. jobs and pay	31	Jobs (54)
Too few new jobs and new industries being created in the U.S.	23	
High government spending and budget deficits	32	Government (53)
Growing government regulations that keep businesses from hiring	21	

National Survey of 950 2012 voters conducted by Democracy Corps for the Roosevelt Institute, October 16–21, 2014.

expenses over which they have no control that could make them cut to the bone, go into debt, go bust, or do something desperate.

I can't afford to lose right now. (non-college-educated woman, Ohio)

Doing okay now but one slip and I could be in trouble. (college-educated man, online)

I'm finally starting to find a little bit of a plateau, but I'm always waiting for the rug to get pulled out from under me. (college-educated woman, Oregon)

Principle Three: People can aspire to a "comfortable life," not middle-class dreams

People are consciously forging more realistic and downsized aspirations for what they want to achieve in their life and for their families. The starting calculation in life's new equation are the jobs that don't pay enough, the disloyal companies, and the lack of social mobility. That produces a new trajectory—one that people contrast with the middle-class trajectory open to previous generations. They know America has changed fundamentally and that they are forming aspirations and goals appropriate for our times.

Americans now seem settled on attaining a "comfortable life." Getting to "comfortable" allows you to enjoy your family, your community, your church, your city, or your hobbies. That aspiration is a downgrade from hopes to become firmly middle-class or to get rich with hard work and enterprise, Horatio Alger–style. It notably lacks the imagery of a social ladder where millions are climbing to an ever higher level. That aspiration has the virtue of being realistic and satisfying, however, reflecting a country that has only produced a 5 percent increase in the median income in three decades and where income mobility trails behind old Europe.

A large majority of Americans—54 percent, according to an NBC/*Wall Street Journal* poll—accept that "the widening gap between the incomes of the wealthy and everyone else is undermining the idea that every American has the opportunity to move up to a better standard of living," while only a minority now accepts that "the United States is a country where anyone, regardless of their background, can work hard, succeed and be comfortable financially." So their own experience confirms the economists' characterizations of this new reality. [48]

That does not mean that people have given up. They have moved to more realistic goals in this new context, though still infused with a great deal of aspiration. Most people are feverishly looking for ways to attain that more comfortable, freer life. They are changing how and where they live, how they consume and what they borrow; they are trying to obtain the right skills, starting businesses or offering services on the side, and using technology to encourage that entrepreneurship. Increasingly, they are hoping to live in communities and metropolitan areas, feeling a strong local identity, joining networks of family and friends, seeking more time for leisure and a better quality of life. [49]

Americans today are very conscious that baby boomers and older generations had a different path and different outcomes, and they have no illusions about those facts. Actually, they almost romanticize what prior generations faced to make a point. That only underscores the clarity of their consciousness about how differently the new economy works. The older generations "went to school on scholarships and had jobs waiting at the end of college" (some-college-educated woman, online); "they could easily acquire houses" (college-educated woman, online); they "were able to save for retirement" and "more companies offered pensions" (college-educated woman, online). Listen to how these online group participants draw the contrast with their parents:

> *My parents could do what they wanted and didn't have to worry too much about money. Jobs were more plentiful, it was easier to get a loan on a new house.* (college-educated woman, online)

> *Their dream was a secure job, a house and higher education for their children. My dream is just to have health care.* (college-educated woman, online)

My dream isn't my parents'. I just want my kids to have an even shot in competition for jobs. (some-college-educated man, online)

My parents were at the height of the American dream: house, good STABLE job, low prices. I'm struggling in all areas. (college-educated woman, online)

What disrupted that path most dramatically was the change in the types of jobs available and the behavior of companies toward their employees. Working people in the past had more "stability" and "better job security." Back then, you might have one job in a lifetime, but now "you cannot rely on your employer for security." Those struggling to do well in today's economy are very conscious that their "parents could work for a company that showed loyalty and took care of them" (college-educated man, online). One man crisply captured the consequences of not having that kind of job: "My parents could work/get an honest job and be able to live a *'normal'* life. That's not the case anymore" (college-educated man, online).

With that understanding clearly in mind, Americans across the class divides are articulating a shared view of the "American Dream" that aspires to a comfortable life. That may seem diminished, yet it gets to something fairly fundamental and unrealized.

In our groups with young people and those without a college degree, people were actively redefining it, and offering real perspective as to why.

Yes, I just think it needs to be altered a little bit, maybe brought back down. (young college-educated woman, Florida)

You can still live the American Dream but you have to reassess your priorities. (young college-educated woman, Florida)

I think sometimes we need to reorganize our dreams and make them a little bit more realistic. (young college-educated woman, Florida)

It's not like it used to be. (non-college-educated woman, Ohio)

Well, to me, I mean, say back in World War II the American Dream was, you know, to have a nice house, 2 kids and a new car and that sort of thing. To me, I don't necessarily think that, you know, the idea of a affording a new house is realistic for a couple of generations maybe. (non-college-educated man, Ohio)

The college-educated in their online discussion were a little more expansive, including good health and a happy family as part of the dream to live comfortably:

The American Dream=being able to maintain self-sufficiency during my working and retirement years. (postcollege-educated man, online)

My American Dream is ensuring that my family has health and that I have adequate means to live comfortably. (college-educated man, online)

The Dream to me means having a stable, happy, comfortable life and livelihood and family. (some-college-educated man, online)

Being able to live comfortably. (postcollege-educated woman, online)

Living debt free and not having to worry about money and providing for my family the way I want to. (college-educated woman, online)

Being able to live the lifestyle that I want without having to worry about finances and not being able to do for myself or others in terms of healthcare, etc. (college-educated woman, online)

What living comfortably means depends on what each person values and their passions: "The American Dream is simply living the life that makes you happy. Mine is teaching and being able to spend time with my family" (college-educated woman, online).

There are a handful of people who describe the American Dream as "working to achieve greatness" or "being rich" (postcollege-educated man and woman, online). The woman punctuated her statement, "Let's be honest. It's having enough money to live the way you want without worry." Even her definition fell within the emerging consensus.

Immigrants to the United States and Hispanics and not an insignificant number of blacks put a lot more faith in conventional notions of the American Dream. Their own recent experience with America and faith in America as a land of expanding opportunity creates a personal trajectory in their mind that is somewhat independent of the new economy. Some of the Hispanic focus group participants in Austin did not embrace a diminished notion of what is possible for their lives: "I mean I'd like to be able to save enough money to have a comfortable retirement, but at the same time I'd like the home ownership, the ability to put my daughter through college, be able to support and care for my elderly parents" (college-educated Hispanic, Austin).

When the moderator then asked the Hispanic participants if the American Dream is different for Hispanics, a number agreed and elaborated:

I think Latinos are generally more family-oriented, so they're going to have more family preoccupations and will allow family to determine more of the decisions, the big decisions are made for people. (college-educated Hispanic, Texas)

I think that Latinos, it's still a little more of like the old economy of having a house, and your family, and everything like that. The yard and the dog. I guess what you see on TV. I think that it's still that way. (college-educated Hispanic, Texas)

I totally agree with that because in fact mine was family-oriented. I said having a job, my American dream is having a good job to be able to provide for my family and having the environment where I can raise my kids to be responsible adults. (college-educated Hispanic, Texas)

In surveys, America's minority and immigrant communities continue to say that America's future includes a great deal of opportunity and mobility. The truth is that new immigrants will always compare America with the countries they left, experience economic gains in their lifetime, and see their children get more education.

But with more than 75 percent of Americans saying today that they are not confident "life for our children's generation will be better than it has been for us," it is good that most people seem determined to find a route to a comfortable life in the new American economy.[50]

Principle Four: Freelancing, independent contracting, and small businesses may provide more income and autonomy

More people are employed independently in contracting, consulting, and freelancing, more are self-employed and own small businesses, and we are a country with very visible entrepreneurs. The increasing role of independent work was clear when focus group participants introduced themselves to the others. Many are working independently or know someone close who is. Pay attention to the college graduates in the groups and online. It is pervasive: "My business is going very well" (college-educated man, online); "I'm also trying to start my own company" (postgraduate-educated man, online); "I am self-employed" (college-educated man, online); "So we have a couple of small businesses on the side" (college-educated man, Oregon); "I've been doing a lot of contract work, and it pays the bills" (college-educated man, Ohio); "I'm a self-employed programmer" (college-educated man, online); "I recently started my own business" (college-educated woman, online).

Independent work is part of their strategies for providing added income on top of full- or part-time work or to supplement a spouse's income. As one woman put it, "If there's no jobs for them to actually acquire then that means that they have to create their own jobs" (college-educated woman, Oregon).

Started part time work for a software company . . . I'm trying to start a motorcycle garage at the same time so I can make ends meet. (college-educated man, Ohio)

*I'm currently a doughnuteer at a well-known doughnut shop downtown.
Going there tonight, then I do Internet marketing consulting on the graphic
design, 3-D animation and illustration side.* (college-educated man, Oregon)

Some see themselves able to achieve greater autonomy in a world where working people have uncertain hours and less flexibility yet also must balance family life and the education and training opportunites needed to get ahead.

*I think it's becoming today way more about being independent, being able to
pursue your own activities.* (college-educated Hispanic, Texas)

*The further I get from working for a corporation the less I want to go back,
because the freedom to make your own decisions is becoming extremely
important to me.* (college-educated man, Oregon)

Many of the college-educated who are well versed and positive about technology see it as a tool to allow the small guy to compete, and some know from experience:

*If you own a small business . . . the ability to use the same technology . . . as
a corporation levels the playing field.* (college-educated man, Ohio)

They're using the efficiency of [new technology] to undercut the entrenched.
(college-educated man, Oregon)

*I guess that's what all these things have done, is to take these larger
corporations' game away from them a little bit. Which I approve of.*
(college-educated woman, Oregon)

*It's more entrepreneurial opportunities that exist because of the Internet and
because of the technology and the social media. . . . It makes it easier to
determine where there's a need that needs to be addressed, and to be able to
come up with a solution for that need. There's also more collaboration of
somebody in Washington State talking to somebody in New York State, and
they form relationships that can turn into money.* (college-educated woman,
Ohio)

*If I didn't have a website, there's a lot of plans I have that I wouldn't even
have because they found me through Google, or whatever online sources I'm
on, or directly through my website. By having that small businesses can take
off a little bit.* (non-college-educated woman, Oregon)

So for many hoping to escape the constraints of this new economy where there is so much competition, little job security, no flexibility, and few pay raises, freelancing and independent business may be the solution.

In making that choice, they may be trying to follow the route many blue-collar workers have taken in manufacturing and construction. Many manual and factory workers are now working in small groups, dispersed in industrial parks, working for small contractors or are small businessmen, Andrew Levison writes in his insightful book. If you look at the construction of single-family homes and small commercial buildings, "you will see instead a collection of pickup trucks and vans with the signs of independent contractors, insulation, sheetrock and heating and air conditioning contractors, grading and foundation contractors, paving installers, trim carpenters, welders, glaziers, roofers, stonemasons, cabinetmaking, landscaping, and security and home entertainment installers." They describe themselves as "hardworking and underpaid manual laborers, as prototypical independent and free Americans and as members of functional local communities." They tell Levison, we're "just country people."[51]

But small businesses took a big hit during the recession—killing 170,000 small businesses between 2008 and 2010—and the number of small businesses is not back to precrisis levels. In focus groups, we found that people fully appreciate that being in business for yourself particularly exposes you to the ups and downs of the economy.[52]

When the economy first collapsed I literally lost half my clients, half my income. My husband was going to school, wasn't earning any income . . . I spent a long time trying to build my business back up, and get my clients back up, and I still haven't gotten back to where I was before. (non-college-educated woman, Oregon)

Or a lot of time you have to take work because that's what's there. . . . My husband does construction and he takes work all the time that's under what he should really make. (non-college-educated woman, Oregon)

I've also found that when I started my business I was definitely living hand to mouth and it took a lot of years for me to be able to buy all the equipment that I needed and get up to the next level. (college-educated woman, Oregon)

My family was in steel, and we really got hit hard, big time. (non-college-educated woman, Ohio)

I'm so afraid of starting a little business. Like, "Oh, my God, how am I going to make sure I make my monthly payment?" (non-college-educated woman, Ohio)

With such limited opportunities in work, the ability for people to connect via the Internet has made working independently much more realistic and worth the risk.

*I have a friend of mine who started up a company, and he definitely
wouldn't have the financier that he does, or even the collaborators if he
didn't have an online presence.* (non-college-educated man, Oregon)

*I sell on eBay, and I sell global, and this last three weeks I've sold to China,
to Russia, to Taiwan, and we chat back and forth.* (non-college-educated
woman, Oregon)

*I have a friend of mine who's starting a small business. With him, he's able
to use Open Source . . . to find information in order to get his business off
the ground.* (non-college-educated man, Oregon)

*There's plenty of websites, there's LinkedIn, there's Business Trip, there's
tons of websites out there that are available for not just social networking,
but for economic networking, business networking, all of it.* (non-college-
educated woman, online)

In her *New York Times* article, Natasha Singer offers an account of a thirty-
five-year-old female navy veteran's participation in the "shared economy" that
allows her to pursue a goal of $25 an hour with "both freedom and uncer-
tainty." She makes her money from driving with her own car, responding to
calls from people using their Uber or Lyft smartphone apps, doing cooking
gigs, assembling furniture, and some accounting contracts for diverse Task-
Rabbit clients. Despite the immense uncertainty and range of compensation,
she creates an independence of sorts, flexible enough for her to organize her
work around her child care schedule.[53]

It is possible that here lies the future. The founder of the Freelancers Union
points out, "People are doing this in the midst of wage stagnation and income inequality, and they have to do these things to survive." As we saw with
the first principle, jobs don't pay enough to live on in the new economy, and
what if that is not temporary? These people may well be the advance guard of
a "new class of laborer, dependent on precarious work and wages," called the
"precariat" by one labor economist.

How precarious, as one can see already, depends on whether your city,
state, or employer is raising the minimum wage to a living wage, whether
individuals are able to get health insurance under the Affordable Care Act,
whether you are treated as a full-time employee with benefits, and whether
groups are organizing the independent workers.

**Principle Five: Technology makes life better but being globally
connected makes the economy more complicated and competitive**
Greenberg Quinlan Rosner and North Star Opinion conducted online focus
groups for the Markle Foundation among those with a four-year college

or postgraduate degree, as well as in-person focus groups in the globally connected high-growth, high-tech-friendly, and high-quality-of-life cities of Austin, Texas, and Portland, Oregon—in short, with the winners of ascendant America in a globally connected world. We asked them, "How is the structure of the economy different from maybe what your parents had?" "What does the term 'new economy' mean to you?"

The new economy means new technology, and that excites them. The new economy also means being globally connected, and they are conflicted about globalization. They understand how disruptive it has been for the types of work available, the amount of pay employers offer, and the fate of small businesses. Technology might level the playing field and create new opportunities, yet they believe it comes with a lot of collateral damage. They lack the enthusiasm for global connection one might expect—and these are the winners.

Many of the online participants immediately associated the term "new economy" with new technology, the Internet, tech companies, and tech jobs, and they believe that is an exciting world.

> The new economy is one that depends more on technology and innovation. (college-educated woman, online)

> There are more internet companies and tech jobs. (college-educated woman, online)

> Certainly technology has us moving economically and socially at a much faster pace. (college-educated woman, online)

> New economy . . . the way the internet and twenty-four-hour news cycles have impact. (college-educated woman, online)

> It's more tech based. (college-educated woman, online)

Two-thirds in the online groups said that the technology leaders and entrepreneurs were leading the adaptation to the forces of the new economy. One person said that Facebook was an example of a company adjusting well to the new economy *because* they were a technology company (college-educated woman, online). They admire Apple, Google, Amazon, Microsoft, and Netflix. They revere the high-tech entrepreneur with an idea who takes risks, attracts investors, and creates value, such as Steve Jobs—"He was amazing" (non-college-educated woman, Ohio). They value that technology and see the impact it has had on their lives. In fact, in focus groups in Oregon they were surprised they were not given iPads to type out their answers to handouts!

In the Austin focus groups, Google was the center of the discussion.

"Google's just everywhere. Like, it's the only company I would sell my soul to. They're in control of my soul. I use Gmail. I use everything" (college-educated respondent, Texas). They invested heavily in technology for "things we all need," including a fiber network that forced old companies such as AT&T to finally build what they should have in the first place. Google gets the benefit of the doubt; as one person added, "I hear they have a good work environment" (postgraduate-educated woman, online).

Among the online focus group participants, a stunning 90 percent said that technology has had a positive effect on the economy. Many can see how technology can help small businesses, and people talk about the new technology jobs and believe the tech industry will provide many new employment opportunities in the future. They are encouraged because "some of the biggest companies, Facebook, Google, Twitter, they were all very small startups and they've become the leading global enterprises" (college-educated man, Texas).

But they are more concerned about who gets to reap the benefits of the tech-enabled economy and whether those who are struggling will see any gains.

Connectivity, but you have to ask who it's serving. (college-educated man, Oregon)

I think it depends on what side you're on. If you're taking advantage of technology. (non-college-educated man, Ohio)

They are especially worried about what happens to those who are unprepared for the digital age. One Oregon college-educated woman asked, "What about people who are not technologically inclined, or savvy? Do they just get left behind?" And another observed the consequences: "I think computers and mechanics have replaced manual labor. People are relieved of jobs and computers and machines don't need salaries!" (some-college-educated woman, online).

Many small businesses just cannot keep up with the growing pace of new technologies, where "it's out with the old and in with the new" (some-college-educated man, online). They know "technology changes much faster than most individuals and/or businesses can keep up with" (postgraduate-educated man, online). People worry about how the smaller companies will fare, including the "mom and pop stores" that "do not do well in utilizing the internet" (some-college-educated man, online). Many think small shops and firms have too few resources and often cannot compete. One college-educated woman wrote online, "Small companies most likely [have not done well adapting to the new economy] because they do not have the resources, manpower and money to do so."

When it comes to globalization, the online college graduates can only be described as deeply ambivalent. Three-quarters said that globalization has had a negative impact on U.S. workers and half that globalization has a negative effect on the economy. In the survey for the Roosevelt Institute, "trade agreements, abuses, and outsourcing to Asia that undermine U.S. jobs and pay" was the second-most-cited economic issue that needs to be addressed, reflecting the broad doubts about globalization. It is, as one person said, "probably good for the world but for us in the United States, probably more bad than good" (college-educated man, Ohio) and "in the short term it's certainly transforming the standard of living here, and not in a good way from what I can tell" (college-educated man, Oregon).[54]

Those with more education and those living in America's globally connected and high-tech cities—people who are integral to the new economy—are just lukewarm about globalization. Most view it as a given:

> *The economy [is] more global and more high efficiency.* (college-educated man, online)

> *It is more globally based now.* (some-college-educated man, online)

> *It is more global. Things in other countries affect our economy more drastically.* (college-educated man, online)

> *Global problems.* (college-educated man, online)

> *It is a more global economy.* (college-educated man, online)

> *You have to be more globally aware now. Speaking Chinese is almost a necessary item on the resume now.* (some-college-educated man, online)

Globalization is associated with more competition for everything, fewer American jobs, and fewer jobs, period. The new economy in this connected world is a "much tougher market now with more competition in everything" (college-educated man, online).

> *It is harder to get ahead. More people competing for the same jobs.* (postgraduate-educated woman, online)

> *Across America, we need to wake up to the fact that we're no longer competing against you and you and you. I'm competing against the guy in China, in India, wherever the lower-cost labor is with a higher education and higher educational standards.* (college-educated man, Ohio)

America and American employees are the losers in this context.

> *U.S. workers, obviously you can make a strong case that it's impacted us negatively because jobs are cheaper elsewhere and we're losing our jobs to those countries.* (college-educated respondent, Texas)

> *From what I know, globalization, in a lot of cases, means things like NAFTA, outsourcing jobs to India and China, which isn't my idea of a good thing. At least not for America.* (college-educated man, Oregon)

This connected global economy has been transformative, to be sure, yet in general those best positioned to engage with it and benefit see it as making life harder, less secure, and more complicated, particularly for the American employees.

> *The economy is a lot more complicated now than it was for my parents' generation.* (college-educated man, online)

> *This "new" economy moves faster with less security than in the past.* (college-educated woman, online)

That ambivalence about the complexity and speed is part of the new consciousness of the new information and technology workers, not just workers in the old industries.

Principle Six: Big business and CEOs are the big winners in the new economy and the principal villains of the piece

CEOs of big businesses play a very negative role in people's understanding of the new economy and dominate the drama. They are the ones that stopped giving raises to anyone except senior executives, outsourced jobs, employed as few Americans as possible, and put pressure on workers. They used their money and influence with government to tilt the economy to work for them. For ordinary people, the CEOs and large corporations have driven the negative changes in the economy—and the economists say they are right.

The intensity of their critique is fairly new in my experience studying public opinion. This is not grounded in the traditional conflict between labor and capital, workers and management; rather, it is rooted morally in the broken compact that has changed the bargain.

The American people are deeply unhappy with the big banks and financial sector that contributed so dramatically to the financial crash and were bailed out by the government. To be sure, the public spreads blame fairly evenly between themselves for taking on too much debt, the banks for making risky loans, and the government for its weak regulatory hand. But while individuals had to put their books in order and deal with the fallout, the financial industry and bankers never paid the price. They believe "The banks do what they want with impunity" and "have bought the government and they get away with a fine and not any jail time" (postgraduate-educated woman, online). No wonder that today they support "increasing the fines and seeking jail time for executives at financial institutions when they break the law and profit from their wrongdoing" more than almost any other proposal to improve economic conditions.[55]

But Americans trust big business even less than the banks. Just 21 percent of Americans have confidence in "big business" according to Gallup. That makes them among the least trusted institutions in American society, above only news on the Internet and TV (19 percent, 18 percent) and Congress (7 percent). By comparison, small business is trusted by 62 percent of people, topped only by the military (74 percent), and even banks are ranked higher (26 percent). Even worse, a paltry 13 percent of Americans say they have "a great deal" or "quite a bit of confidence" in "large corporations"—below the level of confidence in the federal government at a time when it was totally deadlocked.[56]

The public is focused like a laser on "CEOs of big businesses." When we tested that fairly neutral term with the public in June of 2015, just 23 percent gave a warm or favorable response—and almost twice as many, 40 percent, were cool or unfavorable. Who would have thought a pro-business America would be so negative about the leaders of its large companies? And who would have thought that its college graduates and working class would unite in this aversion to America's corporate leadership?[57]

What is going on?

People have watched or experienced the successive restructuring of American businesses, and companies have emerged as pretty hard-hearted and disloyal—both to their employees and to the country. Americans are very conscious that companies pulled out of the compact where hard work would pay off. CEOs are paid record bonuses and "Companies are making record profits with a smaller workforce" (college-educated man, online) by paying as little and employing as few as possible. One college graduate wrote: "New economy means more personal responsibility and not relying on the company that you work for" (college-educated man, online). These were some of the most heated remarks in the face-to-face discussions with college graduates in Portland, Cleveland, and Austin.

What I've noticed is that corporations take advantage of people who are getting towards retirement. I have a stack of rejection letters about this big.

College-educated and non-college-educated have very similar views of CEOs of large businesses

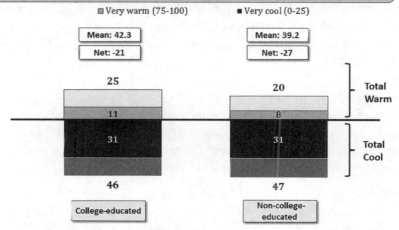

Now, I'd like you to rate your feelings toward some people and organizations, with one hundred meaning a VERY WARM, FAVORABLE feeling; zero meaning a VERY COLD, UN-FAVORABLE feeling; and fifty meaning not particularly warm or cold. You can use any number from zero to one hundred, the higher the number the more favorable your feelings are toward that person or organization. If you have no opinion or never heard of that person or organization, please say so....CEOs of large businesses.

Very warm (75-100)   ■ Very cool (0-25)

	College-educated	Non-college-educated
Mean	42.3	39.2
Net	-21	-27
Total Warm	25 / 11	20 / 8
Total Cool	31 / 46	31 / 47

National Survey of 950 2012 voters conducted by Democracy Corps for the Roosevelt Institute, October 16–21, 2014.

To get a job when you're over fifty is almost impossible. (college-educated woman, Oregon)

It seems to me like bigger companies, institutions, have less loyalty towards their employees, which means at any time they could get laid off for newer, younger employees. (college-educated Hispanic, Texas)

Is it better to put your life in the hands of a company that now is most likely going to screw you over? (college-educated woman, Oregon)

There's no loyalty anymore. (college-educated man, Ohio)

The working-class men and women are quick to call it what it is: greed.

The greed of the large corporations, that's their bottom line, profits. Not bettering the American people or the economy, or the middle class. I hate to say that but it's the truth. (non-college-educated man, Ohio)

I think there again the key word is "greed": they're been selling out all our jobs overseas where they can take advantage of poor people over in other countries where they can pay them a nickel where it could cost them a dollar over here, so everybody's selling out.... I think they could do a better job at trying to keep our workers, keep the jobs here in America. (non-college-educated white man, age fifty)

It seems like corporate America is all about the mighty dollar and not about the long term but today. (non-college-educated white man, age fifty)

There was a noticeable cry for a "company that respects and values you as a worker and takes care of you as well as you work for them" (college-educated man, online); but today, companies "are not able to understand the real needs of simple families" (college-educated woman, online). They remember a time when it wasn't this way.

> *There used to be a time where you built a business, you had your employees, you took care of your employees, you had a relationship with them. Now you're like a number, and the whole thing is to be able to make your money before somebody takes it away from you.* (college-educated woman, Ohio)

> *No heart, no . . . nothing. Just that change in my short time of living, seeing companies going from that family-oriented, togetherness, knowing each other, knowing the employees, just the attitude change and just the impersonalization and all of that, it's amazing to me.* (college-educated woman, Ohio)

Because the big companies have played so central a role, the citizenry is following the money. Just a third of Americans say they are satisfied with the "size and influence of major corporations." The voters had already moved to that conclusion before the financial crash, but about half the country was satisfied just as George W. Bush was assuming office in 2001.[58]

CEO compensation and tax avoidance have become powerful symbols of what is wrong in the country. More than 60 percent of the country expresses a great deal of concern about the fact that CEOs earn 273 times as much as the average worker, that corporate CEOs give themselves multimillion-dollar bonuses and pensions, and that big corporations such as Verizon and G.E. pay no income tax in some years.[59]

If you want to hear animated focus groups, you should listen to people talk about how today's top 1 percent, big businesses and CEOs, use their money and lobbyists to make politics and politicians work for them. They describe the game as "rigged."

> *[The top 2 percent are] holding us hostage and then they've got the money to buy the politicians to get what they want.* (non-college-educated man, Ohio)

> *The best way to put it unfortunately is the general concept of our elected officials being there to support their constituents and the people that have elected to put them in office and unfortunately I think the reality is that too*

*many times they're placing their votes with people that line their pockets
from special interest groups.* (non-college-educated man, Ohio)

*The problem is you have corruption on these high levels where you have
these people who are, you know, laundering money or they're giving
themselves these multimillion-dollar annual bonuses and they're cutting
wages or they're cutting jobs or they're outsourcing jobs.* (young woman,
Florida)

*Congress, these bank owners, bank people, you know, the finance, they need
to have a cap on their income so if they make money it means the prices are
going to go up in order for them to get their raises.* (non-college-educated
woman, Ohio)

When a man in suburban Philadelphia learned that those at the top pay a
lower effective tax rate, he expressed his disgust for "the bad guy that pays
less in taxes than his driver," saying, "That makes me hate the guy" (college-
educated man, Pennsylvania).

Another man was upset because he thought the government "has not done
enough to prevent the exile of good jobs from this country," but then thought
better of it: it was "probably on purpose" because they are likely in on the
"Global Plan" (college-educated man, online). "They're all bought, they're
all puppets" (college-educated woman, Oregon).

No wonder the set of problems related to inequality, the top 1 percent,
and the power of Wall Street and business interests over Washington is the
second most prominent in the consciousness of voters in Democracy Corps's
polling for the Roosevelt Institute.[60]

Everyone is restructuring their behavior and thinking about the economy to
parallel the changing nature of work. Some remain angry and resentful, and
others are resigned and depressed, yet most are pursuing individual strategies to get to stability or success in this new economy, and most would support local and national policy changes if government was not so dysfunctional
and corrupt.

The American public is looking for the leaders of the country to say they
understand the new rules and offer a vision of how things will be better for
them and the country. In Great Britain, all parties are competing to address
the cost-of-living crisis, starting with the price of natural gas. Yet in America, no national leader has stepped into this role, as Bill Clinton did when he
promised to govern on behalf of the "forgotten middle class." Barack Obama's
cramped portrayal of inequality or episodic discussion of the middle class and
the conservatives' denialist reaction to the shrinking middle class and rising
inequality have left the citizenry to their own devices in understanding and
grappling with the new economy.

And the public is very sophisticated and conscious of how much business and government conspire to shape the fortunes in the outcomes in the new economy. Impacting that principle will be central to addressing America's central contradictions.

5 CONTRADICTIONS OF THE NEW SOCIETY

The great social transformations that are changing the country come with a high social price that badly tarnishes America's great promise. The contradictions in our cultural exceptionalism are no less foreboding than those that arise with our economic progress. And as with the escalating economic problems, the citizenry will ultimately demand that leaders and parties "get it" and take up an agenda relevant for these times.

America's cultural exceptionalism comes with a pluralism of marriage types, or what Richard Reeves calls a "multiplicity of marital shapes." He rightly points out that "the legalization of same-sex marriages is only the latest modulation, after divorce, remarriage, cohabitation, step-children, delayed child-bearing, and chosen childlessness"—and he might well add the huge rise in the number of individuals who never marry. Those changes in the shapes of marriages and families are central to the ascendant values and the changing way of life among Millennials and those in the growing urban centers.[1]

Yet many of these marriage shapes come with a high price tag. The surge in the number of people living in unmarried households, children raised by a single parent, and the decline of the traditional family and breadwinner role have serious, troubling consequences.

Working-class men, whether white or black, earn less than they did thirty years ago and are single later in life. When working-class men are on their own for longer, they earn lower wages and drift to the margins of the labor and marriage market. While working women are earning more than thirty years ago, they are still challenged by the pay gap with men, dominate in the lowest-paying, growing occupations, and make less in a lifetime because they still do the bulk of the housework and child care and thus work fewer hours. Unmarried women are the most challenged because they struggle to manage work and to raise young children with the added insecurity of just being on their own.

Pointedly, one of the biggest blockages to upward mobility and diminishing inequality in communities and nationally is the number of children raised by single parents. Kids raised by a single parent learn fewer skills and key values at an early age and are much more likely to end up in poverty, while a child raised by two parents is more likely to finish high school and college and get to a middle-class income level. More black children are being raised by single mothers, yet the sharp upward trend today is entirely the result of what is happening with working-class single mothers, regardless of race.

Nonetheless, it is very difficult to begin a frank discussion of the social costs produced by the decline of traditional marriage because they are produced in part by the changing gender roles, the sexual revolution, and the growing secularism that are integral to America's ascendant trends. And these social changes are still contested.

Yes, there are some conservatives who recognize the tension. Nick Schulz, conservative economist and chief editor of the American Enterprise Institute's online magazine, has declared "the collapse of the intact family is one of the most significant economic facts of our time," but acknowledges that "because the debate about family structure is so thoroughly tied up in the culture war" it cannot be legitimately debated. He laments that it is "tied up with the country's often bitter politics of race, feminism, and sexual politics," not to mention the politics of religion.[2]

But it is hard to set aside the ideological debates when social conservatives are waging a full-scale culture war contesting the ascendant trends. They are challenging the sexual independence and economic autonomy of women and the growing secularism that has less certitude about what is right and what is wrong behavior. As I write, social conservatives are suing to limit the contraceptive coverage in the Affordable Care Act on religious grounds and moving to bar abortion or make it virtually unavailable in all the states where they exercise political control. Every new piece of legislation bogged down in the Republican-controlled Congress is weighed down by new attempts to limit abortion. That real-time battle against the new freedoms prevents a constructive public discussion of how to address the very real social costs, though the problems will only worsen without reforms.

This moment is not so different from when Daniel Patrick Moynihan, a prominent academic and urban policy adviser to President Richard Nixon, released his 1965 report, "The Negro Family." He asserted that the "fundamental problem" facing the black community is the state of the family, which is "the basic socializing unit" because "by and large, adult conduct in society is learned as a child." "The evidence—not final, but powerfully persuasive—is that the Negro family in the urban ghettos is crumbling." He acknowledged with great eloquence the powerful legacy of virulent racism and discrimination shaping black communities as the root of the problem, but he also insisted that "so long as this situation persists, the cycle of poverty and disadvantage will continue to repeat itself." With the black "illegitimacy" rate growing from 16.8 percent in 1940 to 23.6 percent in 1963, well above the 3.1 percent rate among whites, he made the case for national action.[3]

Moynihan came under withering attack for seeming to put the blame on blacks themselves and for diminishing the pressure to mitigate the effects of so many years of legalized racial discrimination and segregation. Just a couple of years after the passage of the historic civil rights laws, it seemed to relieve pressure to desegregate the schools and urban areas and to take affirmative action to offset entrenched racial discrimination in education and employment.

Indeed, I joined that pushback from the margins as a new political science assistant professor in urban studies at Yale University. I had studied with Nathan Glazer and Edward Banfield, and James Q. Wilson had been my PhD thesis adviser at the Department of Government at Harvard. They were the principal intellectuals allied with Moynihan, who stressed values over condition. With my own research in poor neighborhoods, I was right to be critical of Edward Banfield's theory of a "culture of poverty" holding people back in America's cities, though on the question of the family raised by Moynihan, I was wrong.[4]

New York Times columnist Nicholas Kristof's recent apology for liberals will be much more effective than mine in getting people to revisit that period: "One historic mistake by liberals in social policy was the condemnation of Daniel Patrick Moynihan's warning in 1965 of the breakdown of the African-American family." It is really basic: children raised by a single parent are three times more likely to live in poverty than those raised by two. "He was not racist, he was prescient," because, as Nick Schulz points out, "when Moynihan claimed there was a crisis in the black family, the illegitimacy rate among American blacks was a little over 23 percent." Today, the proportion of non-marital births is now 29 percent among whites and 44 percent among white workers.[5]

It took the breakdown of the family among the white working class to get America's attention again. So be it.

Working-class men have been hit the hardest by the decline of stable industrial jobs with decent pay and benefits sufficient to support a family. "Less-educated workers are in trouble, and men are in trouble, and less-educated men are in deep trouble," Jonathan Rauch wrote in The National Journal. Rauch cites one MIT labor economist sounding the alarm: "It has reached a very extreme point." These men are being steadily marginalized by the economic changes but also the social transformations that delayed the age when men married and that undermined the traditional breadwinner role—one where men took great pride in being able to support the family and children.[6]

Many of the ascendant groups have trouble viewing their frustration and depression as legitimate. Books such as Michael Kimmel's Angry White Men are concerned with the most extreme and "entitled" voices "who refuse to even be dragged kicking and screaming into that inevitable future." They seek to further marginalize these working-class men, not to recognize their marginalization as part of the contradictions of these times.[7]

During that period, women moved into higher education and the labor force and made gains in income and inroads into more skilled careers where they were previously unrepresented. At the same time, they were pulling back from the traditional wife and homemaker roles, and even marriage and motherhood altogether in some cases. Women still dominate the lowest-paying occupations, are underrepresented in the highest ones, and face a wage gap and a lifetime income and achievement gap as they still bear the largest share of responsibility for home and child care. Nonetheless, they see growing opportunities and are adapting by learning new skills and constructing family arrangements that work for them.

Working mothers, whether married or single, are managing work and family without the barest of social support—something that is provided in every other developed country in the world. America has witnessed nothing short of a revolution in women's role in the economy and the character of the family. Yet, no new federal law has been passed since the Family Leave Act in 1993—requiring large employers to allow unpaid family leave. That is hard to understand, since there are so many models for doing it better. With social conservatives still contesting many of these social changes and business successful at resisting regulation and new mandates, America uniquely leaves working women with no help on day care, paid sick days or paid leave, or anything else. But they are poised to demand reform.

MARRIAGE

Unmarried households became a majority in the country in 2011. Many trends led to this tipping point for marriage. People are marrying much later; just one in five of those under thirty years of age is married today, compared to three in five in 1960. Those who never marry will soon be half of the unmarried. About half of working-class marriages still end in divorce. As a result, the number of unmarried couples, childless households, and single people is growing faster than the number of married couples with children in every state—a fact highlighted by the conservative American Enterprise Institute.[8]

The marriage rate falling to half of the country is in part driven by other demographic changes, since minority populations experience a lower marriage rate and minorities are becoming a greater share of the total population. While racial discrepancies persist, the decline in marriage is now strongly evident in all communities. Over the past half century, the proportion of blacks living in married households dropped by half—from 61 to 31 percent. Hispanics saw a decline in marriage rates that was 6 points less dramatic but nonetheless significant, starting at 72 percent, comparable to the level among whites at the time, and falling to 48 percent. The fall among whites was 5 points less than among Hispanics, declining from 74 to 55 percent—and among low-income working-class whites, it has fallen to less than half.[9]

People are postponing or abstaining from marriage, and that is also true

Marriage rates by race and ethnicity, 1960–2011

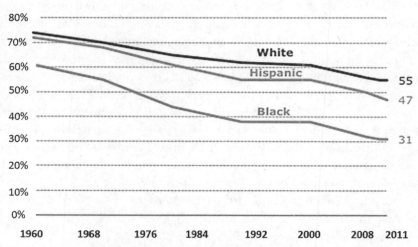

| % currently married among adults ages 18 and older |

"King's Dream Remains an Elusive Goal; Many Americans See Racial Disparities," Pew Research Center, August 22, 2013, p. 29. Note: White and black adults include only those who reported a single race. Asians, Native Americans, and mixed-race groups not shown. Source is the Pew Research Center's tabulations of 1960–2000 Decennial Census and the American Community Survey (IFUMS).

of childbearing, though to a lesser extent. In 1960, only 5 percent of children were nonmarital births, with one-third of marriages precipitated by a pregnancy, but in 2008 that share of births reached 41 percent. While cohabitation used to follow marriage, it is more and more a prerequisite for marriage among the college-educated and an alternative among the non-college-educated today, as two-thirds of couples now live together before marrying. In fact, half of children born outside of marriage are born to cohabitating parents, though nearly two-thirds will be separated when their kids reach ten years of age.[10]

Marriage, or at least "traditional marriage"—a household with two parents, marriage before children, a male breadwinner, and a female homemaker—has been driven low by diverse economic and cultural forces and, as David Ellwood and Christopher Jencks understate it, "some changes may even be irreversible." Ellwood and Jencks believe that three factors altered at least the *timing* and the *order* of marriage and childbearing. First, the link between marriage and childbearing was weakened by the Pill and legalized abortion, which "gave couples, and particularly women, far more control over the timing of births." That allowed them to consider other factors including their changing economic options. Second, noneconomic incentives to marry became less important because "changing sexual mores"—in part driven by the sexual revolution, which "destigmatized premarital sex"—"made it more acceptable for unmarried couples to engage in sexual activity and live together." And third, Ellwood and Jencks believe the dramatic changes in gender roles, which allowed more women and women with children to work, increased the financial benefits from delaying childbearing.

Each of these dynamics allows economic considerations to become more important to decisions about when people marry and have children, and the combination is pretty powerful: "If women gain greater control over the timing of parenthood and if they have more opportunities in the labor market, some of them will find it advantageous to delay childbearing. If women are delaying childbearing, many will delay marriage as well." This explains why more-educated women are more likely to delay childbearing than less-educated women, which in turn explains why they are also delaying marriage longer. On the other hand, less-educated working-class women "see few economically attractive mates" in an economy where working-class men are less assured of a stable, good-paying job, and "this might lead them to delay marriage but not childbearing." All of these conspire to deal a "fatal blow to the traditional model of marriage," concludes Richard Reeves, policy director for the Center for Children and Families.[11]

But it has not dealt a deathblow to the institution of marriage itself—which "is undergoing a metamorphosis." The "old form of marriage, based on outdated social roles and gender roles, is fading. A new version is emerging—egalitarian, committed and focused on children." College graduates, led by the women, "are reinventing marriage as a child-rearing machine for a post-feminist society and a knowledge economy," which means shared responsibility for parenting, home, and earnings. Reeves concludes, "It's working, too."[12]

Well, it's *not* working among the working class and those without a four-year degree, though they are equally committed to getting married. Three-quarters of all Americans say marriage "is very important" or "one of the most important things" to them, and among the unmarried, nearly half of both the college-educated and those with a high school diploma or less want to get married, a commitment that defies class lines and recent history. Half a century ago, marriage rates were no different for the working class and the middle class, but in 2010, almost two-thirds of college-educated adults were married, while just under half of those with less education were.[13]

"The lack of economic security" is a "key reason people don't get married," the Pew Research Center concludes. More than a quarter of never-married adults cite not being financially prepared as the main reason they are not married. And a stunning 78 percent of never-married women say a steady job is the most important thing they are looking for in a potential spouse—and that tops all other considerations. But many of these women are bound to be frustrated as a good man by this criterion is harder and harder to find. For every unmarried woman, there are but 0.65 unmarried employed men.[14]

The changed prospects for traditional marriage along with the changes in the economy have left the institution of marriage decimated among non-college-graduates and the working class. Conservative author Charles Murray tells the story of the lower-income, working-class whites—the bottom 30 percent. More than 80 percent were married in 1960, though less than half were fifty years later. The marriage rate for those at the top, on the other hand, has stabilized in the mid–80 percent range. The concept of being "never married" hardly existed before, yet now it has reached a quarter of those at the bottom. Divorce has accelerated, reaching one-third of low-income whites in 2010, while the divorce rate stabilized just above 5 percent among those at the top. The number of nonmarital births accelerated during this period for everyone except those with a four-year degree, rising highest among the least educated.[15]

Moreover, lower-income and working-class whites report that they are less happy in their marriages and just less happy, period, as economic troubles tend to push people apart. They are increasingly less trustful of others and are substantially less involved now in their community, civic organizations, even their churches: more than 55 percent attended church regularly in the late 1970s, but now it is closer to 40 percent. These patterns are utterly reversed for those at the top 20 percent, reinforcing just how much this alienation from marriage and community predominates among those at the bottom of the socioeconomic scale.[16]

These social trends in marriage rates and children raised with an absent parent have shaped the fortunes and misfortunes of blacks for a long time.

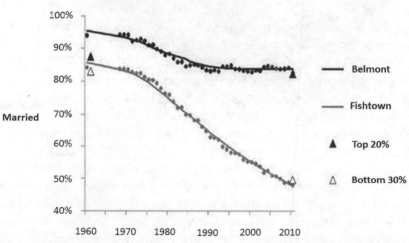

White marriage rate by income

Charles Murray, Coming Apart: The State of White America, 1960–2010. (New York: Crown Forum, 2012), p. 154, Figure 8.3.
Source: IPUMS, sample limited to whites ages 30–49.

White non-marital birth ratio by mother's education

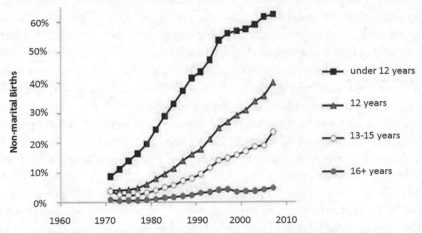

Charles Murray, *Coming Apart: The State of White America, 1960–2010* (New York: Crown Forum, 2012), p. 161
Figure 8.9 Source: Author's analysis of alternative years of the Natality Public Use Files of the Centers for Disease Control, beginning with 1970. Sample limited to white women.

The result is that 28 percent of black Americans live in poverty. Among black men, 41 percent do not graduate high school and 11 percent of black men over 20 are unemployed. In almost all respects, the increased poverty and blocked mobility among blacks is a product of compounding social trends more than race specifically, according to almost all the social science studies cited in the debate. But how do you begin to break the pattern of poverty and blocked mobility created by these powerful social conditions when more than 25 percent of nonincarcerated black men have a felony conviction, a huge obstacle to gaining employment?[17]

A daunting one in six black men between the ages of 25 and 54 dies prematurely or is imprisoned, according to unique analysis provided by the blog *The Upshot* under the headline "1.5 MILLION MISSING BLACK MEN." Black men in the United States are more likely to be imprisoned or die prematurely from homicide, accidents, heart disease, and other diseases. The result is that there are only 83 black men for every 100 black women, though among whites, the number "missing" does not vary for men and women.[18]

The marriage gap also has immense economic consequences. In 1960, the median income gap of married households was 12 percent greater than that of unmarried households; by 2008, it was 41 percent: $77,000 versus $54,000. Marriage just matters: a single-earner in a married household now makes $63,000, but that shrinks to only $53,000 if you are unmarried.[19]

Conservative Nick Schulz is not exaggerating when he declares "the collapse of the intact family is one of the most significant economic facts of our time."

"Nobody doubts that where marriage is, poverty tends not to be; the statistics are stark," writes Annie Lowrey, economic policy reporter for *The New York Times*. She offers a stream of simple but powerful facts that make the economic consequences for families and children painfully clear: "Almost no marriages in which both partners work full time fall below the poverty line; about one-third of households headed by a single mother are poor. One in eight children with two married parents lives below the poverty line; five in ten living with a single mother do." Putting economic issues aside, "children raised by two parents are less likely to have behavioral problems, be asthmatic or hungry; they are more likely to achieve at school and so on." And a recent study of parents found that those living in poverty were "twice as likely to report chronic pain and mental distress" as those from families earning $75,000 or more, and those in poverty were three to five times more likely to be extremely stressed or in extreme pain. By the time they are young men and women, children raised by married parents are 44 percent more likely to go to college.[20]

The father being absent is "similar to the effect of having a mother who did not finish high school rather than one who did," according to a new assessment by Sara McLanahan and Christopher Jencks. The absence of a father produces "increased antisocial behavior, such as aggression, rule breaking, delinquency, and illegal drug use" and a teenager less able or willing "to exercise self-control." These effects are harder on boys than girls, it seems, though the effects are similar for black and white children with an absent parent.[21]

These conditions of the family and marriage contribute to an elevated inequality in the country and reduce the prospects that those born on the bottom rungs of the economic ladder will reach the top ones. That is the stark conclusion of the authoritative work conducted by Raj Chetty, Nathaniel Hendren, Patrick Kline, and Emmanuel Saez on intergenerational mobility at the level of community and nationally.

Measures of family structure are the most important factors in their study, which calculated the proportion of adults who are married, the proportion who are divorced, and the proportion of children living in single-parent households. All three measures are highly correlated with upward mobility, but the proportion of children living in single-parent households has a correlation of -0.76 and, they write, it "is the strongest correlate of upward income mobility among all the variables we explored." Moreover, the correlation between upward mobility and family structure is clear at the individual level and at the community level. So children of married couples have greater upward mobility when they live in communities with fewer single parents, and less upward mobility in communities with more single parents.[22]

In practice, Kathleen Gerson shows in her book *The Unfinished Revolution* that the family today is dynamic and "changes daily, monthly and yearly" as children grow up in married, divorced, or remarried households with stepparents, or some sequence of those family types. But those differences over a lifetime have profound consequences for inequality and upward mobility, as Reeves shows. Children in the lowest quintile born to parents who are continuously married have a not inconsiderable one in five chance (19 percent) of ending up as an adult in the top quintile, but that probability is cut in half to 10 percent if their mother was married, though not continuously; it is cut in half again to a mere 5 percent when the mother has never married at all stages in the child's life.[23]

The college-educated and those with the highest incomes seem fully aware of the social trends and are renewing marriage with a focus on parenting. In fact, college-educated women are more likely to get married, marry later, marry better-educated men, have more resources, and have fewer children, and less than 10 percent have children outside of marriage, according to James Heckman's work on the American family. By age three, their children demonstrate dramatically higher performance on standardized tests than the children of mothers with a high school education, even those with some college education. That gap is apparent for both white and African American children.[24]

And what is the reason for the sustained gap? Their college-educated

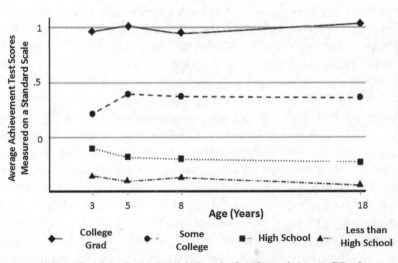

Average achievement test scores of children by age and their mother's education

James J. Heckman, "The American Family in Black and White: A Post-Racial Strategy for Improving Skills to Promote Equality," National Bureau of Economic Research, March, 2011, p. 14.

Returns to investment in human capital

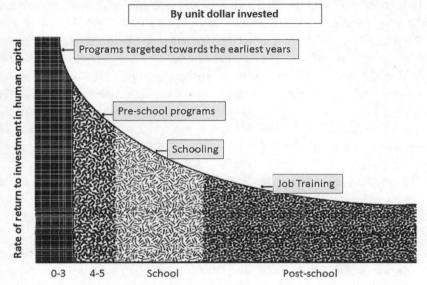

James J. Heckman. "The American Family in Black and White: A Post-Racial Strategy for Improving Skills to Promote Equality," National Bureau of Economic Research, March, 2011, p. 24.

mothers are spending more time with their children at a young age and teach their children good behavior and values in addition to cognitive skills.

When Heckman looked into the most cost-effective programs for raising future skill levels—which will in turn determine the opportunity for advancement—he found that early childhood investments produce a significant return on investment in human capital. Programs are most effective when you reach children under three years but also in preschool years. That is when children learn "soft skills" and foundational behaviors, and they are "as predictive, if not more predictive, of schooling, wages, participation in crime and participation in healthy behaviors as cognitive skills."[25]

You do not have to convince the people living in the most challenging working-class, low-income, and poor neighborhoods with high concentrations of single parents of the value of children learning "soft skills" early. They know the value of good parenting and the importance of values learned at home. But they face untold obstacles, and being on your own makes it very hard to keep kids on the right path.

When I conducted surveys in the black, Hispanic, and white working-class neighborhoods in Chicago, people across the board gave very high support to this statement: "We should not expect city government to raise a child, teach them good values, or make sure they do well in school. We need parents to be responsible for their children." And when thinking about addressing the violent crime that receives so much national attention, they lamented that there were so many guns on the streets and not enough jobs, but also that parents were not spending more time with their children.[26]

President Barack Obama went back to Chicago after the tragic, random murder of fifteen-year-old Hadiya Pendleton, weeks after she proudly performed at the president's inauguration. He reached out to the community and was embraced back when he spoke about his own single mother, the great challenges facing families, and the need to promote marriage and fatherhood. The work to build the ladders of opportunity found in good communities, he declared, "starts at home."[27]

> There's no more important ingredient for success, nothing that would be more important for us reducing violence than strong, stable families—which means we should do more to promote marriage and encourage fatherhood. Don't get me wrong—as the son of a single mom, who gave everything she had to raise me with the help of my grandparents, I turned out okay. But . . . we've got single moms out here, they're heroic in what they're doing, and we are so proud of them. But at the same time, I wish I had had a father who was around and involved. Loving, supportive parents—and, by the way, that's all kinds of parents—that includes foster parents, and that includes grandparents, and extended families; it includes gay or straight parents. Those parents supporting kids—that's the single most important thing. Unconditional love for your child—that makes a difference.

He concluded his message by speaking to the parents: "If a child grows up with parents who have work, and have some education, and can be role models, and can teach integrity and responsibility, and discipline and delayed gratification," then you have given "a child the kind of foundation that allows them to say, 'My future, I can make it what I want.' "

WORKING-CLASS MEN MARGINALIZED
In the post–World War II decades of the 1950s and 1960s, a man completing high school was assured a low- or middle-skill job with decent security and could marry and expect to play the breadwinner role in the family. Now, working-class men can expect to make dramatically less compared to the wages of the nonworking class, and they are pulling back from both the labor force and marriage. While 90 percent of male college graduates are in the labor force, just three-quarters of high school graduates and two-thirds without a high school degree are. In 1960, only 10 percent of male high school graduates never got married, but that has surged to 25 percent today.[28]

While men are growing marginalized, women are on the move, adapting to the new economy and the evolution of gender roles and marriage, taking risks, and getting more education, even as they struggle to find jobs that pay enough to live on and support their families.

Women are surging into higher-education institutions of all types. Remarkably, the number of women who enter higher-education programs is greater than the number of men who apply. Women earned more bachelor's degrees than men by 1982, more master's degrees by 1987, and more doctoral degrees by 2006. In 2010, women were receiving 57 percent of the BA's, 63 percent of the master's degrees, and 53 percent of the doctorates. This gender gap is evident for every race. The student body of traditionally black colleges such as Fisk and Howard universities are about two-thirds female, and Clark University has reached 75 percent. Among the Hispanic graduates of Boston public schools, 64 percent are female.[29]

And falling behind in the knowledge economy has consequences. Look how it has impacted wage gains over the past thirty years.

Compared to three decades ago, women with a postgraduate degree saw a remarkable 33-percentage-point increase in income, and college graduates saw an impressive 23-point gain. Women with some post–high school education saw a very modest 8-point advance, while the incomes of those women with high school diplomas just stood still between 1979 and 2010.

But the incomes of men are on a very different trajectory. Male high school graduates got creamed, their income falling 20 percentage points, and those with some college education lost ground as well. Men had to get at least a four-year degree to pick up any income gains over this thirty-year period. The incomes of college-educated men grew 12 percentage points—though that is 10 points less growth in income than for women with a comparable degree. If you focus on the longer period from 1970, when working-class wages faltered, the median earnings of male high school graduates fell a shocking 41 percent.[30]

The proportion of people in middle-skill jobs in the country has declined as opportunities for such employment have fallen over the past thirty-five years, and while almost the entire decline in women's employment in middle-skill jobs was due to their increased representation in high-skill jobs, for men, half of the middle-skill workers moved to less-skilled ones.[31]

As David Brooks noted powerfully, "The financial rewards to education have increased over the past few decades, but men failed to get the memo." No wonder more than two-thirds of women say they have "more opportunity to get ahead in society" than their mothers, while less than half of men say that when comparing themselves to their fathers.[32]

These differing responses are playing out in the context of broader trends in American society, where many more prime-age workers say they are looking for more leisure time and shorter hours and many fewer people are saying "work is important and gives a feeling of accomplishment." This important

Change in real hourly wages by education level, 1979–2010

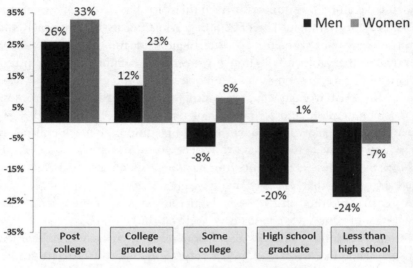

"Diverging Fortunes for Men and Women," *New York Times*, March 20, 2013. For workers ages 25–39.

cultural shock could plausibly explain why the male working class may seem less industrious—but it does not. That is the key finding of Andrew Cherlin's important study *Labor's Love Lost*. From 2006 to 2012 many more working-class men were looking for more leisure time in a job compared to two decades earlier (1985 to 1994), though the problem is that college-educated men—and women, too—were shifting priorities to the same degree. Cherlin speculates that college-educated men who are in high demand do not act on their new priorities, while male non-college-graduates who are not in high demand are able to act by withdrawing from the labor force. Women who see themselves as catching up in a changing labor market also respond differently.[33]

While men "have proven remarkably unable to adapt," Hanna Rosin notes that "this generation of women has adapted to the fundamental restructuring of the economy." Whereas women today "are more fluid," the men "are more likely to be rigid" and seem "like immigrants who have physically moved to a new country but who have kept their minds in the old one," speaking their native language and following the old mores.[34]

The delay in marriage age and the change in work opportunities have delayed formative transition points in the lives of working-class men that will have consequences. While most of the focus has been on women as gender and economic roles change, the changes for men are life-changing, too.

"Marriage, work, and fatherhood remain a package deal in most men's minds (if not in their lives)," the Institute for Family Studies writes. As Kay Hymowitz explains in *The Wall Street Journal*, "Not so long ago, the average American man in his 20s had achieved most of the milestones of adulthood: a high school diploma, financial independence, marriage and children." She might have added that in earlier eras, many had fought for their country, too. But "Today, most men in their 20s hang out in a novel sort of limbo, a hybrid state of semi-hormonal adolescence and responsible self-reliance." And it has "become obvious to legions of frustrated young women," Hymowitz observed in *The Wall Street Journal,* that this "doesn't bring out the best in men."[35]

With the median marriage age pushing toward thirty for men and more not marrying, Stephanie Coontz writes, "marriage no longer organizes the transition into regular sexual activity" and men are less intent on building up "human capital whose returns will later be used to support the marriage."[36]

Now, men "who are not committed to families," Michael Jindra writes, "enjoy all the options that a consumer culture gives them, have more independence and freedom, and thus are found in a wider array of subcultural activities that take men away from consistent work and commitment to families."

Interestingly, it is the younger men that are leading the secession from the labor force and working fewer hours, Tyler Cowen writes, because they "cannot find satisfying work at a wage they are happy with." These are reinforcing trends that take them on a different path than the women and delay their adapting to these tremendous challenges.[37]

The state of working-class men has real economic and cultural content, though they are also increasingly pushed to the margins by other trends and other groups whose issues are seen to be more "legitimate." Nonetheless, the problems of the marginalized working class are very real.

WORKING WOMEN ON THEIR OWN

These revolutionary social transformations put women fully into the workforce while they continue to take primary responsibility for raising children and caring for the household, and yet there has been barely any reform of work and family policies to help them manage it. That growing gap will put work and family issues at the forefront of the public agenda. That is one of the core contradictions that America will have to face if it is to realize the benefits of its economic and cultural changes.

Working mothers are the sole or primary income provider in four in ten households with children, and as a result of the social transformations, half of working women are unmarried. Three in ten mothers are single mothers, two-thirds of the unmarried do not have a college degree, and more than 60 percent of unmarried mothers earned less than $30,000 in 2012. They are on edge financially, but with only the barest help from a father or government.[38]

What responsibilities wives and husbands take on has changed dramatically since the 1960s, but the incompleteness of the changes has only raised the pressures on the women who are fully in the labor force. In 1965, mothers were putting in eight times more hours on housework and four times as many hours as the father dealing with child care. Now it has changed. But women are still putting in twice as many hours as the men on both. That is a revolution in family responsibilities, though with more women spending more hours on paid work and many women unmarried, it is a growing, not a lessening, nightmare.[39]

How parents use their time in 1965 and 2011

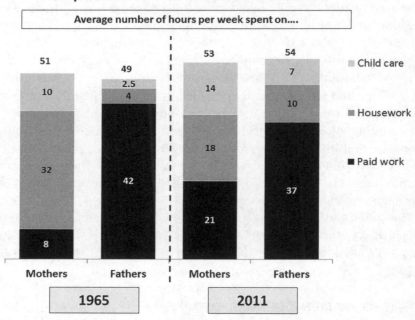

Kim Parker and Wendy Wang, "Modern Parenthood," Pew Research Center, March 14, 2013.

The incomplete revolution in gender roles and changes in marriage are shaping how women participate in the labor market, often diminishing their career prospects and long-term income. Working mothers are choosing to reduce hours at work, work part-time, interrupt their careers, and even quit their jobs to deal with young children at rates much higher than for working men.

Women with children just cannot put in as many hours of paid work as men do. These women are working twenty-one hours a week, compared to thirty-seven hours for fathers. A quarter of working mothers are working part-time, which is twice the proportion for men and four times that for working fathers.[40]

The choice to work part-time might well be necessary for mothers struggling with the time commitment of parenting or the costs of child care, but that choice is profoundly impacted by your economic resources, whether you have the security of a college degree, and whether you have a husband or partner helping you out. Half of unmarried mothers want to work full-time, twice the figure for married mothers. A majority of married moms say the ideal is working part-time. Among working women earning less than $50,000, 63 percent say "I'd prefer to be home with my children, but I need the income so I need to work."[41]

Working women and working men are making different choices in the face of these pressures. Fully 42 percent of mothers reduced their working hours at some point in their working life to deal with the needs of children or another family member, compared to just 28 percent of fathers. A very striking 27 percent of working mothers have quit a job and 13 percent turned down a promotion to deal with family needs. Only 10 percent of working fathers report doing either.[42]

And these choices have real and perceived consequences. A majority of working mothers (51 percent) say that being a working parent has made it harder to advance in their job or career, but just 16 percent of working fathers believe that for themselves. That may be because men and women experience very different reactions in the workplace to their changed status as a parent. According to New York Times writer Claire Cain Miller, "One of the worst career moves a woman can make is to have children" because "mothers are less likely to be hired for jobs, to be perceived as competent at work or to be paid as much as their male colleagues with the same qualifications." On the other hand, men are rewarded for having a child and "are more likely to be hired than childless men, and tend to be paid more after they have children."[43]

Working women and working men are struggling with these issues because the United States provides almost no help, despite these revolutionary changes. After President George H. W. Bush vetoed a similar measure, the Democrats rushed to enact the Family and Medical Leave Act in 1993, and it was the first bill signed by President Bill Clinton two weeks after assuming office. The new law provided up to twelve weeks of unpaid family leave to care for a new child or sick relative for full-time employees of large and medium-size businesses. President Clinton wrote on the twentieth anniversary of the law, "To this day, I received more thanks from citizens for the FMLA than any other single piece of legislation I signed into law"[44]

In any case, that historic law allowed for only *unpaid* leave, and no new major legislation expanding protections for working parents has been enacted in the following twenty-two years. Even though social and economic changes have proceeded at an accelerating pace in the subsequent years, the amount of leave time afforded has not been extended and it is still unpaid. This fact symbolizes both how much working parents are on their own and how isolated the United States is in the developed world when it comes to supporting families, despite the progress of a gender revolution in the labor market and in marriage.

Government-supported time off for new parents in 28 countries

Leave, in weeks, allowed by federal law

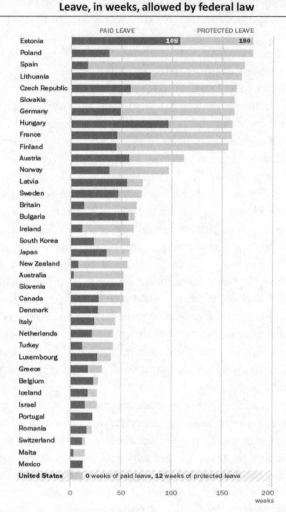

Gretchen Livingston, "Among 38 Nations, U.S. Is the Outlier When It Comes to Paid Parental Leave,"
Pew Research Center, December 12, 2013.

The United States ranks at the very bottom of all OECD countries when it comes to government-supported time off for new parents because it does not provide a penny of paid leave when a child is born. Estonia tops the list with 108 weeks of paid leave, followed by Hungary, with just under 100. Nearly all the other former members of the Soviet bloc in Eastern Europe offer at least 50 weeks, and the core of the Eurozone—Germany and France—gives new parents just under 50 weeks. Asian competitors such as Japan and South Korea give just under and over 25 weeks, respectively. Canada provides our neighbors to the north with roughly 25 weeks of paid leave, and to the south, Mexico matches America's commitment to 12 weeks of protected leave, but it is paid.[45]

It is paradoxical that America would stand alone with no paid leave because it is both the richest and one of the most religiously observant countries, yet it has not addressed social policy in this area so central to parenting, a child's life, and marriage. For working parents it is not just a paradox, it is also an everyday struggle.

With such paltry leave protections for new parents, more working parents must rely on child care in early years. In the OECD countries, the average cost of full-time child care for a two-year-old for a two-earner family is about 27 percent of their annual income. In the United States by contrast, it is over 40 percent. And that is assuming two incomes! And women hardly exaggerate when they look for comparisons: child care costs exceed college tuition in thirty-one states. No wonder this has emerged as a point of exasperation in what seems like an endemic cost-of-living crisis.[46]

The last time the United States attempted to create universally available child care for working parents was in the early 1970s. Congress passed with the support of the Nixon administration and support from both parties the Comprehensive Child Development Bill to provide universal day care. Though after conservatives mobilized against it, President Nixon vetoed it. Social conservatives asserted the law would undermine the traditional male breadwinner and female homemaker family, and with fears about communism looming at the height of the Cold War, the law would commit "the vast moral authority of the National Government to the side of communal approaches to child rearing over against the family-centered approach."[47]

Since that veto, the federal government has neglected to address the issue with the exception of providing some tax credits for child and dependent care and block grants to the states to help the very poorest with child care. And in this age of austerity, spending has been cut and reduced further by inflation, meaning fewer children are covered and the states are busily reducing eligibility, increasing copays, and decreasing reimbursement rates.[48]

So working women understand that they are on their own, and they have personal strategies to overcome the lack of support and take advantage of what opportunities are out there.

That is why I was so taken with Hanna Rosin's account of "Bethenny" at the outset of her book *The End of Men: And the Rise of Women*. Bethenny was single, "twenty-nine and ran a day care out of her house (hence, the Cheerios). She was also studying to get a nursing degree and raising her daughter, who was ten." "Bethenny seemed to be struggling in the obvious ways," as you would expect given her financial and family challenges. Rosin tells us, "Later I saw her at checkout, haggling over coupons. But she did not exactly read as the pitiable single mother type." She was proactive.[49]

Bethenny was like so many working-class and unmarried women I have observed in focus groups sharing stories about pursuing more schooling, taking on extra work, and finding ways to avoid expenses by sharing with neighbors and making creative living arrangements.

Women are adapting to the times and making progress. According to David Brooks, women are doing better than men after divorces—their incomes rise by 25 percent—and woman-owned small businesses are more likely to outperform male-owned businesses and survive the recession.[50]

The women are getting on with their lives and finding solutions, but a traditional marriage is not the primary one. When asked whether she wanted to be married, Bethenny replied, "Kind of." There was Calvin, the father of her daughter, though he was basically invisible now. As Bethenny tossed her daughter a granola bar she added wryly, "But Calvin would just mean one less granola bar for the two of us." Rosin observed, "There was genuine pleasure in that laugh, a hint of happy collusion in hoarding those granola bars for herself and her daughter."[51]

Instead of becoming economically dependent, women are playing the leading role in transforming marriage and parenting with the sense that they must move to adapt to new realities or get stuck in the wrong marriage.

Despite all these changes, virtually all young adults want "to create a lasting marriage or marriage-like relationship," and ideally, a marriage where the goal is for both the man and the woman to be working and pursuing a career as well as sharing responsibilities for parenting and home care, according to Kathleen Gerson's research for her book *The Unfinished Revolution*. Other studies show that 69 percent of unmarried Millennials would like to get married. But Gerson's critical finding is that both young women and young men are doubtful that they will find a partner who can meet that goal and thus pursue "second-best fallback strategies as insurance against worst-case fears." Even though their hopes align, "There is a gender divide lurking below the surface." For both young women and young men, making sure you have a good job and career is the most important goal, and that leads to divergent fallback strategies.[52]

Because young women in this new economy are uncertain that men are able to earn enough and will contribute at home, most are committed to "self-reliance over economic dependence within a traditional marriage." This is true of 60 percent of white women and of middle- and upper-class women, too, but rises to more than 80 percent of working-class and poor women and 100 percent of African American women in her study. "Hoping to avoid being trapped in an unhappy marriage or deserted by an unfaithful spouse, most see work as essential to survival." To hold out for the right partner and the right kind of relationship, women today must be resourceful and focused on finding work that allows them to be independent.[53]

While most people in the country think men and women are equally focused on pursuing their careers, among Millennials both men and women think women are more focused on their careers. The women, by almost three to one, say they are more career-oriented (28 to 10 percent). On college campuses, Rosin observed, many women welcome the "hookup culture" because it gives them the freedom to focus on their education and future professional careers.[54]

While most men join women in saying they prefer an egalitarian relationship with shared responsibility for income, home, and child care, the difference is that the men are content to fall back to a breadwinner role. That is why Gerson describes them as "neotraditional men." Men are doing more housework and parenting than in the past. One in five children under five with a working mother has a father as the primary caregiver; almost 10 percent of all households with minor children and one-quarter of single-parent households are headed by a father alone, more than ever before.[55]

But almost 30 percent of men still prefer a marriage where the man is the primary breadwinner and the woman has primary responsibility for the home.[56]

So with men and women on these divergent paths, it matters a lot if there is a pay gap where women are making less than men for their work. The economy is incredibly challenging for the vast majority of working women and working men, as we saw in chapter 4, though working women are doubly challenged because they dominate employment in occupations that are growing and low paid, such as home health care, food services, and retail. Two-thirds of those earning less than $10.10 per hour, the proposed federal minimum wage, are women. And for those women employed in restaurants in major cities, bring into the equation that 90 percent report experiencing sexual harassment at work and half say it happens weekly.[57]

Men still dominate higher-paying occupations in fields such as law, medicine, and science and engineering. They still dominate employment in manufacturing and construction, where pay is above the median.[58]

Men are also still dominant in public office. In the U.S. Congress, only twenty senators and just 18 percent of the House of Representatives are women. At the state level, women account for just 10 percent of governors and 24 percent of state legislators. Men are still dominant in university teaching, where women hold only 44 percent of the tenured positions, and only 24 percent of women in academia are in tenure-track positions. Men still dominate at the C-suite level in America's corporations, as female CEOs run just 4.2 percent of Fortune 500 companies. And only 19 percent of the board members of American corporations are women, though at least they do not work for Japanese companies, where only 3 percent of corporate board members are women.[59]

A Harvard Business School study of male and female graduates shows how much choices about family responsibilities block women from reaching the highest levels of companies. The women and male graduates begin with very similar career goals, though the men are much more likely to end up in senior management positions. The male graduates are able to pursue their goals because 60 percent expected their careers to take priority over those of their wives, who would have the primary child care responsibility—and that is what happened to them. Starting out, only about 20 percent of the female graduates thought their husband's careers would take precedence, though it did for twice that many. Half of the women thought they would handle a majority of the child care, but three-quarters ended up caring for the children. And those different family experiences had a decisive impact on salary and whether one reached senior management.[60]

Employers and government could do what Google did when it extended paid maternity leave from twelve to eighteen weeks. That ability to afford to care for a newborn led to a decrease by 50 percent in the number of new moms choosing to leave Google. It turns out it was better for Google to do more to keep their experienced new mothers at work than to train new employees. In short, extended paid leave allowed working women to stay in the labor force and maintain their seniority at their company, Google said.[61]

While the gap in wages for men and women has nearly closed for Millennials—woman's hourly earnings are 93 percent of men's—the pay gap continues to matter in so many ways. Women work fewer hours than men because women are still dealing with the majority of the responsibility for the home and children. And with all due respect to the Millennials, the pay gap is alive and well for older generations and in occupations where women predominate. Nine in ten nurses are women, yet women nurses earn $5,000 less than men, and that gap, even controlling for specialty education and working hours, has not narrowed in 25 years, according to a report in the *Journal of the American Medical Association*. Among all workers, women's hourly earnings are 84 percent of men's—and the cumulative effect of decades of lower pay and even less shared responsibility by men for home and child care plays out in retirement with lower Social Security benefits for women.[62]

So women have not drunk the Kool-Aid. They see opportunity and are adapting, though they firmly believe the playing field is tilted against them. A large majority of women (62 percent) believe men earn more than women for the same job, yet fewer than half of men believe that (47 percent).[63]

What about the prospects for getting a top-level job? Professional and working-class women have very different points of view about the opportunities before them. A nearly universal 71 percent of college-educated women think it is easier for a man to get a top-level job in business and government, but that drops to a still considerable 47 percent of women without a college degree. By the way, working-class, non-college-educated men are the most likely to say that it is easier for women to get those top jobs.[64]

This is the bottom line: a majority of women believe they have less opportunity than men and that the country has yet to achieve equal opportunity for women and men.[65]

Working women focus on what they must do in this new economy and they are adapting, though getting almost no help from government or employers in managing work and family, which makes life all that much harder. That they believe the playing field is tilted against women, particularly as they move farther up the job and status ladder, may well prove politically explosive very soon and force a focus on a reform agenda.

When one reflects on the contradictions of the new economy, liberal and some conservative commentary concludes that the country will be forced to address them or there will be some kind of mental or political breakdown. But will that be true for the contradictions in our society? Will the country be forced to address the marriage crisis, the numbers of children raised by a single parent, and the state of both working-class men and working women on their own? These contradictions also produce slower economic growth, more financial stress, people scrambling to survive, more poverty, and less upward mobility. They produce family breakdown and the breakdown of social solidarity, but will that stir a new politics with radical new ways to address them?

When working-class men are so economically, culturally, and politically marginalized—increasingly disconnected from church, community, and family, and unable to adapt to change—how do you get the country mobilized to address their condition as a national priority?

When college-educated women and college-educated men have rallied in recent years to strengthen their marriages to raise children in two-parent households, how do you get them to address the marriage crisis that is now largely a problem of the working class and the poor?

Yet it is just such growing contradictions that create the ingredients for a change in the public agenda and revolution in family policy.

Part III

POLITICAL DISRUPTION

6 REVOLUTIONS AND COUNTERREVOLUTION: THE BATTLE FOR AMERICAN VALUES

The seismic transformations happening in America today—increasing racial diversity, rising immigration, growing secularism, evolving family structures, and swelling metropolitan centers—are not simply economic and demographic changes. They matter so much because they are tied to revolutions in America's values, particularly the values held among Millennials and those living in the cities. These revolutions have produced a furious counterrevolution and battle for America's values—though it is a counterrevolution that cannot prevail.

Among the ascendant groups and in the regions where they dominate culturally, people are more likely to value equality, equal rights, and fairness. They are more empathetic and worry more about harm to the vulnerable. They want to see compassion for those in need. They are more open to diversity, differences, outsiders, and newcomers, people that live different lifestyles and are from different cultures. Tolerance is a virtue. They value a kind of individualism that signifies individual autonomy, self-expression, and sexual freedom for men and women. They welcome the emerging pluralism of family types and reject the traditional family and its roles. They honor education beyond its instrumental value. Education is the key to individual fulfillment and opportunity. And science and technology are the keys to learning discoverable truths.

They consciously do not turn to traditional authority for moral absolutes and they devalue those who depend on faith-based conclusions.

Those battling against these seismic transformations in values honor an individualism that is grounded in personal responsibility, self-reliance, self-restraint, and self-discipline. If the individual is not encouraged to learn self-direction and self-reliance, they think, that person will become idle and dependent. Accordingly, they value industriousness, conscientiousness, and those governed by a strong work ethic. Their beliefs are grounded in their faith. They seek purity before God and admire those who live a sanctified life. Thus they honor marriage and the traditional family, with the man playing the breadwinner role. And they honor faith-based moral absolutes and respect traditional authority. They value patriotism, love of country, and those who defend it from our enemies. U.S. citizens come first.

And they deride those who fetishize diversity, multiculturalism, and misplaced compassion, and who cannot understand the primacy of faith in making moral judgments.

These revolutions and the counterrevolution are producing an increasing cultural and political polarization in America, though the polarization is hardly symmetric. History is on the side of the ascendant revolutions, and thus the opponents must never let up and, indeed, must engage with increasing intensity if they are to forestall the Armageddon. When we look back and ask how America became so polarized and gridlocked, we will likely focus on 2004, when the culture war was joined so strategically.

Defenders of traditional values have been able to wage a counterrevolution of increasing ferocity by encamping in the twenty states of the South, the Appalachian Valley, and parts of the Plains states and the Mountain West. These are the most race-conscious, Evangelical, religiously observant, and rural parts of the country. From this base, conservatives have fervently joined the culture war to reassert endangered values and warn of the high risks of the new mores.

Because race and religion are so central to the conservative counterrevolution, America continues to battle over modern social transformations taken for granted in most developed countries, to the bewilderment of large parts of the country. To be sure, America's civil, women's, immigrant, and gay rights revolutions have fundamentally changed the country, though they are all still contested by conservatives from the conservative heartland and thus unfinished.

The debates over public policy get red-hot because they become the scorecard that signifies what values are to prevail. The ascendant majority takes for granted that the country will invest in education, promote equality, build a stronger safety net, support the growing marriage diversity and acceptance of gay marriage, honor America's immigrant diversity, and get moving on addressing climate change.

To stop the revolutions, Republicans are battling to restrict access to abortion and even contraception and against demands for equal pay for women. They are defending the institution of marriage and religious liberty as the Supreme Court accepts the legality of same-sex marriage. The Republican Party continues to resist voting rights for blacks and Hispanics and battles to reverse President Obama's actions to give legal status to undocumented immigrants, including even the "DREAMers" who came to the United States as minors. They battle to end unemployment benefits and Obamacare subsidies, which they view as welfare undermining the incentive to work.

Consider the Republicans' obsession with contraception. The birth control pill is used by 82 percent of women of childbearing age, yet conservatives took the fight to limit the contraceptive coverage in the Affordable Care Act up to the U.S. Supreme Court. That "Obamacare" covers birth control without copays seems an "implicit endorsement of a value system that says it's perfectly O.K. to have sex without the goal of having a baby," it occurred to Linda Greenhouse in her *New York Times* column. She concluded rightly that this is "a war not on religion or on women but on modernity." For those battling against these revolutions, this is a battle over race, gender roles, faith, and America.[1]

That is largely why Republicans have been able to build intensity and electoral turnout in their base in each successive electoral contest and sweep the twenty states of the GOP conservative heartland in the so-called off-year elections of 2010 and 2014. The Republican base has a rising stake in forestalling a Democratic win, and thus for them all elections are national. And with the rural bias in the U.S. Senate and House elections, Republicans sit atop the U.S. Congress and dominate off-year elections for now.

But the revolutions and counterrevolution produce the opposite result and trend in presidential elections, as we shall see in the next chapter. Dialectically, the Republicans' growing success in mobilizing for the off-year elections only increases the probability that Democrats will win in the next national, presidential election. And Republican control of the U.S. Congress and total Republican control of nearly half the states will only compound the party's problems. Its efforts to nullify the president's executive order on undocumented immigrants, repeal the Affordable Care Act, make abortion illegal, block the president's actions on coal and climate change, and limit the right to vote will only further alienate the Republican Party from the country.

Democrats will not produce a landslide national election that shifts the partisan plates until they get serious about battling for reforms that address the country's growing economic and social contradictions. Only then will the broad coalition of ascendant groups become equally invested in defending their vote and values.

We are truly in an "interregnum," like the one described by Antonio Gramsci, when "the old is dying and the new cannot be born," during which "a great variety of morbid symptoms appear."[2]

RACE AND THE COUNTERREVOLUTION

The battle over American values is rooted in race, America's black-white history, and America's growing racial diversity.

The public believes that white America is on the brink of becoming a minority in an increasingly diverse country. The country erroneously thinks racial minorities already constitute 49 percent of the population—well above the actual figure, 37 percent. While all races expect America to become a minority-majority nation, white Americans believe racial minorities count for 48 percent right now and that they will form a 63 percent majority in 2050—10 points above the census projection.[3]

The rub is that African Americans, Hispanics, and Asians welcome the growing diversity and are confident in its collateral benefits for the country. So are college graduates, those with advanced degrees, liberals, and unmarried women. The same is true among the Millennials—a generation that is not only diverse, but is also increasingly entering into interracial marriages such that one in five newlyweds marries out. That the great majority of Millennials say Barack Obama is "mixed race" rather than African American underlines their identification with this postracial world.[4]

However, the three groups in the country most wary of diversity and becoming a minority are white conservatives, white Republicans, and white Evangelicals. White seniors and the white working class are none too excited either.[5]

It is hard not to conclude that their reaction to this growing racial diversity reflects a deep racial consciousness and aversion to racial minorities. A striking 62 percent of Republicans and white born-again Evangelicals believe more diversity will cause "crime and problems in our neighborhood [to] go up" at a time when crime rates are plummeting to the lowest levels in decades. By contrast, just a third of liberals and college graduates and only a quarter of postgraduates expect diversity to bring higher crime rates.[6]

In my work with white working-class voters and Reagan Democrats, I called for Democrats to take much more seriously the threats these voters faced as they sought to protect their families and neighborhoods. It was very easy for the elites and professors to lecture whites on school busing and crime from their protected enclaves. But much has changed over the past thirty years, and these new findings are of a different character—as the expected "problems" with growing diversity are detached from the real problems facing their communities.[7]

For white conservatives, racial diversity changes the political balance, and political control will come at the expense of whites. About 60 percent of Republicans, white conservatives, white "born again" Evangelicals, and white seniors also believe that racial minorities will use their hold over government to discriminate against whites. Yet just a third of college graduates and Millennials and a quarter of postgraduates think that.[8]

For many conservatives, the worry is what these racial minorities will demand of government. Four of five Republicans and three-quarters of white Evangelicals say growing racial diversity means "there will be too many demands on government services." An intense bloc of 36 percent of Republicans say this is "completely true"—affirming how much the reaction against diversity is a fear that the new majority will use its political power to expand government and spending on behalf of the now ascendant minorities.[9]

To be fair, majorities of racial minorities and Millennials also worry about the demand on government services, though many fewer than for Republicans and without intensity. It likely reflects a genuine competition for services. We have seen this in prior generations as earlier waves of immigrants and minority groups came to worry about competition from newer arrivals. We have seen this in Britain as well, where black immigrants from Jamaica and Pakistan come to resent the new asylum seekers from Somalia or workers from Poland and worry that they are overloading the schools and the National Health Service.

What does not seem to be driving the conservative reaction is worry that growing diversity threatens their job or wages—the flash point for racial and ethnic tensions for most of our history. About 60 percent of Republicans and the white working class say with this diversity "there will not be enough jobs for everyone." But a like number of African Americans and half of Hispanics and Millennials think that, too. The response reflects worries about the job market shared by everyone, rather than a worry that racial minorities will compete for their jobs.[10]

Most important, the ascendant groups view the rising diversity as potentially ushering in a new stage of tolerance and multiculturalism in America. Fully 70 percent of college graduates, Millennials, African Americans, Hispanics, and Asians say it will bring a time of greater acceptance and tolerance. But Republicans balk at that future. Barely a majority of Republicans think "people will become more accepting of their differences and more willing to find common ground." White conservatives and white southerners are more likely to agree with one conservative columnist's diagnosis: "We have fetishized diversity, tolerance, compassion, and niceness"—the "left-wing pseudo-religion."[11]

The response of Republicans, Evangelicals, and white southerners to this growing racial diversity is deeply embedded in America's unfinished white-black history.

Slavery left us with a legal system of race domination and segregation well into the middle of the twentieth century, until challenged by a massive civil rights movement that eventually succeeded in directing the power of the federal government toward efforts to redress the past and get closer to equal opportunity. This turn was possible because major leaders in both national parties considered equal rights part of their legacy and both parties genuinely competed for the growing black vote. The Civil Rights Act of 1964 deepened the country's commitment to equality and barred racial discrimination in public accommodations and government facilities and by employers and government agencies.[12]

Since 1964, however, nearly all Republican presidential nominees put the grievances of white voters at the forefront of their campaigns. Barry Goldwater voted against the Civil Rights Act and Ronald Reagan strongly opposed it, saying it was "humiliating to the South." He parodied "welfare queens" when he ran. Richard Nixon was determined to restore "law and order" and called on the "silent majority" to make itself heard. George H. W. Bush put Lee Atwater at the top of his campaign and ran a flood of "Willie Horton" ads that depicted a convicted black murderer on weekend parole killing again. John McCain had to restrain running mate Sarah Palin from attacking Obama for his association with Rev. Wright. Mitt Romney's promise to enforce onerous immigration policies that would lead the undocumented to "self-deport" and his disdain for the "47 percent" made clear for whom he would govern.[13]

More recently, Republican signals to aggrieved white votes have been matched by serious efforts to deny blacks the right to vote. During four successive presidential elections, the country watched dramatic television coverage of African American voters forced to wait in long queues to cast their votes in the critical swing states of Florida and Ohio, where Republican governors and secretaries of state created shortages of voting machines, limited early voting, and challenged ballots at voting places. Republican state leaders were even accused of blocking traffic to make it difficult for blacks to get to their polling stations. With Republican secretaries of state battling with the U.S. Justice Department and federal courts to bar early voting or to purge voter rolls close to the election, the Republican Party has sent a defining signal about its views of the universal franchise for black citizens.

When Republicans gained control of many new states after the 2010 elections and in the lead-up to the 2012 presidential election, they passed a blizzard of laws to greatly restrict voting. They limited when people could register and vote, required government-issued photo identification that perhaps one in ten voters did not have, and reversed reforms that allowed people with criminal records to regain their right to vote. That set up a huge battle in the courts.[14]

In 2013, the conservative Supreme Court overturned Section 4 of the Voting Rights Act, which required states with a history of discrimination to get preclearance from the Justice Department when changing election laws. Republican-controlled states in the South rushed to implement new regulations on registration and voting, with a disproportionate impact on blacks, Hispanics, and the poor. In 2013, eight Republican-controlled states passed voter ID laws, and others are considering adding mandatory proof of citizenship, such as a birth certificate or a passport, which minorities often lack, in order to vote. Remember, this was 2013, not 1964.[15]

"What we see here is total disrespect and disregard for constitutional protections," declared the head of the Georgia NAACP. Republicans say in their defense that this is about addressing the potential for fraud, though that does not pass the smell test. Half of the ten states with the highest black turnout in 2008 and seven of the twelve states with the largest Hispanic growth over the past decade passed restrictive voter laws by the spring before the 2012 elections.[16]

Conservatives are taking these steps because they fear that the electoral power of minorities will translate into increased demand for government spending on social programs. Rather than rewarding hard work and self-reliance, that will increase idleness and dependence on government. For white conservatives, this is a values argument, not just political calculation or budget policy.

With the unemployment rate near 7.4 percent, Senate Republicans blocked an extension of unemployment insurance for the long-term unemployed. Senator Richard Shelby of Alabama explained, "People, if you pay 'em for years and years, they won't look for a job." And on the fiftieth anniversary of the War on Poverty, Paul Ryan's Budget Committee issued a report declaring defeat. It began by citing the breakdown of the family as the main cause of persistent poverty and blamed counterproductive social benefits for leading people into "the poverty trap."[17]

Ryan also declared that the subsidies in the Affordable Care Act compound this values problem facing the country. Ryan reflected conservative opinion Web sites that equated the health care reforms with welfare. From the start of the public debate, they set off alarms with their headlines: "OBAMACARE PUTS FAMILIES MAKING $192,920 ON WELFARE" and "OBAMACARE IS GOING TO BE THE BIGGEST EXPANSION OF THE WELFARE STATE IN U.S. HISTORY." They warned that seventeen million people will get subsidies to purchase health insurance and twenty-one million will be put on expanded Medicaid rolls. It "would eventually put most Americans on the dole, converting middle-class Americans into lifelong welfare recipients and government dependents." With America in decline, "the number of Americans that are able to independently take care of themselves will continue to go down."[18]

And it was no surprise then that when the Congressional Budget Office concluded that the availability of subsidized health insurance in the individual market would lead some to choose to reduce their working hours, conservative critics pounced. Paul Ryan elaborated on the misplaced values: it is "inducing a person not to work who is on the low-income scale, not to get on the ladder of life, to begin working, getting the dignity of work."[19]

At the heart of this concern is a view of the ethos of these minority populations that have grown less self-reliant and demanding of support. Buried in Phil Robertson's interview with *GQ* about *Duck Dynasty* was an observation that the blacks he knew growing up in Louisiana, "Pre-entitlement, pre-welfare," were "happy" and "godly"—"no one was singing the blues." Ryan's racial assumptions were evident when he said, "We have got this tailspin of culture in our inner cities in particular of men not working. And just generations of men not even thinking about working or learning the value and the culture of work."[20]

In the face of Republican hostility and continuing challenges to the right to vote, civil rights organizations, the NAACP, and the black churches and fraternal orders are on the march as part of a continuing battle for black advancement. That effort has produced a consistent and high level of black turnout regardless of the election and in spite of the new restrictive laws. Ohio—where Republicans doubled down on every conceivable restriction and produced the requisite queues—became the one state in the country where black turnout in 2012 exceeded the extraordinary 2008 levels. Blacks have turned out at a higher rate than whites and other minorities with comparable socioeconomic standing for some time, and in 2012 their overall turnout rate trumped white turnout for the first time.[21]

Blacks comprised a still very insistent 12 percent of the 2014 off-year electorate, as they view their values and rights as still protected by the ballot.[22]

Each new video of a police officer shooting an unarmed black man and the resulting protests confirm for the community that race matters and that the job is unfinished. Each week brings another Eric Garner in a chokehold beseeching, "I can't breathe," or a twelve-year-old Tamir Rice shot in a playground. They know that blacks are three times as likely as whites to be searched at a traffic stop and three times as likely to be arrested—and that Ferguson, Missouri, is more normal than not.

Then a white supremacist pictured with symbols of apartheid-era South Africa and the Confederacy murdered nine black congregants in a bible class, "the beating heart" of the black community, as President Obama described it in his eulogy. And today's generation would be reminded of its history, a church "burned to the ground because its founder sought to end slavery," a pulpit where Martin Luther King preached against Jim Crow laws, and steps where the "marches began." The president reminded America these lost lives matter for everyone "who cares about the steady expansion of human rights and human dignity in this country."

When America celebrates Martin Luther King Jr.'s birthday and the anniversary of the March on Washington, we do not hear the formulaic and requisite speeches given on most national and ethnic holidays. That is because there is a real sense that hard-won civil rights and social gains are not secured, despite the election and reelection of an African American president. Ministers and civil rights leaders are again calling on their congregants, allies, and country to reaffirm and defend equal rights, tolerance, and social justice against the renewed attacks. The continuous legitimation of equal rights in black-white history has made the principle of equality more available as a value and tool as women, immigrants, and gays joined their struggles to shape America's diversity.

FIGHTING THE SEXUAL REVOLUTION AND SECULARIZATION OF AMERICA

America is one of the few developed countries where religious attendance has become one the strongest correlates of partisan political preference. That intertwining of faith and partisanship has grown ever tighter through two periods of growing polarization on social issues. The first period was shaped by the actions of President Ronald Reagan and President Bill Clinton between 1983 and 1996. President George W. Bush's 2004 values election campaign launched the second decade-long period of polarization that includes the current contentious period. Karl Rove's culture war took the religious sorting of the country to a new level.

The potential for such polarization was there because the battles over the family, sexuality, and the role of women played out in a country where religion remains important for at least 40 percent of the country and particularly for Evangelicals.

The first period of religious polarization began when President Reagan and President Clinton traded executive orders on abortion. Within hours of being sworn in as president in 1993, Bill Clinton reversed five executive orders regarding abortion, family planning, and stem cell research. This included reversing both the gag rule that prohibited government-funded family planning clinics serving low-income communities from counseling on abortion, and the "Mexico City policy," which prohibited U.S. aid to international clinics that used their own funds to provide counseling or referrals for abortions. He commented at the time, "As a result of today's action, every woman will be able to receive medical advice and referrals that will not be censored or distorted by ideological arguments that should not be a part of medicine." Shortly after taking the oath of office, President Clinton also tried to change the long-standing prohibition against gays in the military, ordering the secretary of defense to draft legislation to overturn existing policies.[23]

Religious conservatives rejected those actions. Influential Evangelical spokesman and Focus on the Family president James Dobson told his followers that Bill Clinton had "debase[d] the presidency" with his "homosexual agenda" and his "hands are stained with the blood of countless innocent babies." Pat Robertson warned of the stark choice this created: "Either we will return to the moral integrity and original dreams of the founders of this nation . . . or we will give ourselves over more and more to hedonism, to all forms of destructive anti-social behavior." A Christian Voice pamphlet commanded its followers to "make sure government is . . . punishing what is wrong and rewarding what is right." And homosexuality was the ultimate wrong, Rev. Jerry Falwell declared, a sin "so grievous, so abominable in the sight of God that he destroyed the cities of Sodom and Gomorrah because of [it]."[24]

As a result, Democratic presidential candidates and congressional party candidates became increasingly pro-choice and Republicans became increasingly pro-life. In the Senate, 80 percent of Democratic senators had already moved to casting pro-choice votes by 1987. Interestingly, almost 40 percent of Republicans still cast pro-choice votes then, though that plummeted to virtually zero by 2005 as the culture war was joined. The House was fully polarized by 2008: about 90 percent of House Democrats were pro-choice though only 10 percent of House Republicans were. Meanwhile, the number of Republican senators who were Baptist or Evangelical jumped from seven to sixteen and the number of House members jumped from ten to forty-one.[25]

The second wave of religious polarization started with Karl Rove's unlikely culture war in 2004 and has only deepened in the subsequent decade. Gay marriage and abortion gave Rove the critical material to ignite the culture war and launch President Bush's polarizing 2004 campaign.

What Rove saw in 2004 was an evenly divided country and a declining bloc of genuine swing voters, and he decided Republicans could win by raising the turnout of the base rather than by working to persuade swing voters across the electorate. His own campaign team described the plan as a radical departure, but Rove was intently focused on the millions of missing Evangelicals who did not turn out in the 2000 national election.

President Bush invited expressions of faith during his time in the White House, including prayer, and said in debates that the Bible was his favorite book and cautioned on evolution, saying, "religion has been around a lot longer than Darwinism." He hired Ralph Reed, the former head of the Christian Coalition, and reached deeply into the religious communities to fuel his campaign: 350,000 of the 1.4 million campaign volunteers were "pro-family" Evangelicals. President Bush promised a constitutional amendment to nullify the Massachusetts decision to legalize same-sex marriage and supported the thirteen states that held referendums to define marriage as between a man and a woman. Evangelical minister Rick Warren wrote to the 136,000 subscribers of his weekly newsletter for pastors, urging them to use the pulpit to compare the presidential candidates on five non-negotiable issues: abortion, stem cell research, cloning, gay marriage, and euthanasia.[26]

The intense cultural battle moved the turnout to 60.7 percent, the highest since 1968 and a 6.4-point surge from 2000. According to Democracy Corps' postelection poll, the strategy raised the Bush vote by 4 percentage points in the Deep South, by 2 points in the white rural areas, and by 2 points among white Evangelicals (reaching 82 percent). The biggest issue for Bush voters was "moral values"—the first time that issue has topped the list. Gay marriage and abortion were at the top of the list of doubts about Kerry among Bush voters. On Election Day a whopping six million new Evangelical voters came out for Bush.[27]

What Rove failed to take into account, however, was the resulting polarization and countermobilization in the non-Evangelical world. The strategy raised the Republican vote in southern and rural red states. But in the presidential battleground, where all the money and organizing were focused, Bush and Kerry fought to a draw. In those states, Bush gained less than a 1-point margin (0.8 percent) compared to his performance in 2000. Kerry came within 118,599 votes in Ohio of winning the presidency.[28]

When contemplating the exceptional changes in America's politics, we will look back on 2004 as the year the legions crossed the Rubicon.

The Democratic Party was beginning to resemble a coalition of the nonreligious and the Republicans a coalition of the religious, and top issues included the family, sexuality, and women, contraception, abortion, and same-sex unions. This was "the glue," Putnam and Campbell write, "holding the coalition of the religious together." The glue needs to be stronger and stronger because the country is moving away from the traditional values on issues such as crime, prayer in school, family, and marriage that once allowed conservatives to win the culture war.[29]

Former Arkansas governor Mike Huckabee spoke to these issues that are very much alive with Evangelicals. He opposed the inclusion of preventive health services without copays in all insurance policies under the Affordable Care Act and called on Republicans to join the battle against government: "If the Democrats want to insult the women of America by making them believe that they are helpless without Uncle Sugar coming in and providing for them a prescription each month for birth control, because they cannot control their libido or their reproductive system without the help of the government, then so be it."[30]

Social conservatives such as Huckabee probably still relate to the wording pollsters used before World War II when a plurality of Americans said it was "wicked" and not just "unfortunate" when "young women have sexual relations before marriage." Today, though, just one in five says premarital sex is "always wrong," while a near consensus has emerged that it is not wrong at all or not a moral issue. Almost half of Evangelicals, though, continue to believe it is "always wrong" to have sex before marriage, underscoring America's continued polarization on the sexual revolution.[31]

That means abortion has emerged as the most central and enduring issue for social conservatives.

A 1973 U.S. Supreme Court decision gave women the constitutional right to abort a pregnancy in the first three months and in later months with more restrictions. The decision extended the right to privacy under the Fourteenth Amendment to make such a decision, in effect accepting the autonomy of women on sexual matters.

That decision propelled the country into a heated and politically polarized national debate about abortion. For long periods, a small majority of about 55 percent have said abortion should be legal in all or most cases and about 40 percent that it should be illegal in all or most cases. About one in four absolutely opposed or absolutely supported abortion.[32]

Yet forty years after the landmark decision, fewer than 30 percent nationally want to completely overturn the decision and less than one in five now say abortion is a "critical issue" for them. That has made it difficult for pro-life candidates to make headway nationally on the issue, but the majority of white Evangelicals now want to "completely overturn" *Roe v. Wade*. That has steeled Republicans, and they have continued to move aggressively to effectively ban abortions wherever they govern.[33]

Regardless of whether voters want this to be the main issue for the political parties, this is the issue where Democratic and Republican members of Congress are most polarized. Leaders from both parties welcome attending pro-life marches or Planned Parenthood conventions, respectively. Democrats link the issue to their attack on Republicans for their "war on women." To energize their Evangelical base in lower-turnout elections, Republicans are adding state referendums to enshrine legal protections for the fetus. In 2014, the fetal personhood amendment was on the ballot in Colorado and North

Dakota. To motivate women voters, Democrats spent $4.6 million on advertising on abortion and birth control alone in the very off-year 2013 Virginia governor's race. And in 2014, Democratic Senate candidates in North Carolina, Iowa, and Colorado ran ads charging the Republican candidates with leading crusades in their states to ban all forms of birth control, backing harsh anti-abortion laws, and voting to defund Planned Parenthood.[34]

In the prelude to the 2014 off-year elections, both Republican and Democratic voters said the biggest factor in their vote was stopping candidates who did not share their own views on the Affordable Care Act and their own views on abortion. The vote on the health care law, we know now, was really an expression of people's views on the role of government, race, and dependence, and the vote on abortion, about secularization and the sexual revolution.[35]

Homosexuality and gay marriage are now a very close second to abortion as an issue sorting the country into camps. A 53 percent majority say they cannot vote for a candidate who does not share their views on this issue. Acceptance of same-sex marriage has advanced at a breathtaking pace over the past five years, and a majority of Millennials describe themselves as a "supporter of gay rights." That is greater than the number who describe themselves as patriotic, religious, or an environmentalist.[36]

Between 2013 and 2014, all religious dominations witnessed accelerating support for gay marriage, especially among black Protestants. The more than 10-point jump in support among black Protestants is a strong statement about the primacy of equal rights and the power of outspoken civil rights and black leaders. The NAACP, the Chicago Urban League, Rev. Jesse Jackson, and President Obama—the first president to publicly support same-sex marriage—have all framed gay marriage as an issue of equity and part of their ongoing struggle for civil rights.

Only white Evangelicals remained steady in their views between 2013 and 2014, and just 27 percent supported gay marriage in 2015.[37]

In a video posted on a church's YouTube page a couple of years ago, Phil Robertson of *Duck Dynasty* warned that homosexuals committed "indecent acts" and that they received "the due penalty for their perversion." For him, their behavior is an insult to God: "They are insolent, arrogant God haters. They are heartless. They are faithless. They are senseless. They are ruthless. They invent ways of doing evil."[38]

If you want to understand the two parties' reaction to this issue, look at what their state attorneys general did when the federal courts overturned state bans on same-sex marriage. In Ohio, Utah, Michigan, Colorado, and New Jersey, Republican officials asked the courts to block any gay unions while they appealed lower-court rulings. They argued that the states have a sovereign right to ban gay marriage and that "nobody knows right now the precise impact same-sex marriage will have on traditional marriage, children, and society at large." They argued that same-sex couples are not *qualified* to marry, as they cannot procreate, that heterosexual couples are better parents, and that banning same-sex marriage promotes "responsible procreation."[39]

In Virginia, Oregon, California, Pennsylvania, Nevada, and Kentucky, the Democratic attorneys general declared that they would not defend the bans in their states. They say that these laws are unconstitutional, violating the equal-protection clause of the Fourteenth Amendment. Virginia attorney general Mark Herring vowed, "as attorney general, I'm going to make sure that the [people] presenting the state's legal position on behalf of the people of Virginia are on the right side of history and on the right side of the law." The U.S. attorney general defended their refusal, saying state attorneys general do not have an obligation to defend laws they view as discriminatory and called gay rights one of the "defining civil rights challenges of our time."[40]

When the Supreme Court granted constitutional protection to same-sex marriages, it overturned the bans in thirteen, mostly southern, states and extended the meaning of equality and tolerance in all fifty. The White House lit up in a rainbow of colors made its own kind of statement to the world.

Yet Republican attorneys general, governors, and presidential candidates bitterly condemned the ruling. Louisiana's attorney general said the ruling "overturns the will of the people" and Mississippi's governor called the new marriage mandate "out of step with the majority of Mississippians." Alabama's chief justice compared the ruling to fateful wrongfully-decided cases and called for a constitutional amendment to ban same-sex marriages. And Texas's attorney general acted to protect county clerks and magistrates who object to same-sex unions on religious grounds. He declared that this 2015 "fabricated" decision created a "new constitutional right," but it "did not diminish, overrule, or call into question the First Amendment rights to free exercise of religion that formed the first freedom in the Bill of Rights."

Score that one for the values of equality, equal rights, marriage pluralism, and tolerance.[41]

The ferocious battle over values will obviously not quiet. As we have seen in this section, social conservatives are very invested in their fight against secularism and the sexual revolution and their defense of faith and marriage. Abortion is the front line in the culture war.

BATTLING THE IMMIGRANT REVOLUTION

Globalization has brought a surge in global migration, and one in five migrants comes to America and moves to one of the metropolitan centers across the country. The United States is increasingly open to the rest of the world due to a comparatively open immigration policy and an increased border security that has led many undocumented immigrants to stop risking trips home and to settle in cities far away from the borders. Universities, high-tech clusters, and metropolitan centers are becoming magnets for the new immigrants, skilled and unskilled alike. Our megacities are 40 percent foreign-born, and every growing metropolitan area has become a vast mix of languages, skin colors, cultures, cuisines, and heritages.

That a large majority of the country currently thinks immigration is good for the country is not just support for keeping the door open. It reflects support for the core value of openness to outsiders, appreciation for rising diversity, and growing support for multiculturalism.

Yet multiculturalism is an acquired taste in the world, even in America. Citizens expect their leaders to protect their national identity, language, traditions, way of life, borders, standard of living, and economic welfare against foreigners and foreign competition and to preserve public services for the citizenry who built them up. The irresistible integration of outsiders only increases the demand that leaders assert the primacy of U.S. citizens and citizenship, U.S. interests, and English as the official language. America first.

The comprehensive immigration reform bill that passed the U.S. Senate in 2013 but stalled in the House, unsurprisingly, produced a debate that reasserted values central to America's revolutions and counterrevolution. In fact, both proponents and opponents elevated the value of citizenship and putting America first. Leaders embraced the centrality of English and the commitment to protecting U.S. borders and labor markets. The proposed immigration legislation would greatly expand immigration, bring the undocumented out of the shadows, and provide a path for legalization of illegals; but it would also militarize the border, levy high penalties on employers hiring the undocumented, require those applying for registered provisional status to pay a fine and pass a background test, and force those seeking citizenship to wait ten years, be proficient in English, and pay back taxes.

The majority of Republican senators voted against the bill, though they were particularly determined to ensure that any newly legalized immigrants could not get government subsidies, including subsidies to buy health insurance under the new health care law until after the ten-year waiting period—something seven in ten Americans support. In fact, three-quarters believe that legal residents should not receive government benefits such as food stamps, Medicaid, and Social Security before they become citizens.[42]

The norm of putting "America first" remains very strong. Many new immigrants, like the immigrants from old and new Europe before them, themselves became ambivalent about the struggles of new arrivals and expressed concern about competition for work and classrooms as well as the lack of proficiency in English. The lack of proficiency in English also concerns naturalized immigrants, and 87 percent of Hispanics think adult immigrants need to learn English to succeed. Today second- and third-generation Hispanics are using English at a faster rate than immigrant groups such as the Germans who preceded them.[43]

The national Republican Party, with the support of southern Democrats, led the fight after World War I to stop the flood of immigration and get the country back to "100 percent Americanism"—which meant stopping the flood of Jews, Poles, Italians, Japanese, and Chinese.

Well, state Republican leaders jumped at the opportunity to play that role in the face of America's current waves of immigration Governor Wilson in California started the two-decade anti-immigration struggle closed by Governor Jan Brewer of Arizona. They sought to transfer enforcement of immigration laws from the federal government to the states, which would supposedly be more vigilant in chasing down the illegals and denying them access to schools, employment, and housing. These efforts were overturned by the federal courts because of evident racial profiling and because they unconstitutionally usurped the federal government's responsibility for immigration.[44]

Nationally, the Republicans' presidential nominee vowed to pass and enforce laws that would make life so hard for undocumented immigrants that they would "self-deport." The House and Senate Republican leaders committed to giving the highest priority to reversing President Obama's executive order legalizing the "DREAMers" and five million additional undocumented immigrants. With the appropriation bill to fund the Department of Homeland Security the hostage, Republican leaders promised to use the Congress's funding authority and the courts to block the president's executive orders. And when that stalled, Republican state leaders worked to limit undocumented immigrants' access to state universities.[45]

The public is nervous about the permeability of the border, particularly when tens of thousands of unaccompanied minors from Central America poured through it in the fall of 2014 and most ended up remaining in the United States. Nonetheless, when President Obama announced his executive order, he declared, "we are and always will be a nation of immigrants" and "For more than two hundred years, our tradition of welcoming immigrants from around the world has given us a tremendous advantage over other nations."[46]

These political battles over immigration have been joined by an expanding pro-immigration coalition, the Catholic Church, and a growing social movement that expropriated the values of early civil rights struggles. On the occasion of the anniversary of the March on Washington, Clarissa Martinez-de-Castro, the director of immigration policy for the National Council of La Raza, observed, "There's continued progress and struggle that needs to happen on the issues that were fought on in the 1960s, and then we have new and different iterations of those struggles, one of them being the immigration issue."[47]

The Republican Party embrace of 100 percent Americanism is embedded in a broadly shared desire to defend the primacy of being an American citizen and protect the American way of life. But that has consequences in the context of the immigration revolution, something the official Republican Party postmortem warned about after the 2012 defeat. A large majority of the country thinks immigration is good for the nation and that it is evidence of a greater openness to outsiders and appreciation for infusions of different ways of thinking that come with more diversity and multiculturalism.[48]

Elected Republicans continue to block immigration reform, but they will have to let it pass at some point—likely after the 2016 presidential election. The Republicans' focus on work, responsibility, faith, and family might well get an audience with some of these newcomers, yet the Republicans are blocked by the threshold attitudes and values that remain central for conservatives.

RED AND BLUE: THE METROPOLITAN CAULDRON

America is being transformed by seismic changes in the country's racial and immigrant makeup, as well as by the mobility of the best-educated and the Millennials, too. They are all meeting in America's metropolises. And, of course, this is all about values. The metropolitan areas are cauldrons for the ascendant values at the heart of the revolutions in blue America.

The big cities have elevated the importance of equality, equal rights, social justice, and opportunity. This is manifest in the primacy of empathy—compassion for those in need and a presumption that successive generations should see expanding opportunity and rising living standards. The cities have elevated the virtue of tolerance, characterized by openness to many viewpoints and by a comfort with diversity, outsiders, foreigners, and different cultures, forming a kind of urban multiculturalism.

The metropolitan cauldron has elevated a distinct type of individualism—one that values individual autonomy and sexual freedom for men *and* women. Marriage is not itself important, yet alongside it is an emerging acceptance of the burgeoning plurality of family types, from single-headed households and single mothers, to LGBT couples and marriages, and that is close to a new value.

All parts of ascendant America, though particularly in the cities, express great faith in education that transcends any reasonable calculation of income gain over a lifetime. They value science, technology, creative occupations, and learning as means to opportunity and fulfillment. They also seek answers to discoverable truths through empiricism and pragmatic problem solving over traditional authority and moral absolutes about good and bad.

The college-educated, particularly among the Millennials, are moving to the fifty largest cities, and women are rushing into college programs and professional schools there. Not surprisingly, an overwhelming majority of the women say a four-year college degree is critical to success. Universities, colleges, and research institutions are integral to the economic success of metropolitan centers, and they shape the values and attitudes there. As a result, big majorities of those living in urban and suburban areas say a degree is critical to success, and even more say that raising the proportion of people with a four-year degree will be good for the economy.

The new immigrants and racial minorities embrace a college education like a lifeline, and thus 70 percent of Hispanics, 61 percent of Asians, and

55 percent of blacks say a four-year college degree is necessary to be success-ful. More than 70 percent of college-educated minorities agree with that, and strikingly, 85 percent of college-educated minorities say they were encouraged by their parents to work hard toward a degree.[49]

Republicans seem to stand apart from the rest of Americans on educa-tion. Just 40 percent of Republicans say that a four-year college degree is es-sential, while remarkably, a pretty big majority of 55 percent believe it is not necessary for an individual to succeed in America. That response must be rooted in values, because a cascade of evidence would lead you to a different conclusion. The Republican response reflects in part what people in the vast rural expanses of the country believe. There, people are more doubtful that a degree is a key to success, though a plurality thinks increasing the proportion with degrees is good for the economy. The white working class is divided right down the middle on these questions.[50]

The metropolitan centers can hardly comprehend that parts of the coun-try continue to contest the importance of education, civil rights, and equal rights for women, immigrants, and gays. The cities put out a welcome mat for the foreign-born, the creative classes, new types of households, and the LGBT community that becomes self-reinforcing. Multiculturalism, racial di-versity, single and unmarried households, secularism, academic institutions, technicians, professionals, the most educated, and the most ambitious of all classes are meant to flourish there.

The metropolitan cauldron is also nurturing a new set of expectations about quality of life. People there express a preference for density, accessibil-ity, active commercial and street life, engagement in public spaces, apprecia-tion for the arts, myriad kinds of culture, and research institutions. Cities self-consciously brand themselves as places that welcome the revolutionary economic and cultural changes and ascendant values that attract new popu-lations, industries, and investment.

Some of the new trappings of this cosmopolitan culture have caught the at-tention of conservatives. Bike sharing, bike lanes, and car-sharing services have produced a surprising derision among conservative commentators who seem to prefer the world of gas-guzzling SUVs a whole lot more. *Wall Street Journal* editorial board member Dorothy Rabinowitz singled out New York's bike shar-ing program and warned "this means something much more"—it is an example of "the totalitarians running this government." She warned that cyclists are "em-powered by the city administration with the idea that they are privileged be-cause they are helping, they are part of all the good forward looking things."[51]

RED AND BLUE: *DUCK DYNASTY*
Previous generations honored "charity, chastity, duty, Godliness, honesty, honor, industriousness, respect for authority, work ethic, and self-reliance," columnist John Hawkins recalled for us. Conservatives like him are determined

to expose the new values and their consequences. They fight back by reminding people of what used to be considered the basics: moral behavior comes from self-discipline and humbleness and purity before God. Government used to confine itself to the basics, too. Instead it is creating a culture of demands where people just want to know what society will do for them.[52]

The contrast in ways of life and values is there for all to see on *Duck Dynasty*, the A&E cable network show that draws fourteen million viewers, considerably larger than the audience for the final episode of *Breaking Bad*. With the feel of reality television, the show captures the lives of the Robertsons, who live in northern Louisiana—where the family is the center of life and the wilderness of the backwoods is near at hand if you want to hunt for your next meal or cut your own Christmas tree. The men, led by patriarch Phil Robertson, own and operate a successful business that sells duck calls to hunters, and are the central characters on the show. The beloved Robertson women also play key roles in the family, with Phil's wife, Miss Kay, running the show at home, where she hosts the large family gatherings.

Beyond the quippy one-liners and amusing antics of the Robertson men, the attraction of the show is the centrality of family, faith, guns, and traditional values—which puts it in stark contrast to other tokens of pop culture that seem to disrespect marriage and the family and draw attention to growing secularism, urbanism, and "immorality." The teachings of Jesus Christ and prayer are routine in the Robertson home, with each show closing with prayer and reflection at the supper table. The church is where the kids are educated, where you celebrate holidays, and where you worship every Sunday.

The Bible is the center point in red America because faith in God allows us to know what is true and to be assured that the right choices will be rewarded and the wrong ones punished. Marriage and the traditional family are the bedrocks of a virtuous, happy, and healthy life and the touchstones for values and well-being. This faith reviles a pop culture that disrespects marriage and celebrates promiscuity and all forms of sordid behavior, such as abortion and homosexuality, which are considered perversions.

There are now credible academic studies that show these values and related attitudes at the heart of these economic and cultural revolutions and the counterrevolution do matter. The values are highly correlated with an increasingly coherent liberal-conservative ideology, and they are highly predictive of the presidential vote in both red and blue states. These values also greatly impact the type of community people want to live in—and that is integrally related to America's emerging polarized politics.

The academics who conducted the research at distinguished universities in the metropolitan centers, unfortunately, sound like the victors in the culture war. They are barely conscious of how condescending they sound. They rightly highlight the importance of values, but it is pretty clear why conservatives bristle when they hear some social science professor pontificate on social trends.

Academics struggle to understand why conservatives hold these attitudes and values, which, to my mind, is not such a mystery. They seem a very plausible response to the revolutionary changes that genuinely threaten their worldview and political and social standing. Academics take it as a given that the white working class is failing to prioritize its growing economic marginality, and even worse, is erroneously rallying to a party most aligned with business interests. That motivates the academics' search for "system justifying" nodes in the brain to explain their conservative political response. Some of the academics have rehabilitated the concept of an "authoritarian personality," which leads them to conclude that "conservatives are, on average, more rigid and closed-minded than liberals."[53]

However, when the academic research focuses on the distinctive attitudes and values in red and blue states, their findings seem right and also predictive of what happens in elections.

Peter Rentfrow, John Jost, Samuel Gosling, and Jeffrey Potter conducted a major new survey of personality traits in all fifty states and developed models to explain the presidential vote in each state in three presidential election years: 1996, 2000, and 2004. As we know, the 2000 and 2004 presidential elections polarized the country, and in the latter, Karl Rove purposefully enflamed the culture war to get to this very end.

Looking at what values or traits were most politicized, the authors found the voters in blue states are "more curious, creative, imaginative, intellectual, and tolerant of differences." Residents in red states tend to be "more traditional, reliable, organized, efficient, and self-disciplined." Though a third dimension, extroversion, is not a predictor of state votes, it does show blue states to be "characterized as more talkative, enthusiastic, energetic, and sociable and less inhibited, quiet, and reserved."[54]

One article in an impressive collection of essays, *Social and Psychological Bases of Ideology and System Justification,* concludes that people living in the urban and industrial Northeast, Midwest, and West Coast regions are "significantly higher in '*creative productivity*' (defined in terms of *creativity, imagination, intelligence, tolerance, and unconventionality*)," compared to those living in the rural Great Plains and southern regions. Those in the Northeast are "higher in *extroversion* (defined by traits such as *urgency* and *energy*)" compared to individuals in the Mountain West. Those in the Midwest are higher in traits associated with being "hardworking."[55]

Authors Jonathan Haidt and Jesse Graham are more respectful of conservative sociological traditions and the moral concerns of political conservatives. They get to a fuller set of dimensions with relevance for ideology and politics. They find that liberals give high relevance to dimensions such as harm to the vulnerable and fairness and not much to other values and moral dimensions. That narrower set of relevant dimensions produce what the authors call a "moral color-blindness" among liberals. They are not able to grant that conservatives have moral reasons to oppose gay marriage and stem cell research.[56]

What the authors call "moral color-blindness" is better described as a secularism that devalues faith-based conclusions and blocks them from lending much importance to sacredness and authority. The strongly conservative, on the other hand, rate all dimensions fairly highly, though they give their highest scores to authority and purity.[57]

These results underscore how deep the value differences are emerging out of America's revolutions and counterrevolution.

RED AND BLUE: THE POLARIZATION OF AMERICA

America's red-blue polarization grows because the economic and cultural revolutions seem ever more certain to prevail, though that only means the counterrevolutionaries must raise the stakes ever more to put off the unacceptable. Conservatives have done just that since 2004, as the odds of success grow inexorably longer. That only raises the stakes even more and the urgency to defend these values and translate them into politics.

This is graphically illustrated in a major survey by the Pew Research Center on "The Political Polarization in the American Public." Instead of using voters' self-placement on a liberal-moderate-conservative scale, they measured ideology according to people's responses to a range of defining political choices on a variety of values issues, including government wastefulness and regulation, corporate profits, helping the poor, addressing racial discrimination, immigration, use of the military, environmental regulation, and homosexuality. The Pew study views ideologies as an expression of political value choices, though those choices are clearly expressions of deeper attitudes about morality, community, and way of life.

The context created by the current economic and cultural transformations is important. Across all these values measures, the country is becoming more liberal and less conservative. When Bill Clinton was elected and Newt Gingrich led his revolution, the percent of the population with reliably conservative views far outnumbered those with reliably liberal views nationally by 30 to 21 percent, though now those with liberal views outnumber conservatives, 34 to 27 percent. The Gallup Poll annual poll on values and beliefs also shows that the conservative advantage on economic and social issues has dropped to its lowest point in years, and on social issues it is now gone.[58]

For the Gallup Poll, midyear 2015 was a kind of tipping point when 60 to 70 percent of the country said gay and lesbian relations, having a baby outside of marriage, sex between an unmarried man and woman, and divorce are all "morally acceptable." Acceptance had jumped 15 to 23 points depending on the issue since 2001, just before conservatives launched the culture war. 2015 was the year a majority of Americans said gays and lesbians are born, not made, and that nearly ends the moral question.

With the values differences so real, the battle over values is translating into real-life choices about where to live, what kind of neighborhood with what kind of people, and openness to the country's new diversity and multi-culturalism.

A stunning two-thirds of the "mostly conservative" and three-quarters of the "consistently conservative" want to live in a community where the houses are larger and farther apart and schools, stores, and restaurants are several miles away. Less than a quarter of consistent conservatives say being near an art museum or theater is important to them. This response is flipped for the ideologically liberal, who are very much part of the growing preference for urbanism and metropolitan centers. More than three-quarters of the consistently liberal prefer to live in communities where houses are smaller and closer together, with schools and stores in walking distance. Nearly three-quarters of consistent liberals also say living near art museums or theaters is important to them.[59]

It is a relief that the country is united in wanting to live near their extended family, to have high-quality schools, and to having access to the outdoors for hiking, fishing, and camping, though they no doubt bring different values filters and priorities to those local institutions and activities.[60]

The most dramatic cultural difference brought out by this unique national survey is whether you prefer to live with people of different racial and ethnic backgrounds or to live with people who share your religious faith. Those factors are at the heart of American's accelerating racial diversity and rising secularism, as well as the conservative reaction. Just a fifth of consistent

Ethnic diversity more important for liberals, faith community more important for conservatives

% saying each would be important in deciding where to live.

■ A mix of people from different religious and ethnic backgrounds
■ Many share your religious faith

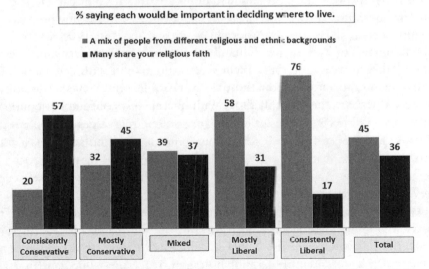

"Political Polarization in the American Public," Pew Research Center, June 12, 2014. Ideological consistency based on a scale of 10 political values questions found in Appendix A of the Pew report.

conservatives say they are looking for that kind of diversity in the communities where they live; almost 60 percent, however, are looking for communities where many people share their faith. In stark contrast, three-quarters of consistent liberals are looking to live in racial and ethnically diverse communities, yet finding those who share their faith is not important to them at all.[61]

That alignment is taking place in a country that is increasingly diverse, immigrant, secular, young, and living in metropolitan centers, which is why conservatives are under siege. Half of consistent conservatives say "It's important for me to live in a place where most people share my political views"—15 points higher than for consistent liberals. And even more, 63 percent of consistent conservatives say it is important that "most of my friends share my political views"—14 points higher than for consistent liberals. Conservatives unhappy with these trends are looking for solidity of friendship and community.

More aligned with developing trends, liberals are less intent on building like-minded communities, though it is still important. Half of consistent liberals live close to most of their friends and one-third want to live in a place where there is an affinity of political views, too. They too are furthering the sorting of the country culturally and ideologically, though with somewhat less zeal than conservatives.

Those numbers do not quite capture the swelling stakes for the supporters of each of the national parties. Increasingly, they think if the other party gets to advance its values agenda, the country is at risk, though it is Republican conservatives that are leading the country to the edge of this perceived national crisis. Now, 27 percent of Democrats say the Republicans "are a threat to the nation's well-being"—but 36 percent of Republicans say that about the Democrats. Half of consistently liberal Democrats say Republicans are such a threat, but they are outdone by consistently conservative Republicans, two-thirds of whom say the Democrats' pursuit of their values and agenda puts the country at risk.[62]

Supporters of both major political parties have become ever more hostile to the other party and fearful of where it would take the country, though Republicans and consistent conservatives are in a league of their own on the perceived threat. The Republican-led culture war has produced dramatic results. A stunning 72 percent of consistent conservatives have an unfavorable view of the Democratic Party, and that has jumped almost 20 points since 2004. A 53 percent majority of consistent liberals are none too fond of the Republicans, but the growth in hostility is half the rate that it is for consistent conservatives, and the level of negativity about the other party 19 points lower.[63]

While the personal response and stakes are higher for conservatives, the nearly complete ideological polarization of the two parties has accelerated since 2004 and is now nearly complete. Since 1994, an increasing number of Democratic voters identify as mostly liberal, reaching 56 percent in 2014. The number of Republicans identifying as mostly conservative surged after

Democrats and Republicans more ideologically divided than in the past

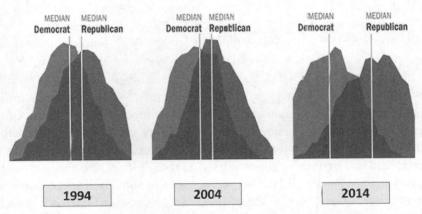

"Political Polarization in the American Public: How Increasing Ideological Uniformity and Partisan Antipathy Affect Politics, Compromise and Everyday Life," Pew Research Center, June 12, 2014, p. 6. Ideological consistency based on a scale of 10 political values questions found in Appendix A of the Pew report. Republicans include Republican-leaning independents; Democrats include Democratic-leaning independents.

2004. That reached 53 percent in 2014, virtually identical to the liberal profile of Democrats.[64]

The launch of the culture war in 2004 brought the thoroughgoing ideological polarization of the two parties. A nearly complete 99 percent of Republicans are more conservative than the median Democrat, and that measure has reached 98 percent for Democrats with respect to the median Republican. That level of partisan ideological unanimity jumped over 10 points for the partisans of both parties since 2004, after remaining fairly steady in the prior decade.[65]

The revolutions and counterrevolution have produced political parties that are ideologically polarized expressions of the emerging values conflict, though the shifts in underlying attitudes and fears are hardly symmetrical. Republicans are more alienated from what they see as the ascendant values, living styles, and multiculturalism, and they want to live in communities where more people share their faith and political views. They are more hostile to the Democratic Party and much more likely to believe that the country is at risk if the Democratic Party wins elections.[66]

That asymmetry has allowed Republicans to overperform in off-year elections since the election of Barack Obama and to build their base in more rural states. It is the Democrats, however, who are aligned with the revolutionary changes that are changing the country and will get to govern nationally, if they take up the huge challenges facing the country.

7 THE DEMOCRATIC ASCENDANCY

The Republican Party is in a death spiral that will mean the end of the Grand Old Party as we know it. The party will feverishly put off the end by entrenching itself in the most rural, religious, and race-conscious parts of the country and by exploiting the constitutional bias in favor of small and rural states, but the Republican Party will face shattering losses at some point. The confirmation of its death will liberate the country and progressive reformers to tackle the huge challenges and contradictions that keep America from realizing its potential. And it will allow a new generation of conservative reformers and modernizers to join the debate, win control of the Republican Party, and chart a new course—though that is for a later chapter and a later time.

The Republican Party is aligned with the oldest, most rural, most religiously observant, and mostly married white voters. Because of the intense battle over American values, big swaths of this diverse country view the Republicans as people with deep convictions about right and wrong, though also as intolerant and not open to America's ascendant trends. The party is virtually off-limits for younger voters and Millennials, for voters in the cities and dynamic metropolitan areas, for mainstream Protestants and the secular, for the foreign-born and new immigrants, and for voters from every racial minority.

And it is worse than you think. The Republican Party is not just doomed because of the inexorability of demographic trends in the country that must reach a tipping point. It is ironically doomed by its strategies to forestall the trends. It is in a pitched fight against the New American Majority.

Fresh from the culture wars, Republicans sustained high off-year turnouts in 2010 and 2014 by constantly raising the specter of President Barack Obama and the grave risks to the country's traditional values if Democrats hold office. They raised the stakes to build turnout among their base, and the predictable consequences played out after the GOP won control of the House of Representatives in the 2010 elections. The actions of the Tea Party–dominated House sent Republican poll ratings into the toilet. And after the 2014 sweep, Republican leaders have promised the base that they will block Obama on his executive action to grant legal status to the undocumented immigrants and will work to repeal Obamacare. And by the way, a large majority of the base of the party says that Congress should start impeachment proceedings against President Obama.[1]

So the more Republican strategies to animate and motivate their voters to win off-year elections succeed, the more they alienate the party from America's burgeoning new electorate.

And Republicans have been able to sustain the intensifying battle for America's values by building a conservative base in the race-conscious and religiously observant South, the Appalachian Valley, across the rural Plains states, and in the Mountain West. It wins in those twenty states by fighting ferociously against government spending for the poor, to stop uncontrolled immigration, to end abortion, and to defend traditional marriage. By winning big in what I call the GOP conservative heartland, the Republicans are able to compete for control of the U.S. Senate and are assured to govern in 40 percent of the states, even though the population of the heartland accounts for only a quarter of the nation. Unfortunately, the more Republicans succeed in solidifying their base of support in the conservative heartland, the more the rest of the country views them as out of touch and from a different era.[2]

American electorate by region

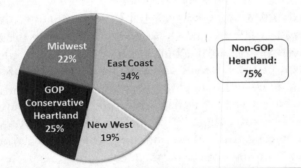

New West: Arizona, California, Colorado, Hawaii, Nevada, New Mexico, Oregon, Washington

GOP Conservative Heartland: Alabama, Alaska, Arkansas, Georgia, Idaho, Kansas, Kentucky, Louisiana, Mississippi, Montana, Nebraska, North Dakota, Oklahoma, South Carolina, South Dakota, Texas, Tennessee, Utah, West Virginia, Wyoming

Midwest: Illinois, Indiana, Iowa, Michigan, Minnesota, Missouri, Ohio, Wisconsin

East Coast: D.C., Connecticut, Delaware, Florida, Maine, Maryland, Massachusetts, New Hampshire, New Jersey, New York, North Carolina, Pennsylvania, Rhode Island, Vermont, Virginia

Democracy Corps' regional definitions created for the Republican Party Project.

The success of these tactics has serious and long-term consequences. They enable the Republicans to pursue a full-throated conservative agenda in the twenty states of the conservative heartland and to block major portions of any Democratic president's agenda in the U.S. Congress. Many of their victories in the states are hard to reverse. But those successes come with a huge price tag, including ceding the presidency, the executive branch, and ultimately the judiciary to the Democrats. These "successes" also obscure the ascendant trends nationally and allow a lot of self-deception about what the Republican Party must do to win presidential elections again.

None of that changes the seismic political transformations that are playing out nationally.

THE WRONG SIDE OF AMERICA'S SOCIAL TRENDS

The Republicans' discomfort with the country's racial diversity and spirit of multiculturalism is translating into stunning levels of support for Democrats among Hispanics, Asians, and African Americans. Republicans were able to win 37 to 40 percent of the Hispanic presidential vote in prior elections—as with Ronald Reagan in 1984 and George W. Bush in 2004—though that has fallen precipitously. Just 31 percent of Hispanics voted for John McCain, an advocate of comprehensive immigration reform, and that dropped to 27 percent for Mitt Romney with his "self-deport" solution to undocumented immigration. The Republican priorities on race and immigration have left the GOP with a barren partisan landscape among Hispanics: only 14 percent identify with the party. That falls to just 12 percent among the Hispanic foreign-born and Millennials.[3]

Despite growing population, the Hispanic share of the vote did not increase in the 2014 off-year elections, likely the result of the president's hesitation to take executive action on immigration. Still, Democrats did take 62 percent of the Hispanic congressional vote—the result of the Republicans' continued anti-immigration agenda.[4]

Among African Americans, Democratic support is more deeply rooted in long-standing voter choices, and no Republican candidate has earned more than 20 percent of the black vote since 1960. Even during the antiwelfare, crime, and affirmative action campaigns of the 1980s, Republican presidential candidates won between 9 and 12 percent of the black vote, and that continued during Bill Clinton's campaigns. But in 2004, John McCain earned only 4 percent of the black vote as 95 percent rallied to Barack Obama's candidacy and presidency.[5]

What is striking is how determined blacks have become to vote in the face of persistent efforts to delegitimize Obama and even stronger attempts to limit their access to the right to vote. Blacks were more than 13 percent of the voting electorate in 2012, turning out at a higher rate than whites for the first time. They also maintained a high share of the vote and steady support for Democratic candidates in the off-year elections. In the 2014 midterm elections, they were 12 percent of the electorate and only 10 percent voted for Republicans. Similar numbers are expected in the 2016 presidential election, as Democrats won that level of support under President Clinton.[6]

Asian Americans are also watching Republicans, and they gave three-quarters of their votes to Obama in 2012. They became part of the diverse racial and ethnic consensus favoring Democrats that year, though they split their votes evenly in the off-year elections.[7]

It is certainly not cool to be Republican among the young and the Millennials. The College Republican National Committee's own youth postmortem described the reactions from their focus groups. The first words that came to mind when young "winnable" Obama voters were asked about the Republican Party included "closed-minded, racist, rigid, old-fashioned," and one young moderate independent woman declared, "I would say your image is all wrong" and "We have the values that we have. So you are going to have to change."

Young voters under thirty years old gave the Democratic presidential candidate 54 percent of their votes in 2004 and 66 percent in 2008. The youth Democratic vote dropped to 60 percent in 2012 when Millennials struggled with the economy, unemployment, and smothering student debt. Still, the Republicans are increasingly shunned by the Millennials: the proportion identifying as Republican fell from 24 percent in 2004 to only 17 percent in 2014 and 13 percent in 2015.

Young voters, as expected, formed 11 percent of the 2010 and 13 percent of the 2014 off-year electorate, though the larger group of Millennials was 21 percent of the electorate in 2012 and will grow to more than a quarter by 2016. Millennials will be 40 percent of eligible voters by 2020, according to exit poll and census projections. And critically, we now know the younger Millennials give the Democrats the same advantage in party identification (+15 points) as the older (+17 points). That answers the question of whether these younger voters had become disaffected with the weak economy under President Obama. And it means that the Millennials' growing proportion in the electorate will tilt the playing field even more Democratic.[8]

Unmarried households are now a majority in the country (51 percent), though two-thirds of the Republican base is married, and conservatives are making marriage more and more central to their values and public policy agenda. Unmarried women have given the majority of their votes to the Democrats in every presidential election since 1988, though in the past two, more than two-thirds voted for Barack Obama.

At the same time, the unmarried women proportion of the presidential electorate has been growing and will reach nearly a quarter in 2016. Yet a very large proportion of them are drop-off voters who take a pass on the midterm elections. Their proportion of the 2014 electorate edged up to 22 percent, though that is still short of the 25 percent expected in the presidential election in 2016.[9]

Less than a quarter of unmarried women identify themselves as Republicans. They feel increasingly disconnected from the Republican Party because of its views of women and families. Unmarried women are overwhelmingly pro-choice on abortion and open to the diversity of family types, including gay marriage. But single women are also literally on their own and find Republican views on the social safety net and government dependency unhelpful. They are the strongest supporters of Medicare and Social Security, equal pay for women, helping working mothers with child care, paid sick days and paid leave, and policies to make college affordable.[10]

The growing secularization of the country and the Evangelical-led battle over American values have upended traditional voting patterns. The new kid on the block is the secular voter or those with no religion. One in five voters does not identify with any religious denomination, and they have emerged as one of the groups with the strongest identification with the Democrats. Seven in ten voted for Obama in 2012, and they were as solid for the Democrats in the midterm elections.[11]

The Episcopalians and Presbyterians dominated the Protestant religious establishment for a century, and they were once the backbone of the Republican Party. Their loyalties are now suspect, however, and just 55 percent voted for Romney in 2012. White Evangelicals have become the largest bloc in the Republican base, as we shall see in the next chapter, and they cast 76 percent of their vote for Romney in 2012. In the 2014 off-year elections, they matched that number for Republican congressional candidates. White observant Catholics gave Obama just 38 percent of their votes, which is well down from previous elections.[12]

The Democrats are deepening their support with the groups that are growing in social and political significance. The rising American electorate of African Americans, Hispanics, Millennials, and unmarried women will constitute 54 percent of the electorate in 2016. If you also include the seculars with no religious affiliation, this rising share of the electorate will increase to 63 percent. Each of these groups is steadily growing and, as of early 2015, two-thirds of them intend to vote for Hillary Clinton, assuming she is the nominee.[13]

The metropolitan areas are indeed cauldrons for these economic and cultural revolutions, making the metropolitan revolution a political one too. A majority of the country now lives in large metropolitan areas, and Obama won 56 percent of the voters in the large metro areas in 2012, including 77 percent of the voters in the urban core and 62 percent in the inner suburbs.[14]

In 2012, Obama won twenty-six of the thirty most populous cities. In the megacities of New York City and Los Angeles, Obama took 82 and 69 percent of the vote, respectively. He won almost all of the big cities outside of the South and the Mountain West, including winning respectably in Sun Belt cities. Romney carried only four of the thirty most populous cities—Phoenix, Jacksonville City, Fort Worth, and Oklahoma City.[15]

The story is even more revealing when one looks at the metropolitan

2012 voting by type of area

	D-2012	R-2012	Share of US Population, 2010
Large Metros	56	42	54
Urban core	77	55	9
Inner suburbs	62	37	19
Mature suburbs	56	43	16
Emerging suburbs	45	53	8
True exurbs	37	61	3
Medium metros	49	49	20
Small metros	43	55	9
Nonmetro metropolitan	40	58	10
Nonmetro non-micropolitan	38	61	6

Ruy Teixeira, "Why Democrats Win the Presidency But Lose The House," *Think Progress*, May 29, 2013.

areas with the highest GDP—the engines of the U.S. economy today. Obama won eleven of the fifteen metropolitan statistical areas with the highest total GDP and nine of the ten with the highest GDP per capita. That economic progress will be fueled by population growth, immigration, rising college-educated populations, and higher concentrations of professional, creative, and STEM (science, technology, engineering, and math) occupations—and those demographic changes will shift those metro areas even farther toward Democrats. This is a pretty foreign place for Republican candidates now.[16]

Mitt Romney carried the small cities with 55 percent of the vote. He dominated the small and medium-size cities in the Sun Belt, getting about 90 percent of the vote in Provo and above 75 percent in Amarillo, Midland, Abilene, and Wichita Falls. Romney performed well in the smaller, old industrial metropolitan areas. For example, he got about 55 percent of the vote in Dayton, Wheeling, Johnstown, and the Cincinnati metro area. All of those are in the Appalachian, Ohio River, and mining areas on the end of the Border South.[17]

In the suburbs, Obama won just over half of the vote compared to Romney's 42 percent, which is a pretty big turn from earlier decades. The transformation of the suburbs is produced by growing diversity as well as the partisan shift toward the Democrats among college-educated white women and professionals.[18]

The growing metropolitan areas—home to the ascendant trends of America—play a big role in the Democrats' new national majority. "The average Obama metro was twice as dense as the average Romney metro," Richard Florida writes, and density is now the highest vote correlation in his

Metropolitan areas overwhelmingly voted for Obama

Metro Statistical Areas with the Largest GDPs	2012 Vote % Obama	Total GDP (billions) 2010	2025	% Growth
Orlando-Kissimmee-Sanford, FL	51.3%	105	194	85%
Austin-Round Rock, TX	51.9%	81	149	84%
Las Vegas-Henderson-Paradise, NV	55.9%	88	160	82%
Charlotte-Concord-Gastonia, NC-SC	48.3%	92	162	76%
Phoenix-Mesa-Scottsdale, AZ	42.9%	182	318	75%
Portland-Vancouver-Hillsboro, OR-WA	57.7%	117	198	69%
San Antonio-New Braunfels, TX	45.3%	85	142	67%
Dallas-Fort Worth-Arlington, TX	40.8%	325	541	66%
Houston-The Woodlands-Sugar Land, TX	43.1%	341	560	64%
San Diego-Carlsbad, CA	51.5%	173	278	61%
Miami-Fort Lauderdale-West Palm Beach, FL	60.6%	236	380	61%
Atlanta-Sandy Springs-Roswell, GA	47.9%	250	391	56%
Indianapolis-Carmel-Anderson, IN	44.4%	92	142	54%
Washington-Arlington-Alexandria, DC-VA-MD-WV	64.4%	392	600	53%
Tampa-St. Petersburg-Clearwater, FL	51.0%	117	177	51%
Denver-Aurora-Lakewood, CO	55.9%	142	212	49%
Seattle-Tacoma-Bellevue, WA	52.7%	211	314	49%
Sacramento-Roseville-Arden-Arcade, CA	51.1%	102	151	48%
Riverside-San Bernardino-Ontario, CA	50.4%	132	194	47%
San Jose-Sunnyvale-Santa Clara, CA	66.8%	127	186	46%
San Francisco-Oakland-Hayward, CA	73.8%	283	411	45%
Minneapolis-St. Paul-Bloomington, MN-WI	54.0%	181	262	45%
Los Angeles-Long Beach-Anaheim, CA	61.7%	732	1,052	44%
Kansas City, MO-KS	47.3%	95	136	43%
Baltimore-Columbia-Towson, MD	54.3%	145	201	39%
Columbus, OH	50.6%	89	122	37%
Cincinnati, OH-KY-IN	40.7%	95	128	35%
St. Louis, MO-IL	53.2%	125	168	34%
Chicago-Naperville-Elgin, IL-IN-WI	61.8%	496	661	33%
Philadelphia-Camden-Wilmington, PA-NJ-DE-MD	62.3%	315	419	33%
Boston-Cambridge-Newton, MA-NH	62.4%	296	393	33%
Providence-Warwick, RI-MA	61.3%	71	94	32%
Pittsburgh, PA	47.9%	116	153	32%
New York-Newark-Jersey City, NY-NJ-PA	61.4%	1,180	1,553	32%
Cleveland-Elyria, OH	57.5%	98	117	19%
Detroit-Warren-Dearborn, MI	60.0%	179	213	19%

Presidential election results by county, 2012; U.S. Census Bureau metro statistical areas; "Urban World: Cities and the Rise of the Consuming Class," McKinsey Global Institute, June 2012.

model. Another study found that voters living in communities with more than eight hundred people per square mile had a two-thirds chance of voting for Obama, but below that they had a two-thirds chance of voting for Romney. Cities with more college graduates are also more Democratic, but particularly those with concentrations of people working in science and technology, business, health care, education, arts, and entertainment. Obama won more than two-thirds of the vote in the country's two high-tech centers, the Silicon Valley area and Seattle.[19]

On the other hand, Romney won 80 percent of those cities with the largest proportions of working-class voters.[20]

The revolutionary changes captured in the large metro areas are moving states out of their traditional Electoral College column and restricting the national Republican Party. The Washington, D.C.-Arlington-Alexandria metro area gave Obama 64 percent of its votes and also put Democrats in a position to win all of the statewide offices. With the Greater Denver metropolitan area giving Obama 60 percent of the vote and the Greater Las Vegas area 56 percent, both Colorado and Nevada moved into the Democratic column. Colorado's new residents are twice as likely to hail from blue as red states, and these "blue state expats now make up 12 percent of the population," according to an Upshot analysis. Blue-state migration is shaping North Carolina at four times the rate of migration from red states, and those blue-state expats now form 16 percent of the state's population. The metropolitan areas surrounding Charlotte and Atlanta gave Obama 48 percent of the vote, and with high African American turnout, North Carolina has emerged as the surprising front line in the presidential battleground, and Georgia may not be far behind.[21]

The close U.S. Senate races in Virginia and North Carolina and the not-so-close one in Georgia in 2014 are part of another story I will describe below. The metropolitan revolution will continue to disrupt the political landscape.

THE DAMAGED BRAND

The Republican Party has emerged with a very damaged brand, defined by its reaction to the ascendant trends and the struggle over American values. Almost seven in ten Americans think the Republican Party has "strong views on right and wrong," and 45 percent say it "shares [their] values." Yet only about 40 percent think the GOP is "open to different kinds of Americans," and less than 30 percent believe it is "open to change." Solid majorities say the party is "out of touch," "too extreme in their views," "force[s] their moral beliefs onto others," and "divide[s] the country."[22]

America has watched the national dysfunction and lack of attention to the country's problems, and they have thrown up their hands, incredulous that anything can happen to make progress in the world of politics. But if one looks at the line representing the thermometer ratings about the parties and their leaders over the past four years, it is hard not to be stunned by the dramatic fall in feelings for the Republican Party, led by distaste for the Republicans in Congress. They have both hit low points for our modern political parties.

The brand deteriorated soon after the Tea Party Republicans took control of the Congress, and over the past two years the Republican Party and the Republicans in Congress have reached a nadir with the public. And as the party begins a new presidential election cycle, just 42 percent view the party favorably. Even fewer, 40 percent, have warm feelings for the Republicans in Congress and only 33 percent say they identify as Republicans.[23]

Republicans viewed much more negatively on brand attributes

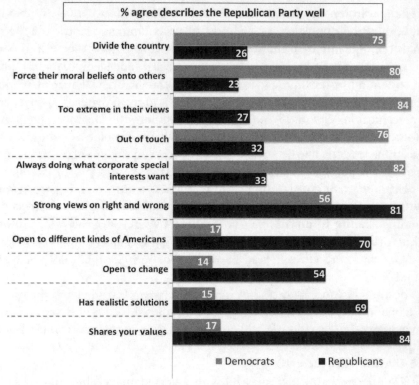

% agree describes the Republican Party well

Attribute	Democrats	Republicans
Divide the country	75	26
Force their moral beliefs onto others	80	23
Too extreme in their views	84	27
Out of touch	76	32
Always doing what corporate special interests want	82	33
Strong views on right and wrong	56	81
Open to different kinds of Americans	17	70
Open to change	14	54
Has realistic solutions	15	69
Shares your values	17	84

■ Democrats ■ Republicans

National survey of 950 respondents and an oversample of 760 Republicans, conducted by Greenberg Quinlan Rosner Research for Democracy Corps' Republican Party Project, July 10-15, 2013.

Favorable ratings for Democrats improve as GOP ratings decline

Now, I'd like to rate your feelings toward some people and organizations, with 100 meaning a VERY WARM, FAVORABLE feeling; zero meaning a VERY COLD, UNFAVORABLE feeling; and 50 meaning not particularly warm or cold.

-□-Barack Obama ●-Democratic Party ▲-Democrats in Congress ◆-Republican Party ■-Republican Congress

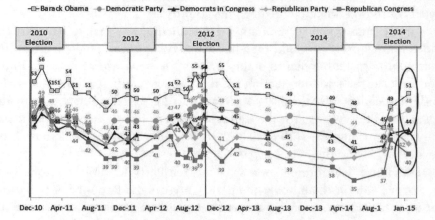

Note: From Democracy Corps surveys conducted in the past 4 years. Data represents MEAN ratings.

As the country watched the new Republican Congress at work and an unending wave of Republican presidential prospects announced their candidacies, the country became even more settled in their contempt for the Republicans and the Democrats' advantage only grew. In the April 2015 *Bloomberg Politics* poll, just 38 percent expressed a favorable view of the Republican Party—with negative judgments far outdistancing the positive by 15 points. At the same time, a near majority of 48 percent offered a positive view of the Democrats. The regard for "Republicans in Congress" had hit historic lows. And by the summer, Democrats had settled into a 9- or 10-point advantage in party identification, which they have largely held since 2010.[24]

The number of Americans identifying as "conservative" has dropped 5 points in surveys for Democracy Corps and the NBC/*Wall Street Journal* in 2015. According to an analysis by the Republican pollster Bill McInturff, conservatives have lost ground with women, young people, Hispanics, the best educated, and voters in the West and the cities. That sounds all too familiar.

The Republican Party has reached this desperate state primarily because of its lead role in the conservative counterrevolution against America's modernizing trends. The country has gotten more polarized and the Republicans more despised, however, because of the party's heated mobilization in off-year elections to keep evil at bay.

"SHELLACKING, THE SEQUEL"

The 2010 and 2014 off-year elections produced nearly identical shellackings for Democrats, though as Ron Brownstein observes, that tells you nothing about what will actually happen in the subsequent presidential election. For Brownstein, these off-year routs were produced by the Democrats' "boom-and-bust coalition of young people and minorities" and unmarried women, and thus they just need to do better with older and working-class voters if Democrats are to win the Congress. That is pretty much right as far as the Democrats go. The party needs to do better with the white working class for sure (and that is discussed below), and they also need their boom-and-bust coalition to be more consistent.[25]

One should keep in mind that the coalition of minorities, young people, and unmarried women was in full bloom and did show up to vote in the 2006 off-year elections, motivated by their deep hostility to President George W. Bush and opposition to the Iraq war. They are not just laggards. Those voters need a compelling reason to vote and defend government, and indeed, they were dispirited thinking about President Obama: more than 40 percent of the Democrats' base voters in 2014 disapproved of how he was doing as president.[26]

What Brownstein fails to ask is why Republicans voted in such large numbers in 2010 and 2014. In an election year when voters just hated Washington, the partisan gridlock and the influence of big-money special interests, and in elections where the low turnout was only matched by the off-year election during World War II, Republicans were motivated to vote. The explanation is crucially important if you want to understand the party's deteriorating brand and diminished presidential prospects.

As we have seen, these elections were just the next battle in the counter-revolution whose urgency only grows, made more vivid by the prospect of President Barack Obama and subservient Democrats being free to implement Obamacare and give amnesty to illegal immigrants. Republican voters view Democrats ever more negatively and think their governance threatens the future of the country. The trends that are changing the electorate are the reason why the Republican base reacts so strongly and why their motivation to vote in election after election grows. Every election is national.

In 2010, Republicans won the House in an unexpected landslide, netting sixty-three House seats and winning the national vote by an 8-point margin, nearly replicating the 6-point margin that allowed them to expand their House majority in 2014. What groups voted and in what proportion looked almost identical.[27]

So, how did the 2010 election story turn out? Within four months of the Republicans taking control of the Congress, the Republican Party's image plummeted, led down by the Tea Party Republicans in the House. Fully two-thirds of the country quickly came to disapprove of how the Republicans were handling their job in charge of the U.S. House of Representatives; 48 percent strongly disapproved at the high point. The Republicans' congressional brand never recovered, and it contaminated the brand of the whole party.[28]

In the 2010 off-year landslide, the Republicans took control of the governors' mansions and state legislatures in the blue states of Michigan, Wisconsin, Iowa, and Pennsylvania, yet none of those states was even competitive in 2012—except perhaps in Mitt Romney's own campaign polling.

What do we think will be the tone of the House Republicans and the great majority of Republican U.S. senators after finally winning control of the U.S. Congress? We know from Democracy Corps polling that the great majority of Evangelical and Tea Party Republicans want to start an impeachment inquiry against the president. We know that 64 percent of Republicans hold very negative views about undocumented immigrants and that they are intent on blocking funding for Obama's efforts to legalize the immigrant "DREAMers." They are still determined to repeal Obamacare before it is too late.[29]

How is the story turning out in 2015? The image of the Republicans in Congress and their leaders has already moved deeply into negative territory. By the time we conducted our first national survey in 2015, Speaker Boehner and Majority Leader McConnell had quickly displaced every other

leader in the race for unpopularity. Twice as many voters view them negatively as positively, and the Democratic Party has quickly moved into a
15-point image advantage with the presidential electorate. By June, Democracy Corps polls showed the two Republican congressional leaders at their
lowest point since 2008.[30]

All Democratic figures and institutions viewed more favorably than Republican

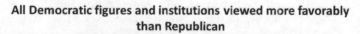

Now, I'd like to rate your feelings toward some people and organizations, with one hundred meaning a VERY WARM, FAVORABLE feeling; zero meaning a VERY COLD, UNFAVORABLE feeling; and fifty meaning not particularly warm or cold. You can use any number from zero to one hundred, the higher the number the more favorable your feelings are toward that person or organization. If you have no opinion or never heard of that person or organization, please say so.

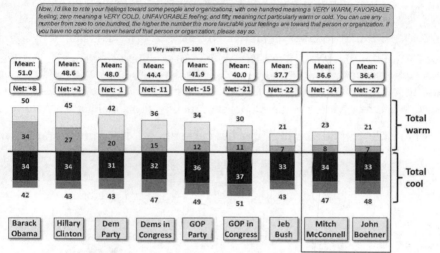

National survey of 950 likely 2016 voters conducted by Greenberg Quinlan Rosner for Democracy Corps, January 7–11, 2015.

In Democracy Corps' focus groups for Women's Voices Women's Vote
held in Florida in the spring of 2015, these swing voters were reading the "Republican Congress" very clearly: "They'll let the country burn to hell if it's
good for the cause"; "I feel they don't care about the middle class, they only
care about the rich"; "If anything, they seem completely closed off, not open
minded whatsoever"; "Just the rich getting richer and one-sided agenda. . . .
I'm not in the Republicans' top demographic."

That is before the full cast of Republican presidential candidates joined
the debate and began airing their full-throated disdain for Barack Obama
and Hillary Clinton. And that is before the Republican presidential primary
voters will have their say, as they did in the aftermath of the 2010 midterms.
The Republican leaders and the party's base voters are fully part of a much
bigger battle that will play out over the next year.

And the presidential electorate knows it. On the night of the 2014 midterm elections, we began simultaneous polls with the off-year and presidential-
year voters, and the stark results remind you: have some perspective. The
bigger dynamics are undiminished. Yes, in the off-year electorate that produced the Republican sweep, Republicans had a 2-point advantage in party
identification. But the Democrats enjoyed a 6-point margin in the presidential

electorate (48 to 42 percent), and that is everything in this polarized country. The Republicans won the congressional vote by 6 points, but in the presidential electorate, the vote for the House would have been fought to a draw.

When we asked about a theoretical presidential contest between Hillary Clinton and Mitt Romney, she trailed him by a point in the off-year electorate that just voted. However, in the presidential electorate that matters for the future, she was winning by 7 points—almost twice Obama's healthy margin in 2012. And when Democracy Corps conducted its first national survey of likely presidential voters in January 2016, she was beating Romney by about the same margin, though in a theoretical race against Jeb Bush, she extended her winning margin to 12 points (52 to 40 percent). She continued to hold about an 8-point lead in Democracy Corps' June survey against either Scott Walker or Marco Rubio. Does that qualify as a "shellacking"?[31]

Hillary Clinton begins presidential cycle ahead of Romney and Bush

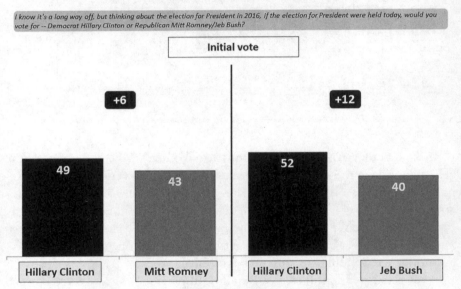

I know it's a long way off, but thinking about the election for President in 2016, if the election for President were held today, would you vote for -- Democrat Hillary Clinton or Republican Mitt Romney/Jeb Bush?

Initial vote

+6 +12

49   43   52   40

Hillary Clinton   Mitt Romney   Hillary Clinton   Jeb Bush

National survey of 950 likely 2016 voters conducted by Greenberg Quinlan Rosner for Democracy Corps, January 7–11, 2015.

There is every likelihood that this midterm story will turn out with the same ending. The 2014 midterm sweep neither changes the national electorate nor puts the Republican Party on a different trajectory. If anything, it makes this bigger story and battle more vivid.

BATTLING FROM THE NEW GOP CONSERVATIVE HEARTLAND

From their base in the South and the Mountain West, conservatives have fervently joined the culture war to reassert endangered values and to oppose new waves of government spending on the social safety net that promises idleness and dependence. America's civil rights, women's, immigrant, and gay rights revolutions have fundamentally changed the country, yet they are also still contested and unfinished because of the resilience of Republican leaders and the party battling on from the GOP conservative heartland.

The Republicans' political resilience is possible because race and racial identity are a special and enduring force in the South and the Deep South and because of the heightened religious observance of Evangelicals concentrated in border states and the Deep South and among Mormons and others in the Rocky Mountain West. Impressive recent academic research shows the persistence of heightened conservative politics in the previously slaveholding counties of the Black Belt across the Deep South and, as Jonathan Chait underscores in his writing on the Obama presidency, race continues to infuse many contemporary issues, from Obamacare to education spending to unemployment benefits.[32]

With race and religion the dominant dynamics in the GOP conservative heartland, virtually all of the other usual demographic lines get blurred. For example, whites in the South—men and women, college and non-college, young and old—all gave President Obama a meager 24 to 30 percent of their votes. That result in the GOP base region reflects their continued battle against the racial and religious trends in the country.[33]

The rest of the country is divided by substantial racial, gender, class, and generational gaps. Obama ran 10 points better with white working-class women than with white working-class men nationally, yet there is no gender

White support for Republicans heavily concentrated in the GOP Conservative Heartland

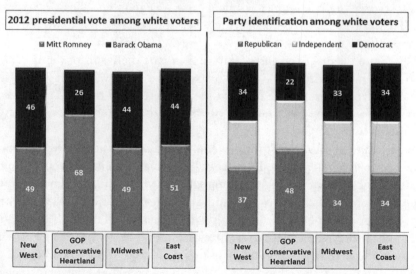

Self-reported 2012 Presidential vote and 2-3-2 Party ID among white voters, based on 6,054 interviews conducted by Greenberg Quinlan Rosner for Democracy Corps, July 2013–November 2014.

gap among the white working class in the Republican South: non-college men gave Obama 24 percent of their votes; the women gave him a grudging 26 percent. Obama ran between 12 and 15 points better among white Millennials than among whites of the silent generation in the Northeast and West Coast states and ran 8 points better among white Millennials in the Midwest.

Yet white college-educated men and white Millennials across the South and Mountain West gave just 30 percent of their vote to Obama—right at the norm for the white Democratic vote in the GOP conservative heartland. While Millennials nationally continue to surprise everyone with breathtaking changes in attitudes and politics, in the Mountain West, white Millennials gave Obama just 30 percent of their votes, and in the South, they gave Obama even less support.[34]

There are cracks in the GOP conservative heartland—led by the modest defection of college-educated white women in the South, who gave Obama 6 points more than the college-educated white men, as well as the college-educated white women in the Mountain West, who gave Obama 12 points more support than the college-educated white men.

College-educated white women have probably played a role in the growing Democratic support in the growing metropolitan centers at the fringes of the South—in northern Virginia, in Atlanta and Tampa in the Deep South, and in Denver in the heart of the Mountain West. In these cities, and in contrast with the GOP conservative heartland as a whole, there is broad receptivity to racial diversity, immigration, multiculturalism, the pluralism of family types, and the independence of women.[35]

In the meantime, the Republicans deepening their support in the most rural and least dense parts of the country and the Democrats growing theirs in the most urban and dense metropolitan areas give the Republican Party a lifeline. That contrast allows them to be overrepresented, even as Republicans lose popularity nationally.

The Republicans' overrepresentation is in part the result of the U.S. Constitution, which allots two U.S. senators to each state, regardless of its size. So while Wyomingites make up less than 0.2 percent of the U.S. population, they are afforded the same number of votes in the Senate as the one in eight Americans living in California.

And while the U.S. Constitution requires that each member represents an equal number of people, the Democrats' growing concentration in the cities leads to the Democrats being underrepresented in Congress. "In many states, Democrats are inefficiently concentrated in large cities and smaller industrial agglomerations," political scientists Jowei Chen and Jonathan Rodden point out, so that "they can expect to win fewer than 50 percent of the seats when they win 50 percent of the votes." Obama won more than 70 percent of the vote in sixty-one House seats while Mitt Romney won that same percentage in only nineteen districts—in some sense "wasting" those voters and margins. [36]

Republicans brought it home by winning control of more governorships and legislatures in the 2010 off-year wave elections and by more effectively gerrymandering the drawing of new seats. Independent analysts show Republicans were particularly successful in creating additional Republican seats in Florida, North Carolina, Texas, Pennsylvania, and Michigan. These district maps will be redrawn in 2021 after the 2020 census though will remain in place through the 2020 presidential election.[37]

Law, geography, and intrigue conspired to tilt the playing field in Washington. Democratic House candidates in 2012 received 1.17 million more votes than Republican candidates, yet Republicans held their 33-seat advantage over Democrats in the House. Republicans won 54 percent of the seats in the House of Representatives with only 49 percent of the popular vote.[38]

With the stakes so high, Republican leaders did not want to leave these results to chance. Most of the states in this GOP conservative heartland passed new laws to limit voting hours and early-voting days, block voting at universities, and issue new requirements for photo IDs and proof of citizenship.

Conscious of the stakes, Republican donors, conservative billionaires, the U.S. Chamber of Commerce, and energy and banking sectors poured money into these off-year and down-ballot races. Again, with the help of the Supreme Court, much of this spending was unlimited by law and unregulated. Conservative Super PACs and unregulated outside groups poured hundreds of millions of dollars of secret money into congressional, U.S. Senate, and state legislative races.[39]

This biasing and rigging of the system combined with the mobilization of conservative voters to defend American values to produce electoral earthquakes. That was particularly true in the rural and GOP conservative heartland states.

Aided by two off-year elections when motivated Republicans turned out in big numbers to fight the national trends, Republicans gained 913 state legislative seats since 2010 and control of 30 state legislative chambers.[40]

While Republicans could benefit from these dynamics in any state, nearly half of the state legislatures that moved into the Republican column were in the GOP conservative heartland states.[41]

When Senators Mary Landrieu of Louisiana and Kay Hagan of North Carolina lost their seats in the 2014 off-year elections, no Democratic senator remained standing in the old South except in Virginia.

So the GOP conservative heartland has played an outsized role in allowing Republicans to hold on to power in a lot of states and in Congress.

Its hold could be loosened if Democrats can win in a wave presidential election in 2016 or 2020—after which new legislative lines are drawn. That could happen as part of the emerging new progressive era. Its hold could be loosened if Democrat voters have a reason to turn out and vote, which is addressed later in this book. The odds would shift if Democrats compete more effectively for white working-class votes. And finally and most important, its hold could be broken if the citizens of these GOP conservative heartland states become discontented with the Republican governing model.

On that last point, there was plenty of evidence of a growing discontent in these states, but the evidence was scattered to the winds by the Republicans' success in nationalizing the 2014 elections. Republican governors swept to victory in the 2010 wave and rushed to enact conservative governing programs. They aggressively cut income taxes for the richest and cut taxes on businesses, while cutting funding for public education and reducing the number of teachers. They also went after their bargaining rights while promoting vouchers and charter schools.

It turns out that the public did not love these policies or the consequences, and Democratic candidates ran competitively during the campaign, attacking the governors and Republican state leaders on their state policies. With the flood of anti-Obama advertising and the consolidation of the Republicans, who remembers? But the discontent was real.

In Kansas, congressional Republicans had a not-surprising good day, winning their races on average by 27 points. By contrast, Governor Sam Brownback was on the same off-year ballot in this deeply red state, and he won by only 4 points. The same was true in Florida; statewide, the Republican congressional candidates won by an impressive 12 points, yet Governor Rick Scott won by just 1 point. In North Carolina, the congressional Republican candidates had a memorable day in a so-called swing state. They won their races on average by 11 points. Yet Thom Tillis, the Speaker of the House who embraced and enacted the conservative North Carolina program, only managed to squeak by Senator Kay Hagan by 2 points.[42]

The doubts about the conservative governing model got lost amid the Republicans' nationalized elections around Obama, yet the numbers do not lie. Those candidates paid a very big price, though not big enough to lose.

CAN THE "REAGAN DEMOCRATS" SAVE THE REPUBLICAN PARTY?

Can the "Reagan Democrats" save the Republican Party, as they helped Bill Clinton's Democratic Party regain its national standing?

Many respected conservative analysts point to the nearly six million mostly working-class white voters who stayed home in 2012 because they were unenthusiastic about the plutocratic Mitt Romney. Some propose that Republicans build on their already high level of support and use populist and nationalist appeals to raise their support and turnout to compete nationally. They are calling on Republicans to find a missing six million new white working-class voters, as they found the missing six million Evangelicals during the culture war.[43]

Democratic and Republican strategists have highlighted the potential strengths of a Governor Scott Walker strategy, precisely because he has the chance to compete for white working-class voters in the old industrial Midwest. "Scott Walker's 2016 strategy is simple," Bob Burnett writes in the *Daily Kos*. "He will seek to defeat Hillary Clinton by mobilizing the resentment of working-class white voters, male and female. Walker will take his adversarial message to swing states such as Colorado, Florida, Iowa, New Hampshire, Nevada, Ohio, Virginia, and Wisconsin; and hope to mobilize a massive turnout by angry white voters. Walker is dangerous."[44]

There is no more oft-repeated statistic than the fact that Barack Obama won just 39 percent of white voters in 2012. "This much is undisputed," Ron Brownstein declared: "In 2012, President Obama lost white voters by a larger margin than any winning presidential candidate in U.S. history." Obama was noticeably weak with a number of groups, though particularly with blue-collar and non-college-educated white men—which Brownstein describes as "once the brawny backbone of the New Deal–era Democratic coalition." Mitt Romney ran as well as Dwight Eisenhower and George H. W. Bush with these key groups, yet Romney did not get close to the White House.[45]

Many analysts and even many Democratic strategists believe the Democrats' weak performance with the white working class is the inevitable result of Democrats embracing the country's growing racial and ethnic diversity, Millennials, and college-educated pro-choice women. Maybe Democrats just did not have to compete for the white working class, brawny or otherwise.

That is misguided, as we have seen in this book. Democrats have every reason to battle for these voters. They cannot tackle the deep problems facing the country unless they are working to change an economy that marginalizes so many lower-wage and middle-class workers and leaves so many working women and working men on their own. It also means battling the corruption of Wall Street and Washington that angers so many working-class Americans.

Even without that turn by Democrats, it is doubtful the disaffected white working class will save the Republican Party from its national misfortune. They have already given at the office.

White working-class voters played the leading role in helping the Republicans hold on in the face of national trends. They were in full revolt against Obama, the elites, and an economy that failed them and led the 2010 and 2014 wave elections. That grim result was part of a broad electoral falloff from 2012, with the Democrats' white non-college vote dropping 7 points, according to Ruy Teixeira and John Halpin.[46]

In the GOP conservative heartland states, the white working class gave Obama just 25 percent of their votes. That gets your attention.[47]

That is the result of a period of polarization and culture war that has shifted partisan loyalties even further. During the 2000 election between Gore and Bush, white non-college voters in the South identified Republican by 10 points, but that margin doubled to 21 points in the polarizing 2004 gay-marriage election, stood at that margin in 2008 when Obama was elected, and surged to a 33-point advantage for Republicans in the 2012 election. By then, just 29 percent of white non-college voters in the South identified with the Democratic Party and produced exactly that vote. In the Mountain West, Republicans were always stronger, starting with a 29-point advantage among white working-class voters in 2000. That slipped marginally to a 27-point advantage in 2004 and to 19 in 2008 before surging to a 35-point advantage in party identification under President Obama. Democratic support sank to only 29 percent of white workers in the western part of the GOP conservative heartland.[48]

That suggests the strategy may be up against its limits. The white working class away from the most religiously observant, Evangelical, and rural areas and deeply race-conscious South is very much in play.

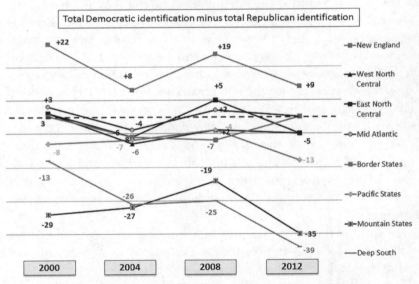

Democratic Party identification advantage among white non-college voters

Based on combined data from national surveys conducted by Greenberg Quinlan Rosner Research for Democracy Corps, 2012.

In all of the other regions, the Republicans' advantage among white working-class voters over time is relatively small or looks very unstable and trending Democratic. At the end of the day, the Democrats had a 3-point advantage among white workers in the East and the Republicans enjoyed just a 5-point advantage in the whole of the Midwest in 2012. The Republicans' strongest advantage, of 13 points, was among the white noncollege voters on the West Coast, a region being transformed by ethnic diversity and a growing white educated population.[49]

The hurdles to reaching the white working class look so daunting because of the success of Republicans in building up huge margins with those voters in the South, Plains, and Rocky Mountain regions. Obama won only 25 percent of white noncollege voters in the South and 33 percent in the Mountain West. And Democrats have been losing ground in political support and party identification with the most religiously observant, racially conscious, and rural white working-class voters in those regions. Voter attitudes there pose very different challenges that do indeed put most of these voters out of reach.[50]

It is important to remember, however, that three-fourths of American voters live outside this GOP conservative heartland. In the rest of the country, the battle for the swing white working class and downscale voters is very much alive. In the East and Midwest, about equal numbers of white working-class voters identify with the two parties, and since 2000, this identification with the two parties has remained very stable. On Election Day 2012, Obama won 40 percent of the white noncollege voters outside the Republicans' regional base. That number still poses a problem, though it would not take major gains with these voters to change the Democrats fortunes in these areas.[51]

The white working-class voter has the chance to play in the Democrats' game because the working class itself is being profoundly changed by America's economic and cultural transformations, and they are among the voters waiting for the political class to step up and address the emerging problems. To start, the white working class comprises just about a third of the presidential electorate—and more than half are women.[52]

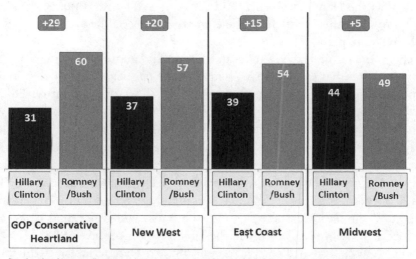

Clinton's presidential vote among white non-college voters in different regions

	+29		+20		+15		+5	
	31	60	37	57	39	54	44	49
	Hillary Clinton	Romney /Bush	Hillary Clinton	Romney /Bush	Hillary Clinton	Romney /Bush	Hillary Clinton	Romney /Bush
	GOP Conservative Heartland		**New West**		**East Coast**		**Midwest**	

Based on the white non-college respondents in a combined national run of 2,379 likely 2016 voters nationwide conducted in November 2014–January 2015. Republican candidates were split between Mitt Romney and Jeb Bush

America's job growth we know is concentrated among registered nurses, teachers, truck drivers, customer service, retail, and sales clerks, home health aides, and fast-food workers—and the average wage for those jobs is dramatically below the country's median income. These workers struggle with jobs that don't pay enough to live on, managing work and kids without help, the pay gap for women, and piecing together multiple jobs to get to a decent income. And at the same time, they live with the social consequences of more unmarried households and more children being raised by single parents—without much help from government. They noticed that things have gone differently for the 1 percent, which gets a lot of help.

If Democrats are championing a reform agenda, today's new working class is as likely to give the Democrats a second look as to turn to the Republicans.

THE FORBIDDING ELECTORAL COLLEGE MAP

The economic and social transformations, the counterrevolution, and the battle over America's values come together to produce this stark red-blue Electoral College map. That map means Democrats are very likely to elect future presidents and govern nationally in the coming period—and thus they may be able to shift the balance in the U.S. courts and advance a reform agenda nationally. The Electoral College map also poses forbidding odds for a Republican Party that must elect a president to block the Democrats' "liberal agenda" and to hold their own coalition of voters. At the moment, the strategies of enflaming culture war, building up the base in the GOP conservative heartland, and stoking emotions to push off-year turnout are turning the Electoral College map bluer.

At some point, the Republican Party will implode, fracture, or get reformed, as the Democratic Party did between 1984 and 2000. For the moment, however, this is still an inside game for the Republicans, as we will see in the next chapter.

This is the result. If the Democrats' presidential nominee did no more than carry the states that Democrats won in all of the past six elections, they would garner 242 Electoral College votes—just 28 short of a majority. Florida brings 29 votes to the table—securing victory for the Democrats before you even count the states that have moved into the Democrats' Electoral College count in more recent elections as a result of the demographic trends and the metropolitan revolution.

One serious analyst puts the probability of Democrats winning the Electoral College after the next general election at 83 to 89 percent. That is based on 10,000 simulations where there is an evenly divided national vote—and Democrats have only failed to win the most votes once since 1988.[53]

Since 1992, Ron Brownstein points out, no Democrat has won fewer

States that have voted for the same party from 1992–2012

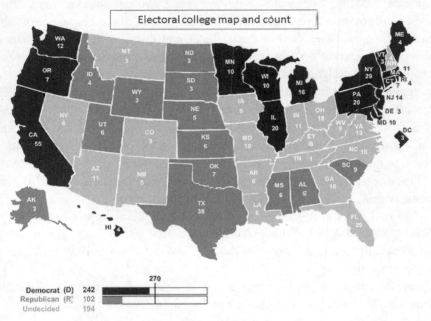

Map made using 270towin.com.

States that have voted for the same party from 2008–2012

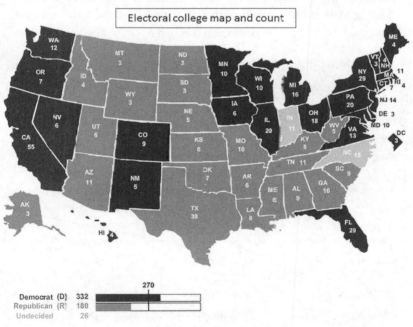

Map made using 270towin.com.

than 251 Electoral College votes—when 270 are needed to win. That is daunting. And two Democratic candidates have reached 365. George W. Bush topped all other Republican presidential nominees when he arguably reached 271 votes in 2000 and 286 in his reelection, "the smallest share of the available electoral votes won by any reelected president since 1804, except Woodrow Wilson," as Brownstein describes it.[54]

Brownstein described the Democrats' "blue wall"—the states that voted Democratic in five consecutive elections that are now six—but that now seems outdated given the trends on racial diversity, immigration, changes in the family, the Millennials, urban and metropolitan area growth, the mobility of the best-educated, and the vast changes in the suburbs.

Obviously, Republicans are focused on the blue-wall states of Wisconsin, Pennsylvania, and Michigan. They do in every election.

The real issue is whether the economic and social trends in the purple states of Florida, Virginia, Colorado, Nevada, and New Hampshire are going to add them to the blue wall. North Carolina and Ohio are likely to remain on the front line.

Ben Highton modeled the trend line for Nevada, Virginia, New Hampshire, and Wisconsin and compares the Democratic candidates' state margins with the national vote margin for every presidential election since 1992. The model predicts the Democratic president would carry these purple states in

Swing states that are becoming more Democratic in their presidential vote

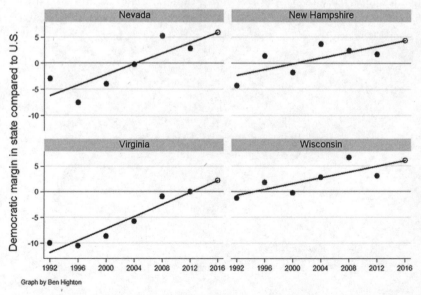

Graph by Ben Highton

Ben Highton, "A Big Electoral College Advantage for Democrats Is Looming," *The Washington Post*, April 28, 2014.

the conservative scenario where Democrats and Republicans split the national vote evenly. In Virginia, for example, where Democrats used to perform dramatically below their national vote, there is an 85 percent chance of Democrats taking the state as the trends rapidly push the state vote margin above the national one.[55]

Obama's 0.9-point victory in Florida in 2012 was surprising to many, though get used to it. If the Democratic candidate simply maintains the same coalition of supporters and is aided by projecting population trends, the Democratic candidate wins Florida by 4 points in 2016. But even that is probably too cautious. Nate Cohn points to the explosive Hispanic growth, driven almost entirely by immigrants from Puerto Rico and Central and South America who are much more Democratic than the Cuban immigrants of the past, and Cubans themselves are now evenly divided in their partisan loyalties. Romney was kept in the game by the aversion of white seniors and the Panhandle to Barack Obama, though that could readily edge back. If the Democratic candidate for president wins whites with the same margin as Kerry did in 2004, for example, he or she would win Florida by 9 points. Think of the implications of the Democrats winning Florida by 9 points.[56]

The Republican Party can barely compete in a national presidential election because of the inexorable trends in the country, and the odds in the Electoral College look more and more foreboding. That is very real for the Republican establishment and its supporters in the business community.

We shall see in the next chapter that the Republican base voters are very aware they are losing the country and any prospect of governing nationally. They are scared to death. That is precisely why the Evangelicals, observant Catholics, and Tea Party supporters have rallied to the counterrevolution and to help Republicans entrench themselves in the GOP conservative heartland and the U.S. Congress. It is showtime.

8 THE END OF THE REPUBLICAN PARTY AS WE KNOW IT

At the heart of the Republican Party's intensified struggle against the current trends in the country are the one-third of the national electorate who say, "I'm a Republican," and the one in five who vote in Republican primaries and caucuses. To understand America's increasingly polarized politics since 2000, you need a scorecard to know who is really calling the shots.[1]

The Republican Party establishment and the allied business elites are focused on how to marginalize the Tea Party, libertarian rebels who shut down the government and defeated establishment U.S. Senate candidates. The national media also thinks the Tea Party is the defining and dominant conservative force in today's Republican Party. They are very wrong, and miss what really drives the Republicans' public agenda.

The religiously devout are the biggest bloc and encompass nearly half of the Republican base voters. That bloc is dominated by Evangelicals who are 29 percent, and observant Catholics, 16 percent of the base. The Republican Party establishment has not dared to challenge their agenda, as they form a fervent plurality and more than three-quarters of Evangelicals vote straight tickets in general elections. Republicans remain resolute and united in their opposition to abortion, Obamacare, and immigration and in their defense of the traditional family.

The Tea Party is also a powerful force in the party, comprising 25 percent of the base, though that understates the strength of these voters. Almost four in ten Evangelical Republicans are also strong Tea Party supporters—and together, Evangelicals and the Tea Party form 55 percent of the Republican base. The Evangelicals cheer the Tea Party because they are the ones fighting hardest against the trends in the country and against President Obama's agenda.

The Evangelicals and the Tea Party are the heart of the Republican Party. About seven in ten strongly identify with the Republican Party, and they are the base segments most likely to vote straight Republican on Election Day.

They do not look like the new American majority. The Evangelical, observant Catholic, and Tea Party base voters are nearly 90 percent white, and two-thirds are married—in stark contrast to a country that is growing more racially diverse and increasingly single.

There is a "moderate" bloc among Republicans—voters who are ideologically or religiously moderate—who are pretty alienated from what they see as the mainstream of the party. They form 25 percent of the GOP base, though they self-consciously split their general election votes between the parties (22 percent of them split fairly evenly, and only 44 percent say they vote *mostly* for Republicans). The moderates are buttressed by the 5 percent of Republican base voters whom I label the "GOP establishment." They are very conservative, pro–small government general election Republican voters, though they are not so enamored of the Tea Party. They would probably rally to a candidate backed by the party's established leaders.

This is a party where Evangelicals, observant Catholics, and the Tea Party are rallying the troops into battle.

Composition of the Republican base

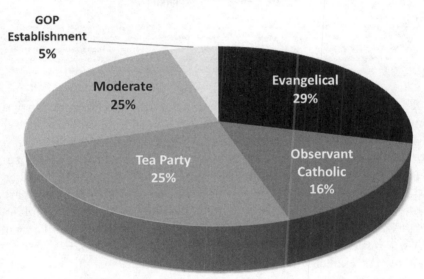

Based on 7,004 interviews conducted for Democracy Corps, July 2013–January, 2015.

In the summer of 2013, Democracy Corps organized focus group discussions with people from the different parts of the Republican base, and we quickly came to appreciate how much they feel they are losing politically—losing control of the country and increasingly powerless to change course. When asked about the direction of the country, their starting reactions were "worried," "discouraged," "scared," and "concerned." While many voters and even some Democrats doubt that Obama is succeeding and accomplishing his agenda, Republicans think he has won. To them, Obama imposed his agenda, and Republicans in Washington let him get away with it. The country is sure that gridlock has won the day, but Republicans see a president who has lied, fooled, and manipulated the public to pass a secret socialist agenda.[2]

Stanley B. Greenberg

How do Republicans feel about the direction of the country?

This is based on findings from the first phase of research for Democracy Corps' Republican Party Project. We conducted six focus groups among Republican partisans—divided into Evangelicals, Tea Party adherents, and Moderates—between July 30 and August 1, 2013. All participants indicated that they voted only or mostly for Republican candidates and were screened on a battery of ideological and political indicators. The groups were conducted in Raleigh, North Carolina (Moderate and Tea Party), Roanoke, Virginia (Tea Party and Evangelical), and Colorado Springs, Colorado (Moderate and Evangelical).

The Republican base thinks they face a victorious Democratic Party that is intent on expanding government to increase dependence and therefore electoral support. It starts with food stamps and unemployment benefits, and expands further if you legalize illegal immigrants; insuring the uninsured through the Affordable Care Act will dramatically expand the number of those dependent on the government. They believe these policies are part of an electoral strategy—not just a political ideology or an economic philosophy. If Obamacare is fully implemented, they fear the Republican Party may be lost forever.

While few explicitly talk about Obama in racial terms, the base supporters are very conscious of being white in a country with a growing minority population. Their party is losing to a Democratic Party whose goal is to expand government programs that mainly benefit minorities. Race remains very much alive in the politics of the Republican Party.

For all that, this is a deeply divided base. Moderates are a quarter of those who identify as Republicans, and they are very conscious of their discomfort with other parts of the party base. The moderates are fiscal conservatives who feel isolated in the party. Their distance begins with social issues such as gay marriage, abortion, and whether homosexuality should be discouraged by society, but it is also evident on issues such as climate change, undocumented immigrants, and the Second Amendment. The moderates are increasingly marginalized in their party as the other segments grow more defensive of views that are increasingly unpopular and under threat nationally.

Evangelicals feel most threatened by the ascendant demographic and cultural trends in America and bring unique intensity to their opposition to what is happening with homosexuals. Abortion is one of the issues where Evangelicals and the Tea Party base are equally aligned and intense—and they have led the charge in that battle against the trends in marriage and independence for women. The observant Catholic bloc is strongly opposed to the growing public acceptance of homosexuality and gay marriage though is less intense than the Evangelicals on this issue. They are less intense in their support for pro-life groups than the Tea Party or Evangelicals and closer to moderates when it comes to measures to prevent global warming; they are also less uncharitable toward the needy and slightly less hostile to Barack Obama personally.

What will quickly become apparent from listening to these voters is how intent they are to battle against the current trends, how high the stakes are for them, and how deeply their emotions run.

FOCUS GROUPS AS REAL LIFE

A few decades ago, a Macomb County focus group participant exclaimed, "No wonder they killed him," after I read a statement by Robert Kennedy. That stopped me and led to a whole new analysis of Reagan Democrats and a new set of conclusions about the core obstacles to Democrats winning working-class white voters again. There were similar moments in the groups with core Republican voters that we conducted during the summer of 2013. This time the most interesting development was how they emerged as affinity groups where the participants worked through their alienation and isolation, not just from the politically correct, liberal-dominated media, but also from other Republicans, family members, and neighbors. If you want to know why Republicans are at war internally, start with their voters who are in turmoil.

The Evangelicals—who seem the most defensive when discussing popular culture, demographic trends, changes in the family, and what is happening in their states—wrote postcards at the conclusion of the groups and commented on what a relief it was to be with people who think like they do.

I'm not alone in the way I view things for the most part. (Evangelical man, Roanoke)

Not by myself in thought process. . . . Thought it was a great conversation and very informative. Thank you for the opportunity. (Evangelical man, Roanoke)

Good to be around like minded people. All of the people feel the country is in trouble due to the Democratic Party. Hope and pray that this will turn around. (Evangelical man, Roanoke)

Democracy Corps conducts homogeneous groups to replicate real-life homogeneity where people can feel free to talk about their feelings and emotions. This is what people say around the water cooler or at a family dinner. Many acted like this was the first time they could express their feelings freely in a safe place—and they did.

The moderates, who are uncomfortable with their own party on social issues, used their private postcards at the end of two hours to express surprise that there are other Republicans who think like themselves. While we did not use the word "moderate" in the focus group script, they did so self-consciously in their postcards.

> *Surprised at other females with fiscal conservative values while also being socially more moderate.* (moderate woman, Raleigh)

> *I was surprised that the group was more moderate on social issues, like I am. It seems that this group focused on the fiscal aspect of Republicanism as the main component.* (moderate woman, Raleigh)

> *Discussions on "hot button" issues and how people with varying background seem to have middle ground.* (moderate woman, Raleigh)

> *Many people are moderate because of $ issues & social issues.* (moderate woman, Raleigh)

> *The common desire for a more moderate political party.* (moderate woman, Raleigh)

I expected that in this comfortable setting or in their private written notes some would make a racial reference or racist slur when talking about the African American president. None did. They know that is deeply non-PC and are conscious of how they are perceived. But focusing on that misses the centrality of race to the worldview of Republican voters. They have an acute sense that they are white in a country that is becoming increasingly "minority," and despite holding the majority in Congress, they feel their party is getting whooped by a Democratic Party that uses big-government programs that benefit mostly minorities to create government dependence and a new electoral majority. Barack Obama and Obamacare are racial flash points for many Evangelical and Tea Party voters.

BARACK OBAMA

For the Republican base, Barack Obama is the starting point for everything that is wrong with the country. Almost 90 percent of the Evangelical and Tea Party bloc "strongly disapproves" of how he is doing his job. For the Tea Party, it is personal, as 87 percent give him the "coolest" personal rating on our thermometer scale. Evangelicals are only slightly less personally hostile, with 83 percent very cool toward him.

Strong disapproval of President Obama among key GOP blocs

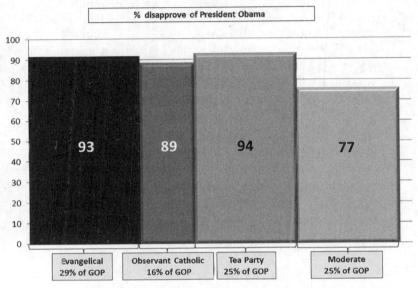

% disapprove of President Obama

Based on 7,004 interviews conducted for Democracy Corps, July 2013–January 2015.

For the Republican base, President Obama is a "liar" and "manipulator" who fooled the country. That offers a visceral separation and a reason not to listen to him. They are frustrated that the country was fooled and reelected the president who is getting his way. They are shocked that people believed him.

They think he is manipulating words, using props and teleprompters to communicate a false narrative to claim success for his governance. The Tea Party participants described him as a "spin doctor," "misleading," "slick," "slimy," "untrustworthy," "condescending," and "an SOB."

He's even slicker than Clinton. (Tea Party man, Raleigh)

I had a concussion so they had to ask me a bunch of questions 'cause my mind wasn't quite working and they said, "Who's the president?" And I said, "an SOB," and he said, "good enough." (Tea Party woman, Roanoke)

When the teleprompter's not there, he really falls apart. So I don't know how much of all of this is him or if it's his staff or whoever the Democratic Party is—and he's just the figurehead. (Tea Party man, Raleigh)

How would you describe President Barack Obama?

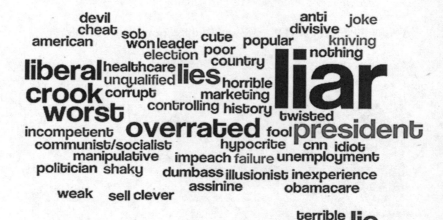

This is based on findings from the first phase of research for Democracy Corps' Republican Party Project. We conducted six focus groups among Republican partisans—divided into Evangelicals, Tea Party adherents, and Moderates—between July 30 and August 1, 2013. All participants indicated that they voted only or mostly for Republican candidates and were screened on a battery of ideological and political indicators. The groups were conducted in Raleigh, North Carolina (Moderate and Tea Party), Roanoke, Virginia (Tea Party and Evangelical), and Colorado Springs, Colorado (Moderate and Evangelical).

The moderates are not very different on this score: "Trying to sell snake oil." (moderate man, Colorado Springs); "He's always campaigning. He's never, it's like you won. Now start leading. Quit campaigning to me" (moderate woman, Raleigh).

When they watched a TV video of the president speaking on the Affordable Care Act, the Evangelical women in Colorado Springs wrote some pretty harsh and dismissive things: "Spin Dr" and "Chronic liar"; "fake"; "lies"; "just a speech"; "liar"; "bullshit." The comments from the moderate men there were almost indistinguishable: "Lies, Lies, Lies, Lies, Lies!!!!!!!"; "lies"; "disregards real facts"; "Socialism"; "Lies, Lies, Lies"; "Health care lies."

The private doubts they wrote on a piece of paper before discussion with the group betray a much deeper suspicion of the president as a person. Many have questions about him being foreign, non-Christian, or secretly Muslim.

Citizenship question. (Evangelical woman, Colorado Springs)

Socialist background. (Evangelical woman, Colorado Springs)

Origin of birth. (Evangelical woman, Colorado Springs)

Background. (Tea Party man, Raleigh)

Muslim; birth agenda; Fake; not true. (Tea Party man, Raleigh)

Not a US citizen. Supports Terrorists. (Evangelical man, Roanoke)

I don't believe he's a Christian. He's a tyrant. (Evangelical man, Roanoke)

Socialist, income redistribution. (Tea Party man, Raleigh)

Lack of relationship with the American people. (Tea Party man, Raleigh)

They wonder about the real motives behind the changes he is advancing.

What is he really thinking? (Tea Party man, Raleigh)

He wants to fundamentally change the country. (Evangelical man, Roanoke)

He is going to try to turn this into a communist country. (Evangelical woman, Colorado Springs)

His motives behind his actions. (Evangelical woman, Colorado Springs)

He supports everything that is against Christianity. (Evangelical woman, Colorado Springs)

The moderate men in Colorado Springs raised as many questions as the other Republicans about who Obama really is:

Only cares about self-promotion, not the AMERICAN people. (moderate man, Colorado Springs)

Hopefully, he doesn't change the Constitution so he can try to get elected again. (moderate man, Colorado Springs)

Feels government can solve any problem. (moderate man, Colorado Springs)

He is masonic Devil Illuminati, Lier can't stand Him. (moderate man, Colorado Springs)

American? (moderate man, Colorado Springs)

Lies and scandals. (moderate man, Colorado Springs)

Muslim? (moderate man, Colorado Springs)

As we shall see below, these questions on character and legitimacy matter so much because these voters think President Obama, Nancy Pelosi, and the Democratic Party are conspiring to push for bigger government and more spending to control the people. The Republican base is united in its opposition to big government programs and wasteful government spending, including the new health care reform law. Evangelical and Tea Party group participants also think he is trying to fool the middle class with a more palatable patina while pursuing a darker, secret, socialist agenda.

Even when he's trying his hardest to appease conservative capitalist-oriented people . . . he still is spouting pure Marxist philosophy. He can't get away from it. . . . I don't know if he can . . . even find a speechwriter that can help him sound like he's actually an American capitalist. (Evangelical man, Roanoke)

Obama's . . . just pure distilled Marxism. (Evangelical man, Roanoke)

We're not on his agenda. And he thinks these are things he should say to appease us, because we're middle class. We want jobs. We care about energy. We care about whatever his talking points are. And yet . . . he can't stop the ultra-liberal Marxist bleeding through what he's trying to say. (Evangelical man, Roanoke)

Republicans believe President Obama is on the verge of using his powers to pursue his agenda without limits. When asked what is going right in the country, a Tea Party woman in Roanoke joked, "Well, we're not a communist nation . . . yet." This fear is evident in the frequent discussions about executive orders and action: "When Congress is gone . . . he just does an Executive Order. He's going to get anything he wants. And there's nobody there that will have the guts enough to stand up to him"; "There's so many secret things that go on—that are—bills are passed and regulations are passed—we never know about" (Evangelical man, Roanoke).

Much more distressing is the idea of the NSA and the IRS being turned against the Republican opponents of the government: "He's turned the government into a spy agency on us" (Evangelical man, Roanoke); "[They are] setting up an organization and a machinery that can control and spy on every asset of our lives, and control it. And once it's infiltrated with all of the little webs . . . you won't be able to undo it" (Evangelical man, Roanoke). Worst of all, they are afraid that the president is getting away with such abuses unchecked.

BIG GOVERNMENT AND DEMOCRATIC DEPENDENCE: OBAMACARE

What unites the current base of the Republican Party is a deep hostility to "Obamacare" or the Affordable Care Act: strong unfavorability is approaching 90 percent among the Tea Party and Evangelicals, and three-fourths of the observant Catholics have strong negative feelings. That is why it was their unifying issue in the U.S. Congress and 2014 off-year elections, and why it will be a litmus test for the Republican presidential primaries in the future.

But the reaction to President Obama's health care reforms is about much more. It embodies their shared revulsion for big government—which has many potential meanings and undercurrents.

Some are straightforward and mainstream. They are opposed to big programs, spending, and regulations that undermine business. That is probably the dominant strand of thinking among the moderates who long for a fiscally conservative and focused Republican Party. Their first associations with government are "big"; "*waste*"; "Regulations. Inefficient"; "Red tape, that's all" (moderate woman, Raleigh). They think big programs go hand in hand with special-interest groups and lobbyists who buy off politicians and push up spending (moderate man, Colorado Springs). Their objections pointedly do not put increased dependence center stage.

Accordingly, the moderates are very opposed to Obamacare because it is big spending; it won't work; it will hurt business and employment. Their first associations are "Stupidity"; "*Job killer*"; "And I say debt, D-E-B-T"; "Job killer" (moderate women, Raleigh).

Many Republicans are also opposed to intrusive government that invades their privacy and diminishes their rights and freedoms—views held in common with many independents, libertarians, and broader parts of the electorate.

However, what elicits the most passion among Evangelicals and Tea Party Republicans is the belief that Democrats are growing big government to create rights to programs and dependence in order to win the electoral allegiance of minorities who will reward the Democratic Party with their votes. The Democratic Party exists to create programs and dependence—the food-stamp hammock and entitlements—for the "47 percent." They freely describe these programs as meant to benefit minorities. Comprehensive immigration reform and the full implementation of Obamacare are now on the horizon, and they fear that citizenship for twelve million illegals and tens of millions getting free health care is the end of the road for their party. To them, that is why Obama and the Democrats are prevailing nationally and why the future of the Republic is so at risk.

The same underlying analysis and reaction are at the heart of their reaction to undocumented and illegal immigration. The Republicans, led by the Tea Party, are about as hostile to "undocumented" immigrants in the United States as they are to Obamacare. More than three in five are extremely cool to them, compared to just one in five Democrats. On the topic of immigration, Republicans speak literally and in graphic terms of being invaded, and the failure to speak English makes them pretty crazy:

Don't come here and make me speak your language. Don't fly your flag. You're on American soil. You're American. (Evangelical man, Roanoke)

You come to our country, you need to learn our language. (Evangelical man, Roanoke)

Why should I put—press 1 if I want to speak in English? You know, everything—every politically correct machine out there says, "Press 1 for English. Press 2 for Spanish." (Evangelical man, Roanoke)

And with the prospect of great political gains, "That's why they want all the illegal aliens legalized," one of the Evangelical men explained.

The most powerful dimension in Republican thinking according to our factor analysis is one that starts with reactions to Obama and Pelosi, then to government programs and activism, and ends with feelings about dependency. This is the predominant and the most motivating dimension of Republican thinking, explaining almost a quarter of the variations in responses to the world they are confronting.

This dimension is animated in the first instance by deep hostility to President Barack Obama, and equally by views of Nancy Pelosi and the Democratic Congress that held sway before the voter reactions in 2010 and 2014. These partisan responses are on the same dimension with a fierce hostility to federal government action on climate change, and importantly, health care reform. While Republicans are desperate to stop "Obamacare" now, future action on climate change is already on the same dimension—as Republican base voters see both as critical areas of government overreach. This is the most emotional and combustible dimension in the Republican identity, explaining the largest proportion of Republican responses across a whole array of topics.

They see the Democrats, led by Barack Obama and Nancy Pelosi, as creating government entitlements and dependence. A lot of people have come out of this economic crisis with different types of benefits that they look at as welfare being abused; especially guilty are those who have misused a food bank or unemployment benefits.

And the entitlement. Everybody seems to feel—And I volunteer at a food pantry. . . . And the thought of entitlement—I didn't get my food stamps, and I need my TANF and I have to get my disability and I have to get my housing. (Evangelical woman, Colorado Springs)

Abused . . . It's too easy to get on it. People who can work won't work, because they're receiving too many government benefits, and it's easier to stay home and cash in on the unemployment and the food stamps. (Evangelical man, Roanoke)

They eat better than I do. (Evangelical man, Roanoke)

That's the whole problem with the whole unemployment and the food stamps: people have taken advantage of it. . . . Now . . . it's a way of living. And that's the problem. (Evangelical man, Roanoke)

I work at Sam's Club . . . lady comes in all the time. All of them: first, fourth, seventh, ninth. "I'm tired of ribeye steaks. Where's your lobster tails? Where's your seafood?" And they're putting it in an Escalade. . . . It's disgusting . . . it's full of graft. It's full of fraud. It's full of abuse. (Evangelical man, Roanoke)

The Democratic Party, they believe, looks to inject government into places where Evangelical and Tea Party Republicans believe matters are better left to family, community, individuals, and churches. They worry that minorities, immigrants, and welfare recipients now believe it is their "right" to claim these benefits. Tea Party participants in particular were very focused on those who claim "rights" in the form of government services without taking responsibility themselves.

Well, on the news, everything is—every minority group wants to say they have the right to something, and they don't. It's life, liberty and the pursuit of happiness. It doesn't say happiness. You get to be alive and you get to be free. The rest of it's just a pursuit. You don't even—you're not guaranteed happiness. You have to work for it. (Tea Party man, Raleigh)

I think that America doesn't give us enough responsibility. I don't think that they let us be responsible for ourselves because we know we have—or people think that there's someone to catch them. (Tea Party woman, Roanoke)

I see a lot of lack of personal responsibility. People are constantly looking toward the government to get what they need. (Tea Party man, Raleigh)

Welfare and making your own money. I think people don't take responsibility for themselves because they know . . . the government will take care of me and my five children while they can't. (Tea Party woman, Roanoke)

This tension between personal and governmental responsibility has emerged as one of the defining values differences between the parties. Three-quarters of Democrats and Democratic-leaning independents say, "It is the responsibility of the government to take care of people who can't take care of themselves." But only a third of Evangelical Christians accept that—the staunchest opponents in the GOP base—and just 38 percent of Tea Party supporters agree. Moderates are aligned with base thinking on this values question (38 percent), but interestingly, 63 percent of the observant Catholics and 51 percent of the GOP establishment accept this safety net role for the government.

This dimension of the Republican consciousness is evident in their consideration of the Affordable Care Act—another entitlement that creates a benefit without the person contributing and taking responsibility, fostering a culture of dependence. This institutional dependence is designed by Democrats to translate directly into votes. It is disheartening, to be sure.

Hatred of health care reform is defining anti-government posture

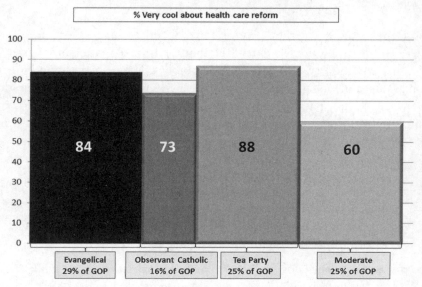

Evangelical 29% of GOP	Observant Catholic 16% of GOP	Tea Party 25% of GOP	Moderate 25% of GOP
84	73	88	60

% Very cool about health care reform

Based on 7,004 interviews conducted for Democracy Corps, July 2013–January 2015.

The government's giving in to a minority, to push an agenda, as far as getting the votes for the next time. (Evangelical man, Roanoke)

They've got their hands in everything. (Evangelical woman, Colorado Springs)

They want us to be dependent upon the government, more so than self-sufficient. And that's what makes them powerful. (Evangelical woman, Colorado Springs)

That's the sort of subculture that the Democrats are creating, is that sense of entitlement, because they want us dependent on them. (Evangelical woman, Colorado Springs)

Obama got elected because he kept saying, "I'll keep giving you unemployment forever." That's why he got elected. Now you can live in this country without a green card. Come on, we'll give you insurance, we'll give you money. That's why he got elected. (Tea Party woman, Roanoke)

There's so much of the electorate in those groups that Democrats are going to take every time because they've been on the rolls of the government their entire lives. They don't know better. (Tea Party man, Raleigh)

They've got a very effective process apparently. They've figured out how to convince the largest number of people to step in line. (Tea Party man, Raleigh)

One of the things the Democrats have done is created a dependency class of loyal voters. (Evangelical man, Roanoke)

The Affordable Care Act is the final act of government-created dependence that will take the Republican Party out for good: "Just looks like a wave's coming, that we're all going to get screwed very soon" (Evangelical woman, Colorado Springs); "It's putting us at the mercy of the government again" (Tea Party woman, Roanoke); "[Our rights] are slowly being taken away—like health care" (Tea Party woman, Roanoke).

EVANGELICALS

Three in ten Republicans are Evangelicals, currently the largest segment in the Republican base, and they are party loyalists through and through. Voting for Republicans has become voting their identity: they are white, married, religious, and older, which puts them behind the times. They talk about how the dominant politics and culture have encroached on their small towns, schools, and churches. They are troubled by the trends and talk with friends, family, and fellow believers about Obamacare, guns, government intrusion, gay marriage, and "culture rot."

It used to be different, a fact illustrated by several men in Roanoke when describing their own towns:

> *It's a little bubble. So everybody—it's like a Lake Wobegon. Everybody is above average. Everybody is happy. Everybody is white. Everybody is middle class, whether or not they really are. Everybody looks that way. Everybody goes to the same pool. Everybody goes— there's one library, one post office. Very homogenous. (Evangelical man, Roanoke)*

It is from that perspective that they view President Obama.

> *I think that his picture of the people in this room would be that we're all a bunch of racist, gun-clinging, flyover state, cowboy-hat wearing yokels. Because we didn't go to Harvard, and we're not from New York, and we're pretty white, we're pretty middle class. We like to go to church, we like our Bibles. And so we're just not him. We're not on his agenda. (Evangelical man, Roanoke)*

They are "pretty white" and "didn't go to Harvard"—and "we're just not [Obama]." The "tolerant" liberals just aren't very tolerant when it comes to them.

In Roanoke, participants remarked that it was refreshing and unusual to be in a room where everyone shared their beliefs—and gave them an opportunity to speak openly about guns, gay marriage, church, and their values. In Colorado Springs, participants remarked that Colorado used to be a conservative state where they could expect that their values and rights would be protected. This seems to be slipping away, as one noted: "We're having to realize that we're going to be in a very politically incorrect minority pretty soon" (Evangelical man, Roanoke).

Rejection of homosexuality by society central for Evangelicals

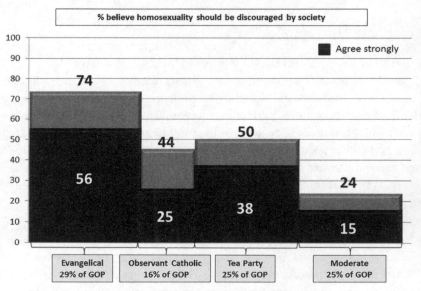

| % believe homosexuality should be discouraged by society |

■ Agree strongly

Evangelical 29% of GOP: 74 (56 Agree strongly)
Observant Catholic 16% of GOP: 44 (25 Agree strongly)
Tea Party 25% of GOP: 50 (38 Agree strongly)
Moderate 25% of GOP: 24 (15 Agree strongly)

Based on 7,004 interviews conducted for Democracy Corps, July 2013–January 2015.

They know that they are the most "politically incorrect" and most disturbed when it comes to this country's acceptance of homosexuality and the gay agenda—which they find to be truly an abomination. Towering above all the other Republican groupings, almost three-quarters of Evangelicals say that "homosexuality should be discouraged by society." Among the current social revolutions, this is their defining and consuming issue.

Giving gay and lesbian citizens of the right to marry the person they love can seriously harm them, and seriously harm the children that they were raising. (Evangelical man, Roanoke)

They've taken what I consider a religious union between a man and a woman—pardon my French—and bastardized it. (Evangelical man, Roanoke)

They believe the dominant national culture promotes homosexuality and makes this "minority" culturally "normal." There is a conspiracy to push "*the gay agenda.*"

> *The fact that it is so prominent, that's day to day. Like . . . that stupid song on 96. . . . It's on every five minutes. The "I can't change" song. It's on constantly. It's [a] song promoting gay and lesbian rights and all that stuff. But it's so prominent. It's every 10 minutes.* (Evangelical woman, Colorado Springs)

> *Like it's a normal way of life. There's a minority of people out there are homosexual, but by watching TV, you'd think everybody's that way. And that's the way they portray it.* (Evangelical man, Roanoke)

> *Somebody's got to say "the gay agenda." That gets thrown around, a lot—that there's this vast conspiracy of gays that are trying to push this. But—you know, to some extent, it almost seems like that, because these things are just moving so quickly along a certain trajectory.* (Evangelical man, Roanoke)

Their kids are under threat from popular culture and in the schools—and the gay agenda seems to have displaced school prayer as the intrusive secularism that is undermining their ability to raise their children right.

> *It's really tough when my 13 year old comes home, and saying, the girls are holding onto hands in school, and the guys, there's nothing that can be done. Which comes back to, Christ is taking—being taken out of schools. They're trying to take anything that mentions the word God out of schools. They could get in trouble, if they bring a Christian book.* (Evangelical woman, Colorado Springs)

> *The schools aren't going to teach your kids the stuff that you want to. We don't need the schools raising our kids. We need to raise our kids, teach them what our beliefs are, what our standards are, our morality is, and let them get an education there, but not raise them there.* (Evangelical man, Roanoke)

> *It's hard when the school is directly opposing what you're trying to teach your kids.* (Evangelical man, Roanoke)

As a result, some have taken their kids out of the public schools and instead placed them in church schools or are homeschooling:

> *My daughter's only one, and I already am making plans for her not to go to school and have that [homosexuals] in her life, because it's*

not—Not only that it's not just something that I agree with, but it's not something that should have to be forced down her throat. (Evangelical woman, Colorado Springs)

Evangelicals believe that their views are unacceptable outside of their small circles of like-minded friends and family because there is a dominant culture that has marginalized them ideologically, linguistically, and culturally. They are very conscious that they are viewed as rednecks by the liberal elite. Take, for example, this exchange between Evangelical women in Colorado Springs:

It becomes hard, because [if you're conservative] you're not allowed to have your opinion, but everybody else is.

You have to agree with another opinion. That's very annoying.

[Does anyone else feel that way? That you're allowed to have certain opinions, but not others?]

Yes. (All around)

[Where does that pressure come from?]

It's from the people who say that we're supposed to be tolerant.

[Who are they?]

The people who are intolerant. It's the left, for the most part. . . . I just recently had a debate on Facebook with a nephew of mine. And he accused me of so much stuff out of one comment. . . . And it was just—He was just clueless on where I stood.

Not surprisingly, the Evangelicals feel besieged and wonder why their own party has not stood up, battled, and won. Republican politicians have lost their way, and there are too many "RINOs" who cannot stop what is happening.

The problem is there's not a party that thinks like us. We don't have a voice in Washington. Or where else? The Republican Party? They might as well just have a D beside their name, as far as I'm concerned. (Evangelical man, Roanoke)

I don't have a party anymore. (Evangelical man, Roanoke)

And the Republicans—a lot of Republicans are just RINOs—Republican in name only. But we've really got to turn this ship around, or we're in deep doo. (Evangelical man, Roanoke)

Above all, they think the leaders of the Republican Party "cave all the time" (Evangelical woman, Colorado Springs). "They're rollovers" (Evangelical man, Roanoke). So thank God *Fox News* and the Tea Party understand the stakes and are fighting them.

When asked about our country's greatest strengths and what gives them hope, the Tea Party is universally mentioned. They say that people are finally "standing up" and "fighting back."

> *Well, I would say, the rise of the Tea Party, that people are getting involved, and they're standing up. . . . People are saying hey, this isn't what's in our Constitution, and it's not what's in our schools. And I think people are taking a stand now, and we need to, before it's too late.* (Evangelical woman, Colorado Springs)

> *America is rising back up and getting a backbone again, and making our voices heard one way or another, whether it's Tea Party, or whatever else. People are being emboldened.* (Evangelical woman, Colorado Springs)

> *They are a group to be reckoned with, because if we're going to turn things around, the Tea Party's going to need to be part of it. And less government and less spending, and throw the rascals out—to quote Ross Perot—is what they're all about. I'm there.* (Evangelical man, Roanoke)

> *I thank God there's enough people getting angry now and it will have to stop. I think people realize that we're going to have to rise up and take control.* (Evangelical man, Roanoke)

> *I'm very proud of them for standing up. It was about time . . . it's given me courage to be able to say what I believe.* (Evangelical woman, Colorado Springs)

In a room full of like-minded others, they become energized and feel ready to fight back and to reclaim what they believe has been taken from them. At the conclusion of the group in Roanoke, the men had formed a serious bond and parted vowing to remain in touch, "These are the kind of people the Tea Party's made of."

Opposition to abortion is a core issue of seriousness among the base of the Republican Party. Nearly three-fourths of Evangelicals give a warm rating to pro-life groups and so do 60 percent of the Tea Party bloc. The observant Catholics are quite warm, though nothing like the intense support of the core of the Republican Party. The pro-life movement and pro-life position are central to the one in ten voters who are the strongest Evangelical–Tea Party supporters.

Stanley B. Greenberg

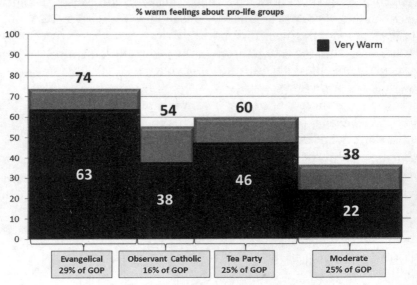

Evangelicals and Tea Party applaud those fighting abortion

% warm feelings about pro-life groups

Very Warm

Evangelical 29% of GOP	Observant Catholic 16% of GOP	Tea Party 25% of GOP	Moderate 25% of GOP
74 / 63	54 / 38	60 / 46	38 / 22

Based on 7,004 interviews conducted for Democracy Corps, July 2013–January 2015.

Abortion millionaires . . . [Planned Parenthood is] making a fortune off of them, of course. (Evangelical woman, Colorado Springs)

We knew when I was 17 weeks pregnant that she had Down's Syndrome . . . half my family pretty much abandoned me because I decided to keep my child so as you can imagine that's a very hot topic and that strictly is a lot of reason I vote for who I vote for is because of abortion and the abortion laws. I don't think in no shape or form you should ever end a child's life. (Tea Party woman, Roanoke)

I don't personally agree on abortion. . . . I've sinned, you know we're all gonna meet the maker. He can deal with them. (Tea Party woman, Roanoke)

There should be no abortions at all. Don't have them. If you don't want them, just don't have kids. (moderate man, Colorado Springs)

TEA PARTY: "FIGHT BACK TO BASICS"

Tea Party enthusiasts form 25 percent of Republican identifiers—and are cheered on by almost four in ten of the Evangelicals (37 percent strong Tea Party supporters) who are depending on their conservative backbone. These are straight-ticket, antigovernment, antiregulation, probusiness voters who are more confident that they can get America back to basics if they fight back. The hot topics among their friends and family include Obama, gun control,

Obamacare, taxes, and government spending. They raise their spirits by joining the battle to get America "back to the Constitution," to American entrepreneurship, freedom, and personal responsibility.

In both Tea Party groups, the phrase "back to basics" was repeated multiple times—as they want to return to a time when they believe government was small, people lived largely free of the government, and Americans took responsibility for themselves.

These are not those times. Government is catering to those who have not earned their benefits or the freedoms of this country. Of all the Republican groups, these were the most anti-immigrant, anti–food stamp, and anti-Obamacare and those who stand to benefit from it. They emphasized food stamps, "welfare" recipients, and illegal immigrants more than any other group. They were also the most anti-Obama, anti–Obama agenda, and anti–Obama politics—because these threaten the basics.

They are conscious that some in the party grumble about how divisive the Tea Party might be in the country, but for the Tea Party Republicans the solution to this internal discord lies in the Tea Party. Many believe that the whole party should rally around this faction.

> The Tea Party is trying to get back to the basics. Then you've got—even within the Republican Party trying to fight the Tea Party. It's like, "Don't fight each other. Let's join together and be one party." (Tea Party man, Raleigh)

> I think [the Tea Party] is good [for the Republican Party]. I think that the rest of the GOP needs to get on board. We need to all agree on some of the basic stuff. (Tea Party man, Raleigh)

> I think it's a good thing, because [the Tea Party represents] core Conservatives. . . . So you've got the Republicans against the Conservatives, and they said, "You need to be more Conservative if you're going to win the elections and get more people." (Tea Party man, Raleigh)

At the center of their opposition to government is a fear that big government is going to invade their rights and undermine their freedoms: "Our freedoms are getting taken away all the time with more regulations and rules and things we can't do. And we let it happen, and then all of a sudden we're not going to have any left" (Tea Party man, Raleigh). They embed the "right to bear arms" in a revisionist history and Constitutionalism.

> I think that our freedom is slowly being taken away from us, like with the gun control and I don't know, just everything. I just fear for our freedom. I don't want to be like the other countries and have to be told what to do and when to do it. (Tea Party woman, Roanoke)

I think we're slowly losing our freedom. You know just by—you can't choose anything, you know when it comes to gun control or anything. . . . I don't think they should take the guns away. (Tea Party woman, Roanoke)

There's talk of the repeal of Stand Your Ground laws and things like that. That's a diminishing right. (Tea Party man, Raleigh)

For me you know our founders . . . we had to rise up and we had to defend ourselves and take over this country and who knows if that has to happen again sometime so I don't want the government—the government already has enough knowledge and stuff about what's going on in my life so if they want to take away all of our rights, I mean I just feel like we're Nazi Germany or something. (Tea Party woman, Roanoke)

Support for the NRA and gun rights nearly defines the Tea Party's consciousness about individual liberties and an encroaching government: more than 80 percent express warm feelings for the NRA. Evangelicals are also overwhelmingly warm toward the pro-gun lobby. The observant Catholic and moderate blocs look more like independents in their thinking on this issue, though the intensity of Tea Party support obscures those differences.

The Tea Party has become the audience and the troops for *Fox News*. Fox is the most viewed cable news network, with 1.64 million total prime-time viewers. But the Tea Party leads all other GOP base blocs in their warm,

Embrace of NRA defining for Tea Party, but also Evangelicals

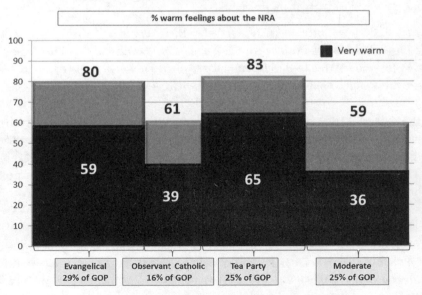

% warm feelings about the NRA

Based on 7,004 interviews conducted for Democracy Corps, July 2013–January 2015.

strong embrace of the network: more than 60 percent of the Tea Party bloc is very warm toward Fox, compared to half of the observant Catholics and a third of the Evangelicals and moderates. The Tea Party women shared their enthusiasm in focus groups:[3]

I absolutely love Bill O'Reilly. (Tea Party woman, Roanoke)

I wish there was more Fox News. (Tea Party woman, Roanoke)

It's great. (Tea Party man, Raleigh)

The Tea Party men in Raleigh confessed that Fox is the only news station they watch.

It's the only news channel I watch. (Tea Party man, Raleigh)

It's the only one I watch. (Tea Party man, Raleigh)

I like it. I'm missing two hours of it. (Tea Party man, Raleigh)

Evangelicals also embrace Fox, and our Evangelical men explained it is the only source for balanced news.

FOX is about the middle. (Evangelical man, Roanoke)

The only one that gives you both sides. (Evangelical man, Roanoke)

I don't think they're trying to make the news. I think they're trying to report the news. It seems like everybody else is trying to make the news. (Evangelical man, Roanoke)

CLIMATE CHANGE

Beliefs about climate change are already a fundamental part of the conscious-ness of the Republican base, and there is the potential for this issue to be-come more divisive than any of the other issues facing the country. Just 39 percent of Evangelicals and a quarter of the Tea Party bloc believe hu-mans are causing the Earth to get warmer. By contrast, climate change is unique because about three in five of the observant Catholics and moderates believe humans are playing a destructive role and "we need to begin taking serious measures." There is potential for real division.

For the Evangelicals and the Tea Party, this is not about how to address a distinct future challenge: it is about faith and values, the role of scientific knowledge, and the value of education and academia. In the focus groups, Evangelicals and Tea Party Republicans are consumed by skepticism about climate science—to the point where they mistrust scientists before they begin to speak.

Humans causing climate change accepted by moderates and Catholics

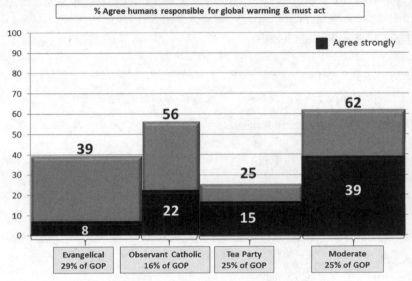

% Agree humans responsible for global warming & must act

Based on 7,004 interviews conducted for Democracy Corps, July 2013–January 2015.

Well, the scientific community in general is minimizing or marginalizing people that are bringing up doubts. . . . You can look in biology, you can look in geology, you can look in chemistry, and you can see that the theory doesn't hold up. And yet the scientific world won't acknowledge that. And if you do say it, and you're a PhD candidate, you can be denied your PhD. You can be denied your master's degree. (Evangelical woman, Colorado Springs)

I think that we're being fed a lot of misinformation. (Evangelical woman, Colorado Springs)

Just like the whole evolution-creation thing . . . I think we waste a lot of time arguing with the science. I think we would all agree that it's the policy that we don't agree with. . . . So that seems to be where we're—we're losing the fight because we're fighting the science. And you can't fight the science. (Evangelical man, Roanoke)

I wonder if they don't put that out there to distract you. (Tea Party woman, Roanoke)

Back in the 70s, there were articles out there that another ice age was coming, and that's just 30 years ago. So now all the articles say, "Hey, it's getting warmer." Well they've already proven the past 12 years it hasn't gotten warmer. (Tea Party man, Raleigh)

You could have 12 scientists on this side talking all about global warming, and you can get 12 scientists that will have the complete opposite. So you're listening and you just don't know. (Tea Party man, Raleigh)

If you look, there was an ice age. So it used to be really, really, really cold, and inevitably it's got to warm up eventually. It can't stay that cold all over forever. And eventually—I think that nature is in cycles. (Tea Party man, Raleigh)

Tea Party Republicans, in particular, are concerned that climate science is another way to force regulations on individuals and businesses.

I think I saw somewhere we have like 100-plus regulations added every day. (Tea Party man, Raleigh)

The politicians and those people—celebrities. Most of them may or may not believe it, but it's an opportunity for them to gain power, make money, push their agenda. They want to regulate everything . . . they want to control it, so this is a great excuse for them to gain that control. And if the world were covered in ice right now, they'd find another reason to gain control. (Tea Party man, Raleigh)

They fear the subsequent costs—both to consumers and taxpayers.

The government will spend you know hundreds of thousands of dollars to check out some bird you know, that's fading away or something. Don't worry about that bird. Worry about the people you know. (Tea Party woman, Roanoke)

I mean I think we have to . . . you know and try to make sure that we're recycling and taking care of our resources . . . but not at the cost of the jobs and our economy. I mean if we regulate down . . . to zero emissions . . . but then a car costs . . . 200,000 dollars, well then we can't afford it all right. (Tea Party woman, Roanoke)

And all those regulations are putting companies out of business and like you're saying, making products too expensive. (Tea Party woman, Roanoke)

Many think that climate change is natural or divine providence and would rather leave decisions about the future of the planet to God.

Planet's been here for millions of years. Temperatures have fluctuated many times. And man is—to think that we could have something to do with changing the weather is giving ourselves way too much credit. (Evangelical woman, Colorado Springs)

Like you said, regardless if we're here or if we smoke or if we fire this or if we drive our SUVs or if we all drive hybrids and electric cars, the climate is going to change whichever way God says it's going to change. (Tea party man, Raleigh)

If you live next to the ocean, your house is going to get messed up. The seawater does rise when it gets warmer. Ice caps melt when it gets hotter. It's scientific fact and it just leads you down the wrong path, like that's something that's bad or not right or not natural, when it's just nature doing its thing. (Tea Party man, Raleigh)

I agree we're warming up slowly, but we have nothing to do with it. It's going to happen if there were no humans or if we were full of humans. It's a natural cycle of nature. (Tea Party man, Raleigh)

Mother Nature has a way of taking care of herself. (Tea Party woman, Roanoke)

"I CAN'T SELL MY KIDS ON THIS PARTY"

The Republican base is deeply divided. Just talk to any persuasion of base voter—the party is a mess.

The GOP is dominated by its Evangelical and Tea Party core, committed to faith, family, and country, the right to life, and small-government conservatism. They are horrified by spending, taxes, and dependence that Democrats expand to engender more political support.

A large majority of observant Catholics, which includes a healthy dose of Catholics and mainline Protestants, disagree with those in their party who say government should not care for the needy and join the moderate bloc in accepting science as the arbiter on global climate change. But those views are now heresy and not open for negotiation among the major Evangelical and Tea Party sections of the party.

For Evangelicals, homosexuality is an abomination, and opposition to gay marriage is a dominant dynamic in the consciousness of most Republican voters. Moderates, on the other hand, are more warm than cool toward gay marriage and closer to embracing it as right. Tea Party Republicans offer a whole range of views on gay marriage, as reflected in their crisp reactions below.[4]

Who cares? (Tea Party woman, Roanoke)

I don't want the government telling me who I'm sleeping with or whatever in my bedroom, so I just don't think it's the government's business. (Tea Party woman, Roanoke)

It's fine with me. (Tea Party woman, Roanoke)

I think it's not important. I mean either way we have so many bigger issues to worry about. (Tea Party woman, Roanoke)

It doesn't hurt anybody. (Tea Party woman, Roanoke)

I don't think the government has any say in it. . . . I personally don't agree with gay marriage, but I don't think the government should say who can get married and who can't. It's not their business. (Tea Party man, Raleigh)

They've got a lot more to deal with than that. (Tea Party man, Raleigh)

The moderates are a quarter of the base and are acutely aware of being a minority in a party that does not value voters who are *only* fiscally conservative. As a result, less than half are straight-ticket voters. Their biggest differences surround social issues—acceptance of gay marriage first and foremost though also contraception, Planned Parenthood, and abortion. They are animated on the gay marriage issue because they know how central this is to the conservative mainstream:

My idea is if they're going to do it, let them do it. (moderate man, Colorado)

From a legal standpoint I don't understand why it's a debate because I think that gay people should actually be allowed to get married. . . . [First] of all every argument I've heard against it has been based on religion and if our government is truly separate from religion then our government shouldn't be able to make laws based on religious beliefs. (moderate woman, Raleigh)

It just doesn't really make any sense why they shouldn't be allowed to . . . have that kind of special bond. (moderate woman, Raleigh)

I mean they're [together anyway]. You know? The world is going to change anyway. And it is changing anyway every day. (moderate woman, Raleigh)

That's what I don't understand, is like they have houses together and they do everything that a married couple would do together and I just don't understand. (moderate woman, Raleigh)

The first gay divorce was filed in Massachusetts—Good, that's what I like. I'd like them to have the same opportunity we have. (moderate man, Colorado)

Doesn't hurt me. It doesn't affect my life. (moderate man, Colorado)

I don't understand why you can regulate what the hell I think and do. This is a free fricken country. There's been homosexuals since the Roman times and before. What the hell are you scared of them? Are you scared they're going to get you? Are you? Are you scared they're going to get your kids? (moderate man, Colorado)

Many of them applaud Planned Parenthood, even though they look around the room first to see if there are others who share their experience and views.

> *I think it's necessary for a lot of different reasons and not saying just abortion, people associated with abortion but I think it does so much more than that they don't get credit for.* (moderate woman, Raleigh)

> *I think Planned Parenthood is great and I think it always has been, just I mean it just offers people options it offers a lot of education.* (moderate woman, Raleigh)

The moderates are in a different country than the Tea Party and Evangelical blocs when it comes to immigration. In our groups, they started the conversation with the implausibility of sending the undocumented home:

> *I mean I don't think it's feasible to say, send everybody home.* (moderate woman, Raleigh)

> *I mean it's a huge struggle to get here illegally so I think if they are here illegally . . . they are not leaving. And that means they are going to be putting a toll on our roads . . . taking up space in classrooms . . . so it would be nice if they were legal and they actually could be contributing to that tax circle. . . . I just think getting them a path to that would be great.* (moderate woman, Raleigh)

In contrast to most of the Republican base, many moderates spoke positively about immigrants as good for the country and the economy. They described immigrants as people with good work values who are able to contribute, not as people looking to become dependent.

> *I need more customers. I need more people to sell things to. I need more people to do business with. And I can see that these people are potential customers. And the jobs they did . . . we won't do. . . . We just flat won't do it. . . . We don't have some of the work ethic they have. . . . I want it to all be legal. . . . I don't mind that they're customers. They can pay taxes.* (moderate man, Colorado)

> *Many immigrants come into our country do better than we do . . . they don't complain.* (moderate man, Colorado)

> *I feel like if we're not going to embrace some sort of path to citizenship we're going to see a cost of a lot of services go up.* (moderate woman, Raleigh)

> *And they work hard and they actually realize the American dream. And a lot of us Americans complain, we won't do what we think we'll do.* (moderate man, Colorado)

When we asked the moderates about scientists, the first words that came to mind included "respected" and "smart." Although some are doubtful about climate change, they do not reject science offhand; rather, those skeptics explain that they simply do not know enough to decide whom to believe: "I'm not smart enough to say [climate scientists are] full of shit. . . . But I am smart enough to know I need to get more information before I say anyone's full of shit. I do know that" (moderate man, Colorado). They were not aware at the time that many climate deniers would use this line to escape being pressed on the issue.

Many of the moderates seem comfortable with regulation of carbon pollution and open to the idea that climate change is one area where government ought to do more.

I'm glad we're starting to do [more on] energy standards, I wish it was higher. . . . I'm glad that we're seeing more efficient cars. I'm glad they passed that to where in 2015, we have to have cars that run more efficiently. (moderate man, Colorado)

Watching landfill and watching vehicle emissions, watching what we're pumping into our rivers, that's very, very smart, period. Regardless of climate change. (moderate man, Colorado)

I mean, that's just part of good stewardship of the earth that we've been given. And I think that you find a lot of Republicans will feel that way too because a lot of Republicans hunt. They're very sensitive to what the environment does to the hunting, you know, the changes that they see and anything like that. (moderate man, Colorado)

The moderates, like other base Republicans, think government is "waste," "inefficient," "regulations," and "red tape." They believe their taxes are too high and the Republican Party should work to make the government more fiscally prudent and effective. But when they see all of the polarization and dysfunction in Washington, they think their own party has taken the lead. They resent the polarization that says "you have to be one side or the other" and keeps the country from getting to "some middle ground" and "what could be good for everybody" (moderate woman, Raleigh).

Everything seems very divided and angry. (moderate woman, Raleigh)

They've been holding everything up in Congress lately. Like, the Democrats proposed this but Republicans just say no. (moderate woman, Raleigh)

I feel like there's a whole lot of talk and not a whole lot of action that just keeps tying everybody up and just this constant circle of just kind of anger and you can't get through it. (moderate woman, Raleigh)

While they continue to appreciate the party's fiscal conservatism, the moderates see a Republican Party that has little room for the moderates and is increasingly closed to a plurality of views and the ascendant trends described in this book.

I think of a white 54-year-old man in a business suit. And my mom. (moderate woman, Raleigh)

I feel hopeful [about the Republican Party] on an economy level. I feel doubtful on a personal rights level, a women's rights level, an environment level. So those two issues. But the rest, economy-wise, budget-wise I feel hopeful. (moderate woman, Raleigh)

I just tend to be a little bit more moderate on social issues. However I'm a pretty staunch fiscal conservative so it's kind of like at least among my peers there's a change in kind of the conservative group. But it doesn't necessarily seem like the Republican Party is changing with it. (moderate woman, Raleigh)

These developments in the party make it difficult for educated young people to identify as Republicans. As one man in Colorado said, "I can't sell my kids on this party." They hear these leaders talking about the "rape crap" and frankly, "I can't sell them on my party. These kids are smart, they know these stupid politicians are saying crap" and should "get out of our bedrooms, get out of our lives and do what they're supposed to do" (moderate man, Colorado Springs).

This research window into the base of the Republican Party underscores the growing fractures that played out in Republican primaries across the country. But that pales before the elevated worries across the base about the growing dangers facing the country and the demands for a bold conservative policy response. The GOP war to repeal Obamacare and end food stamps and unemployment benefits can only be understood within this Republican world. The same is true for Republican resistance to addressing climate change and immigration and why Republican attorneys general are appealing their defeats on gay marriage in the federal courts. The GOP-controlled states are competing with each other to effectively ban abortions and allow concealed weapons everywhere.

Out of the dynamics of the Republican Party emerge their policy priorities in the face of America's many challenges.

Part IV

ADDRESSING AMERICA'S CONTRADICTIONS

9 THE CONSERVATIVE INTERREGNUM

Will the Republican Party step up to address America's growing challenges at this tipping point? Based on everything we know about its philosophy, values, and politics, the answer is almost certainly no for now.

The Republican Party brings to this moment a small-government model of low taxes and low regulation that gives business as much freedom as possible. This model is premised on a belief in individual responsibility as self-reliance and a belief in individual liberty that requires freedom from government intrusion. Growing government spending is like an irresistible pot of gold that invites a feeding frenzy of special interests and that invites dependence and a weakening of the public character.

In practice nationally and in the states, the Republican Party prioritizes reversing the Affordable Care Act and obstructing government action to address climate change. It cuts funding for food stamps and views unemployment benefits as just a new form of welfare and dependence. It is aggressively cutting funding for education and science. It is still contesting the voting rights for racial minorities, the new roles for women, and America's pluralism of families.

Over the past three decades, a network of outside conservative groups have fed Republican leaders and activists a rich diet of ideas on the welfare state, supply-side economics, and business regulation, and the Evangelical churches rallied them to oppose abortion and to stand against the forces of secularism. That entangling of business, faith, and politics has produced an orthodoxy, Thomas Mann and Norman Ornstein write, according to which conservatives are "the reflexive champion of lower taxes, reductions in the size and scope of the federal government, deregulation, and the public promotion of a religious and cultural conservatism."[1]

The Koch Brothers committed to spend almost $900 billion—as much as any national political party—in the 2016 presidential election and proceeded to audition candidates to see who should carry their conservative banner into the election. That externalized the Republican campaign in a way we have never seen before. Charles and David Koch are not at all shy about their views on energy and climate change, on low taxes and small government, and on the need to prioritize deregulation. They want to see which candidate can best articulate that vision and agenda, and Marco Rubio, Rand Paul, Ted Cruz, Scott Walker, and no doubt others auditioned before wealthy donors at Koch-sponsored meetings in Palm Springs and New York City. The Republican presidential candidates unapologetically defended these billionaires as "job creators" and praised their constructive role balancing the influence of Hollywood and the liberal media on behalf of Democrats.[2]

The top conservative thinkers downplay inequality and the problems facing the middle class and press instead for a focus on the poor, whom they think liberalism has failed. The liberals hold out a safety net that invites idleness, and they show a disdain for marriage that leads to a growing number of children raised by single parents and in poverty. Conservatives think that if the safety net provided less security and comfort, people would become more self-reliant and seek out work. Thus weakening the system of social insurance should be part of the strategy for reducing poverty.

Republican presidential hopefuls in 2016 started to mention inequality, middle-class anxieties, and persistent poverty, particularly because they could use these to take an ironic bite out of President Obama for his hypocrisy and failed economic plan. "The recovery has been everywhere but in the family paychecks," Jeb Bush observed. "Today, Americans across the country are frustrated. They see only a small portion of the population riding the economy's Up escalator." Marco Rubio highlighted the recovery: "What really happened is a bunch of the recovery over the last several years has gone to such a small segment of the population." *Washington Post* writers observed that the candidates sounded more like John Edwards than Mitt Romney.[3]

For all of them, highlighting these problems is a way of saying President Obama's big-government policies have failed on their own terms. "Income inequality has worsened under this administration," Rand Paul pointed out, and "President Obama offers more of the same policies—policies that have allowed the poor to get poorer and the rich to get richer."[4]

And only a few of the presidential campaigns ventured very far beyond conservative orthodoxy on how to address these issues. A few conservative leaders in the House and Senate have ventured out and supported extending the earned income tax credit to the unmarried, and some have proposed a very large expansion of the child tax credit—both programs that can aid the poor and the lowest-wage workers. The Republican House majority leader Eric Cantor felt inspired to give a speech titled "Make Life Better" to "make sure every American has a fair shot at earning their success and achieving their dreams."[5]

They were taking up policy ideas and broader goals developed by a network of intellectuals and conservative reformers, highlighted in separate major pieces by Sam Tanenhaus and E. J. Dionne on the "Reformicons." As it turns out, the policy innovation did not go beyond tax credit proposals already supported by President Obama. And their plans to support the traditional family and to block grant relief to the poor so states may take greater responsibility hardly open up new conservative territory. As Dionne concluded, they were "more engaged in rebranding than rethinking."[6]

When Michael Tomasky reviewed all the presidential candidates' new books, including those that talked about the "opportunity gap," he was struck by how few mention the word "wages" or discuss "wage stagnation." If they talk about inequality, it is to criticize liberal thinkers for inviting "class envy." Their focus is mostly on the persistence of poverty and the moral decay that has accompanied the decline of the two-parent family. That equips these candidates with a fairly limited set of policy tools, as they tiptoe into the debates about America's deepest problems.[7]

When the Speaker-in-waiting, Eric Cantor, was ignominiously defeated in a Republican primary, the reformers were shattered. As Tanenhaus observed, "the narrative of the newly in-touch GOP met the cold reality of politics, with its pitiless winnowing of winners and losers." It was an abrupt reminder that the low-tax, small-government, probusiness conservatives rule in the Republican Party. They do not have much patience with this talk about all Americans getting "a fair shot." They want to know what you are doing to strengthen the counterrevolution against big government.[8]

The price of entry for all the Republican presidential candidates in 2016 is to propose huge tax cuts that add between $1.5 and $2.4 trillion to the deficit over the next decade and shower benefits on the very richest. Most of the candidates embrace the traditional conservative supply-side approach and want to dramatically cut top tax rates, move to a flat tax, or cut or abolish taxes on inheritances, corporations, capital gains, or dividends. Marco Rubio and a smaller bloc of conservatives, on the other hand, joined the debate about the struggles facing families by proposing to expand the child tax credit from $1,000 to $3,500. In today's Republican Party, though, any such proposal to help families has to be more than matched by inventive ways to cut taxes for business and top earners. No longer worried about the added trillions this would add to the deficit, Rubio also proposed to end taxes on capital gains and dividend income, cut the corporate tax rate, abolish taxes on foreign income, and offer tax breaks to "non-corporate businesses"—a device that helped send the Kansas state budget into crisis.[9]

· When any of the presidential candidates talk about reform in some area, they move quickly to demonstrate they hold to a deep red worldview. Rubio moved to make sure the wealthiest and businesses would be the principal beneficiary of his tax plans and opposed the comprehensive immigration reform law that he had voted for in the Senate. Jeb Bush, compromised by his support for Common Core and perceived moderate stance on immigration, quickly surrounded himself with the foreign policy team that gave us the Iraq war and promised to repeal President Obama's executive orders that granted legal status to millions of America's immigrant "DREAMers."[10]

With America needing leaders to address these deep problems, it is fair to conclude there is a conservative interregnum.

RED AND BLUE VISIONS

Governor Rick Perry of Texas and Governor Bobby Jindal of Louisiana have been on the front line arguing that the country faces a choice between the governing models in the red and the blue states. There is "the vision common in blue states, where the state plays an increasing role in the lives of its citizens," Governor Perry points out. Taxes are on the rise there, pension programs are "out of control," and "jobs are leaving by the truckloads." Without much caution, he quotes Thomas Jefferson in a call to arms against that blue-state model: "a little rebellion now and then is a good thing."[11]

Republicans govern very differently, guided by very different values. There is "a vision common to red-state America where the freedom of the individual comes first, and the reach of government is limited," Perry observes. In the red states, "taxes are low, spending is under control, jobs are on the rise." Perry calls out the names of the governors in the GOP-controlled states and asks, what is the common denominator? He answers his own question: conservative governors "know the freedom of the individual must come before the power of the state." They "trust the people more than the machinery of government."[12]

While head of the Republican Governors Association, Governor Jindal hailed the reforms conservative states had advanced against the liberal tide. "Whether it is showing the way without an income tax, whether it's cracking down on frivolous lawsuits, whether it's cutting down on government spending, whether it's growing the private-sector economy instead of the government economy," Jindal proclaimed before the Texas state legislature, "you have shown the country that conservative principles work.[13]

Governor Jindal is unapologetic about inequality. He scorned President Barack Obama, who talks of "class envy and warfare," "equality of outcomes," and insists on "demonizing those that have been successful." The "rich are evil, unless they are from Hollywood."[14]

What the president and liberals want is to use the issue of inequality to grow "government spending, borrowing, and taxes." So if they get their way, liberals will "manage the slow decline of this great economy" and "further [divide] the existing pie." Disaster is inevitable because the liberals want "government to explode"—"to pay everyone; to hire everyone; they believe that money grows on trees." And the left thinks "debts don't have to be repaid."[15]

Demands on government are what will drive the country to ruin. Jindal builds the case by posing a series of questions: "Where do you go to if you want special favors? Government. Where do you go if you want a tax break? Government. Where do you go if you want a handout? Government. This must stop." He predicts, "At some point, the American public is going to revolt against the nanny state."[16]

Blue America believes "people of faith are ignorant and uneducated; unborn babies don't matter; pornography is fine; traditional marriage is discriminatory."[17]

Red America, Jindal assures us, is determined above all else to restore self-reliance and teach people not to ask anybody else to pay their way. Under such circumstances "freedom is still alive."[18]

So at the heart of the conservative counterrevolution, E. J. Dionne writes with such clarity, is "a pure and radical individualism."[19]

It is so powerful because it sits at the heart of Red America's contest against Blue America and its determined battle for America's values. This radical individualism produces an antitax conservatism that sees all government as a threat to individual liberty and any government regulation as a mortal threat to business success and market competence. There is little appetite for any project that uses government or even for discussion of any major national problem, lest it invite a collective or governmental response or more government spending. Where conservatism used to want to empower local communities, this extreme individualism seems to resent both state and local government as well. They are just as capable of burdening business and creating dependency.

As Evangelical Christians were mobilized to battle against today's growing national threats, their conservatism, too, became more individualistic and hostile to government. In William Jennings Bryan's day, the fundamentalists and populists gave voice to Christ's social gospel about rich and poor and the needs of community. As Dionne points out, they held out the promise of individual salvation, as the white Evangelical churches do today. But now, as we pointed out in chapter 8, Evangelicals have embraced the Tea Party and its extreme individualism because they are the only ones fighting against Obama and the threats to America's values. That bond and alliance between the Evangelicals and the Tea Party is hegemonic within the GOP and creates a modern Republican Party with a unique brand of conservatism.

This modern-day conservatism does not have much use for William F. Buckley Jr. and his ideological colleagues at *The National Review* who appealed to both libertarians and traditionalists by promoting both liberty and virtue. One colleague who went into the Reagan administration described the mission as "utilizing libertarian means in a conservative society for traditionalist ends." Conservatism's appeal is more than just making it possible for individuals to get rich.[20]

Today's conservatives do not have much use for the brand of conservatism presented by George W. Bush. His faith-based initiatives sought to elevate local civic efforts to aid the poor and vulnerable, and his race-to-the-top education reforms aimed to raise student achievement with accountability. Their skepticism is rooted in an ascendant individualism "that simultaneously denigrates the role of government and the importance most Americans attach to the quest for community."[21]

Today's Republican Party has emerged as an "insurgent outlier" that does not grant the legitimacy of its political opponents, Thomas Mann and Norman Ornstein write in *It's Even Worse Than It Looks*. Put that kind of purposeful ideological party in the America constitutional order with separation of powers and you have a "formula for willful obstruction and policy irresolution." They are waging a "guerrilla war" to oppose the president, of course, though as Jonathan Chait points out, they are battling to restore America's values, and that seems to justify a "procedural extremism." It precludes today's Republicans listening to Joe Scarborough to emulate electorally successful conservatives, like Dwight Eisenhower, Ronald Reagan, Richard Nixon, and George W. Bush who put "pragmatic conservatism" ahead of "reflexive purity." To win, they accommodated the New Deal and Social Security and grew government programs and federal spending. That formula is not under consideration.[22]

The new conservatives in government brought a brinkmanship that shut the federal government down in 1995–1996 and again in 2013. The insurgent House leader Newt Gingrich sought to coerce President Clinton to accept cuts in Medicare. The Tea Party–dominated House threatened to have America default on its debts and to force changes in the Affordable Care Act. They shut the government down for sixteen days. Prominent Republicans said their central mission is "to make Washington . . . inconsequential."[23]

It is little wonder that the principal narrative offered by the Republican candidates for president amounted to little more than a mantra about small government and empowering the "productive citizens and private companies" that "would bring back prosperity and solve the nation's problems on their own." Mitt Romney was not apologetic about the central actors in the comeback. "Corporations are people, my friend," he said with such revealing clarity. And when he considered running again and with the same lack of self-consciousness about the rich—what Peggy Noonan described charitably as his "clunkiness"—Romney "leaked his interest in running: to mega-millionaires and billionaires in New York. 'Tell your friends.' "[24]

With the Republican Party embracing this radical individualism and extreme hostility to government, government institutions, and blue America, Republicans nearly disqualify themselves from the public debate about what America should do in the face of these great challenges. That will have to wait until after there are convulsions in the Republican Party that lead to Republican reform presidential candidates who really challenge this narrow conservatism from the inside and win, as Bill Clinton did when he led the reform of the Democratic Party. Then the conservatives' version of the Democratic Leadership Council will matter. Until then Republicans will be aggressively promoting the conservative governing model wherever they can.[25]

THE REPUBLICAN STATE MODEL

Pay careful attention to what Republicans did when they took full control of state governments after the 2010 midterm wave. They translated this radical individualism, antitax, small-government philosophy into huge spending cuts, particularly from education, reduced aid for low-paid workers and the poor, and slashed regulation and tax cuts for corporations and the richest. This is not theoretical or posturing for elections. This is what they choose to do when unfettered by political opposition or Constitutional checks and balances. They moved with stunning clarity and impact.

On the judicial front, Ron Brownstein points out, governors and attorneys general in virtually every Republican-controlled state joined the suit to overturn the Affordable Care Act, block any judicial encroachment on traditional marriage, and overturn President Obama's regulations on climate change. With a handful of exceptions, all have refused to expand Medicaid coverage among those with a lower income. While all states cut public-sector jobs with the economic crash, the GOP-controlled states cut more deeply, and more important, they pushed to restrict the bargaining rights of public workers and moved against the teacher unions and teacher tenure. They expanded the rights of gun owners, severely limited abortion access, and restricted the voting rights of racial minorities, foreign-born citizens, and college students.[26]

The first priority of Republicans in their states was cutting spending. All but four states in the country cut public services during *and after* the financial crisis. That is the key to understanding Republican priorities in these states: 728,000 public-sector employees, almost half in education, lost their jobs *after* the economy began to recover in June 2009. And over 70 percent of the public-sector jobs eliminated in 2011 came in twelve solidly red states.[27]

The Republican-controlled states led the way, slashing spending beyond what was needed and declining to use their "rainy day" funds to forestall cuts. In Texas, the Republican-controlled legislature, fueled by Tea Party supporters, passed a $172 billion two-year budget, an 8.1 percent decrease from prior spending levels. The budget cut $4 billion from public schools, $1 billion from higher education and financial aid to more than 40,000 students, and eliminated 5,600 state employee jobs. In the face of a $23 billion shortfall and a no-tax-increase budgetary policy, Governor Rick Perry and his allies in the legislature refused to avail themselves of more than $3.2 billion of the $9.7 billion rainy-day fund. GOP-controlled states oversaw a 22 percent decrease in education spending while state tuition rose 31 percent on average.[28]

While education spending was cut almost everywhere to balance budgets, twelve states simultaneously cut corporate taxes and taxes on the wealthy, ensuring spending cuts would be larger than necessary. Cutting government further to cut taxes is ideologically driven. Accordingly, Louisiana, South Carolina, and Iowa joined Texas in refusing to use their massive rainy-day funds to avoid drastic cuts in state spending on vital public services. These GOP-controlled states have gone a step further, seeking to lock in the new spending levels and legally bar future tax increases through constitutional amendments.[29]

While workers and unions were struggling financially, the U.S. Chamber of Commerce and the National Association of Manufacturers joined with the Club for Growth, the Koch brothers, Karl Rove's Americans for Prosperity, big corporations such as Wal-Mart, FedEx, and Exxon Mobil, as well as the tobacco and pharmaceutical industries, to strike a fatal blow. In the GOP-controlled states, public employees and teachers in particular lost collective bargaining rights, and Michigan, the birthplace of the UAW and progressive unions, became a "right to work" state.[30]

The poor, however, were hit the hardest, and by design, consistent with the ascendant values in the Republican Party and its conservative regional base. A majority of Republicans believe people are poor because of a lack of effort on their part, while a majority of independents and Democrats believe people are poor because of circumstances beyond their control. Republicans believe government efforts to raise people out of poverty have been stymied by society's growing indifference to marriage, which further underscores the poor's lack of virtue. Though there are many poor and low-wage whites in this world, there is a strong sense that blacks and other racial minorities "cry the blues" and feel entitled to aid. Republicans are even more distinctive in believing the rich got their riches through hard work and are virtuous.[31]

Republicans have moved to bring virtue and responsibility to work by slashing the safety net. These policies are actually meant to cause a little pain—to make sure people who are getting any kind of government benefit struggle to get it and to purge any sense of entitlement. The GOP-controlled governors and legislatures have largely refused or fought expansion of Medicaid under the Affordable Care Act to cover more of the poor and low-wage workers. A striking two-thirds of poor uninsured blacks in the country live in these "refusenik" states, where almost six million residents will not get health insurance.[32]

In this new brave new world, unemployment insurance—a state-administered, contributory program that provides workers up to twenty-six weeks of benefits if they lose their job without cause—is now seen as welfare. That equation was only affirmed when millions were thrown out of work by the financial crisis and many remained unemployed through the Great Recession. Republicans determined that extended unemployment benefits removed the incentive to work. While the national unemployment rate stood at 9 percent at the worst of the Great Recession in 2009–2010, the U.S. Chamber of Commerce lobbied for unemployment insurance reform, "pressuring workers," in the EPI's words, "to take any job offered, no matter how low the wages or how poor the conditions."[33]

A bloc of seven Republican-controlled states permanently reduced the number of weeks the unemployed can apply for benefits; some reduced the level of benefits as well. Under Wisconsin's new law, the unemployed must wait a week before collecting benefits. Under Tennessee's new law, the unemployed may stay out of work for only thirteen weeks before being required to take a job paying 75 percent less than their previous positions; and they must certify every week that they applied for at least three jobs that week.[34]

Child labor has become virtuous in this new world. Four Republican-led states lifted some restrictions on child labor, endorsing Newt Gingrich's conclusion that child labor laws are "stupid." Idaho acted first and now allows kids from twelve years of age to work up to ten hours a week. Jack Kingston, the Republican chairman of the House Appropriations Subcommittee for Agriculture and Nutrition and a recent candidate for the U.S. Senate from Georgia, proposed that kids from poor families receiving free lunches at school "pay a dime, pay a nickel" or "sweep the floor of the cafeteria" to "instill in them that there is, in fact, no free lunch." He elaborated, "[I] think what we would gain as a society in getting people—getting the myth out of their head that there is such a thing as a free lunch."[35]

Each of the Republican governors has battled to take the model as far as they could—and often to the limits of their own popularity.

Kansas

A Tea Party favorite and leader of uncompromising pro-life Republicans during his time in the U.S. Congress, Governor Sam Brownback announced that Kansans were "leading an American Renaissance—a return to the virtue and character that built this state and a great nation in the first place." This starts with a vow to "rebuild our families" and realize the solution is not government, it is God: "Our dependence is not on Big Government but on a Big God that loves us and lives within us."[36]

To that end, he made radically cutting taxes and spending the centerpiece of his platform. The governor's stated goal was to totally eliminate the personal income tax and the earned income tax credit for the working poor and to cap spending increases at 2 percent a year, requiring major cuts in spending.[37]

The Tea Party governor had to struggle to win the support of some moderate Republicans who were allied with former senator Bob Dole, a Republican who respected President Eisenhower's moderate conservatism. Nonetheless, Governor Brownback cut taxes by $1.1 billion and eliminated the income tax for small businesses while cutting welfare by nearly half. He announced, "Our new pro-growth tax policy will be like a shot of adrenaline into the heart of the Kansas economy."[38]

The Kansas model is more than a little tarnished, as the promised economic miracle failed to produce a surge of new jobs and state revenue. Jobs grew only 3.4 percent between 2011 and 2014, the second-lowest rate in the region and well below the national average. Colorado job growth, for example, was 8.2 percent. With reports of growing poverty, the governor offered policies that cut the safety net and promoted marriage. He proposed waiving the marriage-license fee for couples who complete eight hours of premarital education and adding a work requirement for food stamps that encourage idleness.[39]

It all reached a point of crisis when state revenues evaporated because of the massive tax cuts. A state court found that school spending for poor districts was so low as to be unconstitutional and ordered that $129 million be restored. The state pensions underfunded and the rainy-day fund depleted, Moody's Investors Service ultimately cut the state's credit rating. At least the governor was able to win the repeal of teacher tenure in his new budget.

Governor Sam Brownback's job approval fell to 33 percent in 2014, and with the endorsement of one hundred defecting Republicans, Democrat Paul Davis lost by only 4 points in this deep red state. His margin was 23 points short of what Republican candidates for Congress averaged on that same ballot in 2014.[40]

After the election, a prospective budget shortfall of $143 million in 2016 forced Governor Brownback and the Republican legislature to consider increasing sales and excise taxes and cigarette and liquor taxes and to slow the reduction of income taxes that was his signature conservative policy.[41]

Pennsylvania

Governor Tom Corbett, swept into office by the 2010 wave, cut education spending by $841 million in his first budget, and twenty thousand teachers lost their jobs. The Republicans' education cuts, however, were not aimed solely at getting to a smaller government or a balanced budget. Its purpose was to reduce education spending for the poor, minorities, and immigrants. The governor scrapped the funding formula that took account of the number of students in poverty and who needed English instruction. This guaranteed that the brunt of the education cuts would fall on the poorest and Hispanic populations.

To forestall the possible political backlash, the state rushed to implement a new law requiring voters to show photo identification at the polls. A Pennsylvania judge struck down the law as imposing an unreasonable burden on voters.

Corbett embraced the GOP state model and moved aggressively to cut taxes on businesses. He cut corporate taxes by $1.2 billion and angrily opposed the Democrats' effort to impose a severance tax on the booming shale-gas industry. "It's the property owner's gas. I'm sorry. It's the mineral owner's gas," he declared. All of this business-friendly policy passed in the name of job creation proved for naught. Pennsylvania fell from seventh in the nation in job creation when Corbett took office to forty-seventh in the spring of 2014.[42]

The governor supported the "Women's Right to Know" Act. It required that women considering an abortion get an ultrasound and required that the abortion provider hand copies to the patient and let them hear the fetal heartbeat—"as long as it's not obtrusive." When asked whether the law goes too far, Corbett offered, "You can't make anybody watch, okay? Because you just have to close your eyes."[43]

Governor Corbett's job approval rating bottomed out at 35 percent in 2014—and he was not returned to office by the voters.[44]

North Carolina

The Republicans swept the North Carolina legislative elections in 2010. When Republican governor Pat McCrory was elected in 2012, he quickly forgot his moderate style as mayor of Charlotte, and state Republicans aggressively made up for lost time. They began by slashing education spending for local schools by $600 million and raising tuition for the state's universities and community colleges. With the exception of a small 1.2 percent raise in 2012, North Carolina teachers had not received pay raises in six years. On top of that, the legislature passed a 2013 law that phased out teacher tenure, a change a judge would later overturn. Republicans persisted, however. They offered to raise pay and restore some jobs if the teachers would forgo tenure.[45]

They moved to reduce the participation of minority and younger voters by requiring a government-issued photo ID at the polls, ending same-day voter registration, reducing early voting by one week, and requiring university students to vote where they registered their car. The governor also signed the repeal of the Racial Justice Act, which had allowed convicted murderers to appeal their convictions based on evidence of racial bias in their sentencing.

Like Pennsylvania, North Carolina passed a law requiring that women seeking an abortion have an ultrasound and hear a provider's description of the image, that abortion clinics qualify as surgical centers, and that the doctors there obtain admitting privileges at nearby hospitals. A federal judge ruled the ultrasound provision an unconstitutional violation of free speech in early 2014. North Carolina Republicans were much more concerned about protecting rights guaranteed under the Second Amendment. The legislature expanded the rights of gun owners so they are allowed to carry concealed weapons in bars, restaurants, and parks.

That all pales in comparison to what the Republicans did on taxes and to the unemployed and the poor. The North Carolina model is truly the model for the other GOP-controlled states. North Carolina immediately cut the maximum weekly unemployment benefit from $535 to $356 and reduced the maximum period of benefits to nineteen weeks—one of the six states that provide fewer than twenty-six weeks of benefits and the second shortest period in the country.

North Carolina Republicans reduced the corporate tax rate and replaced the progressive income tax with a flat 5.8 percent income tax rate that cut taxes dramatically for the top fifth of income earners. At the same time, they abolished the state earned income tax credit for 900,000 low- and moderate-wage workers. Conservatives faced no ideological backlash when they raised taxes for the poor and those with a low income. Without embarrassment, the conservative state model cut taxes and regulations for the rich and corporations while cutting benefits for the poor, for those with a low income, and for racial minorities.[46]

These initiatives formed North Carolina's response to the national debate over how to produce a faster economic recovery, raise stagnant incomes, and reduce inequality. Governor McCrory confidently touted the "Great Carolina Comeback" as evidence that his economic experiment was a success and a viable model for the country. But voters did not get the memo: only 37 percent thought the state was headed in the right direction in mid-2014 and the governor's approval rating stood at only 39 percent. The leader of the State Senate, Thom Tillis, defeated the incumbent Democratic senator, Kay Hagan, by only 2 points, even as Republican congressional candidates in North Carolina won by 11 points.[47]

Louisiana

Genuine in his embrace of an exceptional individualism and the market and his contempt for government and government spending, Governor Bobby Jindal proposed abolishing the income tax and cutting taxes on business and the energy companies. He proposed radical changes in how to fund education. In fact, he said the amount of education spending is unimportant. He proposed instead that every state education dollar follow the student. It did not matter whether he or she went to a traditional public or charter school, joined an online program, or went to a private, parochial, Christian, independent, or home school. The "public" option was barely mentioned, and Jindal was hardly disappointed when he closed the last four public schools in New Orleans. He was disappointed, however, when a state judge found the voucher at the center of his individualized education policy unconstitutional, and the public turned against it as well.[48]

The public and civic reactions were not pretty. When the plan was strongly opposed by business groups, the tourist industry, religious groups, and the voters, Jindal was also forced to abandon his plan and to propose a higher sales tax. When withdrawing the legislation, the governor observed, "It certainly wasn't the reaction I was hoping for."[49]

Governor Jindal's approval rating stood at only 32 percent during this troubled period in 2014 and, interestingly, his disapproval rating of 53 percent was as low as President Obama's in Louisiana at the time.[50]

When the budget shortfall produced by Jindal's policies produced a projected $1.6 deficit for 2016, the governor proposed a 40 percent cut in funding for the state universities to the horrified reaction of nearly everyone. Undeterred, he insisted on his red vision: "We made the intentional policy decision we think it'd be better to shrink government and cut taxes."[51]

The Republican-controlled states are a vital conservative laboratory for policies Republicans would implement in the face of our nation's challenges. Clearly, the public is looking for something very different, even in these very conservative states.

EDUCATION

The evidence is conclusive. Completing a four-year college degree has an immense positive impact on the prospect of remaining employed, wages and benefits, lifetime earnings, and much more. Consider hourly wages, the most basic material measure. In 2013, a graduate with a four-year college degree made 98 percent more an hour than someone without a degree—and the gap in favor of more education has been growing. The gap was 89 percent five years ago, 85 percent ten years earlier, and 64 percent at the outset of the 1980s, when the median income began to stagnate. In short, four-year-college graduates now earn twice as much as those without a degree, and that advantage is certain to grow.[52]

Rising value of a college degree

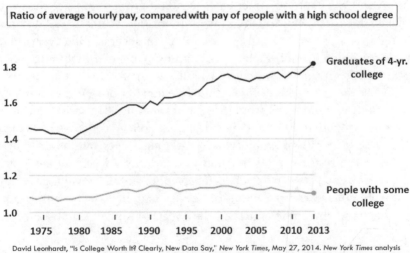

Ratio of average hourly pay, compared with pay of people with a high school degree

David Leonhardt, "Is College Worth It? Clearly, New Data Say," *New York Times*, May 27, 2014. *New York Times* analysis of Economic Policy Institute data. Labels reflect group's highest level of education. "Graduates of 4-year college," for instance, exclude people with graduate degrees.

We know that education has continual material consequences. In June 2014, the United States reached a milestone when the country finally returned to the employment level it had before the financial crisis and the Great

Recession. The unemployment rate fell that month to 3.2 percent among graduates with at least a four-year college degree and to 5.5 percent among those with some college education; by contrast, in that same month, it moved up to 6.5 percent for high school graduates and to 9.1 percent for those who never graduated from high school.[53]

Getting a four-year degree profoundly improves prospects for social mobility. If you are a child born to a household in the lowest quintile of income earners, completing four years of college gives you a 26 percent chance of ultimately ending up in the top 40 percent of income earners and a 54 percent chance of making it into the middle quintile. But if you do not complete a four-year degree, you have a 50 percent chance of never getting out of the bottom quintile. Breaking out requires a four-year degree, nothing less.[54]

Among blacks, unemployment remains higher than for whites at every level of education—and that remains part of the unfinished business of the country. Yet the unemployment rate for blacks with a four-year degree or more is only 5.7 percent—about half that for blacks with some college or a high school degree and a fourth of the unemployment rate for those who did not finish high school. A four-year college education just matters.[55]

So if we are to begin to address any of the great challenges and opportunities before America, we must dramatically improve our approach to education—expand early education, enhance student learning, allocate more resources and talent to poorer communities, broaden college preparation, and make education affordable.

As we saw in chapter 6, America's ascendant groups embrace the value of a college education. Majorities of racial minorities, women, and city dwellers agree that a bachelor's degree is essential for success. Like everyone else, they worry about the obstacles to obtaining a degree, including whether they can afford it, but they believe it will pay off for them personally and will improve the economy because it raises the number of well-trained workers.

Republicans stand apart from the rest of the American scene on this issue and are most likely to believe that a four-year college degree is *not* essential to economic security and mobility: a remarkable 55 percent majority believe it is not necessary for success in America, and only 40 percent say that it is necessary. The gap between Republican perceptions of the advantages of graduating from college and the economic reality may be as wide as the gap between them and climate scientists on the effects of human activity on climate change.[56]

The Republican Party is a low-tax party that believes cutting taxes is the principal route to a strong economy, economic opportunity, and mobility. That is reflected almost literally in the Next America Poll reported by Ron Brownstein in the *National Journal*. He asked people which policies will do more "to improve the economy in your community"—"spending more money on education, including K through 12 schools and public colleges and universities" or "cutting taxes for individuals and businesses." Republicans back cutting taxes by a landslide margin, 55 to 38 percent, with very similar results in the rural areas and among white working-class men.[57]

They are very isolated. Three-quarters of Democrats and half of independents choose education spending over tax cuts. So do landslide majorities in the urban and suburban areas, two-thirds of racial minorities, and 60 percent of women and young people. The Republican embrace of tax cuts over all else is tone-deaf.

The Republican posture, however, is all too real. Republican governors of the GOP-controlled states competed with each other to reduce education spending. Between 2008 and 2014, fourteen states cut per-pupil spending on education by more than 10 percent. All but one of those was controlled by Republicans. California cut education by so much because Republicans in the legislature blocked all tax increases, including those meant to fund education. Governor Jindal sought to cut state funding for the state's universities by 40 percent and Scott Walker sought to cut it by 13 percent—a full $300 million over two years. Hardly in awe or respectful of the state's elite research university, the governor pushed for the college system to better "meet the state's work-force needs." He was in a race with other GOP heartland governors, Fareed Zakaria writes, who had more disdain for a "liberal education."[58]

If you want to know whether Republicans bring the same approach to the budget and economy nationally, look at the latest Paul Ryan budget for 2015, "The Path to Prosperity." It represents what Republicans would do if they could: cut $5.7 trillion in taxes for the wealthy and corporations and balance the budget over the next ten years. It raised no new taxes and closed no tax loopholes. It cut spending by $5.1 trillion, guided by Republican priorities. It slashed discretionary domestic spending by 24 percent over the coming decade, though it centered its cuts on investments in education, training, infrastructure, and science and technology research—the keys to sustained growth and global competitiveness. They took their biggest budget ax to education and training programs, which were cut by 47 percent. And while college costs were skyrocketing, the Ryan budget eliminated the mandatory funding for Pell grants and froze the maximum award for the next decade.[59]

All but twelve Republicans in the House voted for these priorities when they passed the Ryan budget in the spring of 2014. And incidentally, the twelve dissenting Republicans thought the Ryan budget was too timid in cutting federal spending.

CLIMATE CHANGE

"Climate change is already affecting the American people in far-reaching ways," the 2014 National Climate Assessment concluded. It describes "extreme weather events with links to climate change" such as "prolonged periods of heat, heavy downpours, and, in some regions, floods and droughts," which "have become more frequent and/or intense." Sea levels are rising, oceans are becoming more acidic, and 2012 was the hottest year on record in the United States. These changes are "disrupting people's lives and damaging some sectors of our economy." Using sixteen climate models to analyze different emissions scenarios, they say the conclusion is "unambiguous": a half century of warming "has been driven primarily by human activity"—namely, "the burning of coal, oil, and gas and clearing of forests."[60]

It is fair to say that climate change has emerged as one of the principal contradictions of America's and the globe's economic progress.

What was exceptional about the report's release was the media coverage. Nearly all outlets described its conclusions about climate change's causes and effects as uncontested and not an issue to be debated and kicked about by politicians and their aligned experts.[61]

What was not exceptional was the clarity of Republican leaders' silence about or rejection of those conclusions. We now know from chapter 6 how central is the refusal to acknowledge the human role in climate change to base Republicans and that a growing majority of Republicans oppose acting to address the growing crisis, including three-quarters of Tea Party Republicans.[62]

Almost immediately after the release of the National Climate Assessment, the Republicans in the House, with just three Republican dissenters, and against the wishes of the Defense Department, barred it from using any funds to implement the recommendations of that report. And for good measure, the House Republicans also instructed the Defense Department to ignore any recommendations of the United Nations' Intergovernmental Panel on Climate Change. "This amendment," the sponsor of the amendment explained, "will ensure we maximize our military might without diverting funds for a politically motivated agenda."[63]

Of the 107 Republican candidates who ran for the U.S. Senate in 2014, only one mentioned climate change on his Web site and acknowledged that humans are to blame. The others did not mention the issue, questioned whether it is happening, or opposed addressing it. It is hard to remember that most Republicans supported the Clean Air Act and other landmark environmental laws. That included conservative U.S. Senators such as James Buckley and Alfonse D'Amato, even Mitch McConnell, though today's Senate Republicans have largely embraced the new orthodoxy.[64]

And after their victory in 2014, they used their supposed mandate to roll back and prevent further action to address climate change. A few weeks after the election, the lame-duck Congress passed an omnibus spending bill that blocked funding for the UN Green Climate Fund (in addition to eliminating a provision of the Dodd-Frank bank reform disliked by Wall Street). And a few weeks into the 114th Congress, all but two Republican senators in the new Republican-controlled Senate voted to pass a bill that would limit President Obama's ability to negotiate at the UN Climate Conference in Paris in 2015 and quash his historic agreement with China on limiting greenhouse gas emissions.[65]

The Republican Party's presidential candidates have also gotten in line. Senator Marco Rubio virtually announced his run for the presidency with an unnuanced denial of the role of human activity on global climate. He expressed contempt for the pack of scientists who are rushing the country to ill-considered government activism that would endanger the economy. "I do not believe that human activity is causing these dramatic changes to our climate the way these scientists are portraying it," the senator from Florida declared. That statement of faith got him back into the conservative mainstream after being dislodged when he voted for immigration reform in the Senate. The interviewer followed up and asked whether the report's conclusion that Florida is facing more damaging hurricanes affected his response. The reporter might also have asked whether the increased competition for water and damage to agriculture in the South led him to reconsider. No. Rubio spoke of climate change as an ahistorical given: "Climate is always evolving and natural disasters have always existed." And probably most important, government activism is ineffective and counterproductive: "I don't agree with the notion that some are putting out there, including scientists, that somehow, there are actions we can take today that would actually have an impact on what's happening in our climate"—though they "will destroy our economy."[66]

The other 2016 hopefuls joined Rubio on the issue. Jeb Bush stayed in the Republican mix by denying the scientific consensus: "It is not unanimous among scientists that it is disproportionately manmade." Scott Walker signed the "no climate tax" pledge, and Bobby Jindal declared that we "must put energy prices and energy independence ahead of zealous adherence to left-wing environmental theory." Rand Paul declined to challenge the GOP status quo on climate change, dismissing scientists as the arbiters of what is happening: he is "not sure anybody exactly knows why" the Earth is warming. Paul Ryan used his authority as chairman of the House Budget Committee to try to remove the EPA's authority to regulate CO_2 emissions and accused climate scientists of playing "statistical tricks to distort their findings and intentionally mislead the public on the issue of climate change."

Rick Santorum has posed a more fundamental challenge to the elite consensus on climate change. He believes that the scientific realm for understanding the world should not be given a higher standing than others and that science has become a new orthodoxy: "The apostles of this pseudo-religion believe that America and its people are the source of the Earth's temperature. I do not."[67]

So imagine the consternation when the Vatican released the encyclical letter of Pope Francis "On Care for Our Common Home" that chides humanity for the "harm we have inflicted" on this earth. After consulting with "scientists, philosophers, theologians and civic groups," Francis affirms the "very solid scientific consensus" on the warming of the climate—a process that was bound to win over doubting Republicans. That he placed the blame specifically on "a model of development based on the intensive use of fossil fuels" meant Republicans would find the backbone to oppose him. While Pope Francis did not mention the Koch brothers he urged action that will disrupt "the worldwide energy system" that is endangering the poor most of all.

Jeb Bush responded quickly, embracing Catholic candidate John F. Kennedy's formulation of the separation of church and state when Kennedy said famously he believed in an America "where no public official either requests or accepts instructions on public policy from the pope, the National Council of Churches or any other ecclesiastical source." Bush declared in a like vein, "I don't get economic policy from my bishops or my cardinals or my pope," though the governor, who kept Terry Schiavo on life support, was not asked any follow-up questions. The devout Catholic Rick Santorum just attacked the pope: "The church has gotten it wrong a few times on science," and "when we get involved with political and controversial scientific theories, then I think the church is probably not as forceful and credible."

Each candidate in his own way showed he knows today's Republican base electorate. In the two critical early caucus and primary states of Iowa and South Carolina, voters said the position they found most unacceptable from a presidential candidate was the belief that "climate change is man-made and action should be taken to combat it."[68]

In some GOP-controlled states, a number of Republican elected leaders are challenging the new Common Core curriculum because it accepts the reality of evolution and the Earth's warming, and now the Next Generation Science Standards are coming under fire for teaching that human activity has contributed to climate change. The standards "handle global warming as settled science," one Wyoming state representative complained. "There's all kind of social implications involved in that, that I don't think would be good for Wyoming." And Wyoming became the first state to reject the standards over climate change, even though the state's committee of science educators had unanimously endorsed them. The legislature barred any spending to implement the standards, and the State Board of Education ordered the state committee of science educators to come up with new standards.[69]

In Oklahoma, the legislature successfully repealed the Next Generation Science Standards because, as one state senator explained, they "heavily promote global warming alarmism and do not prepare students for work in STEM fields." In South Carolina, educators watered down the standards for climate change and evolution, though it remains to be seen whether that will be enough for the Republican legislature and governor, who will have the final word.[70]

The dynamics of the Republican Party will not allow it to play a serious role mobilizing the country and its resources to address this growing national and global challenge.

WHITHER THE MIDDLE CLASS?

In December 2011, President Obama traveled to Osawatomie, Kansas, the same small town where Teddy Roosevelt gave his 1910 "New Nationalism" speech. Obama gave his own major speech and finally elevated the challenges of the middle class to being "the defining issue of our time."

> *This is a make-or-break moment for the middle class, and for all those who are fighting to get into the middle class. Because what's at stake is whether this will be a country where working people can earn enough to raise a family, build a modest savings, own a home, secure their retirement.*

We have to build a nation "where we're all better off" and where every citizen can believe "that hard work will pay off, that responsibility will be rewarded, and that our children will inherit a nation where those values live on."[71]

The conservative intellectuals' reaction looked very much like their more recent response to Thomas Piketty's book on inequality, which I will discuss later in this chapter. They knew that if the public agenda centers on the state of the middle class and inequality, the voters will not be listening to the Republican Party.

First, they rushed to attack the president for waging "class warfare." They accused him of "scare-mongering targeted at the middle class" and trumpeting "the overstated problems of the middle class." They alleged this class warfare will have the "shameful effect of unnecessarily raising Americans' economic anxiety levels," and further, they point out, with crocodile tears, that this ferment will delay "a full recovery."[72]

The conservative analysts engage in asymmetric warfare to undermine the legitimacy of this concern for the middle class. They recalculate the components of middle-class income to include social insurance or tax credits to show that things are better than you think. That is just a bait and switch, of course, because they then propose to eliminate those very programs that they think increase dependence among the poor. At the end of the day, the conservatives say America has no idea which policies could raise middle incomes, though it is all too clear which would be effective.

Conservative writers showed breathless excitement about the study authored by Richard V. Burkhauser, Jeff Larrimore, and Kosali I. Simon for the National Bureau of Economic Research titled "A 'Second Opinion' on the

Economic Health of the American Middle Class." Their research inspired *The Washington Post* editorial page to run an op-ed piece by Ron Haskins under the headline "THE MYTH OF THE DISAPPEARING MIDDLE CLASS." Scott Winship wrote a piece in *The New Republic* headlined to get a response: "STOP FEELING SORRY FOR THE MIDDLE CLASS! THEY'RE DOING JUST FINE." *Fox News* headlined their online contribution, "SORRY, MR. BIDEN MOST MIDDLE CLASS AMERICANS ARE BETTER OFF NOW THAN THEY WERE THIRTY YEARS AGO."[73]

Their key starting point is refuting the assertion of "middle-class decline," "the vanishing middle class," and the conclusion that "things have gotten worse for middle-income Americans." They have focused like a laser on President Obama's observation in Kansas that "over the last few decades, the rungs of the ladder of opportunity have grown further apart, and the middle class has shrunk" and Council of Economic Advisers chairman Alan Krueger's indisputable observation that there are fewer people clustered around the median income and more at the top and the bottom.[74]

That is beside the point. Burkhauser and his collaborators spend a lot of time factoring in changes in household size, posttax income, transfers such as tax credits and food stamps, and health insurance. They believe that those in the middle of the income scale saw their income rise 37 percent over these three decades. That is about 1.1 percent a year and very close to the consensus calculations of the Economic Policy Institute, the Center for American Progress, the Council of Economic Advisers, and economists from the major banks.

They fail to note what a change this represents from the post–World War II period that shaped the baby boomers and others. And disingenuously, they fail to note the contrast in fortunes with the top 1 percent. That line does not appear anywhere.

Perhaps most egregious is their lack of curiosity about what periods produced this 37 percent gain for the middle class over three decades. Well, it turns out that half the income growth came in the period dominated by Bill Clinton's economic and tax policies. During the Clinton period, it grew by 16.8 percent, double the average for the Republican presidents (8.3 percent). I wonder why that was not mentioned?[75]

Moreover, after all of their calculations to factor in tax credits and food stamps, it is only during the Clinton period that the Gini coefficient—the standard measure of inequality—improved. The top five percent did okay, their income going up 15.1 percent, though that was a touch *less* than for the middle quintile, which gained 16.8 percent. The Reagan period brought a dramatic worsening of these numbers for the middle, second, and bottom quintile, and the George W. Bush years were just terrible for everybody.[76]

Had they paid attention to the political periodization, they might have at least speculated as to what policies made such a difference in mitigating or entrenching the problem. Instead, they present these political periods as "business cycles," without any evident curiosity about the correlation.

The research did not display data or talk about the top 1 percent. Those heralded top earners do not even get a line in Burkhauser's graphs. In a *Washington Post* op-ed, Ron Haskins lists the Democrats' charges, including that the country is "wracked by inequality," and miserably fails to explain it away. That "is partly true," he says, "mostly because those at the top of the income distribution have pulled away from the rest of us." Well, other than that, Mrs. Lincoln, how was the play?[77]

Not having the line for the 1 percent or having examined the political periodization and its implications for policy, senior Atlantic Council fellow Douglas Besharov told a sympathetic interviewer, "No one has the slightest idea what will work. The cupboard is bare."[78]

But the cupboard is hardly bare. The conservative public intellectuals and op-ed writers themselves are enthralled with the Burkhauser recalculations precisely because they take into account the following items: the earned income tax credit; the value of all "public transfers," including food stamps, welfare, Pell grants, Social Security, and other government-provided cash assistance; and Medicare and Medicaid. Their higher bars that are meant to show how well off is the middle class are really bars showing how government activism can raise incomes and raise people out of poverty.

Ron Haskins marvels in *The Washington Post*, "the bottom 20 percent had about 25 percent more income in 2007 than in 1979. Even the bottom is moving up." Yes, they moved up, though they moved up only under the policies advanced under President Clinton. The income of the bottom quintile rose 23.2 percent during the Clinton-dominated economic period, while growth for these earners was only 0.4 percent under Reagan and 2.2 percent under Bush.[79]

Did the conservative economists notice that the Ryan budget decimates food stamps, seeks to eliminate or limit refundable tax credits, caps Pell grants, tries to repeal the Medicaid expansion under the Affordable Care Act, and aims to privatize Social Security and turn Medicare into a voucher? Did they notice that the leading Republican governors are competing to abolish the state versions of the EITC, slashing food stamps, refusing to expand Medicaid, cutting unemployment benefits, and shifting the cost of higher education onto students? Did they notice while they were cutting taxes for the wealthiest that they raised the tax burden on the poor and the middle class? Of course they noticed, as they are fully paid members of the conservative policy discussion. The truth is they think the decline of the family and the growth of dependence are the real problems facing the country, not the decline of the middle class. Food stamps and tax credits might well "lift the poor out of destitution," but they simultaneously "discourage the upward mobility of poor

The income effects of tax credits, food stamps, grants and other government programs

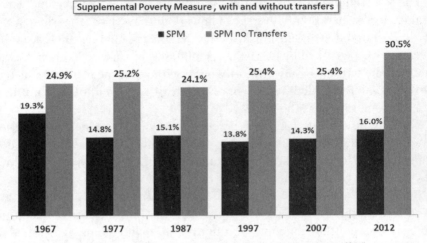

Supplemental Poverty Measure, with and without transfers

■ SPM   ■ SPM no Transfers

*The SPM takes into consideration tax payments, work benefits, and in-kind benefits in its estimates of family resources

Liana Fox, Irwin Garfinkel, Neeraj Kaushal, Jane Waldfogel, Christopher Wimer, "Waging War on Poverty: Historical Trends in Poverty Using the Supplemental Poverty Measure," National Bureau of Economic Research, Working Paper 19789, January 2014.

children." Social insurance programs such as unemployment benefits, food stamps, and refundable tax credits are inadequate incentives, if not disincentives, to "work, marriage, and saving." That does not concern the "left," these conservatives write, which "does not want to confront the important issues of family instability, criminality, and personal responsibility in limiting life chances."[80]

The Republican agenda to address poverty begins with getting the country back to a discussion about values. "There are the deserving poor and the undeserving poor," according to Bob Woodson, president of the Center for Neighborhood Enterprise and adviser to Paul Ryan on poverty. He laments that it "became politically incorrect" to make that distinction, and praises conservatives who are now "returning to some of the old values that served people very effectively until the welfare reforms of the 1960s."[81]

And their poverty agenda goes back to a discussion of big government creating dependence and undermining values. Liberals have grown "the welfare state" and "entitlement state," and those produced their own revolutionary changes, Nicholas Eberstadt writes in *National Affairs*. The great American experiment has been corrupted by an "entitlements machine" that has "recast the American family budget over the course of just two generations." By 2012, over one-third of Americans were on means-tested programs, by his calculation. That is the rub. That number is double the level in 1983 and before the Affordable Care Act began enrolling the uninsured. This growing "mass dependence on entitlements" is "corrosive" because it is associated with the spread of so many pathologies. That portends badly for the country, Eberstadt concludes.[82]

In mid-2015, the graph line representing rising public support for the Affordable Care Act crossed the falling line representing the opposition to the new health care law. And then the U.S. Supreme Court in a 6 to 3 decision validated the funding mechanism and rationale for the Act, defeating the last serious challenge to Obamacare. For liberals, that reminded them of the incompleteness of the social safety net and the centrality of health care to struggling families. For conservatives, it is a confirmation of their warnings about growing dependency and what it will mean for the country's moral fabric.[83]

POVERTY AND MARRIAGE

Conservatives used the fiftieth anniversary of Lyndon Johnson's War on Poverty to take up the plight of the poor and particularly those living in the inner cities—read, the black and minority citizens at the heart of our metropolitan diversity. In the "The War on Poverty: A Progress Report" hearing of the House Budget Committee, Chairman Paul Ryan asked Eloise Anderson, secretary of the Wisconsin Department of Children and Families, how SNAP (Supplemental Nutrition Assistance Program) could be improved, and she shared a touching story: "You know, a little boy told me once that what was important to him is that he didn't want school lunch, he wanted a brown bag because the brown bag that he brought with his lunch in it meant that his mom cared about him." That someone else made up the story is less important than the fact that Ryan repeated the story as fact during a speech at CPAC or that the *National Review* and others reprinted and defended it. Indeed, Ryan's Budget Committee report on the War on Poverty concluded "perhaps the single most important determinant of poverty is family structure."[84]

America has so many children in poverty, the editors of *The National Review* argue, because parents are not meeting their responsibilities to their children. Citing genuine scholarship, they write, "Children of single-parent homes, which are overwhelmingly single-mother homes, are not only more likely to be poor but are more likely to stay poor." It is also true that children living in communities where single-parent households are prevalent are less economically mobile, even if their parents are married. The editors somehow conclude from this that programs "intended to help the poor" end up "mak[ing] the lives of the poor worse in significant ways, mainly by encouraging the long-term dependency that concerns Ryan and others."[85]

Paul Ryan described the "tailspin of culture in our inner cities" that is driving large populations, particularly black men, out of the labor force. *The National Review* defended his statement and offered the unemployment rates of whites and blacks in cities such as Milwaukee and Detroit as evidence that

Ryan was victimized for telling the truth. They elaborated further, saying that most of these young blacks "are born out of wedlock," and part of a perversely effective system "for producing poverty."

"The evidence regarding poverty, single motherhood, and economic mobility . . . is as close to 'settled science' as the social sciences have to offer," they write. They urge liberal elites to bring the same standard they bring to climate change and prioritize taking action to promote "marriage, work and stability."

Progressives need to listen because these changes to the family "have significant social costs," as Andrew Cherlin described so vividly: "Children face instability and complexity in their home lives, and adults drift away from the institutions that historically have anchored civic life." Finding ways to reverse these trends could not be more important. In chapter 12, I urge progressives to take up a reform agenda that promotes parenting, a greater role for the church, early childhood education, paid family and sick leave and child care, and higher wages.[86]

Conservatives still have trouble getting heard on their social agenda by the new America. Each prospective Republican presidential candidate for 2016 begins with the need to restore traditional marriage as the best anti-poverty program. Unfortunately, government programs to encourage and support marriages among those most likely to separate have not been successful, just as programs to promote abstinence before marriage have been ineffective.[87]

The public does believe marriage is a good thing and favors policies that encourage it, as long as they do not punish or disadvantage those who are unmarried or in nontraditional relationships, and voters oppose any "marriage penalty" in the tax system. But real unmarried people, working women, and working men are looking pretty desperately for help with child care, paid sick leave, and financial assistance so they can afford skill training and college rather than the offer of a moral ladder leading to marriage."[88]

About half the public supports prioritizing a Republican agenda that responds to the problem of marriage breakdown and unwed mothers with policies that "encourage people to marry, giving them higher tax benefits, and oppose kids being born out of wedlock." About half the public also acknowledges these problems and instead wants a government agenda that "helps them with child care, paid sick days, and paid family leave." And it is the unmarried women here who matter the most on this question. When you ask them, twice as many and with intensity say, please, we need help.[89]

That the current Republican offer falters when it gets to financial help with child care tells you a lot about today's Republican Party. The culture war leaves many conservatives cautious about seeming to reward women for working over caring for a child, a symbol of the traditional family that has been lost.

That blockage is evident in Abby McCloskey's thoughtful article on conservative policies that could raise incomes for working women and increase their labor force participation. Not surprisingly, she champions lower marginal tax rates and marriage earnings sharing. More surprisingly, she pushes for greatly increasing EITC payments and for higher benefits for single women. And finally, she recommends help with child care—a formidable cost for mothers and a blockage to rejoining the labor market. Gerald Ford signed the Child and Dependent Care Credit in 1976 and President George W. Bush expanded the credit in 2001. So McCloskey puzzles out loud and without answering her own question, "Why aren't conservatives who are interested in increasing employment taking up the cause of child-care subsidies?"[90]

Consider what happened in Britain in 2015. With two weeks before the election and the parties deadlocked in public opinion polls, *The Financial Times* reported, the Conservative Party prime minister David Cameron visited a nursery school and promised to double the hours of free child care if he got back to Downing Street. With his political life at stake, he did not hesitate to make this critical conservative offer.[91]

The central policy debate among conservatives in America, by contrast, is still rooted in the dynamics of the GOP base and a morality that still describes the children of single parents as "born out of wedlock," without quotation marks, and are shocked to hear "OUT-OF-WEDLOCK BIRTHS ARE THE NEW NORMAL." They try to spotlight and restore the old normal, highlighting the benefits of maintaining the old sequence: "finish high school, get a job, and get married before having children." Despite the unmistakable benefits, you cannot get there. The "same secularization of society that allowed stores to be open on Sunday destigmatized out-of-wedlock birth so that the mothers felt free to keep their children."[92]

Thus, conservatives have treaded carefully on government intervening to tilt the balance. They have entertained policies that tax divorce and make tax credits available only to the married. And while Ross Douthat supports these policy changes, he is skeptical that they can succeed without deeper moral pressures: "Social pressure would probably have to become more explicitly moralistic to influence the deeper trends toward non-marital childrearing."[93]

Douthat welcomed Robert Putnam's new book, *Our Kids*, because it "recognizes the social crisis among America's poor and working class" and most important, Putnam "is attuned to culture's feedback loops." At a time when the safety net was much thinner, "lower-income Americans found a way to cultivate monogamy, fidelity, sobriety and thrift to an extent that they have not in our richer, higher-spending present." Putnam and I would probably agree with Douthat that "a cultural earthquake that makes society dramatically more permissive" is a big part of the explanation. Putnam and I would also add equality for women and the collapse of the male-breadwinner traditional family as part of the explanation as well. Disingenuously though,

Douthat says he is just looking for liberal elites to recognize that "culture shapes behavior," when what he is really looking for is for them to condemn or judge the moral choices people are making. He says conceding the role of culture "doesn't require thundering denunciation of the moral choices of the poor." Instead, "our upper class should be judged first" for its "present ideal of 'safe' permissiveness" when working-class families are in so much trouble. In truth, then, Douthat's policy prescriptions cannot help but depend centrally on moral suasion grounded in a sense of lost virtue.[94]

Nearly alone among conservatives after the Supreme Court decision on gay marriage, David Brooks urged a radical, yet still pious course. "Put aside a culture war that has alienated large parts of three generations from any consideration of religion or belief. Put aside an effort that has been a communications disaster, reducing a rich, complex and beautiful faith into a public obsession with sex. Put aside a culture war that, at least over the near term, you are destined to lose." Get to work instead mending the social fabric in a country where communities and families are in flux and children in need of help. "Social conservatives could be the people who help reweave the sinews of society," he writes powerfully.

That Republicans continue to escalate the culture war is over-determined for now. The Evangelicals and Tea Party are the dominant majority politically in the Republican Party and observant Catholics are battling for their worldview against a modernist pope. And the Republican Party is hardly losing the culture war in the GOP conservative heartland, as you can see in the response of its governors and attorneys general to the Supreme Court decision. Until there is a major political disruption, conservatives will continue their role defending a lost morality.

That need to moralize and stigmatize, however, makes it very difficult for conservatives to forcefully enter the national policy debate on an issue where new thinking is clearly needed when it comes to achieving more personal responsibility and more responsible parenting and better care for children.

WHITHER *CAPITAL IN THE TWENTY-FIRST CENTURY?*

The conservative think tanks, commentators, and newspapers treated the English release of Thomas Piketty's *Capital in the Twenty-first Century* as the next fad, the next manufactured attack on the 1 percent, and the next wave of liberal "PC scientific tenets." They describe an American left that "has worked itself into another one of its frenzies about income inequality." The reaction might not have reached the level of "Beatlemania," blogged Scott Winship of the Manhattan Institute and public adviser to Paul Ryan on economic mobility and inequality. But Piketty "has inspired the Washington analog of teenage frenzy," he wrote, and added with irony that D.C. is home to 28 percent of the nation's top 1 percent. The reaction to Piketty was like "I

Want to Hold Your Hand" among "a certain crowd that is convinced that inequality is a dire economic problem."[95]

Rush Limbaugh, not surprisingly, was a touch more direct: "Some French socialist, Marxist, communist economist has published a book, and the left in this country is having an orgasm over it." "He's a wuss" who has arrived to support President Obama's push against inequality, "as if there's some moral sin in income inequality," "in capitalism, and therefore there is a moral sin in the United States of America." You knew this "inequality" gig would end with Barack Obama showing his contempt for the U.S.A.

"To the extent that there is any concentration of wealth taking place in this country," it is not by capitalism but by government! Why are the richest counties in the nation in the suburbs of Washington, D.C., as Limbaugh points out? It's because "wealth is being concentrated in the hands of people who are in or associated with government." Conservatives' preference is to see this inequality thing as a pet project of the rich liberal elites, such as George Soros, Tom Steyer, and Jeffrey Katzenberg, who are well represented among lists of America's richest and biggest givers to the Democrats.[96]

The conservatives view this as a fad because they do not view inequality as problematic and certainly view other issues as much more serious. For example, when an interviewer for *Business Insider* asked Winship about the gap between the top 1 percent and everyone else, he said it might be growing, though quickly added, "Whether I think that's a problem, I'm not at all sure." He does not grant the knock-on effects of a growing gap: "I don't think that the evidence that rising inequality has produced societal problems is very compelling."[97]

Conservatives were quick to attack Piketty for not including tax benefits, social insurance, and income transfers that improve the position of the middle class—the very programs they choose to cut because of their perverse incentives to idleness and dependence. They were most shocked that Piketty ignores the "huge Obamacare subsidies" that Republicans are intent on repealing if they get the chance. Jared Bernstein calls this "the transfer defense." He finds that Piketty's argument still holds up after you consider taxes and transfers. As it turns out, conservatives unwittingly are making the case for the effectiveness of government: almost all middle-class income growth came over many decades from government transfers and tax policies.[98]

Then conservatives got into Piketty's data and relished arguing that the top 1 percent took a bit of a hit during the economic crisis and that the rich and the poor rise and fall together. One piece in *The National Review* highlighted the fact that the top 1 percent saw their income fall 16.3 percent in the financial fallout from 2007 to 2012. They reference a study from the Cato Institute that urges readers not to be distracted by the abrupt changes because the "rich and poor rise together." We should take comfort in the fact that "when the top 1 percent's share rises, the poverty rate falls."[99]

Chris Giles, the economics editor of *The Financial Times,* challenged some of Piketty's data choices and showed how some of those choices produce very different results, particularly for Britain. Piketty defended his conclusions, citing newer data not available in the book. *The Economist* called the match for Piketty, concluding, "Nor have [Piketty's] findings that wealth concentration is, once again, rising been fatally undermined" by Giles's analysis.[100]

Above all, conservatives seek to delegitimize inequality as the central point for social critique and policy-making. "The most important problem with talking about income inequality is it focuses on relative income to the exclusion of absolute income," writes one conservative columnist at *Forbes,* who then asks, "[Is] it better to live in a country with some income inequality, where those with low incomes have adequate food, shelter, and opportunity?"[101]

It is pretty clear that Republicans will not be working through policies to address the growing inequality in the country, leading even David Brooks to acknowledge, "This is a moment when progressives have found their worldview and their agenda." He challenges conservatives to get into the national debate by at least acknowledging the problem and raising the inheritance tax, then offering an agenda that gets serious about improving human capital while addressing the "fraying social fabric" that contributes so critically to "low economic mobility."[102]

James Pethokoukis of AEI and *The National Review* goes much farther into the intellectual consequences of the book. He believes Piketty makes a powerful case that "private capital accumulation inevitably leads to the concentration of wealth into ever-fewer hands," and "now Marxism's fundamental truth is reasserting itself with a vengeance, a reality borne out in both Piketty's own meticulously gathered data and in business pages replete with stories of skyrocketing wealth for the 0.001 percent and decades of flat wages for everyone else." The triumph of the left's public intellectuals will drive "the economic agenda pushed by Washington Democrats and promoted by the mainstream media."

John Maynard Keynes and Friedrich Hayek joined the debate in the 1930s, although Hayek retreated when Keynes published *The General Theory of Employment, Interest and Money.* The debate was only carried on by Milton Friedman and Anna Schwartz in the 1960s. Fearing statists have won the moment, Pethokoukis asks, "who will make the intellectual case for economic freedom today?"[103]

The conservative *New York Times* columnist Ross Douthat concedes that if the growing inequality remains unaddressed, it could prove politically disruptive, as Piketty writes about. Douthat, however, does not think America will fall into a new period of class turmoil, as during the Gilded Age, because of "the power that even a weakened 99 percent (or 90 percent, or for that matter 47 percent) can exercise through the ballot box." America will be spared such a crisis because the public will rally to reform. The center-left is "more powerful and better-positioned" than the "radical left" to lead and to implement the "corporatist tax-and-transfer policies" that will be needed. They will "tax *enough,* redistribute *enough,* to maintain the richest nations' social peace, and avoid violent labor-capital conflict by making even the relatively poor feel like they have too much to lose from such upheaval."

Douthat believes America will be okay because the Democrats are winning national elections, not the Republicans, reminding conservatives that Paul Ryan and his conservative approach were "on the ticket that *lost* the last presidential election." The ball is in the Democrats' court, and Douthat hopes they will get on with the job of mitigating the economic inequality problem.[104]

And if they make progress perhaps that will also allow the country to turn to another "inequality-related crisis"—"one that's more about social and cultural and moral capital." Douthat is right that the country needs radical critiques and solutions here, too, though conservatives are still blocked by their battle against the sexual revolution from leading in bringing these reforms.

It will obviously fall to the Democrats for now to tackle America's greatest challenges and to find ways to engage the country in the mission.

10 FROM REAGAN DEMOCRATS TO THE NEW AMERICA

The American people want a politics that is relevant to their lives, that acknowledges their struggle for something better, and that produces a government that will help and mitigate some of their privations. Unlike the politicians who have tiptoed into this new century, the public is ready to rally for bold reforms and join a building wave that can transform this era.

You can see this readiness in Democracy Corps' major national survey conducted at the outset of the 2016 presidential cycle. A large majority of the country embraces a bold reform narrative that demands leaders confront the special interests' hold on government and puts the problems of the middle class center stage. People get excited by leaders who understand their lives. The new American majority is hungry for leaders who know how hard it is for people to piece together multiple jobs to make ends meet—and so is calling for drastic improvements in wages and employment rights. Voters want leaders who appreciate the horrific cost of college and will make college more affordable, and they want leaders who understand how bewildering and difficult it is to balance work and have a family, and will therefore offer adequate social supports. They are ready to see deep investments to rebuild American infrastructure and modernize the country—if it is serious in scale, long-term, and independent of a Congress dominated by special interests and self-seeking politicians. And they understand that this is one way that government can produce good-paying jobs.

And the American people are ready to tax the richest and disrupt their special deal with government. They bring to this period a special disdain for the overpaid CEOs and the crony capitalism that makes government work for big business and special interests. The rich paying their fair share in taxes is nearly a first principle of economic reform and getting to a good society.

They are ready for government to help—if the stables can be cleansed. They know government today is bought and sold to the biggest donors and that it wastes hundreds of billions of dollars at the behest of special-interest lobbyists. The American public is excited when leaders begin with reforms that restore democracy and get government to work for the middle class again.

So the public really is ready for an era of government activism beginning with reform. The Republicans are so consumed with fighting off their own demons that they are barely relevant for America's growing majority. But are the Democrats ready to lead?

A NARRATIVE FOR THESE TIMES

The new American majority at the heart of the ascendant trends, swaths of working people, and the broader American public are waiting for leaders who understand the principles of the new economy. Democratic leaders will win their strong support, this section shows, when they commit first to take their broom to the corruption and special-interest waste in government. Support will be stronger still when the narrative and agenda they advance asks the CEOs of big businesses and the top 1 percent to pay their fair share of taxes so government can work for the middle class. And finally, the narrative gains special standing when it includes an economic agenda for working women and working men, replete with bold reforms that finally address the unaddressed economic challenges facing people and the country.

At the outset of the 2016 presidential election cycle, I tested such a middle-class economic narrative. The narrative begins with the recognition that people are drowning, jobs don't pay enough, and people are struggling to pay the bills despite all their hard work. At the heart of the narrative is an intention to use government to help. That includes help with making college and child care affordable and ensuring equal pay for working women. It also includes tax credits for low-wage workers and the middle class and a promise to protect Medicare and Social Security. It ends with a call for an economy that works for working people and the middle class again.

When we tested the narrative in January 2015 in a poll conducted for Democracy Corps and Women's Voices Women Vote Action Fund, more than 70 percent of presidential-year voters said they found it convincing, and almost 40 percent responded with intense support. More important in the context of the national elections, that narrative tested about 20 points more convincing than a conservative economic narrative that faulted Democrats for leaving so many people struggling and offered a small-government route to growth as well as a conservative narrative that pushed back against government overreach.[1]

The Democratic economic narrative speaks to the new American majority, what we have called the rising American electorate. Fully 78 percent of the growing coalition of young people, unmarried women, and minorities said the narrative was convincing, dramatically higher than the share of the vote they gave Democrats in the best years. Unmarried women were moved in particular. A stunning eight in ten found it convincing, and nearly half chose "very convincing." The narrative got its strongest generational support from the Millennials, but it was nearly matched by the enthusiasm of the baby boomers.

Public embraces bold Democratic economic narrative; not the Republican one

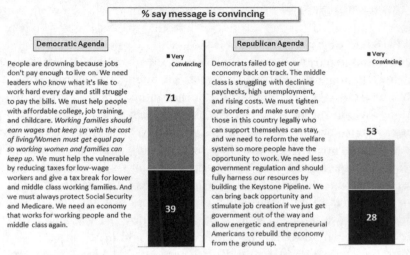

| % say message is convincing |

Democratic Agenda

■ Very Convincing

People are drowning because jobs don't pay enough to live on. We need leaders who know what it's like to work hard every day and still struggle to pay the bills. We must help people with affordable college, job training, and childcare. *Working families should earn wages that keep up with the cost of living/Women must get equal pay so working women and families can keep up.* We must help the vulnerable by reducing taxes for low-wage workers and give a tax break for lower and middle class working families. And we must always protect Social Security and Medicare. We need an economy that works for working people and the middle class again.

71

39

Republican Agenda

■ Very Convincing

Democrats failed to get our economy back on track. The middle class is struggling with declining paychecks, high unemployment, and rising costs. We must tighten our borders and make sure only those in this country legally who can support themselves can stay, and we need to reform the welfare system so more people have the opportunity to work. We need less government regulation and should fully harness our resources by building the Keystone Pipeline. We can bring back opportunity and stimulate job creation if we just get government out of the way and allow energetic and entrepreneurial Americans to rebuild the economy from the ground up.

53

28

*Half of the sample heard the Democratic agenda with "working families," half with "working women and families." The combined result is shown.

National survey of 950 likely 2016 voters conducted for Democracy Corps and Women's Voice Women Vote Action Fund and The Voter Participation Center, January 7–11, 2015.

The middle-class economic narrative also got the attention of white working-class voters. They have not been great fans of government activism in recent decades, and they have only been giving Democrats about a third of their votes. Yet an impressive 71 percent of white non-college-educated women embrace this narrative, 41 percent strongly. Moreover, the white working-class women find the Democrats' middle-class economic narrative slightly more convincing than the Republicans' conservative, small-government economic narrative.

While white working-class men respond less intensely to middle-class economics, 62 percent still find the middle-class economic narrative convincing—and that is only 5 points below their support for the competing, small-government conservative economic narrative.

Independents gave a slight edge (60 to 55 percent) to the Democrats' middle-class economic narrative that has government activism on behalf of the working and middle classes at its core.

What really empowers the Democratic economic narrative, however, is a commitment to reforming politics and government. That may seem ironic or contradictory, since the narrative is calling for a period of government activism. But of course it makes sense. Why would you expect today's government to act on behalf of the ordinary citizen? And why would you expect people who are financially on the edge, their wages flat or falling, and paying a fair amount of taxes and fees, to not be upset about tax money being wasted or channeled to special interests?

During the 2014 election cycle, we watched concern about big money in politics grow. Democracy Corps tested a middle-class narrative that explicitly called out leaders who listen more to "the richest who show up with big money" and called for an "economy here that works for working people and the middle class again, not just those with the big money." The middle-class economic narrative got more voter support when it included that critique of big money.[2]

We have arrived at a tipping point at the outset of the 2016 election cycle, however, where the demand to reform government is equal to or stronger than the demand to reform the economy. More accurately, reform makes it possible to use government to help the middle class. Reform must come first.

In a straight test, the presidential electorate is as enthusiastic about a reform narrative as the Democrats' middle-class economic one.

Reform and economic messages are equally successful

% say message is convincing

Democratic Agenda — ■ Very Convincing

People are drowning because jobs don't pay enough to live on. We need leaders who know what it's like to work hard every day and still struggle to pay the bills. We must help people with affordable college, job training, and childcare. *Working families should earn wages that keep up with the cost of living/Women must get equal pay so working women and families can keep up.* We must help the vulnerable by reducing taxes for low-wage workers and give a tax break for lower and middle class working families. And we must always protect Social Security and Medicare. We need an economy that works for working people and the middle class again.

71

39

Democratic Reform Agenda — ■ Very Convincing

There is too much money in politics and government. Big corporations and lobby groups spend millions getting their candidates elected, and then get tax breaks and special laws that protect their special interests. Billions are spent on government programs that are often outdated or don't even work--but special interests and government bureaucracy protect them. We need leaders who will clean up Washington by restricting the campaign dollars that come in, changing programs that don't work and using that money to help middle class working families--not big campaign donors.

72

40

**Half of the sample heard the Democratic agenda with "working families," half with "working women and families." The combined result is shown.

National survey of 950 likely 2016 voters conducted for Democracy Corps and Women's Voice Women Vote Action Fund and The Voter Participation Center, January 7-11, 2015.

The first part of the reform narrative focuses on big business and big interests that give big money to politicians and use lobbyists to win special laws and tax breaks that cost the country billions. The second part emphasizes how special interests and bureaucracy protect out-of-date programs that don't work. The bottom line of the narrative is that reform frees up money so government can work for middle-class and working families, not the big donors.

Most important, when voters hear the reform narrative first, they are dramatically more open to the middle-class economic narrative that calls for government activism in response to America's problems.

When voters hear reform message first, voters are dramatically more supportive of economic message

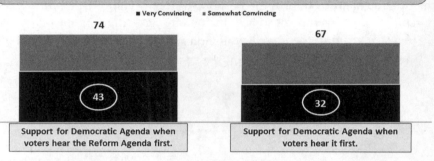

Reform Agenda: There is too much money in politics and government. Big corporations and lobby groups spend millions getting their candidates elected, and then get tax breaks and special laws that protect their special interests. Billions are spent on government programs that are often out dated or don't even work—but special interests and government bureaucracy protect them. We need leaders who will clean up Washington by restricting the campaign dollars that come in, changing programs that don't work and using that money to help middle class working families—not big campaign donors.

Democratic Agenda: People are drowning because jobs don't pay enough to live on. We need leaders who know what it's like to work hard every day and still struggle to pay the bills. We must help people with affordable college, job training, and childcare. (Working families should earn wages that keep up with the cost of living/Women must get equal pay so working women and families can keep up.) We must help the vulnerable by reducing taxes for low-wage workers and give a tax break for lower and middle class working families. And we must always protect Social Security and Medicare. We need an economy that works for working people and the middle class again.

■ Very Convincing   ■ Somewhat Convincing

74

67

43

32

Support for Democratic Agenda when voters hear the Reform Agenda first.

Support for Democratic Agenda when voters hear it first.

National survey of 950 likely 2016 voters conducted for Democracy Corps and Women's Voice Women Vote Action Fund and The Voter Participation Center, January 7-11, 2015.

Among voters who heard the reform message first, 43 percent described the middle-class economic narrative as very convincing—11 points higher than when they heard the economy message first. Among white working-class voters in particular, the order effect produced a 13-point jump in intensity for the Democrats' middle-class economic message (from 27 to 40 percent).

ECONOMIC REFORM AGENDA FOR WORKING WOMEN AND WORKING MEN

A large majority in the country supports big changes in economic and social policy to address the building challenges facing the country, people, and families. Support is particularly strong with the rising American electorate and unmarried women who face these problems most acutely, though support is high and intense with independents and the white working class, too. The country really is ready for a bold reform agenda.

The economic reform agenda is gaining support because of the public's deep understanding of the new economy, their changing families and communities, and their astute perception of who government really works for. These policies are becoming more and more politically relevant and are increasingly on the public agenda because voters are insistent that America's disruptive changes be met by disruptive new policies.

At the top of the agenda are protecting Medicare and Social Security, the existing social safety net that so many people depend on. Voters know it is at risk and being frayed, and protecting it from elite meddling is front and center. There is also support now for a whole new regime for protecting and helping working families and working mothers. With women fully in the labor force though earning less for many reasons, equal pay matters. So does help making college affordable—the key block to upward mobility in their view. The public is ready for a long-term government plan to modernize America by investing in infrastructure, building schools, and broadband to create good jobs. And finally, the voters put reform of government itself at the very top. That includes limiting the role of money, though equally, making sure government is spending in the interests of the people.

Bold progressive agenda gets strong support

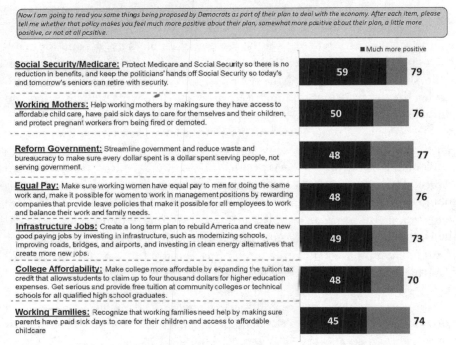

Now I am going to read you some things being proposed by Democrats as part of their plan to deal with the economy. After each item, please tell me whether that policy makes you feel much more positive about their plan, somewhat more positive about their plan, a little more positive, or not at all positive.

■ Much more positive

Social Security/Medicare: Protect Medicare and Social Security so there is no reduction in benefits, and keep the politicians' hands off Social Security so today's and tomorrow's seniors can retire with security. — 59 / 79

Working Mothers: Help working mothers by making sure they have access to affordable child care, have paid sick days to care for themselves and their children, and protect pregnant workers from being fired or demoted. — 50 / 76

Reform Government: Streamline government and reduce waste and bureaucracy to make sure every dollar spent is a dollar spent serving people, not serving government. — 48 / 77

Equal Pay: Make sure working women have equal pay to men for doing the same work and, make it possible for women to work in management positions by rewarding companies that provide leave policies that make it possible for all employees to work and balance their work and family needs. — 48 / 76

Infrastructure Jobs: Create a long term plan to rebuild America and create new good paying jobs by investing in infrastructure, such as modernizing schools, improving roads, bridges, and airports, and investing in clean energy alternatives that create more new jobs. — 49 / 73

College Affordability: Make college more affordable by expanding the tuition tax credit that allows students to claim up to four thousand dollars for higher education expenses. Get serious and provide free tuition at community colleges or technical schools for all qualified high school graduates. — 48 / 70

Working Families: Recognize that working families need help by making sure parents have paid sick days to care for their children and access to affordable childcare — 45 / 74

National survey of 950 likely 2016 voters conducted for Democracy Corps and Women's Voice Women Vote Action Fund and The Voter Participation Center, January 7-11, 2015.

Support for these policies that advance middle-class economics is very strong. On average, about 75 percent say they are more positive about a Democrat advancing them, though even more significant is the nearly 50 percent who are much more positive.[3]

And if you want to understand whom the public is turning to at this tipping point, consider that on average the top policies in the Republican offer test about 6 points lower in intense support and 7 points lower in overall support. The top Republican policies involve reforming Congress so they are required to achieve fiscal balance or lose their perks and helping small businesses.

And indeed, help for the self-employed and for independent contractors is one of the unaddressed problems in the new economy.

1. It's Medicare and Social Security, stupid!

SOCIAL SECURITY AND MEDICARE: Protect Medicare and Social Security so there is no reduction in benefits, and keep the politicians' hands off Social Security so today's and tomorrow's seniors can retire with security.

The elites have grand plans to cut and "reform" Medicare, Medicaid, and Social Security to "rein in out-of-control spending"—and that is the bulk of the cuts at the heart of the Ryan budgets passed by House Republicans. They are at the heart of most of the bipartisan commissions that have made their "bold" recommendations. Well, the voters see that very clearly, and protecting the safety net for retirees is at the top of the popular agenda, and for many voters nothing is more urgent than stopping the elite and conservative plans. That is particularly true for baby boomers, who are in the front line. It is also among the top priorities of unmarried women, white working-class men and women, and Independents.[4]

The security of retirement benefits and the social safety net is a growing issue in every election because people are now reaching retirement more dependent on those benefits. Many are still working because they have no choice. At the close of the U.S. Senate election in Louisiana in 2014, Democracy Corps explored how Mary Landrieu might get more of the white vote. Among the approaches raising the most serious doubts about her competition was an attack on Landrieu's opponent, Republican Bill Cassidy, for not understanding what people face at this point in life. And despite her defeat, this issue will be close to the surface in every election to come.[5]

Cassidy is a doctor, yet he voted to end the Medicare guarantee, which would force seniors to negotiate with insurance companies and cost them thousands more out of pocket every year. He also voted to cut Social Security benefits and to raise the retirement age to seventy, even though the average life span for poorer Louisianans is only sixty-seven.

The policy agenda in these disruptive times begins with protecting and preserving the most important and legitimate parts of the social safety net, yet with people retiring with fewer assets, pensions, and homeownership, the reform agenda will almost certainly move to increasing Social Security benefits. For now, just keeping the elites from tampering with the safety net would be a big victory. However, that just may not be enough in this new economy.

2. Helping working families and working mothers

WORKING FAMILIES: Recognize that working families need help by making sure parents have paid sick days to care for their children and access to affordable child care.

WORKING MOTHERS: Help working mothers by making sure they have access to affordable child care, have paid sick days to care for themselves and their children, and protect pregnant workers from being fired or demoted.

The disruptive changes to the traditional family and marriage and to the role of women in work are a volatile combination—particularly when the regime of support for working women and working mothers dates from a previous era. Woman know they still have the primary responsibility for the children and have to work fewer hours because of it, and neither employers nor the government have done anything to help them balance the impossible.

The electorate gives impressive and intense support for the simple policy of helping working families with paid sick days to take care of their kids and affordable child care and helping working mothers with the same things, in addition to providing protection for pregnant workers. The policies are simple, though achieving them would require an all-new regime for dealing with work and family, with immense benefits for working women.

Support for the offer for working families is strongest in the rising American electorate, unmarried women, and white working-class women. Helping working mothers is embraced more by Millennials who are of childbearing age and, perhaps ironically, white working-class men. Help for working mothers gets some of the most intense support: 50 percent saying they would be much more likely to support a Democrat.

When we started testing a range of policy initiatives on their own—paid family leave, affordable child care, paid sick days, and protecting pregnant workers—none of them tested off the chart. That all changed when we brought them together under the broader and long-overdue recognition that working mothers need help. The cluster of policies takes on the unaddressed problems of discrimination against pregnant workers and new mothers, the reality that companies are being allowed to fire or demote these women, the fact that working mothers need to make use of child care to work while costs soar through the roof and they aren't guaranteed paid sick days when they need to care for an ill child or other family member.

An agenda for working mothers and working families began to test stronger in the 2014 election cycle as women voters in particular became increasingly exasperated with the lack of help.

When President Obama made this cluster of policies a centerpiece of his

His paid sick day proposal gets a big rise from all

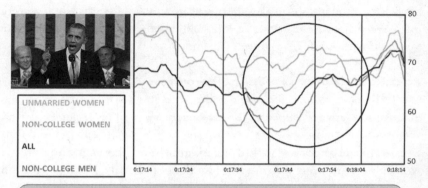

> Today, we're the only advanced country on Earth that doesn't guarantee paid sick leave or paid maternity leave to our workers. Forty-three million workers have no paid sick leave. Forty-three million. Think about that. And that forces too many parents to make the gut-wrenching choice between a paycheck and a sick kid at home. So I'll be taking new action to help states adopt paid leave laws of their own.

State of the Union research was conducted on January 20, 2015, by Greenberg Quinlan Rosner Research for Democracy Corps and Women's Voices Women Vote Action Fund. Participants were 61 white swing voters nationwide who split their votes fairly evenly between Democratic and Republican candidates over the past several Presidential and Congressional elections, though there were slightly more Obama voters than Romney voters. The group's self-identified partisanship was 33 percent Democratic, 34 percent Independent, and 33 percent Republican. The group included 27 women and 34 men, including 13 unmarried women.

The president's child care proposal spikes with working class and unmarried women, and $3,000 tax cut gets the men

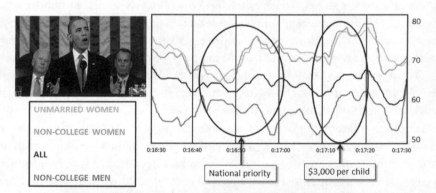

> It's time we stop treating childcare as a side issue, or a women's issue, and treat it like the national economic priority that it is for all of us. And that's why my plan will make quality childcare more available, and more affordable, for every middle-class and low-income family with young children in America -- by creating more slots and a new tax cut of up to $3,000 per child, per year.

State of the Union research was conducted on January 20, 2015, by Greenberg Quinlan Rosner Research for Democracy Corps and Women's Voices Women Vote Action Fund. Participants were 61 white swing voters nationwide who split their votes fairly evenly between Democratic and Republican candidates over the past several Presidential and Congressional elections, though there were slightly more Obama voters than Romney voters. The group's self-identified partisanship was 33 percent Democratic, 34 percent Independent, and 33 percent Republican. The group included 27 women and 34 men, including 13 unmarried women.

middle-class economics, unmarried women and white working-class voters rushed to support him. They turned their dials dramatically up at each point.

How steep the lines go is a measure of how much America is at a tipping point and ready to finally address what's happened to the family and working women with a reform economic agenda.

3. Equal pay and equal rights for women

EQUAL PAY: Make sure working women have equal pay to men for doing the same work and make it possible for women to work in management positions by rewarding companies that provide leave policies that make it possible for all employees to work and balance their work and family needs.

Seismic changes brought women fully into the labor force—though they are doing more of the lowest-paying jobs, are able to put in less time because of child care, and are facing discrimination up to the highest levels, so equal pay is becoming a flash point. A policy agenda for working women focused on equal pay is now in the top tier of policies among all likely voters and the new American majority and even higher for the white working class and independents. With about three-quarters of voters nationally saying that this initiative makes them more positive about the Democratic Party's economic plans, and nearly half saying so strongly, you have to accept that something is going on.[6]

When we asked voters in a poll of the most contested House seats to imagine what priorities a candidate for office might champion that might inspire them to vote for them, it surprised me how inspirational the idea of equal pay was for women. It inspired 60 percent of college-educated and non-college-educated women and almost two-thirds of white unmarried women. It inspired half the independents and nearly 40 percent of Republicans.[7]

You knew something had shifted when Republican congressional candidates running in blue states or districts began endorsing equal pay in principle to show they were attuned to this new world.

The great majority of Republicans, though, were surely not on board. When President Obama issued an executive order requiring that federal contractors comply with some provisions of the Paycheck Fairness Act, Republican leaders in Congress challenged him. They went to great lengths to show that the "pay gap" was exaggerated. Every Republican senator voted to block the Senate from taking up the equal-pay law.

Democracy Corps tested the power of an attack centered on this issue in the fall of 2014 in North Carolina, where state Speaker of the House Thom Tillis was challenging Senator Kay Hagan. The attack noted that "more and more women are breadwinners for their families, but women make just 77 cents for every dollar men make. Thom Tillis is opposed to requiring equal pay for women who do the same job as men." The hit also attacked Tillis for letting insurance companies charge women higher premiums than men and not covering preventive care. Well, nearly two-thirds of likely voters in North Carolina said this raised serious doubts about voting for Tillis, with nearly 40 percent saying it raised very serious doubts. When we applied a regression model to see which attacks could shift the vote, Tillis's position on equal pay and women's equality was far and away the strongest.[8]

Opposition to equal pay costly

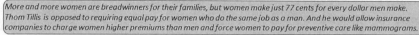

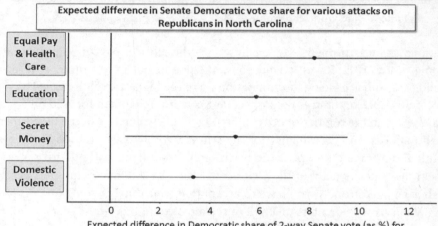

Expected difference in Democratic share of 2-way Senate vote (as %) for agreement with attack message compared to neutral opinion

Survey of 1,000 likely voters in the 12 most competitive Senate races across the country conducted by Greenberg Quinlan Rosner Research for Democracy Corps and Women's Voice Women Vote Action Function, September 20–24, 2014, including an oversample of 1,200 voters across Georgia, Iowa, North Carolina, and Colorado conducted September 12–October 1, 2014. Marginal effect estimates based on responsiveness to each message, comparing very serious doubts responses to no real doubts.

Senator Kay Hagan did run ads later in her campaign on Tillis's opposition to equal pay, and in the end Tillis defeated Hagan by 2 points—which is much closer than the 11-point margin across the congressional races in North Carolina in 2014.[9]

4. Affordable college education—starting with free tuition

AFFORDABLE COLLEGE: Make college more affordable by expanding the tuition tax credit that allows students to claim up to $4,000 for higher-education expenses. Get serious and provide free tuition at community colleges or technical schools for all qualified high-school graduates.

The first principle in the new economy is that jobs don't pay enough to live on and people are looking for ways to make more. People should not underestimate the underlying power of this point and how intensely people are pursuing personal strategies such as further training to deal with it. Women in particular are moving into colleges at all levels. So help making college affordable is part of the top tier of reforms to offset the contradictions of this new economy. These initiatives are virtually the top policy change for the Millennials.

The voters see the proposal to expand tax credits for college students and provide free tuition for community colleges and technical schools as a potential game changer as the political class is forced to focus on the affordability of college. That was reflected in the dial-meter reaction of white working-class and unmarried women voters who gave this policy offer their strongest positive turn-up on their dial meters.[10]

His free community college proposal produced the biggest response

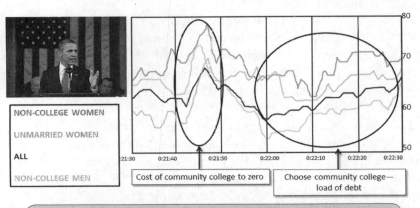

NON-COLLEGE WOMEN

UNMARRIED WOMEN

ALL

NON-COLLEGE MEN

Cost of community college to zero

Choose community college—load of debt

...lower the cost of community college – to zero.
Forty percent of our college students choose community college. Some are young and starting out. Some are older and looking for a better job. Some are veterans and single parents trying to transition back into the job market. Whoever you are, this plan is your chance to graduate ready for the new economy, without a load of debt.

State of the Union research was conducted on January 20, 2015, by Greenberg Quinlan Rosner Research for Democracy Corps and Women's Voices Women Vote Action Fund. Participants were 61 white swing voters nationwide who split their votes fairly evenly between Democratic and Republican candidates over the past several Presidential and Congressional elections, though there were slightly more Obama voters than Romney voters. The group's self-identified partisanship was 33 percent Democratic, 34 percent Independent, and 33 percent Republican. The group included 27 women and 34 men, including 13 unmarried women.

5. Long-term infrastructure investment to rebuild America and create middle-class jobs

INFRASTRUCTURE JOBS: Create a long-term plan to rebuild America and create new good-paying jobs by investing in infrastructure, such as modernizing schools, improving roads, bridges, and airports, and investing in clean energy alternatives that create more new jobs.

America will only get to its growth potential and create American jobs if it makes comprehensive long-term investments in rebuilding and modernizing its infrastructure. As we shall see here, the country is ready to rally around leaders who make that case and offer a vision. But understand that voters are cautious because they think politicians and government are corrupt and short-term in their thinking and select projects for political gain. That is why they are cautious about activist government—unless the reform starts with changing politics and government first.

In this first survey of the 2016 cycle, the top-rated initiative for the new American majority—the rising American electorate—was a plan of long-term investment in infrastructure to create jobs. It is hard to understate the strength of their support. Fully 73 percent were positive, but almost half were intense in their support. Support is also high among white non-college voters and white unmarried women, who are seeing the potential for job growth that could help them.

At the same time, you cannot underestimate the importance of the term "long-term." For many voters, the concept stands in contradiction to politicians and government that operate short-term and with a focus to get re-elected. In the focus groups with working-class men, "long-term" meant structure and goals—things that could not long survive politics, special interests, and Washington dysfunction.[11]

The voters' theory about politicians and government is not very different from the dominant theory among senior executives and thought leaders on why there are so few large infrastructure projects. They think politicians get elected on a short-term basis and the benefits and social gains from infrastructure are long-term. Politicians and governments operate with a short time horizon when budgeting, but infrastructure requires long gestation, planning, and execution. Politicians get punished immediately by voters for unpopular tolls and gas tax increases, while the gains in efficiency and safety accrue socially and long-term. As one head of global infrastructure told us, "Politicians don't think in seven-year or ten-year cycles. They think in terms of the next election cycle."[12]

They might just as well have been speaking about infrastructure to a pretty typical American working-class voter in Virginia Beach: "I don't think we've ever had a long-term plan for anything"; "we have never had a long-term plan to fix what's wrong and we need to but of course our government changes every four years so it's something they'll need to work on."[13]

I think that infrastructure leaders and political leaders are just misreading the ordinary voter. The ordinary politician may be focused on the short-term, but the ordinary voter is very focused on the "long-term" social and economic consequences of government decisions in their communities and for the nation.

Consider voters' reaction to the national debt, for example. They thought rising deficits threatened key long-term government commitments such as Social Security and left the United States ever more beholden to China. They were very cautious about Keynesian policies—"stimulus" or "giving the economy a jolt"—even if those were indeed the best way to get to growth. They thought politicians were throwing money at problems, trying to bribe voters like themselves, or paying off special interests and moneyed donors.[14]

The argument that "growth requires public investment in things like transportation, science, and education" did not begin to prevail over the argument that economic health requires more spending cuts until recently in the United States. The public's surprising support for austerity during the economic downturn was part of a conviction that Americans live off debt and had to take their medicine for their long-term health.[15]

The public also did not rush to support public investment in infrastructure because they were much less critical of its quality than were civil engineers. Even though they gave America's infrastructure a D+ grade, a majority of Americans say they are satisfied with the condition of the transportation infrastructure in their own area. And if you want them to support more taxes to support improvements, an even larger majority thinks the gasoline tax has gone up every year. The federal gas tax, however, has not been raised since 1993.[16]

At the end of the day though, the most important reason the public holds back from investment is their distrust of politics, politicians, and political processes that control infrastructure decisions. A striking 85 percent of the public thinks transportation funding decisions are political, and more than 60 percent believe that strongly. They deeply dislike "earmarking" of transportation projects by members of Congress. They have no reason to believe that political leaders are selecting the best projects or doing what is good for the long term.[17]

When President Obama was first elected, he took his Economic Recovery and Reinvestment Act to the Congress and the country. It included $30 billion for infrastructure improvements, including $26 billion for 12,000 bridge, highway, and road projects, $1.3 billion for aviation improvements, and $18 billion for traditional transit and high-speed rail under the clean energy projects category—timed to be spent quickly, over about two years. The voters at that point understood the context and timing. At the time, two-thirds of the public thought "increased spending on infrastructure such as highways and public buildings" would be helpful in fixing the country's economic problems.[18]

But when he later took his jobs bill to the Congress with additional infrastructure spending to give a short-term stimulus to the economy, barely half the country supported it. The president described it as "a jolt to an economy that has stalled" and said that it "answers the urgent need to create jobs right away," and the public questioned the efficacy of such short-term policies and short-term jobs.[19]

You win the public for infrastructure when voters see independence from the political process, long-term plans, and a larger economic or national purpose. In the context of highways and bridges, there is almost 60 percent support for public-private partnerships to fund new infrastructure: "allowing private companies—with government oversight—to fund, build, and maintain a roadway for a specific term." The same is true for a national infrastructure bank: "an independent, nonpartisan entity of the government tasked with evaluating and choosing transportation infrastructure projects based on merit and financing those projects with public and private funding."[20]

The public rallies to support infrastructure investment on a large scale when it is part of a plan and is meant to address a big national goal. Two-thirds agree with the following statement, 38 percent strongly:

> *Our principal economic challenge is not the deficit but our hesitation to strongly invest in our future economic capacity. Trillions of dollars of capital is idle and millions are unemployed, and that's wrong. We need to put this money and people back to work right now rebuilding our nation's energy, transportation, and water systems. This is the best way to grow the economy and reduce our debt burden.*[21]

Three-quarters of voters say they feel more positive about a leader who commits to addressing our "massive public investment deficit."

> *We have a budget deficit, but the fact is we also have a massive public investment deficit—in roads, sewers, schools, trains, renewable energy, and other basic parts of our communities. To be competitive, we need to rebuild the infrastructure that is vital to our economy. This will create jobs, help business compete, improve our communities, and generate revenues that can help pay down the budget deficit.*[22]

The public is looking for leaders who will defy the corruption and short-termism and act to rebuild and modernize the country for the long term. This is a moment for leaders to catch up with the ordinary voter.

6. Tax the richest so they pay their fair share

FAIR TAXATION: Raise taxes on those with the highest incomes and close corporate tax loopholes and special-interest subsidies so they pay their fair share of taxes.

A resounding two-thirds of presidential-year voters say we should raise taxes on the top earners and close their tax loopholes and subsidies simply so "they pay their fair share." A large bloc of 42 percent support that strongly—including 50 percent of the rising American electorate and 58 percent of unmarried women. Independents, too, think it is time for them to pay: 62 percent support it, 40 percent strongly. And among white non-college-educated voters, who gave Obama only about 36 percent of their votes, 65 percent say the time has come for the rich.[23]

The American people strongly believe that the country should be raising taxes on those with the highest incomes, closing tax loopholes, and ending special-interest subsidies so the richest pay their fair share of taxes. It is at the top of the list when it comes to addressing the challenges in the new economy. The voters believe the tax system is a product of a corrupted political system that shapes everyone's economic fortunes.

Liberated in his last two years in office, President Obama presented a budget for 2016 that included raising taxes to pay for infrastructure projects, two years of free community college, and tax credits for students and parents of children and dual-income households. The Republican leaders of Congress dismissed it immediately as class warfare, and in Senate majority leader McConnell's words, "another top-down, backward-looking document."[24]

Democratic leaders this time had already advanced their own tax reform initiatives, which included a financial transaction tax and limits on tax breaks for the top 1 percent of earners—and they applauded the president's turn to middle-class economics. Perhaps Democrats will be less timid in putting such tax increases front and center.[25]

The fact is that starting with President Bill Clinton every Democratic nominee has advocated raising taxes on the rich and won. Clinton came into office after the Reagan tax cuts that heavily cut top-end rates and acted like a starting gun for CEOs to begin taking the lion's share of the economic gains. The cut in tax rates and the inheritance tax restructured the incentives for corporate behavior, and voters watched skeptically.

It is virtually a rule that Democratic candidates run for president on raising taxes on the wealthy because tax policy, to be frank, is effective: when Republicans cut taxes, it helps the top and disadvantages the bottom; when Democrats raise taxes and close loopholes, it works, too—and that is what Democrats have done.

In his economic plan, Putting People First, Bill Clinton proposed raising taxes on families earning more than $200,000, closing corporate tax loopholes, and preventing companies from deducting CEO salaries of more than $1 million. The plan specifically proposed expanding key programs targeted at the lower- and middle-income people—community development block grants to rebuild urban infrastructure, a network of community development banks to give loans to low-income entrepreneurs and homeowners, funding for continuing education and job training programs, and expanding the earned income tax credit. Importantly, the plan would pay for these programs by *raising tax rates for the wealthiest individuals and corporations.* Clinton proposed eliminating tax breaks for excessive CEO compensation, multinationals that abused offshore tax havens, and drug companies that raised prices faster than the rate of income growth.[26]

Bill Clinton ran on raising taxes on the wealthy and promoted it with powerful rhetoric that left you thinking, "Finally, the average guy is going to get a break." On the campaign trail, he put a lot of heat and rhetorical brilliance behind his plans: "I have news for the forces of greed and the defenders of the status quo—your time has come, and gone. It's time for change in America." He reminded people that he "was raised to believe that the American Dream was built on rewarding hard work," but "for too long, those who play by the rules and keep the faith have gotten the shaft." The government doesn't get it because it has been "hijacked by privileged private interests" and the administration in Washington is animated by an economic philosophy that says, "you make the economy grow by putting more and more wealth into the hands of fewer and fewer people at the top."[27]

In case you missed it, the Clinton campaign's advertising in the last two months of 1992 made the case. "Only the rich are doing better because for twelve years we've been dominated by selfishness and greed and a concern for the short run." So "We're going to ask the rich to pay their fair share so the rest of America can finally get a break."[28]

Barack Obama ran for president famously proposing to let President Bush's tax cuts expire for those earning over $250,000 and pledging no tax increases for those earning less than that. Our surveys at the time showed that posture to be exceedingly popular.

Obama of course won that election in 2008, but you may not have noticed that he won an even bigger win on taxes. Note this: Obama won the tax issue by twice the margin that he won in the actual election. On Election Day, 53 percent of voters thought Obama would do a better job on taxes—13 points more than the 40 percent who preferred John McCain's approach. The tax issue helped him in the election, as it did for President Clinton before him.[29]

The 2008 election provides even clearer proof on the issue. Obama used the inelegant phrase "spread the wealth around" in an impromptu exchange with Joe Wurzelbacher, who became known as "Joe the Plumber." I'm sure his campaign advisers groaned, as this was not his organizing theme, but John McCain would make sure he owned it in the next two months. McCain raised Joe the Plumber nine times in the third presidential debate, took Joe Wurzelbacher to his campaign rallies, and elevated him in the campaign's advertising—until he was the total topic of the campaign's final paid advertising.[30]

This attack was the closing argument of the McCain campaign. They put

$5.7 million behind their "Joe the Plumber" ad, airing it 12,750 times. It began with the Obama exchange. "Spread the wealth?" asks the announcer, followed by a series of individuals on camera, "I'm supposed to work harder just to pay more taxes. Obama wants my sweat to pay for his trillion dollars in new spending." The announcer brings the ad and the campaign to a close: "Barack Obama: higher taxes, more spending, not ready."[31]

The Joe the Plumber debate reminds us how misplaced our admiration for John McCain was. For all that effort, McCain lost the tax issue and the election.

The American people come to the tax debate with a strong set of values and their own common sense. For them, there is no new economic policy that does not address the tax code in a fundamental way.

The embrace of higher taxes for the richest so they pay their fair share when framed under Clinton's historic legacy strikes many Americans as an "inspired" idea that would lead them to support a candidate who proposed it.

> Go back to the tax rates under Bill Clinton so those earning more than $250,000 and CEOs pay a new higher 40 percent tax rate so those who have done so well pay their fair share of taxes.

A striking 50 percent of Americans in the most contested House districts in 2014 described that as an "inspired" idea that would lead them to consider a candidate, while another 22 percent supported going back to Clinton rates even though it was not a factor in their vote.[32]

So the public is ready for a new tax regime.

In truth, President Obama consistently enacted tax and economic policies that favored working people and the poor. He got Congress to lower Social Security payroll taxes for two years and won an expansion of the child tax credit and the earned income tax credit. He won expansion of Medicaid and new subsidies to help working people purchase health insurance. And he also got Congress to raise taxes on top earners and investment income to pay for the Affordable Care Act and to repeal the Bush tax cuts for those earning more than $450,000. As Paul Krugman wrote, "While America remains an incredibly unequal society, and we haven't seen anything like the New Deal's efforts to narrow income gaps, Obama has done more to limit inequality than he gets credit for."[33]

While the public is a bit uneducated about Barack Obama's tax policies, it is totally clear-minded about the administration's posture toward the big corporations and economic sectors that sank the American and global economies. The public thinks he has worked hand in glove with the big banks— to rescue them and promote their interests, even as they did almost nothing for those with underwater mortgages. What was scary for voters was presidential candidate Barack Obama rushing to Washington to meet with Democratic and Republican leaders and the Treasury secretary at the White House to support the bailout of Wall Street banks. They ultimately bailed out the auto industry, too. And the Obama administration defended the payment of bonuses at the big banks, and no Wall Street executive was ever prosecuted for the deceit and the damage.

Some of these actions were no doubt critical to America avoiding another Great Depression and America's financial sector rapidly gaining health, though overall they created a deep impression that government was there for the most irresponsible big businesses.

In the spring of 2010—a good year into the implementation of the American Recovery and Reinvestment Act—Democracy Corps asked voters, "Who are the main beneficiaries of the Economic Recovery Act?" Almost half, 45 percent, said the unemployed benefited a lot or some from the act, and a lesser amount, 34 percent, said the middle class was benefiting. But three-quarters said the big banks and financial institutions were the beneficiaries and 50 percent said they benefited *a lot*—more than eight times the number who said that for the middle class.[34]

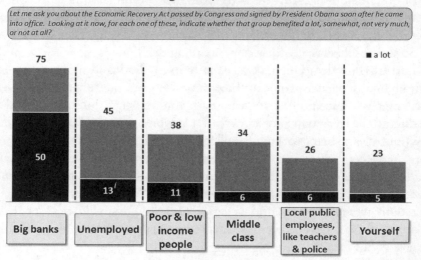

Which groups benefited from the Economic Recovery Act?
The big banks, of course.

Let me ask you about the Economic Recovery Act passed by Congress and signed by President Obama soon after he came into office. Looking at it now, for each one of these, indicate whether that group benefited a lot, somewhat, not very much, or not at all?

■ a lot

Big banks	Unemployed	Poor & low income people	Middle class	Local public employees, like teachers & police	Yourself
75	45	38	34	26	23
50	13	11	6	6	5

Web survey of 2,671 adults nationwide conducted by Greenberg Quinlan Rosner Research for Citizen Opinion and the Center for American Progress, April 18–19, 2010.

When the voters looked at the president's approach to the economy, they looked right past the Economic Recovery Act itself to the larger set of policies that revealed who the government really worked for. Maybe the public was more right than wrong.

7. Reforming money and politics

As we showed earlier, support for the economic agenda is much stronger if it is predicated on reforming government and politics. The public understands what role money plays in getting government to rig the system and the consequence for the middle class and inequality. They realize that political inequality is integral to economic inequality. They are connecting the flood of spending on campaigns to the principles of the new economy and the paralysis of government in the face of growing need. The scale of the corruption is embodied in the record-breaking flood of unregulated and legalized secret spending.

All of this has led to a new level of public revulsion and support for fundamental reforms. Super PACs are not arcane institutions. They are known by more than half of the voters and detested: seven times as many people react to them negatively as positively.[35]

That public consciousness has been expressed at every juncture. It is evident in the public's rallying to higher taxes on the rich, to eliminating special-interest tax loopholes, and to treating investment income the same as wages. It is even evident in their mundane though considered reaction to short-term stimulus projects that look like they are part of the same system decision-making that has been corrupted by elite access.

The public knew that the *Citizens United* Supreme Court decision was a sham from the outset. They never accepted that spending to influence the outcome of elections was constitutionally protected free speech, or that corporations were people, or that campaign donations should be deregulated. When the Supreme Court made its groundbreaking decision to allow corporations or outside groups to spend unlimited amounts of money to influence elections, the public was opposed from the beginning—eight in ten Americans opposed the ruling, 65 percent strongly just weeks after the decision.[36]

The public very quickly concluded that the new fund-raising regime of big donors and secret money damaged something fundamental. Two-thirds were convinced it "undermines democracy"; 54 percent believed that strongly. Just a third accepted the counterargument that "money is always going to be spent in campaigns" and that this flood of secret money allows all candidates and points of view to be heard. Indeed, Republican defenders argued that this was business as usual and "just the way campaigns are run today." That does not pass the smell test, however. Two-thirds of the public concluded that this system is "wrong" and "leads to our elected officials representing the views of wealthy donors who finance Super PACs, instead of representing all of us." Half of Republicans also concluded that this funding regime is "wrong."[37]

For the public, the consequences of this legalized system of secret and unlimited donations are self-evident. When they are asked which of the following has the most influence on members of Congress, the public puts "special-interest groups and lobbyists" and "campaign contributors" in a league of their own: 59 percent say the first has the most influence and 46 percent the second most. They are seen to wield the most influence in Washington, as political parties pale in power: just 29 percent choose party leaders as most influential. And when it comes to the "views of constituents," only 15 percent say that they matter the most.[38]

The election of 2014 hit a tipping point in people's tolerance for massive unregulated money and watching such pervasive negative advertising. Super PACs spent $348 million and 501(c)(4) organizations spent at least $118 million in 2014 to influence the House and Senate races, and it moved voters to a new place on reform. Voters now seem ready to reward politicians who offer the boldest possible reform of the campaign financing system and punish those who take huge amounts of money from the top 1 percent and billionaires and then proceed to protect their tax breaks and lower rates while failing to make changes critical for the middle class.[39]

The obvious starting point for reform is simple transparency. A nearly universal 85 percent of independents and both Republicans and Democrats would require corporations, unions, and nonprofits to disclose their sources of spending when they participate in elections. You know you have reached a threshold for reform, however, when three-quarters of voters in these states flooded with campaign money support a Constitutional Amendment to overturn the *Citizens United* ruling.[40]

You know this system is corrupt and the public is ready for fundamental reforms when 61 percent support "a plan to overhaul campaign spending by getting rid of big donations and allowing only small donations to candidates, matched by taxpayer funds." That campaign finance reform wins over a majority of independents and 38 percent of Republicans. The American citizenry has become progressively more supportive of using public funds to empower small donations and barring big and corporate donations.[41]

Even in the face of charges that this is "welfare for politicians," voters rally to a candidate who argues, "We need a government of, by, and for the people—not government bought and paid for by wealthy donors." Nearly 60 percent of voters in the Republican-leaning 2014 Senate battleground states preferred such a reform position, and that was true with independents and supporters of both parties.[42]

What is new is that advocates for reform increase their chance of getting the public's attention and winning elections as a reformer.

To measure the electoral power of these campaign finance reforms, we conducted an experimental exercise with voters in the Senate battleground survey that faced a deluge of campaign advertising. All of the respondents in the survey heard a proposal to publicly fund campaigns and half the respondents

Reform advocates win the public debate—even when attacked as "welfare for politicians" with taxpayer money

Now I'd like to read two statements about this proposal. Please tell me which comes closer to your point of view, even if neither is exactly right:

We need a government of, by and for the people - not government bought and paid for by wealthy donors. It's time we let big donors and private companies pay their fair share of taxes, rather than paying for politicians who will write them special tax breaks. By replacing large contributions from CEOs, PACs, and lobbyists with small contributions from everyday Americans and limited public funds, **we'll make every voice count in Washington.**

Paying for elections with tax dollars is just welfare for politicians. It means politicians will use billions of our taxpayer dollars to fund their campaigns instead of other important issues. **Tax money will go to bumper stickers, yard signs, and even negative attacks,** and the proposal would require a costly bureaucracy to police our speech. It leaves the super PACs alone, which means it won't really clean up politics. This is not a good use of our tax dollars.

	Total (+26)	Democrats (+45)	Independents (+22)	Republicans (+11)
	59	70	56	50
	43	58	40	31
	33	25	34	39
	22	17	24	26

Survey of 1,000 likely 2014 voters across the 12 most competitive Senate battleground states conducted for Democracy Corps and Every Voice, July 12–16, 2014.

also heard a debate about *Citizens United* and candidates' positions on campaign money. While the full sample responded positively to the campaign finance proposal and shifted toward the Democratic candidate, the half that also heard about *Citizens United* shifted even farther. The Democratic candidate who proposed to overturn *Citizens United* and attacked the Republican candidate's positions on campaign money performed even better because the candidate made gains with independents, moderate Republicans, and the white working class.[43]

Proposals to reform campaign funding are now testing in the top tier of issues for Democrats. Two-thirds of voters nationally were more positive about an economic plan when it proposed to overturn *Citizens United* and bring in public funding of campaigns.[44]

Campaign finance reformers are winning the argument when the public hears them, and voters across the political spectrum are embracing proposals to dramatically change how America's elections work. They are ready to support proposals to go after the money and undermine the special interests' influence, which is crowding out the role of ordinary citizens. And the voters seem poised to punish candidates who are part of this corrupt nexus and to reward leaders ready to clean the stables.

One of the most effective campaign attacks we tested linked big donations to politicians advancing the interests of wealthy donors who used unlimited secret money to make sure the billionaires and CEOs paid no higher taxes and their loopholes were protected.

> (The named Republican candidate) supports the Supreme Court's decision to allow wealthy special interests and big corporations to spend unlimited amounts of secret money to buy elections, taking the power away from regular citizens and putting it in the hands of just a few billionaires. (GOP candidate) made sure CEOs paid no higher taxes and that their loopholes are protected, while working men and women struggle.

The power of this attack comes from the centrality of the corrupt Washington and Wall Street nexus to the new economy. While working men struggled, the Republican candidate was helping government work for big corporations and special interests.

When Democracy Corps tested this attack in Louisiana, North Carolina, Georgia, Iowa, Colorado, and the other Senate battleground states, it was among the most powerful attacks on the Republican candidates. In Louisiana, for example, two-thirds of white persuadable voters said this raised serious doubts about Bill Cassidy, and 40 percent had very serious doubts.[45]

Secret money buying a government that works for big corporations, not working people, is strongest attack

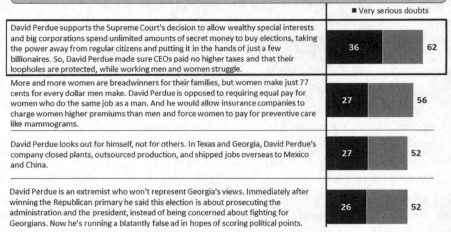

Now I'm going to read you some things that Republicans like David Perdue and in your state are trying to do. These could decide whether you vote in November. Please tell me whether it raises very serious doubts, serious doubts, minor doubts, or no real doubts in your own mind about David Perdue when you are thinking of voting in November.

■ Very serious doubts

David Perdue supports the Supreme Court's decision to allow wealthy special interests and big corporations spend unlimited amounts of secret money to buy elections, taking the power away from regular citizens and putting it in the hands of just a few billionaires. So, David Perdue made sure CEOs paid no higher taxes and that their loopholes are protected, while working men and women struggle.	36	62
More and more women are breadwinners for their families, but women make just 77 cents for every dollar men make. David Perdue is opposed to requiring equal pay for women who do the same job as a man. And he would allow insurance companies to charge women higher premiums than men and force women to pay for preventive care like mammograms.	27	56
David Perdue looks out for himself, not for others. In Texas and Georgia, David Perdue's company closed plants, outsourced production, and shipped jobs overseas to Mexico and China.	27	52
David Perdue is an extremist who won't represent Georgia's views. Immediately after winning the Republican primary he said this election is about prosecuting the administration and the president, instead of being concerned about fighting for Georgians. Now he's running a blatantly false ad in hopes of scoring political points.	26	52

Statewide survey of 456 white persuadable likely voters in Louisiana conducted by Greenberg Quinlan Rosner Research for Democracy Corps, October 11–14, 2014.

Of course, none of the Democratic candidates ran that ad.

That tells you that the Democratic Party may need to be reformed, too, and that the public is far ahead of the politicians. *Are* the Democrats prepared to enact the reforms to tackle the roles of big money, big business influence, and the rising inequality that nexus furthers?

This is really the same question asked by Thomas Edsall in a series of tough op-eds in *The New York Times*. In the end, those challenges really empower those who lean into reform. As the public understands, reform begins with going after the money and the corruption of government.

Sure, the Republican Party is much more dependent on the billionaires and richest donors. Yet it is the Democrats who want to mitigate inequality and limit the growing influence of the top 1 percent and they too have grown increasingly dependent on their donations. Since 2000, a quarter of the Democrats' contributions have come from the billionaires in the top .01 percent. And since 2008, about half of Democrats' campaign money came from the top .01 percent and the largest donors.[46]

Democratic fundraising increasingly from super and large donors

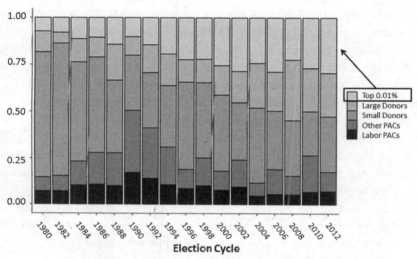

Election Cycle

Thomas B. Edsall, "Can the Government Actually Do Anything About Inequality," *The New York Times*, September 10, 2013. Data from the Federal Election Commission and the Internal Revenue Service.

That dependence on the largest and billionaire donors is very real and only underscores how Democrats must make a visible break with the big-money and corporate, special-interest influence over government. For the public, that is a precondition for inviting a government activism that can address our biggest economic and social problems.

BEYOND THE REAGAN DEMOCRATS

Democrats will likely get the chance to lead this era of reform simply because they are aligned with the ascendant trends and the new American majority and Republicans are battling ferociously against them. The Constitution allows them to avoid catastrophic defeat by overrepresenting rural parts of the country where Republicans deepen their support.

Having the national stage, however, does not mean that Democrats will build a politics around people's current struggles and be willing to battle against the inertia and against the powerful forces dominating government. To lead reform, Democrats will have to embrace a disruptive political project focused intensely on the current and emerging contradictions.

Bill Clinton's formula for winning the national vote and the Electoral College lay in reclaiming the votes of enough of the declining white industrial male workers and combining that with the votes from the Democrats' growing liberal cultural coalition—a product of the civil rights and women's movements, the influx of immigrants, and the protests against the Vietnam and Iraq wars. President Clinton and some in the Democratic Leadership Council described this formula as "running to the center," though as a pollster and strategist for Clinton, I never did. I described it as a formula for building a progressive majority from the bottom up—and it did allow Democrats to win again in the industrial Midwest and run better in some parts of the South.

The measure of success for candidate Bill Clinton was his ability to win over the "Reagan Democrats" in Macomb County, Michigan, at the heart of the unionized auto industry. Bill Clinton famously ran to govern for "the forgotten middle class," and winning back and running respectably with those working-class voters set Democrats on a course to build a winning national coalition in five of the past six elections.

Barack Obama has evolved the formula in a pretty fundamental way. He embraced the new diversity and changes in gender roles and the family, which built the Democrats' electoral support among America's new majority. Obama could get by with just 36 percent of the white working-class in 2012 because the Democratic formula increasingly depends on the two-to-one support the party gets from minority voters, new immigrants, Millennials, and unmarried women, as well as the party's big majorities among the college-educated and professional women.[47]

So in the end, Obama's big election victories in 2008 and 2012 were the political triumph of the ascendant trends. In 2008, the huge crowd in Grant Park celebrating the election of a young, mixed-race president was celebrating a changed America. The next Democratic president might celebrate victory in New York City as a million people gather in Central Park and hundreds of millions around the world watch. This, too, would be a victory of the new America.

Any new Democratic president will very quickly discover, however, as Barack Obama did all too soon, that the American mood can easily darken. Two-thirds will very quickly say the country is headed in the wrong direction. This was Obama's experience by 2010. Whether that occurs again will depend on how the new president decides to address the growing economic and cultural contradictions described in this book, and if he or she embraces the reform agenda described in this chapter—a project Obama did not undertake as the defining challenge of his presidency.[48]

When President Obama assumed office after the economic collapse of 2008, he did not view it as a Roosevelt moment when a Democratic president might have educated the public on the fundamentals of the new economy and advanced a bold reform agenda. The financial crisis and Great Recession forced him to focus like a laser on the economy and to enact Wall Street reforms, but restructuring the economy was not the defining project of his presidency and he never educated the country on his economic path.

Obama's political project was transcending the division of the country into blue and red America and the resulting dysfunction in Washington. President Obama won the party nomination running as an outsider demanding change, aligned with the forces mobilized to oppose George W. Bush and the Iraq war. He won the nomination fully aligned with the country's rising cultural liberalism and racial diversity, but what animated him was his exasperation with Karl Rove's culture war that had willfully polarized the country since 2004. Even when the president turned his focus to the middle class late in his presidency, he reminded the country, "We are still more than a collection of red states and blue states," and "together, we can do great things." In the end, his presidency will have made critical progress on health care, climate change, and tax equity, but his political project was more transitional to the new politics centered on the new majority and bold reforms.[49]

The American citizenry and new majority celebrate the ascendant trends, values, and changing way of life, but they live the contradictions. They struggle daily with the pay gap and work that doesn't pay enough to live on, piecing together several jobs and participating in the freelance economy while managing work and kids, many of them as single parents. The majority live with the social consequences that arise from more and more households being unmarried; from the reality that working-class men today face a dimmer future than their fathers did; and from the lack of public policies that support women who are fully in the labor force. All the while they are watching the top 1 percent use their money to influence political connections and rig the system so the economy works in their favor, not for the working and middle class.

With those problems unaddressed, the public simmers, waiting for political leaders who "get it" and who will reform government and bring real changes. Large percentages of the new American majority—the progressive base for change—believe the country is headed in the wrong direction and still give Obama high disapproval ratings. So while Republicans are deeply engaged in a battle against the changing trends, the new American majority is much less engaged because they see politics failing them. The rising American electorate could be the Democrats' salvation—but that electorate first has to be engaged and motivated to vote.

The new political formula for a real national electoral majority does not depend on winning the "Reagan Democrats" or a "forgotten middle class." We now know that identifying with the emergent trends and joining the battle for American values will still leave the Democrats short of the momentum they need to bring change. Democrats have to show they get it and have finally joined the battle over the central contradictions of our times and advance a reform agenda. Then, they will have a majority that defends its gains year in and year out.

Part V

NEW PROGRESSIVE ERA

11 THE PROGRESSIVE ERA: "TO CLEANSE, TO RECONSIDER, TO RESTORE, TO CORRECT THE EVIL"

America in the two decades closing out the nineteenth century was a wonder, an emergent powerhouse industrializing at a breathtaking pace, sucking in immigrants from across Europe to work in its mines and factories, and building the first railways connecting New York City and San Francisco. It was poised to be the exceptional nation, economically, culturally, and militarily ascendant. The twentieth century was to be "the American century."

But exceptionalism then, as now, came with deep contradictions that threatened the sustainability of the American model. America's Industrial Revolution brought industrial monopolies and ever more political corruption. It brought longer hours at subsistence wages for farmers and laborers, and terrible living conditions in teeming slums and such a level of inequality that it became known as "the "Gilded Age." Toss into the brew the spreading union strikes and police violence, the nativist anti-immigration campaigns, and the populist, socialist, and progressive revolt and you had a formula for growing instability. That only deepened the industrialists' resolve to defend the new economic order. Before the turn of the century, "muckraking" investigative journalists exposed businessmen and politicians' special deals that nurtured the endemic corruption at the heart of the Republican and Democratic parties.

The next twenty years and four national elections would be transformative. Presidents Teddy Roosevelt and William Howard Taft at the head of the Republican Party, the La Follette Republicans and Bryan Democrats from outside, and President Woodrow Wilson as head of the Democratic Party would bring bold reforms that would mitigate some of the worst outcomes of the industrial era. The radical reforms would reduce inequality, improve living and working conditions for the working class and new immigrants, and make it possible for them to edge up the social ladder. They also limited the influence of the top industrialists and saved democracy from the systemic corporate corruption of government. Even more important reforms would have to await the election of Franklin Roosevelt. Nonetheless, the progressive revolt against the industrial titans and party bosses brought a period of progressive governance and reforms that allowed America to develop in a very different way. America standing astride the twentieth century would not have been possible without this era of reform.

The radical reforms of the progressive era were not achieved in one presidential election or presidential term. The reformers first triumphed and governed with a progressive agenda in key cities and states. Nationally, it took four presidential elections and three presidents with varying commitments to reform that grew bolder and inevitable with time. The voices of muckraking journalists got heard over the tabloid and yellow journalists. Local reform clubs, charities, churches, and some notable philanthropists organized to improve living and working conditions. And together they won the intellectual argument about the nature of this new economy. Progressives came to be hegemonic in civil society before they were ascendant politically.

America has been dealt a not dissimilar hand today, and Democrats and reformers will be called upon to address the dark side of America's progress. They will have to battle for radical reforms that will allow America to realize its great potential.

The story of the Industrial Revolution in the last decades of the nineteenth century is really an American story of unprecedented economic growth and emerging global dominance. That story began in Britain and had no precedent. All developments in human history that came before the Industrial Revolution barely budged upward the rate of economic output and progress. America would dominate an extraordinary surge in human productivity and economic growth.

Thomas Piketty graphs that story with real historical data. For the first millennium since the beginning of the Christian calendar, the growth rate of world output hovered near zero. While world output grew 0.1 percent between 1000 and 1500, and 0.2 percent between 1500 and 1700, the per capita growth rate remained unchanged until 1700. Total global economic output did not grow more than 0.5 percent a year, and per capita growth did not rise above zero until the 1700–1820 period. However, output tripled with the Industrial Revolution (1.5 percent) and per capita growth reached almost 1 percent. In North America, the per capita rate of growth surged to 1.6 percent a year during the Industrial Revolution, almost twice the global per capita rate at the time.[1]

The disruptive change that began with the steam engine and portable power, Ian Morris writes, "reduces" everything that came before "to insignificance." Muscle power, wind, and water have inherent limits. It was the portable steam engine that burst those limits. Look at what happened with cotton. Steam power greatly accelerated the production of cotton as the cotton gin separated the sticky seeds from the cotton fiber on America's plantations. America's African American slave labor was integral to this first industrial era as production of cotton bales surged from 3,000 in 1790 to 178,000 in 1810 to 4.5 million in 1860, a year before the Civil War began.[2]

Other inventions slashed the cost of a telegram by 100 percent between the Civil War and First World War, and the first telephones that came into operation in 1876 allowed communication to advance with lightning speed. The steam engine brought the rapid expansion of the railroads that fueled a burgeoning trade among the states, and by the turn of century 200,000 miles of rail crisscrossed America. With steam power, ships could sail much greater distances and made possible the development of an Atlantic economy that American industrialists would dominate.[3]

The United States and Germany, Morris writes, led the next phase of the Industrial Revolution because they were much more systematic in the application of science to new technology. This would soon be an "age of oil, automobiles, and aircraft." The internal combustion engine was invented in Germany in 1885, and by 1913 America was producing one million cars a year.[4]

Because of the technological advancement, Europe and America began "to claim a share of global output that was two to three times greater than their share of the world's population," Piketty writes, "simply because the output of each person was two to three times greater than the global average." Starting in 1870, however, this became an American story. Its share of total world output rose dramatically—doubling to 24 percent—while the European share went flat and then declined between 1913 and 1950. Meanwhile, America's rising share of global output continued unabated. The Industrial Revolution really did make America ascendant.[5]

The Industrial Revolution also triggered a massive human wave in the second half of the nineteenth century. An unimaginable 168 million acres of land were cleared—comparable to clearing the whole state of Texas—to make way for the new Americans. Almost one in five of Great Britain's 27-million-person population would immigrate to America between 1851 and 1880. That sounds an awful lot like the one in five global migrants who have recently ended up living in the United States. Germans and Scandinavians joined the British and Irish immigrants who would take up one-third of the manufacturing jobs.[6]

In 1800, two-thirds of Americans were employed in agriculture. That fell sharply to 41 percent by 1900 as people flocked to the cities to work in the new factories. New York City grew from 79,000 in 1800 to 2.5 million in 1890, and Chicago, a "prairie town" of 30,000 in 1850, was the sixth-largest city in the world and home to almost 1 million people well before the turn of the century.[7]

The World's Fairs of 1893 in Chicago and 1904 in St. Louis showcased America's self-confidence as the leader of this new industrial era and America as a beacon to the world. The fairs promoted American business, and twenty million people came to St. Louis to see the newest products and technologies on display. Also on display were the leading industrialists, who would play an increasingly central role in this period.[8]

Standing prominently atop this new order was an emerging class of industrialists whom Morris aptly describes as "a new, steam-powered class of iron chieftains." The steam engine "had unleashed a storm of moneymaking" by industrialists who grew their empires and profits, while the "workers who made the money saw precious little of it." Nonetheless, the new industrialists were very conscious of their virtues and contributions to the nation. They fought bitterly to defend their enormous wealth and freedom to be entrepreneurs.[9]

Cities were at the heart of this American revolution. One observer wrote eloquently, "all the Central States, all the Great Northwest roared with traffic and industry; sawmills screamed; factories, their smoke blacking the sky, clashed and flamed; wheels turned, pistons leaped in their cylinders; cog gripped cog; beltings clasped the drums of mammoth wheels and converters of forges belched into the clouded air their tempest breath of molten steel. It was Empire."[10]

That churning simultaneously grew the dark side of cities, the homes of the country's diverse immigrant population. Of the 1.7 million living in Chicago in 1900, more than three-quarters were first-generation immigrants. For most, the new life in America was better than for their families in the impoverished rural areas of southern and eastern Europe and Ireland, though 40 percent did return to their native countries. America would win out. Over a half century, the new immigrants would establish stable communities.[11]

The industrialists got their labor force for the mines, railways, and factories in the cities by recruiting families from the most impoverished and rural parts of Europe. The recruitment as families would prove disruptive, too. While young single girls worked in the factories for very low wages in unsafe conditions, all the females were expected to marry and take over the very hard work at home. The husband was genuinely the male breadwinner with all the respect and legal status; his role was to earn enough to keep his family above subsistence. But the wives were still expected to earn more for the home by sewing, taking in boarders, or selling rags in addition to their labor-intensive chores. Unions, progressives, philanthropists, and enlightened employers worked for a higher family wage and for laws requiring kids to be in school and limiting female employment.

The working and living conditions in the heart of America's Industrial Revolution, however, were a scandal in the making. The factory buildings and housing were built shoddily as local officials ignored building codes. The surging populations jammed into tenements where people lived in squalor and were at risk from epidemics of contagious diseases. That horror did galvanize local groups, charities, and the churches to work for change. The progressive Republican Jane Addams launched the national settlement house movement, and she won the support of wealthy donors, intellectuals, philanthropists, and a host of female volunteers. She opened the Hull House settlement house in Chicago's Little Italy, though it also served the Germans and Jews, Greeks, Irish, and French Canadian immigrants in their neighborhoods.

Hull House battled for child labor laws and to protect immigrant women who were being pushed into sexual slavery. They worked to establish building codes and to expand health inspections, sanitation, and rubbish removal—and to get those, they had to challenge the local party bosses, whose corrupt relationship with landlords and factory owners allowed them to escape inspection.

The settlement house movement was on the front line of the push for reform in the cities and became a platform for progressives fighting for working people. At age twenty-five, Frances Perkins volunteered at Hull House and worked closely with Jane Addams, and would later become FDR's secretary of labor and America's first female cabinet secretary. This was where she met the writer Upton Sinclair, the famous muckraker who worked undercover in the factories and wrote the best-selling novel *The Jungle*. It depicted the struggles of a Lithuanian immigrant family that worked in a meatpacking factory with brazenly unsanitary and desperate working conditions. The book caused a sensation and led to the passage of the Pure Food and Drug Act in 1906, one of the first major progressive reforms at the national level.[12]

The workers organized and fought to establish unions to affect their working conditions and terms of employment. They pushed back against pay cuts, demanded safer working conditions, and wanted a say in the speed of the production process. The industrialists opposed any recognition of labor unions, wanted the freedom to speed up the production process, and above all, to institute a twelve-hour workday. The longer hours would allow them to employ only two shifts of workers, which business management professionals told them would be maximally efficient and profitable in a very competitive world—just as the workers, the unions, and their allies were demanding an eight-hour day as a new norm.[13]

With workers and owners on a collision course in these closing decades of the nineteenth century, the country witnessed pitched battles between striking workers and armed police, militias, state National Guard units, and sometimes the U.S. Army. Authorities resorted to widespread violence in Chicago, Baltimore, Pittsburgh, and St. Louis to put down the Great Railroad Strike of 1877. That hardly ended the industrial unrest. The coal strikes in 1884 were joined by 132,000 United Mine Workers in Pennsylvania, Ohio, Iowa, West Virginia, Tennessee, Kentucky, Missouri, Alabama, and Colorado, and 25,000 miners joined the strike in Illinois. And in 1886, Doris Kearns Goodwin estimates, 600,000 workers were out on strike.[14]

The industrialists atop this new economic order created huge trusts—gigantic corporate monopolies—that allowed them to dominate America's industrial economy. They succeeded by dramatically eliminating competitors and achieving enough market power to push up prices, or in the view of the industrialists, "stabilize prices." The trust was wholly a product of a special deal between the industrialists and government. To start, the federal government maintained high tariffs on a broad range of specific products and commodities to protect America's industry from foreign competition. It blessed or turned a blind eye to market practices that allowed the big companies to drive competitors out of business and establish preferential rates for favored companies while setting higher rates for farmers. Finally, at the federal, state, and local levels, government used violence to suppress worker demands for higher wages.

The industrialists kept these corrupt deals hidden from public scrutiny, the investigative journalists would write, "by manipulating local political machines and wooing legislators and journalists." The companies made big payoffs, though small payoffs, such as passes for a legislator and his friends and family to travel free on the railroads, were also effective.[15]

Andrew Carnegie gave America its first billion-dollar corporation, achieved with American ingenuity at manipulation, taking advantage of favorable government policies and new technology, and defeating all competition. He began his career in finance, using insider information to make investments. He became a broker for the shares of overcapitalized companies, sold stocks at inflated prices, and took a cut off the top for himself, which he used to start his iron business. Faced with overproduction and instability, Carnegie used his market power to cut special deals with the Pennsylvania Railroad and bridge companies at the expense of his competitors. This domestic steel industry became viable because the federal government imposed a high tariff on imported steel in 1870. With that advantage, Carnegie visited the Bessemer steel plant in Sheffield, England, and introduced their advanced technology in his new steel plant near Pittsburgh. And when the railroads shifted from iron to steel, Carnegie realized a yet bigger fortune. He was not just the right person in the right place at the right time.[16]

John D. Rockefeller would surpass all the other "robber barons," achieving a net worth of $1 billion by 1913—2 percent of the country's GNP at the time. Very talented and daring, he viewed himself as a man of rectitude, though this self-image masked the breathtakingly dishonest and brutal market practices that allowed him to crush his rivals, an exposé by *McClure's Magazine* concluded. Ida Tarbell described the Standard Oil Trust as "the most perfectly developed trust in existence; that is, it satisfies most nearly the trust ideal of entire control of the commodity in which it deals."[17]

Rockefeller started his oil refining business in Cleveland, expanding his control of the market and eventually establishing the Standard Oil Company. In 1871, he joined what Tarbell called "a remarkable scheme" to force foreigners to purchase refined U.S. oil instead of crude, which could be refined more cheaply abroad. He established a secret partnership with a large portion of the oil refiners and shippers. That allowed them the power to negotiate rebates with the railroads for themselves and impose price penalties on their competition. He then forced twenty-one of twenty-six refineries in Cleveland to sell out to him. With such market dominance, he cut output to keep prices up. At the same time, the railroads conspired to stop exporting American crude oil, forcing Europe to buy America's refined oil products.[18]

Rockefeller's business model and fortune were made possible by his "power in state and federal government, in the press, in the college, [and] in the pulpit," Tarbell writes. He was tireless in fighting against any "legislation directed against combinations."[19]

John Pierpont Morgan emerged as the most respected Wall Street banker, known for his "sobriety and responsibility." As Jackson Lears writes, he was American capitalism's assured leader in time of crisis. He looked on the booming railway industry as a kind of Wild West, and he worked to get rid of the weak players. He backed the "natural monopoly" in each region where the state governments were happy to play a helpful role by granting state charters and rights-of-way. In a process that became known as "Morganization," he shifted investments in the railroad from bonds to equities. That consolidated the financing of these industries in the Wall Street investment banks.[20]

In the late 1880s, J. Pierpont Morgan joined two other railroad owners and merged their holdings into a trust—the Northern Securities Company—putting control of half the rail mileage in the United States under his control. Journalist Ray Stannard Baker wrote in *McClure's* at the time that "You can now ride from England to China on regular lines of steamships and railroads without once passing from the protecting hollow of Mr. Morgan's hand." It was the largest railroad corporation in the world.[21]

An America powerfully shaped by its frontier and new immigrant experience was transformed by an Industrial Revolution that left it as divided as old Europe. It has never witnessed such an extreme inequality again—until today. During America's first century as a country, the top 1 percent owned between 25 and 32 percent of the wealth. However, the Industrial Revolution allowed the top 1 percent to increase its share remarkably to 45 percent between 1870 and 1910.[22]

In reality, this was a difficult period for many businesses, with endemic low prices, frequent economic crises, and rampant business failures. Many of the trusts, such as the "rope trust," went bankrupt in the economic crisis of 1893, and the economy fell into depression. Andrew Carnegie, John D. Rockefeller, and J. P. Morgan argued that the trusts' efforts to cut costs and wages and eliminate competition, with government help, were prerequisites to America's economic hegemony. At one point it was an argument accepted by Theodore Roosevelt.

The workers and farmers were harder to convince of the value of the trusts, and they fought against them and the high tariffs. At a time when the great majority of Americans were living near subsistence, the government embraced policies that produced higher rail fares and production costs for farmers and higher prices for consumers. That sparked a rising popular resistance that helped propel the populist William Jennings Bryan to the Democratic nomination for president.

For America's industrialists, the election of 1896 would be a titanic battle that would decide the fate of the new industrial order and the role of the federal government.

The industrial magnates got behind William McKinley, whose first speech in the U.S. Congress was on the need to maintain high tariffs. That was the animating issue for them, and McKinley was an unapologetic candidate of industry and finance and champion of an economic nationalism that benefited the workingman, too.

His campaign manager was wealthy businessman Mark Hanna, who rallied America's industrial magnates to bankroll an unprecedented campaign to win the presidency. The railroad companies provided almost a million people with special discounted fares to hear McKinley speak on his porch in Canton, Ohio, and the Republicans spent $3.5 million on the campaign, nearly all of that raised in New York City. Paul Krugman is right to remind us that what the Republicans spent on that election is equivalent as a share of the GDP to $3 billion today, more than in any election in U.S. history. The billionaire donors to the post–*Citizens United* Republican campaigns look like pikers by comparison.[23]

It was a good investment. After McKinley's victory in 1896, money poured into the New York Stock Exchange, and the number of corporate mergers surged. Wall Street became the primary source of investment capital, and the number of investors doubled. Wall Street financed the "triumph of the trusts" and the concentrated control over industries after 1900 that gave us U.S. Steel, International Harvester, American Tobacco, Standard Oil, and Carnation Milk.[24]

The industrialists were not shy about pushing further concentration after defeating the populist forces in 1896, though popular opposition was hardly suppressed and reformers were making themselves heard in both parties. It would take two decades of growing progressive momentum in civil society and in the cities and states, but eventually conservatives would be put on the defensive. The public demanded that leaders address the excesses of the industrial order, and progressives would ultimately win control of Congress and the presidency. "A new political movement rose from the flames," Michael Wolraich wrote, "and triggered one of the greatest explosions of change in U.S. history: income taxes, labor law, women's suffrage, campaign finance reform, environmentalism, industrial regulation, the Federal Reserve and other reforms that define modern America." These reforms made it possible to restrain the industrialists and create an industrializing America whose excesses are checked and bounty more broadly shared.[25]

The impetus for reform came in civil society, and the "socially responsible reporter-reformer" played a big part, as described in Doris Kearns Goodwin's account of Taft and Roosevelt. The pioneers of investigative journalism—Lincoln Steffens, Ray Stannard Baker, William Allen White, and Ida M. Tarbell—were all recruited to *McClure's Magazine*. It was priced to sell, and circulation hit a quarter million. The magazine, Goodwin writes, "would play a signal role in rousing the country to the need for political and economic reform, animating the Progressive movement." In an exchange of letters with President Teddy Roosevelt in 1908, Steffens explains his zeal for exposing the corrupted link between business and government: "Trace every case of corruption you know to its source, and you will see, I believe, that somebody was trying to get out of Government some special right; to keep a saloon open after hours; a protective tariff; a ship subsidy; a public-service franchise." Those are the "principal evils" that the muckraking journalists worked to expose.[26]

Many journalists would form close relationships with and advise the most prominent progressive leaders. As a police reporter, Lincoln Steffens accompanied New York City's new reform police commissioner, Teddy Roosevelt, on his raids, and they talked often during Roosevelt's time as commissioner and later at the White House. Steffens also formed a personal relationship with governor and then senator Robert La Follette of Wisconsin and admired his impatience and bolder approach to winning reforms. Ray Stannard Baker's writings were important to Teddy Roosevelt, and later Baker worked hard to see President Woodrow Wilson succeed.[27]

Herbert Croly founded *The New Republic* as a political weekly in 1914 to build on the ferment for reform generated by the temperance, suffrage, anti-trust, and trade union movements and by the huge progressive electoral battles. Croly's new progressive insight was that Thomas Jefferson's individualism could only be realized with the help of a strong central state. He spent many hours with Teddy Roosevelt after his third-party race and launched the political weekly to "serve as a transmission belt of ideas, carrying the thoughts of intellectuals to a much broader and, therefore, much more meaningful audience," Franklin Foer wrote for the magazine's uncertain hundred-year anniversary. A young Walter Lippmann joined the magazine in 1914, and he would advise President Woodrow Wilson and help with his work to fashion a liberal postwar order.[28]

Republicans Teddy Roosevelt and Senator La Follette fought bitterly and were contemptuous of each other's methods and motives. Nonetheless, they finally broke the conservatives' hold on the Republican Party. Teddy Roosevelt was self-consciously a "practical man" who compromised to get things done. "He pushed for change one small step at a time" and cut deals with the trusts and the conservative leaders of both the U.S. House and Senate. Roosevelt declared, "Nothing of value is to be expected from ceaseless agitation for radical and extreme legislation"—a reference to Senator La Follette's call for bold action. Roosevelt believed "in "fighting one evil at a time" and trusted people "who take the next step; not those who theorize about the two-hundredth step."[29]

But a short decade later, Teddy Roosevelt would embrace the whole package of reforms with the same zeal and boldness as his former adversary.

What kept the pressure on national leaders was the early success of uncompromising progressive leaders who defeated the conservatives in key states. They insisted on regulating business abuse, and even more important, on enacting democratic reforms that allowed them to rally popular support to defeat the conservative backlash. At the local level, Jackson Lears writes, "Progressive mayors were often the best at revitalizing democracy—partly through the innovation of 'home rule,' which freed city governments from conservative and often corrupt state legislatures, and partly through the encouragement of citizens' engagement in policy-making." Mayors Tom Johnson of Cleveland, Sam Jones of Toledo, and Hazen Pingree of Detroit increased popular participation, offered social services once provided by the party machines, regulated business, and took control of public utilities.[30]

Their achievements inspired large-scale reforms in the states. In 1905, Governor La Follette of Wisconsin demanded that the state's legislature pass Wisconsin's own railway bill, regulate corporate lobbyists, and require railway companies to open their books to state auditors. He threatened to remain governor and not take up his U.S. Senate seat unless the legislature passed his program of reforms.[31]

Many states would try to emulate the "Wisconsin idea." They taxed the railroads, outlawed rebates, and required lower shipping rates. They regulated the public utilities and authorized the state to take public ownership, if need be. Wisconsin went further and enacted a state income tax, established housing codes to get rid of slums, raised the compulsory school age to sixteen, and passed a state minimum wage law. The goal was reforms that improved living conditions and wages and allowed a family to live above subsistence. They wanted to make sure the worker and farmer got a fair deal.

To make progress, La Follette understood you had to break the power of local party machines and expose their corrupt ties with business. He introduced the referendum that allowed the public to vote directly on issues and direct primaries for all offices and state delegates to party conventions to circumvent and weaken the established parties. And by 1912, twelve states had followed Wisconsin and introduced direct primaries.[32]

Progressive reformers in the states also worked to reduce social abuse and violence and to help the new immigrants have more stable families. That put them in the middle of the battle over temperance. Many of the women reformers fought to bar the sale of alcohol to protect women and children from drunken husbands and from wife beating. It also undercut the party local machines that used alcohol and the local saloons to "buy" the votes of immigrant workers.

Reformers were very focused on protecting women and the family, and prohibition had the support of progressives, populists, suffragists, the NAACP, Protestant congregations, and the Industrial Workers of the World. By the time the national Prohibition movement got taken up at the federal level, nearly two-thirds of Americans were already living in "dry" states. That was part of the progressive momentum in civil society.[33]

Woodrow Wilson, the president of Princeton University, ran for governor of New Jersey in 1910 and swept to a surprising victory. He apparently was paying close attention to the reformers in the cities and states, as he quickly repudiated the party bosses who nominated him. Wilson introduced, Lears writes, "a statewide corrupt-practices law to prevent business-government connivance, a Public Service Commission to set utility rates, a workmen's compensation law, and the empowerment of municipalities to use initiative, referendum, and recall."[34]

The country's growing disdain for the conservative defenders of the old order and support for the reformers produced the wave off-year election of 1910. Democrats won massively to take control of the Congress, and progressive Republicans held their seats against the wave. La Follette was triumphant: "In the beginning, our program of legislation was viewed with alarm and denounced as visionary, extreme, radical, and a menace to capital and to business interests. Today, the justice, the wisdom, the economic soundness of every Wisconsin law to which the progressive movement gave being, has conquered opposition and compelled approval in every enlightened commonwealth in America."[35]

The demand for radical progressive reforms and change became the common sense of the era, nurtured and flourishing as a model in the cities and states, even as conservatives and industrialists blocked change nationally. The stark contrast between progressive reforms in the states and conservative roadblocks nationally became a motivation for Teddy Roosevelt, who was considering running for president again. He delivered his "New Nationalism" speech in Osawatomie, Kansas, and declared, "so now the great special business interests too often control and corrupt the men and methods of government for their own profit. We must drive the special interests out of politics"—putting that task of attacking this essential evil on the same level as the task of confronting slavery.[36]

He then embraced in a powerful rush all the policies that the insurgents and state reformers had advanced: "tariff overhaul, workmen's compensation, child labor laws, direct Senate elections, voter referendums and recalls, minimum wages, maximum workweeks, workplace safety regulations, physical valuation of *all* corporations, graduated income and inheritance taxes, environmental conservation, and public disclosure of campaign donations." He would ultimately run as the candidate of the Progressive Party after the Republicans scorned him.[37]

Running under the banner "New Freedom," Woodrow Wilson won an extraordinary victory in a three-way presidential contest and would now work with a Congress where progressives from both parties were the majority. In his inaugural address in front of the U.S. Capitol, the new president declared America's duty "to cleanse, to reconsider, to restore, to correct the evil" before it.[38]

After being sworn in by the chief justice, President Wilson made clear he would attack the tariff system that "makes the Government a facile instrument in the hand of private interests," including a banking and currency system suited to fifty years earlier; an industrial system that "restricts the liberties and limits the opportunities of labor, and exploits without renewing or conserving the natural resources of the country."[39]

Over the next four years, the big progressive majority from both parties marginalized their conservative wings, and after two decades of impasse, the progressives proceeded boldly. They moved immediately and slashed tariffs by a third and barred Congress from favoring particular industries. The Federal Reserve Act was created in 1913 to issue currency, create a national banking system, and counter the dominance of the private banks. By 1913, three-quarters of the states had ratified the Sixteenth Amendment, permitting a federal income tax, and an income tax bill was passed. The Clayton Antitrust Law of 1914 outlawed price discrimination and gave the president the ability to block corporate mergers—eliminating one of the original abuses of the industrialists that had motivated the progressive reaction.

In 1914, enough states had ratified the Seventeenth Amendment, and in future elections U.S. senators would be directly elected by the people. The conservative Supreme Court overturned the new laws that barred the use of child labor in manufacturing, though the reformers were able to establish an eight-hour day, overtime pay for railway workers, and workmen's compensation for federal employees. Before very long, the Nineteenth Amendment gave women the right to vote.[40]

Congress also enacted the Eighteenth Amendment barring the manufacture, sale, and transportation of alcohol, despite President Wilson's objection. Keep in mind that progressive reformers such as Eleanor Roosevelt supported Prohibition to protect women and children from abusive men, because alcohol was addictive and degrading to urban life—one of the dark social consequences of America's Industrial Revolution that progressives set out to mitigate.

The country would repeal the Eighteenth Amendment thirteen years later, but for better or worse, progressives and the country were seeking to address the social as well as the economic consequences of America's rapid industrialization and Gilded Age. In this case, it overreached. In other places, though, the program underreached and would have to wait for the "New Deal" and a new Supreme Court that would accept reforms that empowered labor and allowed much higher taxes on the richest. Still, these bold progressive reforms fundamentally changed American capitalism and democracy and allowed America's dominant century.

America today is at a comparable tipping-point moment.

12 MOMENTUM FOR REFORM

America today is at a tipping-point moment comparable to the one before the progressive era. Like the earlier progressives, reformers today are building momentum in society, charities, and churches, creating models of reform in the cities and the states, and building toward major changes that can shift the trajectory on inequality, challenge the tightening bond of business and government, and expand democracy. If the first progressive era is any guide, the big issues will not be settled in one presidential election, though each election will embolden the reformers to build an era of reform.

MOMENTUM FOR REFORM

The momentum for reform in the progressive era became irresistible when leaders and activists in all domains became aligned on the central questions— what was wrong, what problems had to be addressed, what values should guide the work of change, and what kind of country we wanted it to be. In short, the momentum for reform moves to a tipping point when reformers have won the argument at the heart of America's disruptive revolutions. They get the main stage to tell us what issues are most important, what must be addressed, and with what urgency.

That I have reached this point in the book and *not* proposed the formation of a bipartisan commission to address the deepest problems is a measure of how much America has changed since Simpson and Bowles's National Commission on Fiscal Responsibility and Reform and the Bipartisan Policy Center's Debt Reduction Task Force. Addressing the deficit and entitlements is not the key to America's renewal. They are part of an age of austerity that has limited America's potential. In any event, today's Republican Party is preoccupied with the battle for America's values and has repudiated every bipartisan policy idea in its policy agenda.

To achieve the radical reforms to check the excesses of the Gilded Age, the progressives of both parties had to break the power of the old stalwart conservatives in both parties. That is why this is a tipping point for reformers who are pressing on for change. For now, Democrats will only succeed in their role if they expose how destructive is the current Republican Party for the country and expose its corrupt strategy to keep the new American majority from governing. Conservatives are waging a guerrilla war against reform. So Democratic reformers will have to press their advantage for change to become inevitable.

If the modernization of the Democratic Party is any indication, the change that allowed for the nomination and election of Bill Clinton took a long time. The Republican Party has not even begun the process.

Democrats only embarked on party reform after their mainstream presidential candidate Walter Mondale lost in a landslide in 1984. A similar moment could come sooner than conservatives expect, and business and the business wing of the Republican Party could insist on much more than the gagging of the Tea Party. It could start with demands on immigration reform, funding for education, and infrastructure investment. Observant Catholics might be listening to Pope Francis about inclusiveness, poverty, and the destructive effects of climate change. Maybe a shattering defeat in both the election and the culture war will allow some of the Evangelicals to follow the path of the mainline Protestants who defend the safety net and immigration, and accept homosexuality, gay marriage, and the need to address climate change. Perhaps some of the less politicized Evangelical churches will grow impatient with the partisan impasse and get to work with others in their community to rescue the working-class family and children.

Until then, the Republican Party is unwavering in its commitment to lower taxes and the smallest possible government, which leaves them with no national project other than waging wars against Islamic extremists and containing Russia and China. Republicans struggle with America's immigrant and racial diversity and view the badly frayed safety net as overly generous and the cause of dependence and poverty. They think the middle class is doing better than you think and insist the jury is still out as to whether inequality really exists or matters that much.

We do not know whether opportunistic presidential candidates co-opting the language of "poverty" and "inequality" will really change the party's trajectory. Their answers will still likely be less immigration, fewer food stamps, and more traditional families.

Republicans are still coming to terms with the sexual revolution and thus are uncomfortable with contraception and making accommodations for working women and single working mothers. They remain unconvinced about the value of education and higher education and have tried to reduce America's funding of education and research. They are very skeptical about science and dismissive of claims about climate change. With deep roots in rural America, they have yet to come to terms with the diversity of our culture, marriages, and lifestyles celebrated in metropolitan areas and among the Millennials and by many major businesses.

Republicans hold their views more deeply, sound more confident, and act more urgently because they are winning elections in the more rural conservative heartland that feels deeply threatened by the ascendant trends in the country. As they lose their grip on the country, as they did in California, they move even farther to the right to mobilize and consolidate their Tea Party and Evangelical bases. Their bases and rural support allow them to govern as real conservatives, particularly in the twenty states where they are largely uncontested by the Democrats, and compete for control of the U.S. Congress for now.

Because they are vociferous, confident, and united in their battle against America's revolutions does not mean the country is listening to them. Today's conservative Republicans have lost the argument on the character of the country and what are the urgent problems to be addressed.

As conservatives rally their forces, keep in mind that seven in ten Americans say rising diversity means Americans will be enriched by exposure to different cultures and that a more diverse workforce will lead to more economic growth and make American businesses more innovative. A majority in the country and nearly two-thirds of the growing Millennial generation say immigrants strengthen American society.[1]

You know conservatives are losing the argument when Alan Greenspan, chairman of the Federal Reserve during the boom years before the financial collapse, makes this confession before the House Committee on Oversight and Government Reform: "Those of us who have looked to the self-interest of lending institutions to protect shareholders' equity (myself especially) are in a state of shocked disbelief." What did he say? Greenspan acknowledged he had lost "faith" that "self-interest would deliver financial stability." Acting as a simultaneous interpreter, Martin West writes: "It is as if the Pope declared he no longer believed in the Resurrection of Jesus Christ." With that, you realize how much was shattered by the crisis. The "established views" of how the advanced "economies and financial systems work" turn out to be "nonsense." "It confirmed," West concludes, "that the financial system is a ward of the state, rather than a part of the market economy." If you are a conservative, that should take you back to the drawing board.[2]

You know there has been a shift in momentum when you look at the reaction to the U.S. release of Thomas Piketty's *Capital in the Twenty-first Century*. It set off intense national debates about inequality. It also exposed how fractured conservatives are on this core problem. Some conservatives minimized the importance of inequality or belittled the frenzy among liberals. Some acknowledged the problem but urged conservatives to be wary of what policies might emerge out of such a debate. Others urged their colleagues to acknowledge the problem and consider innovative conservative ideas to lessen inequality or rethink their opposition to the inheritance tax or other measures. One even suggested that conservatives defer to the liberals and accept that Democrats will likely govern nationally in the medium term and let them mitigate the worst consequences of inequality.[3]

You know momentum has shifted when economic and social science research at distinguished universities and institutes show an inescapable story since World War II. When Democrats hold the presidency. the economy and median income grow decidedly faster than when there is a Republican president, and income inequality and poverty are mitigated. When conservative economists joined the debate on the state of the middle class and inequality, they confirmed the same post–World War II historic pattern. Critically, they confirmed that low-tax policies never produced a period of economic growth. They are simply naked when it comes to their defining policy on the economy. You can see the shift in momentum when the public puts cutting taxes at the very bottom of the list of policies to help the economy and a large majority wants to raise taxes on the richest.

Paul Krugman's provocative columns and headlines—"RETURN OF THE BUMS ON WELFARE"; "THOSE LAZY JOBLESS"; "THE DEFLATION CAUCUS"; "THE FISCAL FIZZLE: AN IMAGINARY BUDGET AND DEBT CRISIS"; "ADDICTED TO INFLATION"; or "OBAMACARE FAILS TO FAIL"—spotlight how archaic are conservative policies and how errant are their forecasts for the economy and social policy. He presses the liberals' advantage among social scientists and economists on the evidence, even if the debate on austerity with the public is still contested.[4]

The *New York Times*'s *The Upshot*, *FiveThirtyEight*, *The Washington Post*'s *Wonkblog*. *Salon*, *The Guardian*, and the next generation of digital sites like *Quartz*, *Vox*, and *Intercept* are creating a new audience for data-based stories on what is really happening in government, the economy, and society, and they are beginning to receive the attention that the investigative reforming journalists had in the progressive era. This new journalism brings an inescapable clarity and authority when they broadcast headlines such as:

"CORPORATIONS USED TO PAY ALMOST ONE-THIRD OF FEDERAL TAXES. NOW IT'S ONE-TENTH"

"BOOSTING SCHOOL FUNDING 20 PERCENT ERASED THE GRADUATION GAP BETWEEN RICH AND POOR STUDENTS"

"AMONG THE POOR, WOMEN FEEL INEQUALITY MORE DEEPLY"

"THE TYPICAL HOUSEHOLD, NOW WORTH A THIRD LESS"

"CHART: THE MINIMUM WAGE IN AMERICA IS PRETTY DAMN LOW"

"THE HEAD OF THE IMF SAYS INEQUALITY THREATENS DEMOCRACY. HERE ARE 7 CHARTS PROVING SHE'S RIGHT"

While many of these writers are not self-consciously social reforming journalists, they expose the stark realities in new and legitimate ways, and their observations begin to create an inescapable conventional wisdom.[5]

And when ordinary citizens began shooting and sharing cell phone videos of the deaths of Eric Garner, Walter Scott, and Freddie Gray at the hands of the police, they forced discriminatory treatment of black youth onto the public agenda.

You know who has the momentum when you consider that the median age of *Fox News* viewers is sixty-nine and rising, and Millennials are much more likely to tune in and get their news from *The Daily Show*. And when conservative talk radio hosts grumbled about Coca-Cola's sixty-second Super Bowl commercial depicting scenes of a multicultural America with "America, the Beautiful" sung by kids in seven languages, the executives pushed back and doubled down.[6]

Something has changed when the Komen Foundation, the leading charity fighting breast cancer with its Race for the Cure, faced a huge public outcry and plummeting race participation when it dropped funding to Planned Parenthood to conduct mammograms. Planned Parenthood is viewed favorably by a not inconsiderable majority of the public.[7]

You know the tide is growing overwhelming when Justice Anthony Kennedy writes for the Supreme Court majority: "Under the Constitution, same-sex couples seek in marriage the same legal treatment as opposite-sex couples, and it would disparage their choices and diminish their personhood to deny them this right." And in a sign of the times, Wal-Mart publicly lobbied an Arkansas governor to veto a religious freedom bill because it is at odds with their views on "diversity and inclusion."[8]

It is game, set, and match when Pope Francis's apostolic exhortation declares, "Just as the commandment 'Thou shalt not kill' sets a clear limit in order to safeguard the value of human life, today we also have to say 'thou shalt not' to an economy of exclusion and inequality. Such an economy kills."[9]

With growing confidence in the momentum for reform, more and more leaders are taking advantage of the emerging space to advocate for change.

LEADING FROM AMERICAN CITIES AND METROPOLITAN AREAS

America's cities and metropolitan areas play an outsized role in generating the country's economic and cultural dynamism and a growing proportion of the citizenry wants to live and work there. Yet these metropolitan areas are also the cauldron for the deepest inequality and blocked mobility, the lowest wages and highest prices, and the poor and working-class families struggling to raise children in single-parent homes. That stark paradox is starting to move and motivate leaders to get on with addressing these deep problems.

The national government is not likely to act, so political, civic, and business leaders in the cities are moving to raise the minimum wage and improve education opportunities and begin to address the problems of working families. As I wrote earlier, many are addressing climate change in pretty dramatic and impactful ways.

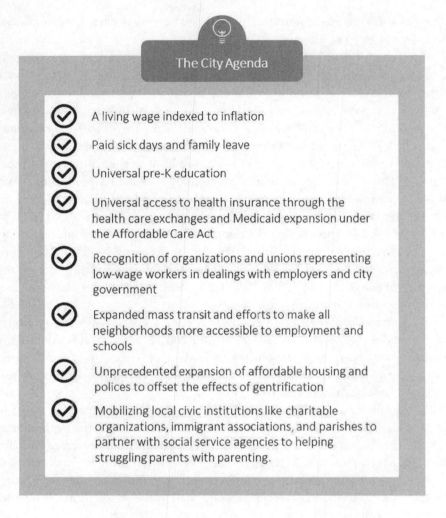

The City Agenda

- ✓ A living wage indexed to inflation

- ✓ Paid sick days and family leave

- ✓ Universal pre-K education

- ✓ Universal access to health insurance through the health care exchanges and Medicaid expansion under the Affordable Care Act

- ✓ Recognition of organizations and unions representing low-wage workers in dealings with employers and city government

- ✓ Expanded mass transit and efforts to make all neighborhoods more accessible to employment and schools

- ✓ Unprecedented expansion of affordable housing and polices to offset the effects of gentrification

- ✓ Mobilizing local civic institutions like charitable organizations, immigrant associations, and parishes to partner with social service agencies to helping struggling parents with parenting.

As we saw in the progressive era, it was cities such as Cleveland, Toledo, and Detroit and states such as Wisconsin that advanced a package of reforms that proved successful and became a model that presidents and parties nationally ultimately embraced.

The truth is that the metropolitan level may be the right place to address many of these issues. Moving the new progressive agenda locally and in the states may allow reformers to build more public support while also making more rapid progress in a period when the national government is distrusted, corrupted, and dysfunctional.

People's life chances are fundamentally affected by their broader metropolitan area, local community, and immediate neighborhood, as Raj Chetty, Nathaniel Hendren, Patrick Kline, and Emmanuel Saez have demonstrated in their groundbreaking work. And just as local factors impact people's chances for intergenerational mobility, they also reveal what kinds of initiatives would be most effective.[10]

And a number of cities and states are beginning to take up the challenge.

If the national minimum wage were gradually raised to $10.10 an hour by 2016 and then adjusted for inflation, 16.5 million people would see a pay increase and 900,000 people would be lifted out of poverty. The Congressional Budget Office estimates that about half a million jobs would be lost as a result, a 0.3 percent dip in employment, though that small downside is contested by studies that take a side-by-side look at the employment measures in neighboring states where only one has raised its minimum wage. Raising the minimum wage to $10.78 an hour would place it at 55 percent of the median full-time wage, up from the current 37 percent and back to where it stood in 1968 before the middle-class compact came undone.[11]

The president's efforts to raise the minimum wage to $10.10 an hour from the current rate of $7.25 were blocked by Republicans in Congress. In the absence of congressional action, he at least raised the minimum wage for federal employees and contractors.

Raising the minimum wage, however, is one of the tools available to cities and states in the absence of federal action, and cities and states are already realizing that there is no reason for them to wait. Cities are attracting the most educated and most affluent, though they are also drawing in more service and immigrant workers too.

Ten states and the District of Columbia raised their minimum wage in 2014, and a like number have scheduled increases starting at the beginning of 2015, with key states such as California, Connecticut, Delaware, Hawaii, Illinois, Massachusetts, Maryland, New Mexico, and New York indexing the level to inflation to keep up with rising costs. The minimum wage is already higher than the federal level in nearly half of the states, though only one of them, Montana, is in the GOP conservative heartland.[12]

Minimum-wage increases were on the ballot in five states in 2014, and the voters passed all of them.[13]

In 2003, San Francisco and Santa Fe became the first cities to establish their own minimum wage. Today, West Coast cities are pushing the bar higher and purposefully above the proposed federal minimum wage. In 2014, Seattle passed a law increasing the minimum wage from $9.32 to $15.00 by 2018—more than twice the current federal minimum wage and approaching a *living wage,* which should likely be the guide if reformers are serious about addressing the fundamental issue of jobs that don't pay enough to live on. San Jose raised its minimum wage to $10.66 an hour and Santa Fe raised its to $10.84; San Diego passed a minimum-wage increase to $11.50 by 2018 and Oakland voted for a $13.19 minimum wage by then as well.[14]

New York City mayor Bill de Blasio signed an executive order to imme-

Minimum wage laws in the states, as of Jan. 1, 2015

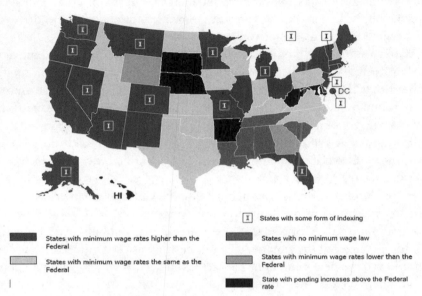

I States with some form of indexing	
States with minimum wage rates higher than the Federal	States with no minimum wage law
States with minimum wage rates the same as the Federal	States with minimum wage rates lower than the Federal
	State with pending increases above the Federal rate

Niraj Chokshi, "Twenty States Raised Their Minimum Wage Today," *The Washington Post*, January 1, 2015.

diately increase the minimum wage for businesses contracting with the city to $13.13 per hour, and that amount is expected to increase to $15.22 by 2019. Mayor Rahm Emanuel in Chicago implemented an executive order to increase the minimum wage to $13.00 an hour for city contractors and sub-contractors. After Illinois voters passed a referendum to raise the minimum wage to $10 an hour in November, Mayor Emanuel pushed the City Council to pass a law increasing the minimum wage to $13 by 2018 and then index-ing future increases to inflation, as recommended by a task force of business and labor leaders.[15]

San Francisco decided these reforms have to lead to a living wage at the end of the day, and it voted in November 2014 to raise the minimum wage from $10.74 to $15.00 an hour by 2018. In Los Angeles, Mayor Eric Garcetti pro-posed to gradually increase the minimum wage to $13.25 an hour and link further increases to the Consumer Price Index, but the LA City Council studied the issue and then raised it to $15.

And to tilt the balance further, some leaders in the cities are starting to recognize organizations and movements that put pressure to raise wages from the bottom up.

Workers in fast-food restaurants such as McDonald's and Taco Bell have made headlines with their one-day walkouts in New York, Chicago, Detroit, Seattle, and Washington, D.C., to highlight their low wages. For all of labor's difficulties nationally, unions have backed Fight for $15 and OUR Walmart and have begun to win minimum-wage increases in major cities and states. And they have had success organizing domestic workers and taxi drivers in cities where elected leaders are supportive.[16]

With this growing momentum to raise the minimum wage and move toward a living wage in the metropolitan areas, businesses will soon take for granted that that is the price of entry and doing business. And that has already begun to happen. McDonald's, Wal-Mart, Target, T.J. Maxx, and Marshall's have announced new base wage rates above the legal minimum. "I really want to assert McDonald's as a modern and progressive burger company," its CEO declared, sounding like he fully identified with this new metropolitan culture.[17]

He has a long way to go to catch up with the CEO of a Seattle-based credit card payment processing company who announced that he would create a new minimum salary of $70,000 over three years, doubling the compensation for a quarter of the employees, while cutting his own million-dollar compensation to the new minimum. This act is unlikely to set an example, though it could help create a new norm in our cities.[18]

With momentum building from the bottom, congressional Democrats nationally have rallied around a $12 minimum wage, while the Congressional Progressive Caucus has committed to the Fight for $15.[19]

States and cities are moving ahead with other unaddressed national challenges as well. We may be looking back on this period and see Connecticut as the Wisconsin of this "new progressive era." Connecticut was the first state to raise the minimum wage to $10.10 and the first to pass a paid sick leave bill. Connecticut now requires businesses with fifty or more employees to provide up to one hour of paid sick leave for every forty hours worked. Between 200,000 and 300,000 employees have taken leave because they were sick, needed a checkup or medical test, or needed to look after a sick child or family member. After successful implementation of the Affordable Care Act, Connecticut brought the proportion uninsured down from 8 to 4 percent, and it is now among the states closest to universal health insurance coverage.

San Francisco, Washington, D.C., Denver, Seattle, New York City, Portland, Oregon, and Newark have all introduced paid sick leave, and California recently passed a law requiring small and large employers to provide three days of paid sick leave a year, which will benefit 6.5 million workers.[20]

A grab bag of states have also expanded preschool education, including red states such as Oklahoma, Georgia, and West Virginia, and more recently Alabama, Michigan, Minnesota, and Montana. The number of children in preschool has doubled since 2002, though still just 30 percent of four-year olds are in preschool.[21]

Some cities are moving to make universal pre-K the norm. In one of his earliest actions, the mayor of Chicago introduced full-day kindergarten in all the public schools. In the 2014 school year, the city expanded pre-K to allow 44,000 three- and four-year-olds to start classes. The mayor of New York City made universal pre-K his signature policy for addressing inequality and increasing upward mobility. Amazingly, at the beginning of the 2014–2015 school year, 51,500 kids enrolled in New York City preschool centers for the first time, only 1,500 short of the goal.[22]

Mayors are prioritizing social mobility because it is the cities where America is most unequal. As we discussed earlier, the metropolitan areas are attracting the most dynamic industries, the best-educated and the most affluent, though they are also growing lower-paid service sector jobs and attracting many new immigrants.

Local leaders are struggling to address the paradox of inequality and learn from the vast differences in upward mobility in different metropolitan areas, as outlined by Raj Chetty and his colleagues. Someone born in the lowest quarter of income earners has the best chance to reach the top of the ladder if they live in San Jose, Seattle, Boston, New York, or Los Angeles. They have the least chance if they live in Detroit or Atlanta. A child born in Atlanta has one-third the chance of one born in San Jose. Moreover, a fairly poor child in Seattle has as much chance of reaching the top as a middle-class child in Atlanta.[23]

This research teaches us that the state of the family and marriage in these cities—including whether children are raised by a single parent—are the biggest predictors of upward mobility. We also know that there is much greater opportunity in cities that are less physically divided by income and race, and where low-income families are less isolated and workers have shorter commute times to reach work. Transportation and segregation matter.[24]

These are huge challenges, and many of today's mayors lead in cities where the family is under stress and neighborhoods are highly segregated. With so much history of class and racial segregation and some mass transit systems built a century ago, creating linkages that bring the city closer together will be a daunting challenge. That means expanding mass transit that links poorer and low-income neighborhoods to their work opportunities and the expansion of affordable housing.

In Chicago, Mayor Emmanuel fulfilled a campaign promise to modernize and expand the Red Line to the mainly African American South Side. In the Seattle metropolitan area, the county mass transit system began giving discounts to its low-wage commuters whose income did not exceed 200 percent of the federal poverty level.[25]

New York mayor de Blasio has committed to expand affordable housing by 200,000 units over the next ten years, as The New York Times keeps reminding him in its editorials. A year later, they applauded his "timely and exciting mission," which is premised on extensive building in more densely populated areas, making more units permanently affordable. The task the mayor has set out is daunting, though this is where all these mayors will struggle to keep these cities affordable for their diverse populations.[26]

The cities and states are pushing ahead with reforms to raise incomes, provide new kinds of support for working women and working men, create a real safety net, and address the challenges facing families. These are the critical contradictions in this period, and the cities and states are setting the new policy agenda for the country.

THE CHURCHES

America is a diverse country undergoing huge changes that can enrich our communities and the nation broadly. America's potential is threatened by the concentration of wealth at the top, though it is threatened just as much by the changes in the family, marriage, and the vast number of children being raised by single parents. The new leaders in cities and states are moving ahead in impressive ways, yet few have highlighted their rescue plans for the family. Reformers need ideas and allies to really begin to tackle what is happening in these communities.

In earlier times, the churches and religious charities were progressive allies in caring for the poor, defending the immigrants, and advocating for change. Progressives could turn to the major churches for inspiration, organization, or as allies in the battle for reform and rights. That changed when the Evangelicals joined the counterrevolution against the sexual revolution and against the demands of blacks, women, and immigrants for equal rights. Since 2004, they have been closely allied with the social conservatives and the Republican Party. The Catholic Church gave such primacy to abortion and innocent life and battling against marriage equality that observant Catholics became an important part of the Republican base. So it has been difficult for Democrats to turn instinctively to the churches as allies in bringing progressive change.

Pope Francis's apostolic exhortation in "The Proclamation of the Gospel in Today's World," however, signaled a marked departure in the Catholic Church's focus and tone. He called on the faithful "to embark on a new chapter of evangelization" as a "Church whose doors are open," like a "mother with an open heart." It should avoid a style that is "obsessed" with a "multitude of doctrines to be insistently imposed."[27]

That was simply his point of entry, however.

The pope thinks that an "economy of exclusion and inequality" kills, as I quoted earlier. He explicitly rejected the economic philosophy that is at the heart of today's conservative Republican thinking. He challenged those who "continue to defend trickle-down theories, which assume that economic growth, encouraged by a free market, will inevitably succeed in bringing about greater justice and inclusiveness in the world." He dismissed that proposition empirically, saying that it "has never been confirmed by the facts."[28]

He also attacked the "crude and naïve trust in the goodness of those wielding economic power" and the lack of charitable feeling inherent in this worldview: "Almost without being aware of it, we end up being incapable of feeling compassion at the outcry of the poor, weeping for other people's pain, and feeling a need to help them, as though all this were someone else's responsibility and not our own." The values associated with such an economic policy lead conservatives precisely to the outcome the pope fears: "its emphasis on success and self-reliance does not appear to favor an investment in effort to help the slow, the weak or the less talented to find opportunities in life."[29]

Pope Francis changes everything.

"We have created new idols," the pope concludes. "The worship of the ancient golden calf has returned in the new and ruthless guise of the idolatry of money," with the following result: "While the earnings of a minority are growing exponentially, so too is the gap separating the majority from the prosperity enjoyed by those happy few."[30]

The pope embraced the core argument of this book: the deepest problems must be addressed if we are to make progress. "As long as the problems of the poor are not radically resolved by rejecting the absolute autonomy of markets and financial speculation and by attacking the structural causes of inequality, no solution will be found for the world's problems or, for that matter, any problems. Inequality is the root of social ills."[31]

Pope Francis accepts that countries have reached a tipping point where powerful forces for progress are running up against the building social ills, with many people at the end financially and struggling to live.

> In our time humanity is experiencing a turning-point in its history, as we see the advances being made in so many fields. We can only praise the steps being taken to improve people's welfare in areas such as health care, education and communication. At the same time we have to remember that the majority of our contemporaries are barely living from day to day, with dire consequences.

It is a "turning-point," the pope believes, because the contradictions and the need to act are both becoming inescapable. In such a world "The joy of living frequently fades, lack of respect for others and violence are on the rise, and inequality is increasingly evident."[32]

It is in the cities, the pope understands, where the multicultural mix comes together to build and innovate and find ways to live in proximity and not to just tolerate but respect and celebrate differences:

> *How beautiful are those cities which overcome paralyzing mistrust, integrate those who are different and make this very integration a new factor of development! How attractive are those cities which, even in their architectural design, are full of spaces which connect, relate and favor the recognition of others!*

He admires the multiculturalism:

> *Cities are multicultural; in the larger cities, a connective network is found in which groups of people share a common imagination and dreams about life, and new human interactions arise, new cultures, invisible cities.*

He praises the cities that open their doors to immigrants and "prove capable of creating new forms of cultural synthesis" instead of "fearing the loss of local identity."[33]

But cities are also segregated and violent, and full of the contradictions we know so well:

> *Cities create a sort of permanent ambivalence because, while they offer their residents countless possibilities, they also present many people with any number of obstacles to the full development of their lives.*

The results are that cities are places for "mass protests" and where people seek "justice" and "a voice in public life."[34]

He also knows about the other contradictions in our culture, such as what is happening with families and people drawing back from civil society today.

> *The family is experiencing a profound cultural crisis, as are all communities and social bonds. In the case of the family, the weakening of these bonds is particularly serious because the family is the fundamental cell of society, where we learn to live.*

And Pope Francis insists, like so many economists concerned with mobility, that the "indispensable contribution of marriage to society transcends the feelings and momentary needs of the couple." He also sees the "depth of the obligation assumed by the spouses who accept to enter a total communion of life" as critical to people's material and spiritual well-being.[35]

In the face of such challenges, society needs charity expressed in "micro-relationships (with friends, with family member, or within small groups)," though it also needs to be expressed in our economy, civil society, and politics. "I beg the Lord," he writes, "to grant us more politicians who are genuinely disturbed by the state of society, the people, the lives of the poor!" They need to begin their work with focus on "the homeless, the addicted, refugees, indigenous peoples, the elderly who are increasingly isolated and abandoned, and many others," including migrants.[36]

Even more important, the pope sees an obligation to advance very specific policies whose goal is to ensure that growth's gains are broadly shared. It is almost as if he has read Joseph Stiglitz when he writes:

> Growth in justice requires more than economic growth, while presupposing such growth: it requires decisions, programs, mechanisms and processes specifically geared to a better distribution of income, the creation of sources of employment and an integral promotion of the poor.[37]

So Pope Francis really does change everything. He has thrown the Catholic Church behind the idea that the country is at a crisis point and all in civil society, business leaders and politicians, must work to offset the economic and cultural contradictions of our progress.

Pope Francis's exhortation should remind us that the church remains the strongest institution in many local communities, and America's religious community is fairly tolerant of religious pluralism and listens to a forgiving God. That includes large parts of the new American majority—the African American community and Hispanics—for whom church congregations are central to daily life, family, community, and politics.

Pope Francis is a natural ally in the battle to win support for an urban agenda to raise incomes and reduce poverty in these multicultural and dynamic metropolitan areas. He will no doubt be an ally in promoting infant health, universal health care as a right, and the need for children to learn skills and values at the earliest ages.

I do not underestimate the importance of that change, though that is the easy part, to be honest. America also needs congregations with more congregants, especially in poor and working-class neighborhoods where church attendance is falling and more people are trying to manage on their own. The family is in crisis. We need more people to marry, more children to be raised in two-parent households, and more parents to take responsibility for raising and educating their children, especially working-class men who have not settled in household roles. Nothing would prove more important to bringing greater happiness, social mobility, and rising incomes. And congregations can help.

We do not yet know whether the Catholic Church will ultimately end up welcoming gay congregants and accepting gay marriage and divorced Catholics. We do know for certain that Pope Francis embraces parents and parenting—and few things are more important to the well-being of children and their future prospects. Few things have as big an impact on social mobility and inequality in cities and the country as single motherhood.

America is being radically shaped by a "two-tier family" structure that is becoming deeply entrenched. "In the upper, college-educated third of American society, most kids today live with two parents, and such families nowadays typically have two incomes," Robert Putnam describes in his powerful book *Our Kids*. "In the lower, high-school-educated third, however, most kids live with at most one of their biological parents, and in fact, many live in a kaleidoscopic, multi-partner, or blended family, but rarely with more than one wage earner." The human toll, cost to society, and immorality of this state of affairs are calculable, as Putnam shows, but who's counting? That ought to be a call to arms.[38]

Francis himself sounds like he is trying to figure out how to help the children and the mothers and fathers who face such challenges. In statements to reporters after a trip to the Philippines, Pope Francis said Catholics do not need to breed "like rabbits." With the pope calling for "responsible parenthood," the Church's social agenda may come to include policies to reduce the number of unplanned pregnancies or to encourage teenagers to delay when they have children.[39]

It is not a foregone conclusion that if churches take up this mission with a sense of moral purpose teenagers will put off getting pregnant, more people will rush to get married, and more children will be raised in two-parent households. In macro terms, the areas of the country with the highest rates of church attendance are also the areas with the highest rates of divorce and single-parent homes. That correlation, however, could be a false one—simply the result of the concentration of non-college, working class, and poorer households in these areas, particularly in the South. However, we really do know that government programs to encourage marriage have not proved particularly effective. Well-funded government programs under George W. Bush that counseled people to marry just did not succeed in increasing marriage rates or keeping parents together.[40]

While making progress is difficult, there is a lot to be done that can reduce the number of unwanted pregnancies, delay childbearing, and improve parenting—particularly if civil society rallies to the compelling need to bring social change. Up until now, the churches have hesitated because the Catholic Church has opposed artificial birth control and fundamentalist denominations have resisted sex education. The reality is that social conservatives tried to block contraceptive coverage in the Affordable Care Act and are still battling to limit its scope.

Will the pope's new emphasis on delaying childbearing and helping struggling parents left behind by the new economy change what is possible? If
yes, here is where progressives should start.

We know we have the ability to reduce the number of unplanned pregnancies and the number of young, single moms. A stunning 60 percent of
their pregnancies are unintended. Half of these were the result of not using any contraception, and nearly as many from inconsistent or incorrect
use. Interviews with women suggest that "many young Americans are drift-
ing into pregnancy," the Brookings social mobility project reports. And
this trend is particularly pronounced among the poor and women without
a high school diploma, though it is also marked for high school graduates
too.[41]

The use of IUDs is extremely effective in preventing pregnancy, indeed,
20 times more than the pill. Black churches are already advocates for the
greater use of birth control and could be mobilized in the effort to expand
their use.[42]

A teenager who delays having a baby for two years and gets a high school
diploma will by age 29 earn $6,600 a year more than a teenager who does
not wait and fails to get a degree. These personal choices have a huge impact
on life chances.[43]

Federal government programs can have a measurable impact. Ron
Haskins, codirector of the Center on Children and Families at the Brookings Institution, points to the Nurse-Family Partnership—a program where
nurses visit mothers to advise on prenatal health, child rearing, and life
skills from before birth until the child is two years old. The participating
mothers "were less likely to abuse or neglect their kids, and more likely to
be working, and their kids were more likely to be healthy and ready for
school."[44]

Sentencing reform is supported by conservative and liberal elected officials and is an obvious starting point that would immediately affect families and parenting in these communities. Reforms could reduce sentences
for nonviolent criminals, rehabilitate ex-prisoners on a much wider scale,
and increase funding for job training and drug rehabilitation.[45]

Policies that expand tax credits and income to poorer families in a sustained way can be life changing. Receiving $3,000 in family income during
the first five years of a child's life has an astonishing impact—an increase in
academic achievement equivalent to 20 points on the SAT and 20 percent
higher income later in life.[46]

To really have a chance, the Catholic parishes, the black churches, and an
array of other congregations would likely need to take the lead in elevating
these issues and in their support for parents and parenting, but progressive
reformers have a big stake in their success too.

Stanley B. Greenberg

AMERICAN BUSINESS

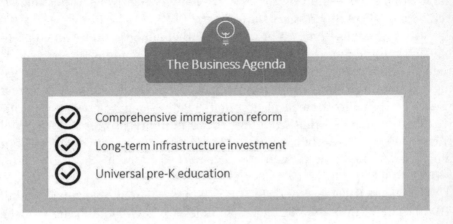

The Business Agenda

- ✓ Comprehensive immigration reform
- ✓ Long-term infrastructure investment
- ✓ Universal pre-K education

The business community is in a position to lead and ally with others in civil society to demand that national leaders of both parties move ahead with three critical reforms that will accelerate America's economic growth and expand opportunity. This is not some liberal wish list for business. The U.S. Chamber of Commerce and major business groups have supported and lobbied for comprehensive immigration reform, long-term infrastructure investment with public-private funding, and funding for universal pre-K in every city and state. Each has won major bipartisan backing. When passed, these reforms would relieve some of the greatest inefficiencies in the U.S. economy, reinforce America's competitive advantage, and help U.S. companies get the labor force they need. And critically for the country, they would expand employment, opportunity, and social mobility.

Think about the potential vibrancy of the American economy if immigration were reformed and the undocumented legalized, if public-private financing were allowing the rebuilding of America long-term, and if all children zero to five were getting early education. These are major reforms that allow America to realize the potential for growth and allow more people to share in the gains.

Business has as much interest in advancing these three changes as Democratic and reform leaders who now put these initiatives at the heart of their economic mandate. But the business community has hardly mobilized to support this agenda in the past few years. They were discouraged by Washington's dysfunction and a Republican Party that has walked away from all three. The current Republican Party cannot even entertain the idea of the "DREAMers" gaining legal status. The Paul Ryan budget cuts infrastructure spending by a quarter over the next decade, and Republicans at the federal and state levels have aggressively pushed for cuts in education funding.

It is not unimportant that the U.S. Chamber of Commerce and its allies spent heavily to defeat Tea Party candidates in the off-year elections and will rally to support "establishment" candidates in the presidential primaries. U.S. businesses cannot wait on the Chamber of Commerce to forsake its role as head of the business wing of the Republican Party. America cannot wait either.

The U.S. business community can only advance this critical agenda if it makes clear how high a priority these changes are and joins with prestigious coalitions to demand action on this three-part probusiness package. They should make clear: "Don't even think of yourself as pro-business unless you are with us on these three priorities."

Comprehensive immigration reform

The vitality of America's economy past and present is fueled by legal and illegal immigrants who contribute as consumers, employees, and employers and who are part of America's unique cultural diversity. The Border Security, Economic Opportunity, and Immigration Modernization Act, passed in the U.S. Senate with a bipartisan, two-to-one vote, would be a transformative law that would strengthen America's economy and add to our diversity even further.

As I described in chapter 2, if this law becomes the law of the land, the population would grow by ten million in ten years and sixteen million by 2033. The twelve million undocumented across the country would gain legal status and be on a path to citizenship after ten years. The "DREAMers" would move quickly into citizenship. There would be no more caps on family-based visas for spouses and minor children. The law would create new guest-worker visas for low-skilled workers in construction and hospitality, and agricultural workers would get immigrant status. It would create a new merit-based visa system that considers skills, employment history, and educational credentials, admitting about 200,000 immigrants a year.[47]

And critically for business, green card limits would be lifted for the exceptionally talented and for those graduates with advanced degrees in science, technology, engineering, and mathematics (STEM) from U.S. universities. The cap for high-skilled workers would also be substantially raised. In addition, the law would create a start-up visa to entrepreneurs abroad who wish to start a company here.[48]

Consistent with our history, this transformative law would increase the real GDP by 3.3 percent by 2023 and 5.4 percent by 2033. With immigrants participating in the labor force at a higher rate than other Americans and paying more of their earnings in taxes, this transformative law would reduce the deficit by $300 billion.[49]

These changes can happen if the next president and congressional leaders insist on it, but that is in the hands of the business community. Comprehensive immigration reform likely had the broadest and deepest support of any reform that has advanced in recent years. There was broad support from religious organizations and associations, from the Catholic Church, the mainline Protestant faiths, Jewish and Muslim associations, the National Council of Churches, and the YWCA. There was support from every immigrant and civil rights group, including the National Council of La Raza and organizations representing Asian Americans and Hebrew immigrants. There was support from Planned Parenthood and LGBT rights organizations. There was support from the unions, including the National Education Association, the SEIU, and the AFL-CIO. But also lobbying for the bill were Facebook CEO Mark Zuckerberg and the U.S. Chamber of Commerce under the hashtag #Ready4Reform. A parade of tech leaders lobbied the Hill for the law's passage. Bill Gates helped found one of the key groups, along with senior figures at Dropbox, Microsoft, LinkedIn, and Facebook.

The U.S. Chamber of Commerce declared on its Web site, "Throughout our history, America has had the opportunity to grow and thrive because we have attracted and welcomed the most talented and the hardest working people to our shores" and argued, "Commonsense immigration reform would boost economic growth, create jobs, and spur innovation and entrepreneurship." The Chamber of Commerce was also instrumental in hammering out the details of the Senate's comprehensive reform bill, negotiating an agreement on guest workers with the AFL-CIO in early 2013.[50]

It is in the hands of the business community whether it is going to use this moment to break the impasse on immigration, but its backing can bring about this transformative change, which would build the momentum and core strength and character of the U.S. economy.

Ten-year infrastructure plan to rebuild America

There is deep understanding in the business community, among economists, and in the country at large that America has been underinvesting massively in its national infrastructure, according to a McKinsey Global Institute report on the "game changing" opportunities available to the United States. That backlog of maintenance and the gradual erosion of the transportation system create massive inefficiencies and backlogs, huge costs for business, and deprive the country of the chance to renew its economy as it did with the interstate highway system fifty years ago.[51]

The starting marker for this debate is the 2013 American Society of Civil Engineers Report Card for America's Infrastructure, which gives America an overall grade of D+. That is up from D in its 2009 report. Our lowest grades are for roads, waterways, and levees, and for transit, aviation, and dams.[52]

The World Economic Forum rates America's infrastructure behind that of all other advanced countries, with America ranked sixteenth on its roads, twelfth on its ports, and twenty-sixth on its power and telephone networks. It is sixteenth overall, which is just the middle of the pack among other OECD countries.[53]

While America lags, the Republicans in the U.S. Congress struggle to pass even a long-term transportation bill, and the gas tax, at 18.4 cents, has not been raised since 1993.[54]

It is hard to believe that the business community has allowed Washington's aversion to any tax increase and Republicans' unwillingness to commit to long-term highway and mass transit funding. It should have taken House Budget Committee chairman Paul Ryan to the woodshed for passing a budget that cuts infrastructure spending by 25 percent. Nor did it push the Obama administration for serious long-term infrastructure investment and creative financing, rather than the modest year-on-year throwaways for the budget.[55]

America needs to raise infrastructure spending by $150 billion to $180 billion a year for fifteen to twenty years, to increase infrastructure spending by 1 percentage point of GDP "on a sustained annual basis to compensate for past underinvestment and set the stage for future growth." That would put America on par with the level of investment of Canada, Sweden, and Australia. That would add 1.4 to 1.7 percent to the annual GDP over the next five years and create up to 1.8 million jobs.[56]

There is no proposal that has won more support across both parties, from liberal and conservative economists and key stakeholders, than moving immediately to make long-term commitments in transport, bridges, highways, mass transit, air traffic control, rail, inland waterways and water systems, the electric grid, broadband, and telecommunications. And that investment should be financed by leveraging government funds with private capital—an infrastructure bank—as is already being done on a large scale in Europe and elsewhere.

Tom Donahue, head of the U.S. Chamber of Commerce, is right to observe that we have moved from "first in the world to middle of the pack" when it comes to infrastructure, and we require long-term investment and an infrastructure bank. So do Simpson-Bowles's bipartisan deficit commission and the bipartisan coalition of officials led by former U.S. secretary of transportation Ray LaHood, former New York mayor Michael Bloomberg, former Pennsylvania governor Ed Rendell, and former California governor Arnold Schwarzenegger. So do Leo Gerard, president of the United Steelworkers, and his cochairman on the Task Force on Job Creation and former corporate CEO Leo Hindery. Their number one recommendation: Create a national infrastructure bank.[57]

Congresswoman Rosa DeLauro, my wife, introduced the infrastructure bank legislation fifteen years ago, and she was inspired by the work of legendary banker Felix Rohatyn, who championed the bank as a much-needed "domestic IMF." The model to emulate, DeLauro points out, is the European Investment Bank, which is currently spending about $100 billion a year on almost five hundred large projects. Like the EIB, $25 billion of U.S. government investment can be leveraged with the sale of bonds to reach $455 billion, though it would have to operate on twice that scale.[58]

The idea has become a rallying point because it has real scale, leverages private funds, and opens the way for public-private partnerships, because it is long-term, and because the project selection is independent of Congress. Business's requirements for taking the lead on this scale of infrastructure development are reforms that streamline and speed up the approval process, insistence on a ten-year plan that investors and stakeholders can work with, and openness to technology and big data that increase efficiencies.[59]

The gains for business and for the country will be immense—and business can lead.

Pre-K

In 2010, the U.S. Chamber of Commerce released a report in which it "calls on [the] business community to be deeply involved to make sure children have the skills to thrive in the global workplace, today and in the future." They addressed all levels of education, but they focused on "the lack of preparation of early learners who enter school for the first time" and "the significant education gap among the groups of students." Citing the studies by the Federal Reserve Bank of Minnesota, they accept that the "capacity for developmental skills begins in the first five years of life." That sets their priorities. "There is a great need for children to enter kindergarten prepared to learn."

They called for much better coordination and effective programs and made clear that "through these efforts, states and localities should strive to provide access to high-quality programs for all children."[60]

In 2011, Barack Obama released his plan to increase funding for pre-K education for poor children and requested $8.2 billion in his budget for Head Start. Republicans were instinctively critical, even though many Republican governors had advanced pre-K programs in their states and business had been supportive. The national Republicans said the program "continues to significantly underperform in certain aspects," but instead of working to improve implementation, they cut Head Start by $400 million and eliminated slots for 51,000 poor preschoolers in 2013.[61]

A number of business groups were supportive of pre-K nonetheless, including a new group, Ready Nation, with backing from John E. Pepper Jr., former chairman and CEO of Procter & Gamble.[62]

The business community pulled back in the context of the political polarization and Republican resistance to government education initiatives, but the U.S. Chamber of Commerce has continued to send signals that the country should act. On its Web site it has a section on pre-K where it offers the following guidance: "13 Things That Business Can Do to Support Early Childhood Education." The list urges all kinds of activity, including learning about the issues, talking to your employees, and getting involved locally. Buried in the middle of the list is Point #6: "Convey to policy makers your support for public investment in early education. As someone who does not have a vested interest in the early childhood education field, business leaders make powerful messengers in support of public investment for effective programs."[63]

It is asking the leaders to use their standing as businesspeople to call for "public investment" in expanding pre-K for children. And many state chambers have taken up that guidance, including seven local chambers in Texas.[64]

In the U.S. Chamber's own terms, it is time for the business community to become articulate again on this fundamental need—because they are "powerful messengers" and must lead so children do come to school prepared and American companies are able to build the kind of workforce they need.

There is a lot of room to make pre-K universal and to make it effective at raising student performance and social skills. A recent estimate by the Social Mobility Project at Brookings shows that 60 percent of parents with some college education or more have their four-year-olds in pre-K centers or classes, while only 50 percent of those with high school diplomas or less do. That percent has not moved up in the past ten years, so this is a moment to press for a change.[65]

The good news is that many red and blue states have been trying to make progress with pre-K, so national businesses have the space to act. Reformers and the business community have a shared stake in a great expansion of the most effective pre-K programs, regardless of whether these are public, non-profits, for-profit companies, religiously based, or even in family homes. Tolerance for that local pluralism may make it possible to make great advances locally despite the gridlock nationally.

DEMOCRACY IN THE TWENTY-FIRST CENTURY

A lesson from the progressive era is that if you dig deeply enough the sources of the worst wrongs are private interests and politicians working out special deals at the expense of the ordinary people and the public interest. Well, the conservative majority on the Supreme Court has made clear that this is the one area where it intends to throw off all spending limits and regulations, empowering Super PACs and giving corporations and billionaires constitutional rights on a par with the First Amendment right to free speech. That leads Darrell West to observe that the federal judiciary has made "freedom to spend" equivalent to "freedom of speech." The reason why this is happening is transparent and does not pass the smell test with citizens. This corruption

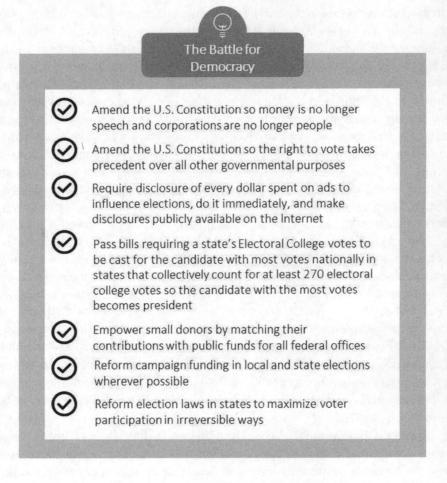

The Battle for Democracy

✓ Amend the U.S. Constitution so money is no longer speech and corporations are no longer people

✓ Amend the U.S. Constitution so the right to vote takes precedent over all other governmental purposes

✓ Require disclosure of every dollar spent on ads to influence elections, do it immediately, and make disclosures publicly available on the Internet

✓ Pass bills requiring a state's Electoral College votes to be cast for the candidate with most votes nationally in states that collectively count for at least 270 electoral college votes so the candidate with the most votes becomes president

✓ Empower small donors by matching their contributions with public funds for all federal offices

✓ Reform campaign funding in local and state elections wherever possible

✓ Reform election laws in states to maximize voter participation in irreversible ways

is at the heart of the current Gilded Age. Thus you cannot cleanse politics of this money until conservatives lose their majority on the U.S. Supreme Court. This will be their last stand.[66]

In the 2012 presidential contest, the two parties and their allies spent about $2 billion, a breathtaking number. Obama, despite raising $218 million from small contributions, worked many campaign fund-raisers, getting contributions of $1,000 or more; Romney, for his part, raised two-thirds of his funds in contributions of $1,000 or more at fund-raisers where he opined about "the 47 percent" who are "the takers." Their Super PACs and the independent groups on both sides spent almost all their funds on TV ads.[67]

Well, the Republicans in 2016 are bringing an innovative American spirit to financing the next election. They have essentially thrown the entire legal system for financing presidential campaigns over the side and turned their campaigns over to Super PACs that can spend without limits and billionaire donors who can give without limits, starting with the Koch brothers, who pledged almost $1 billion through their Super PACs and allied groups. Jeb Bush created a Super PAC, Right to Rise, that will be run by his closest personal adviser and take over the advertising, direct mail, and data-gathering functions normally performed by a candidate-directed campaign. It can raise money from the super-rich without limit and had raised tens of millions of dollars before Bush had even declared his candidacy. Senator Ted Cruz launched a clutch of four tightly held Super PACs with "strong personal and family ties to Senator Cruz." They started with over $30 million from donors who were promised "influence and control over expenditures." Governor Scott Walker directed his long-time adviser to run his Super PAC, named the Unintimidated PAC. Walker also created a tax-exempt 527 committee to raise and spend unlimited amounts of money on campaign issues. A Marco Rubio Super PAC began with a $10 million contribution from a billionaire auto dealer in Miami.[68]

The billionaire megadonor takeover of the Republican Party has the full imprimatur of the U.S. Supreme Court, though the citizenry knows this is a corrupt deal to maintain and magnify the power of the 1 percent over government.

The broader conservative assault on democracy also includes, amazingly, limiting the right to vote. It took its most brazen forms in *George W. Bush v. Albert Gore Jr.*, the Supreme Court case that put Bush into the White House, and the gutting of the Voting Rights Act, freeing most southern states from having to seek preclearance on changes in registration laws. In between and in nearly every election Republican secretaries of state are trying to limit access to the polls and the ballot. They have put the right to vote on a par with the right of states to ensure the integrity of elections and to prevent fraud. The result of new voter ID laws is to make it harder for the poor and minorities to vote. This thuggish and undemocratic work still left Democrats with the lead in the popular vote in four of the past five national elections, but that only raises the stakes if Democrats win again. Republican secretaries of state are moving to limit voting hours and early voting, and Ohio will continue its role at the front line of this battle.[69]

The conservative jurists do not waver on this assault on democracy. Some have wavered on the constitutionality of the Affordable Care Act, the constitutionality of state efforts to bar gays and lesbians to marry, and the constitutionality of the death penalty. They do not waver on the question of democracy.

As we know from the progressive era, you can only bring this scale of reform if the public feels revulsion with the corrupt deals at the heart of the system and if you open up the process to reclaim democracy. That came with exposure by reforming investigative journalists, changes to the Constitution, and presidents who changed the Supreme Court.

The reforming journalist's role has been taken by *The Washington Post*,

The New York Times, *Salon*, *Vox*, *Open Secrets*, and the academics who dig into campaign finance records and tax returns. Under the spotlight of today's investigative journalism, the corrupt connections become more visible and the pressure for change has been building.

In his in-depth Opinionator piece for *The New York Times*, Thomas B. Edsall documents the flood of conservative money going to the secretive Super PACs and independent committees. He also documents the Republicans' Putin-like effort to erase any sign that they were once enthusiastic supporters of disclosure and transparency in campaign finance. That is gone. The current Republican Party platform, Edsall points out, supports "the free speech right to devote one's resources to whatever cause one supports." Today's Republicans have elevated the First Amendment and, as a result, conservatives have found religion when opposing campaign finance regulations. This is why they have brought the gears of the Federal Election Commission to a halt.[70]

The top 1 percent for their part wants to stay out of public view because their policy preferences are so out of step with the average citizen, we now know from Darrell West's book *Billionaires*. The differences are stunning, and the implications for democracy beyond challenging. Just 27 percent of the public would cut Medicare and funding for education and highways to reduce the budget, though 58 percent of the 1 percent would. A nearly universal 87 percent of the public would spend whatever is necessary to ensure that all children have good public schools. Just 35 percent of the 1 percent aligns with that public consensus. About half the country (53 percent) would provide jobs for all who want to work, but only 8 percent of the 1 percent would.[71]

The 1 percent and big donors dominate the financing of both parties, and they use their money, Joseph Stiglitz points out, to impact the government's policy priorities and rig the rules to their advantage. Many of the billionaires have mastered politics more than entrepreneurship. Stiglitz is eloquent on this point: "we have a political system that gives inordinate power to those at the top, and they have used that power not only to limit the extent of redistribution but also to shape the rules of the game in their favor, and to extract from the public what can only be called large 'gifts.' " Stiglitz stands in awe of their inventiveness: "Those at the top have learned how to suck out money from the rest in ways that the rest are hardly aware of—that is their true innovation."[72]

Stiglitz is wrong about the public, however. It knows the system is rigged and would overturn the whole corrupt system. As we saw in the previous chapter, the public detests the Super PACs and wants to regulate what the 1 percent and business can give as contributions. They scorn the idea that campaign contributions have anything to do with free speech. And three-quarters would support a constitutional amendment to overturn the main decision of the Supreme Court on campaign funding.

There is no argument to win, as the public is aligned with a constitutional revolt against the corruption at the core.

This is a moment not unlike the progressive era, when the Supreme Court threw out all efforts to regulate hours of work. The progressives limited their eight-hour day and restrictions on child labor to the railroads when regulating interstate commerce. But it took the Labor Standards Act in 1938 and new justices to bring the change. Hopefully, it will not take two decades to reduce the influence of big donors, though it might.

Any Democratic president in this period has to make constitutional change his or her starting point. They should use the prospect of constitutional change to educate the country on the state of American democracy and the corruption that undergirds our inequality and struggling middle class.

Many were surprised when Hillary Clinton's presidential campaign announced that campaign finance reform would be one of the four pillars of her policy agenda. "We need to fix our dysfunctional political system and get unaccountable money out of it once and for all—even if that takes a constitutional amendment," Clinton said. Her campaign chairman was heard to say that "the country needs justices who believe as much in the right to vote as in the rights of corporations."[73]

The Democrats should also battle for transparency in hopes that the crudeness of unlimited, secret donations becomes an embarrassment in an age where transparency is assumed in every aspect of life. Do Republicans begin to lose their allies in the private sector and civil society because of the obscene level of campaign donations and obscene level of campaign advertising? Is their opposition to transparency so illegitimate in this Internet age that Republican conservatives are delegitimized?

Everyone knows that Republicans will maintain control in at least twenty states in the GOP conservative heartland and will keep any constitutional amendment from being ratified. Advancing reform is meant to build public consciousness of the role of money and put Republicans on the defensive. There are some real changes that can happen at the national, state, and local levels though. You can have immediate disclosure on the Internet of every contribution in real time, and with outside groups, you can require disclosure of every large contribution used to fund the advertisements they are airing.

We can also establish independent, public funding of campaigns that matches small donations and limits large ones—and the public now supports such a change. Under this proposal, federal candidates would collect a large number of small contributions from individuals in their home states or districts, and these contributions would be matched on a six-to-one basis by public funds. Anyone making a small donation would get a refundable tax credit of $25, each candidate's public funding would be strictly capped at a certain amount, and all donations would be limited and disclosed.

And it is possible that the president of the United States will be elected by a majority of the voters rather than by the Electoral College. This is not a fantasy. States that send a majority of the electors to the Electoral College can pass legislation instructing their electors to vote for whichever candidate received a majority of the national popular vote. Ten states and the District of Columbia, which collectively have 165 electoral votes, have enacted the National Popular Vote Bill, which will be activated as soon as it has been enacted by a total of 270 electoral votes. Instead of the presidential candidates and campaigns focusing on the eleven states that now constitute the battleground, they will then have to focus on the states and media markets where large populations are concentrated, and every vote will count. That will enable candidates to build the popular momentum for reform so that we can begin to address the contradictions that hold America back. Restoring democracy and the power of a popular majority is what makes it possible to sideline the new billionaire oligarchs, the principal obstacles to reform.[74]

THE PRESIDENTIAL AGENDA

Though the momentum for reform has been building intellectually and through the concrete changes pushed by business, churches, and local leaders, it will fall to presidents to get the scale of reform necessary for this to be considered a new progressive era. It is the president who has to forge a politics and advance a mission that allows for America's renewal.

What America will actually need to do to take on its economic contradictions is not that complicated. The unaddressed problems have been building up for a long time, but given what has worked historically, it is pretty clear what a president needs to champion to put the country on a very different path. "Simple changes—including higher capital-gains and inheritance taxes, greater spending to broaden access to education, rigorous enforcement of antitrust laws, corporate-governance reforms that circumscribe executive pay, and financial regulations that rein in banks' ability to exploit the rest of society," in Joseph Stiglitz's straightforward list, "would reduce inequality and increase equality of opportunity markedly." He adds simply reversing the "underinvestment in infrastructure, basic research and education at all levels."[75]

Any Democratic president will call for the money changers to be expelled from the temple.

A new Democratic president will applaud the mayors and governors who are bringing critical changes and urge the country to devolve power and spending to the states, cities, and neighborhoods that are leading the reforms.

He or she will welcome Pope Francis and the religious communities that are allies in the struggle against poverty, strengthen local communities, and help children.

A Democratic president will applaud the business community that has rallied such broad support for comprehensive immigration reform, pre-K, and infrastructure. Those fundamental changes will dramatically affect the American economy.

Though perhaps most important, a Democratic president will speak about our national aspiration, not at all fearful that it will invite a greater government activism. America can build great things, can create a shared prosperity, and can ask that all contribute to the common effort.

The country, as we have seen earlier, is ready for a national project after our aspirations have been so diminished by austerity and the cramped conservatism that has dominated Congress and many states. The new president might quote Rosa DeLauro, who said:

> The chapters of our American success story have always been written in stone and mortar, iron and steel, granite and fiber-optic cable. When Thomas Jefferson doubled the size of the nation with the Louisiana Purchase. When Governor DeWitt Clinton of New York, even during the financial crisis known as the Panic of 1819, pursued the Erie Canal for his state. When Abraham Lincoln invested in the Transcontinental Railroad, Franklin Roosevelt the Tennessee Valley Authority and rural electrification, Eisenhower the National Highway System.[76]

The agenda of any new Democratic administration will include a fundamental change in taxes, a new economic agenda for working women and working men, a new national approach to education, and a new commitment to an economy that operates at a fuller level and brings about full employment. Each is a nearly radical break from the current course but very much a part of the new common sense.

From 39.6 to CEO compensation

The Democratic reform agenda will include as a start a higher, simple tax rate on the top-income earners. That is a defining starting point for progressives that the public is clamoring for and makes possible their family and investment agenda. It is also the most effective thing they can do to mitigate inequality and fundamentally change the incentives for CEOs and companies.

The top tax rate under President Bill Clinton was 39.6 percent for all income. In other words, capital gains were taxed at the same rate as salaries and wages—removing many of the incentives for gaming the system. As we know, the Clinton decade was the only period since 1980 when those in the middle-income range made serious gains, where gains were more broadly shared, and where the bottom quintile and the poor did particularly well. Adopting that kind of tax reform sends a message about hard work being valued as much as investment at the heart of Democratic economic policies.[77]

The lesson is pretty clear: restore the top tax rate to 39.6 percent and defend the expanded earned income tax credit that Presidents Reagan and Clinton

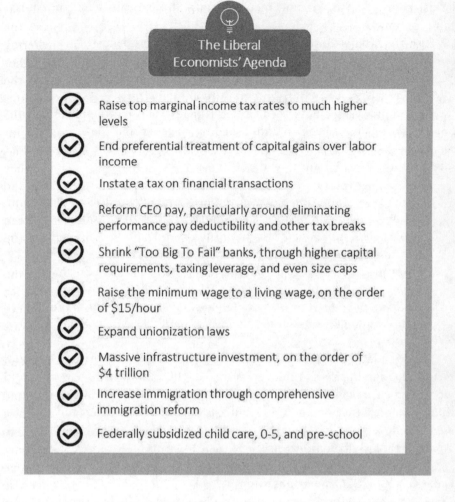

The Liberal Economists' Agenda

- ✓ Raise top marginal income tax rates to much higher levels
- ✓ End preferential treatment of capital gains over labor income
- ✓ Instate a tax on financial transactions
- ✓ Reform CEO pay, particularly around eliminating performance pay deductibility and other tax breaks
- ✓ Shrink "Too Big To Fail" banks, through higher capital requirements, taxing leverage, and even size caps
- ✓ Raise the minimum wage to a living wage, on the order of $15/hour
- ✓ Expand unionization laws
- ✓ Massive infrastructure investment, on the order of $4 trillion
- ✓ Increase immigration through comprehensive immigration reform
- ✓ Federally subsidized child care, 0-5, and pre-school

championed and the refundable child tax credit that George W. Bush expanded in his presidency. With President Obama having won a mandate twice for raising taxes for those earning more than $250,000, the next Democratic president can almost certainly win a mandate for this critical starting point.

Remember that the Affordable Care Act was paid for in part with a 0.9 percent Medicare surtax on employment income of more than $250,000 and a 3.8 percent investment tax on capital gains.

And with a Democrat and any bipartisan commission certain to propose raising the Social Security payroll tax cap—now $117,000—and with the median state income tax on the top 1 percent at 5.5 percent, the top rate will move to well over 50 percent.

Stiglitz cites economists who say that a 70 percent top rate would be most efficient, and that is what the top rate was before President Reagan enacted his breaks, Thomas Piketty points out mischievously and accurately.[78]

There is indeed an emerging consensus among all Democrats about a dramatically more progressive tax code. In his State of the Union address, the president proposed to increase the capital gains tax rate, to stop sheltering those with $100 million estates from inheritance taxes, and to place higher taxes for the wealthiest to the tune of $320 billion over 10 years. At the same time, the Democratic ranking member of the House Budget Committee announced the Democrats' support for a financial transaction tax. And the Center for American Progress released a "Report of the Commission on Inclusive Prosperity," cochaired by Lawrence Summers, that cites Thomas Piketty and calls for a "more progressive" long-term tax system. As a start, they propose tougher rules on corporations' overseas income, taxing estates, and rooting out special-interest "tax expenditures." In a separate interview, Summers proposes making the mortgage interest deduction a tax credit, instead of a deduction—which would dramatically shift the tax benefit from the top quintile to middle-class homeowners.[79]

That contrasts, of course, with the Republican presidential candidates who have assured their billionaire donors that they intend to cut their taxes further.

Reformers need to educate the public about the appropriateness of inheritance taxes. Only five million Americans pay the inheritance tax at a top rate of 40 percent, and even still, the public is ambivalent about taxing in this way. For many, it looks like it is changing the rules after a lifetime of work or looks like a tax on small businesses.[80]

And the next Democratic president will have to build public support and alliances in civil society to take dramatic action on climate change. Major international corporations such as Nike and Coca-Cola are beginning to speak out about the costs of climate change. Exxon Mobil and Wal-Mart have already priced a carbon tax into their long-term budget, and other companies, such as Microsoft, Walt Disney, Google, and General Electric have also assumed a carbon tax in their strategic planning. A carbon tax should be used to affect incentives for turning to clean energy, not to address other public priorities—and thus any revenue should be fully returned to individuals in some method that builds support.[81]

The public, on the other hand, would quickly rally to a Democratic administration that was eliminating $500 billion of special-interest subsidies and tax breaks to support broad-based investment or long-term deficit reduction. The Congressional Budget Office has identified $1.5 trillion of "tax expenditures" in the federal budget. Many have a broad social and economic purpose. Many do not—and the top 1 percent of households get a disproportionate share of such breaks. They are nearly as important as the tariffs of an earlier era that invited special interests to feed at the trough.[82]

Also critical to the Clinton decade were the earned income tax credit and the refundable child tax credits that were expanded under President George W. Bush and President Obama. They reduced the number of working people and children in poverty and supplemented the income of low-wage workers. These are tools that work, and Democrats have proposed making the expansion of these credits permanent and indexed for inflation. And they have proposed greatly expanding the tax credits for child care, dependent care, and college tuition.

With "stagnant middle-class incomes," CAP's Commission on Inclusive Prosperity proposes a plan of "temporary tax relief" for those earning between $23,000 and $95,000—those that earn enough that they do not benefit from the existing signature policies for low-wage workers like the EITC. The commission supports a plan of short-term tax credits for the middle class.[83]

Congressman Chris Van Hollen, the ranking Democrat on the House Budget Committee, has proposed higher taxes on top earners and a financial transaction tax to finance a "paycheck bonus credit" for the working and middle class. Each worker would receive a tax credit of $1,000—or $2,000 in dual-income homes—each year to buttress family income.[84]

The last time the minimum wage was increased was in 2009, the last in a series of gradual increases from $5.15 to $7.25 an hour enacted in 2007. To keep up with inflation, the national minimum wage must rise well above the $10.10 proposed by President Obama and would have to be indexed to inflation so it does not lose its value, as it has over the past two decades. Democrats nationally are now supporting a national minimum wage of $12 an hour.

There is emerging consensus among progressives that reform has to include ways to foster greater unionization. The Commission on Inclusive Prosperity suggests that unions give employees in the middle quintile a "wage premium" of 20 percent. That will require a National Labor Relations Board that is creating a more favorable climate for organizing and a president of the United States who always highlights the value of worker representation. It will require that local officials take the lead in supporting unionization in their communities. And it will require that unions up their game in trying to represent working people in this new economy.[85]

The lesson from the Clinton decade and from Piketty's account of an America with a much higher top tax rate is very clear. These policy levers work very well. We know how to reduce inequality and give CEOs different incentives while helping the poor and the middle class to do a lot better. As Stiglitz observes, "We can achieve a society more in accord with our fundamental values, with more opportunity, a higher total national income, a stronger democracy, and higher living standards for most individuals."[86]

The goal of reform has to be to get corporations more focused on long-term performance and less focused on core competencies, the traditional way to maximize short-term stock-market gains. The current securitized system leads to the shedding of production and employees. To change the time horizons of corporations, reform has to break the link of CEO compensation from the short-term stock value. Progressives have also proposed dropping quarterly reporting, increasing transparency, restricting hostile takeovers, and expanding employee stock ownership. The last demonstrably increases company productivity and employee loyalty.[87]

Those lessons need to be brought into the reform of corporate governance. This is one of the most important steps toward rising wages, encouraging corporate investment, increasing research and development and production, and the creation of more apprenticeships and jobs. In one study cited by the Commission on Inclusive Prosperity, privately held firms invested about 10 percent of total assets, compared to just 4 percent of the publicly listed firms. Reform means changing the rules of corporate governance or changing the incentives to achieve a similar result, despite the securitization of American companies since the 1980s.[88]

The most important and practical step would be to go back to the original reform that barred companies from deducting CEO pay above $1 million—though this time, that exclusion should apply no matter what the form of compensation, including stock shares. There is no reason not to bar corporations from deducting any executive compensation over $1 million, and their corporate tax rate could be linked to reducing the ratio of CEO to average employee pay. Corporate boards need to be reformed so they operate independently of the CEO and so they include employee representatives, as in Germany.[89]

The federal government changed the laws and regulations in the 1980s and 1990s and helped produce this unique pattern of CEO compensation and declining investment. Reversing those reforms can produce a very different result and trajectory for the American economy.

Franklin Delano Roosevelt

The Roosevelt Institute under the auspices of Joseph Stiglitz brought together thirty-six prominent liberal economists from the universities, think tanks, the labor unions, and Congress to meet in Washington in April 2015. They discussed inequality and economic performance, with the purpose of getting to a policy agenda that would be released by the Roosevelt Institute. They were asked to pick policies in the areas of taxation, macro and monetary policy, financial markets and corporate governance, international trade and finance, mobility and opportunity, market power, and labor market institutions that would reduce inequality and improve economic performance. From this whole list, ten policies were selected as the top priorities for a political agenda.

The liberal economists' list of policies looks very similar to the agenda that has emerged from this book to be addressed at the presidential level. The liberal agenda starts with raising the top marginal income tax rates, making sure income from wages and capital gains are taxed at the same rate, and introducing a tax on financial transactions. Indeed, that is the top priority that I address in the next section—as it is emerging as the starting point to addressing America's deepest economic issues.

The liberal economists would then address the CEOs, corporations, and banks that are so unpopular with the public. Top of the agenda is reforming CEO compensation, which we know is central to the public's new economic consciousness. Next, they would begin to address the financialization of corporations and the role and size of big banks that have produced less domestic investment and job creation and put the economy at risk.

These economists would raise the minimum wage to $15 an hour and reform labor laws to allow more workers to become unionized, going directly at the problem of jobs that don't pay enough to live on. Combining that with $4 trillion in infrastructure investment and comprehensive immigration reform will raise economic performance and create good-paying jobs.

Finally, the liberal economists would include a new package of work and family policies, including subsidies for child care for children ages zero to five and preschool education. That, too, is part of the liberal agenda.

The Franklin Roosevelt tradition remains very much alive in the emerging debate about what reforms can address our deepest problems.

Economic agenda for working families

With jobs not paying enough to live on, a reform agenda will include aggressive use of tax credits and increases in the minimum wage that can really raise wages. People are looking for help with affordable education and training, and relief from the overwhelming student debt burden.

While this may not seem radical, a Democratic president will have to affirm that he or she is protecting the existing social safety net, particularly for retirement—and may even advocate increased Social Security benefits. That will not please the pundits and elites whose retirement is not at risk and who will attack the president for coddling spoiled retirees. The president will be able to educate them about some facts of life. Life expectancy is not rising for working-class Americans, so raising the retirement age has very unequal and painful consequences. Working women will be getting lower Social Security benefits than men because they have worked fewer hours and interrupted work to take care of children. And with employers scaling back private pensions, two-thirds of Social Security beneficiaries sixty-five or older rely on it for the majority of their income.[90]

The whole area of work and family is different. There is a brewing explosion that will put this area of reform at the center of a Democratic president's agenda.

The public is ready for America to finally address one of the building contradictions of the new economy: women are now fully in the labor force and are the sole or primary breadwinner in four in ten households with children, yet they continue to carry most household and child-rearing responsibilities and they get little help from businesses or the government. And that is a building scandal that may bring a new Fair Labor Standards Act. The Fair Labor

Standards Act of 1938 finally got rid of child labor, established legal working hours, and created a federal minimum wage. This one will have to deal with paid sick days, paid family and medical leave, the right to ask for workplace flexibility without retaliation, protections against discrimination for pregnant workers, and equal pay for women.

Heather Boushey, head of the Washington Center for Equitable Growth, is one of the few economists who understands what is possible. She writes, "Together, this collection of new policies can lay the foundation for a new strategy for economic growth as well as a new broadly progressive political coalition that can be as transformative and as durable as FDR's New Deal."[91]

The reform agenda would have to include a national effort to achieve universal access to child care. A new Child Care Act like the one Nixon proposed would create federally supported child care centers for lower-income families and subsidies and tax credits for the middle class. President Obama and congressional Democrats have already proposed tripling the child care tax credit to help working families.[92]

Some of the new proposals have financing arrangements that try to minimize the burden on employers or to share the costs. Under the proposed Healthy Families Act, for paid sick days employers and employees pay into a fund, just like unemployment insurance. In one study cited by Boushey, nine out of ten employers said the requirements for employees having paid family leave had no effect or had a positive one. However, with the major business organizations so opposed to paid family leave and so successful in stopping any new reforms for two decades, a Democratic president may try something radical and more akin to Europe. He or she could propose a Working Family Fund, financed from general or dedicated revenue. That may actually be the game changer that pushes business to come on board.[93]

The agenda would also include the Paycheck Fairness Act sponsored by Congresswomen Rosa DeLauro that ensures equal pay for men and women, which came within two votes of becoming law. It puts discrimination against women on the same level as discrimination based on race, with the same remedies.

At some point that might include affirmative action policies that begin to break the huge predominance of men in the big technology companies, tenured university positions, and CEOs. Companies such as Google, Facebook, and Apple, *The New York Times* editorial board points out, seem to mainly employ white and Asian men, and the paper calls for much more affirmative action. With women holding only 16.9 percent of corporate board positions, two dozen American companies, including Bloomberg, DuPont, and DeLoitte committed in 2014 to appoint boards that are 30 percent women. Unfortunately, in studies in Norway, where this became the law, there was no increase in female CEOs, no decrease in the gender gap, and no expansion of family-friendly policies. At some point very soon, America will be contemplating a more comprehensive approach to affirmative action.[94]

Equal pay and equal opportunity have to be the entry points, though other aspects of the new economy have discriminatory effects. Women dominate in jobs that pay well under the medium income and women are more likely to work part-time because of family demands, just to name two. Much of the agenda for working women and working men is focused on providing more support and protections on those jobs.

Finally, Democratic presidents will remind people of the absolute centrality of the Affordable Care Act that barred charging women more than men for insurance, got rid of preexisting conditions, provided free health preventive services, and created a marketplace where individuals can buy subsidized insurance. With almost a third of Americans employed in consultancy, freelance, and small businesses, with women more likely to be working part-time, the new subsidized marketplace allows them to carry their insurance with them, independent of any particular company. It is a huge change that is part of the new agenda for working women and working men.

National commitment to renew American education

The next president will need to mobilize the country behind a fundamental change in how America educates its next generation and how it changes access to higher education. The reforms will be very big and opposition will be great, though as with new tax policies, we have a pretty good idea what the toolbox looks like to make a big difference. It is critical that the president rally the country around the need to renew a country that has periodically done radically new things with education.

I think what is happening with education rises to the level of "crisis," though I am aware that talk of the "American education crisis" has been *en vogue* for more than half a century. Josef Joffe's *The Myth of America's Decline* recalls the 1950s "Johnny can't read" campaign. A simple Google search for "American crisis in education" produces 378 million entries.

Joffe is right to point out that America is more vast and diverse and is home to huge immigrant and minority populations and that first- and second-generation immigrants score lower than their native-born counterparts for reasons that have nothing to do with the quality or resources at that school. If you control for these kinds of demographic and cultural differences, the United States rises to number seven on the Program for International Student Assessment (PISA) rankings.[95]

But to say that America's ranking is understandable does not change the fact that America with all its demographic and cultural changes is falling off the educational charts with real consequences for people and the growth and competitiveness of the economy. These shortcomings begin at the earliest grades, and faltering college education and graduation rates are undermining social mobility and pushing down working-class incomes.

America used to lead the world with its most educated population, though that is a distant memory now according to McKinsey's Global Institute Report—and that needs to become part of the public consciousness. Among America's preretirement population, 41 percent had a college or tertiary education, and that put America on the level with Israel and Russia and in third place in the global ranking. That is twice the level of college penetration for that age group in all the OECD countries. But our Millennials, those now twenty-four to thirty-five years old, have the same level of college education as the baby boomers. There have been no gains. The 41 percent with college education is just above the OECD average today for that age group. Great Britain has reached 45 percent with that level of education; Japan is at 56 percent and South Korea at 63 percent.[96]

With tuition averaging $8,655 at public universities and $29,000 at private colleges, college has become part of the problem rather than the solution. For people from families in the top fifth of earners, the cost of college has gone up from 6 to 9 percent of family income from 1971 to 2011. That is significant, though for those in the bottom fifth, it has jumped from 42 percent to 114 percent of family income.[97]

The cost has stalled American's progress into college, and that has only widened the gap between the top and the bottom. Between 1979 and 2012, the gap between a family with two college graduates and a family of two high school graduates has grown to $30,000 a year. Less than a third of American adults now achieve a higher level of education than their parents, and in that measure of mobility, we trail the aspiring world. And of course, those who get to college have built up $1 trillion in student debt that saps them as consumers and delays them marrying and forming households.[98]

Those widening gaps alone warrant the term "crisis."

U.S. students scored 487 on PISA, and that is at the center of the discussion. That is below the OECD average and well below Canada at 527 and Germany at 513. I will not tell you what Shanghai, Singapore, and Hong Kong scored, because they were special cases, but South Korea? Its score was 546.[99]

But I do not think that it should take the Shanghai comparison to mobilize for this crisis. That score is kind of a marker for everything that could be done differently.

A plan for renewing American education has to start at the earliest age based on the convincing material in chapter 5. That means a huge increase in support for the WIC (women, infants, and children) programs and for any of the effective early-childhood education programs, as well as support for universal pre-K education. These policies were in the liberal economists' agenda because all the research confirms we must invest at as early an age as possible.

When it comes to K-12 education, America is not without a lot of guidance on how to make major improvements, according to the McKinsey Institute. Between 2003 and 2011, education reforms in Massachusetts, New Jersey, Texas, and Maryland produced huge gains, and their students' test scores were right up there with Germany's. But Arkansas, Hawaii, and New Mexico also made big gains, as well as Washington, D.C., though from a much lower base.[100]

The next president would be well served to set aside all the built-up conventional wisdom and demand empirical results from the reformers, and as a start, embrace what has worked. Common Core has so much promise and the teachers helped create it, so the states and foundations should be committing big resources to getting it implemented right. Student testing is out of control, and as Marc S. Tucker, author of a report on education accountability, wrote on teacher evaluation, "There is no evidence that it is contributing anything to improved student performance." The regime of testing, however, comes with a price: teachers feeling less professional, contributing to high teacher turnover.[101]

The same goes with charter schools. Some, such as Knowledge Is Power Program (KIPP) schools, are achieving results. New Orleans's charter schools seem to be successful in the aftermath of Katrina. But there are plenty that are underperforming. In Chicago, impressively, it is the public schools rather than the charter schools that have produced the striking gains in the past two years.

If one looks at the McKinsey Global Institute recommendations or *The New York Times* editorial board's exploration on effective teaching, you start with paying teachers much more and treating them as well-trained serious professionals, including moving away from teachers' colleges and raising standards at universities. That is the lesson from Finland that has had the best results and from McKinsey's global comparison. In the United States, a high school teacher gets paid 72 percent as much as all college graduates, putting American teachers on a par with Italy and the Czech Republic. In all OECD countries, it is 90 percent—meaning teachers' salaries nearly match those of other college graduates. German teachers earn slightly more. But teachers in South Korea are making 130 percent and earn a lot of respect, along with their students' impressive performance.[102]

McKinsey recommends further that America expand apprenticeships and make its nondegree programs more effective for meeting the skill needs of companies. Probably the most important goal though would be to make students more successful in the existing two- and four-year programs, where graduation rates are pathetic. It would help if many more of those graduates were in STEM specialties. And it would help if more cities followed Chicago's example and abolished college tuition for graduating high school students with at least a C+ average.[103]

That should be a model for other cities as leaders think through the role of metropolitan areas in building the momentum for change.

To get abrupt changes in education, the federal government needs to take up President Obama's plan to make the first two years of college free across the country. His plan has the potential to help some 9 million students, though they have to maintain a C+ average, be in school half-time, at least, and make "steady progress" toward a degree.[104]

Obama's proposal is just a wedge into the huge issue of college affordability that is undermining Americans' presumptive access to higher education and stalling America's presumed social mobility. Between 2008 and 2012, state funding for public colleges was cut by 5 percent or more in 26 states. Over the last decade, tuition costs at public schools have surged almost 80 percent, and unpaid student debt has doubled since 2007. That has left 40 million Americans with student debt, averaging $32,500 per student. Senator Elizabeth Warren described student debt as an "economic emergency that threatens the financial futures of Americans and the stability of our economy."[105]

Bold reforms have to include the cancellation or refinancing of student debt to free a generation to get on with its life choices as well as the reform of college costs so America can get back on track as a country of opportunity.

America is not without guidance from our own experience and globally on how to address its education crisis. It is waiting for leaders to make it their cause.

A national commitment to a fuller economy and full employment

The United States is formally committed to achieving full employment, as well as price stability, and that is embedded in U.S. law. Founding the U.S. Federal Reserve was one of the major achievements of the progressive era, and the Fed was given the dual mandate to minimize inflation and maximize employment. President Harry Truman introduced the Employment Act of 1946 with the purpose of revising the mandate to include "full employment," though conservatives successfully weakened the law. In 1977, however, President Jimmy Carter and a Democratic Congress passed the Full Employment Act that made that goal the law of the land.

In fact, the country has only achieved acceptable gains in income and reduction in poverty when the country was at full employment in the late 1990s. While the American economy is growing at a rate that impresses the world, it could operate at a higher level that pushes companies to operate at fuller capacity, brings many more people into the labor force, reduces unemployment, and raises wages.

Larry Summers and Paul Krugman point out that we only got close to these goals when aided by banking, stock, and housing bubbles. There is growing recognition across ideological perspectives that the financial crisis wiped out a huge amount of economic value comparable to the amount of spending in the world wars, and economic output is falling endemically short of projections and capacity. The economy is on a trajectory 14 percent short of the precrisis trend and the IMF has warned countries globally that potential output in the developed countries will slow to 1.6 percent between 2015 and 2020. While demographic trends could play some role explaining this slowdown, the dominant factors are rising inequality, stagnant wages, and unemployment that produces insufficient demand, as Martin West confirms.[106]

The result may indeed be the "secular stagnation" that the Commission on Inclusive Prosperity now treats as settled science. Larry Summers co-chaired the commission with Ed Balls who led the British Labour Party's fight against austerity. Highlighting the dramatic decrease in public investment over the last five years, the commission presses leaders to show "political courage" and "increase how much we are investing in infrastructure to raise potential and actual gross domestic product." They recommend $100 billion a year of public investment over ten years, surprising Robert Kuttner, editor of the liberal journal *The American Prospect*, who described their proposal as "some surprisingly strong medicine." The commission also accepts Martin West's conclusion about currency that "the global market for the US dollar is rigged." The weaker dollar means less employment and a downward pressure on wages, and that is why the commission concludes that the WTO needs to be amended because it has proved so ineffective in limiting currency manipulation.[107]

A broad range of economists and the IMF have settled on the need for large increases in investment spending for research and development, education, banking that supports small and medium-size businesses, and above all, investment in infrastructure. With reforms that limit political blockages and distortions, they urge the creation of public-private partnerships to finance the modernization of America's infrastructure to promote greater economic growth and employment.[108]

Are the country's elected leaders ready to make the turn from austerity to a much higher level of investment?

Democratic presidents will have to reclaim and revitalize the goal of full employment that tilts the playing field to the advantage of employees. That the last time America really achieved that goal was under President Bill Clinton is good reason to reclaim it. That does send signals about openness to higher inflation targets to the Federal Reserve and Europe. It is also a signal to America's global companies and Asian powers that America will be energy rich and will dramatically increase investment in education and infrastructure to renew the country. It would incentivize American companies to build and create American jobs. And most important, it would push up income gains from the bottom and middle to give the American middle class the purchasing power to get the engines moving.[109]

The era of radical, progressive reforms at the turn of the twentieth century made possible America's ascent and claim on exceptionalism. It disrupted the Industrial Revolution, which was just that. The steam engine and portable power produced a surge in human productivity and economic growth not seen since the beginning of time. Waves of immigrant families left impoverished parts of Europe, as well as Mexico and Asia, to work in America's mines, railroads, and factories. They moved increasingly to the burgeoning cities and tenements, where living and working conditions were scandalous. With industrialists pushing for longer hours and lower wages, families figured out new ways to survive, and unions led strikes that were mostly crushed by the police and the army.

The frontier and immigrant experience produced an individualistic and egalitarian ethos, yet the new industrialists ruthlessly drove out competition and created legal monopolies that enabled them to fix higher prices. They bought off government officials at every level. The industrialists won high protective tariffs that pushed out foreign competition. All of this came at the expense of farmers and workers, who made the industrialists fabulously wealthy. This was rightly called a Gilded Age.

That America was not sustainable.

America was able to dominate the twentieth century because a democratic revolution and an era of progressive reform mitigated some of the worst excesses and enabled more Americans to share in America's promise. The work of the unions, the settlement house movement, the journalist social reformers, and local and state progressive leaders built the momentum for reform. In a two-decade period, America would regulate the trusts and working conditions, prohibit the sale of alcohol, enact an income tax, introduce party primaries and direct election of U.S. senators, keep public lands out of the hands of the private interests, and dramatically reduce tariffs to break the corrupt ties of business and government. Obviously, the job of reform was not completed until the New Deal, but the progressive era reforms changed the trajectory of America.

The progressive era of bold reforms happened because of the work of President Theodore Roosevelt and his ally President William Howard Taft, both

Republican reformers, the Democratic candidate William Jennings Bryan, who stretched his appeal to reach the urban workers, and ultimately, Woodrow Wilson as progressive governor of New Jersey and as the Democratic presidential nominee at the time of the progressive electoral wave.

Today America is being transformed by revolutions in energy, digital technology, advanced manufacturing, and big data, by immigration, and by seismic changes in racial diversity, in the family, and in gender roles. Those changes are crystallized in the growing metropolitan areas and the rising Millennial generation. With America open to immigration and multiculturalism, it is poised to lead and to be exceptional again. But first it must address the dark side of that progress. Long-term wage stagnation leaves people in jobs that don't pay enough to live on, while CEOs and the top 1 percent take all the gains in income and wealth. And the top 1 percent has been given license to buy elections and the government to rig the rules even further. Marriage and working-class families are in trouble, with a growing number of children raised by single parents. Working-class men feel marginalized, while working women face huge hurdles managing work and family and earning equal pay and must get by without help from employers or the government.

Well, America's new majority is demanding a politics and an agenda that addresses these huge challenges. The public argument is now centered on these issues, and a new data-driven social critique is making itself felt. The momentum for reform is building in America's cities and states, in the churches, and in some sectors of business. And the public is ready to support a Democratic political project centered on these challenges, including going after the big money and special interests and asking the top 1 percent to do their part.

And that means the current and future Democratic presidents will get to play a historic role shaping a reform era. President Barack Obama rescued the economy from the financial crisis and the Great Recession. He signed the Affordable Care Act, which is dramatically reducing the number of uninsured, reducing health care costs, and giving women and the self-employed new security. President Obama and state attorneys general made the fight for marriage equality, and now gay marriage is constitutionally protected in all fifty states. His legalization of the "DREAMers" could not be overturned by Congress, and he has delegitimized the anti-immigration forces.

Those are critically important gains and a starting point for addressing the problems of America's new economy. And these successes reflect his identification with the ascendant demographic trends and values in America, rather than the real-life contradictions people are struggling with every day.

It will fall to future Democratic presidents to take up the mantle of reform. The next president will come to power when the conservative forces are still very strong and desperately battling to slow the ascendant trends. The country does not yet know whether the next Democratic president will be a Theodore Roosevelt or a Woodrow Wilson—both of whom played honorable and necessary but very different roles in the triumph of reform. Ultimately, Democratic leaders will take the stage and play both roles if America is to see the scale of change that is possible and required if all are to benefit from America's ascent.

The next president might take note of the choices Theodore Roosevelt made in 1905.

Let us imagine that a newly elected Democratic president is preparing to drive to the U.S Capitol to deliver his or her first State of the Union address to a joint session of Congress. The president will likely have read and taken some lessons from President Roosevelt's first and second State of the Union messages, delivered to Congress after his 1904 election to a second term. His pragmatic side tempered his "progressive spirit" since he was well aware that the Congress itself, the Supreme Court, and conservative Republicans in the states constrained what he could accomplish. The House and Senate leaders then were deeply opposed to those progressive changes, as Roosevelt acknowledged in his message: "I am well aware of the difficulties of the legislation that I am suggesting, and of the need of temperate and cautious action in securing it. I should emphatically protest against improperly radical or hasty action."[1]

While not expecting Congress to enact bold reforms, Roosevelt said that it should at least take some critical first steps to reform, such as requiring that the rail owners charge everyone the same rates and not discriminate against farmers or smaller manufacturers. At least get that done, Roosevelt urged Congress. The legislation lurched through Congress, and ultimately they produced a bill that many progressives hated, the Hepburn Act of 1906. Roosevelt would applaud the compromise because it at least outlawed free railroad passes and strengthened rules against rebates—practices used by railroads to empower favored industries and bribe legislators—and established the principle that the federal government could regulate and oversee railroad rates.

In 2017, there will be very great pressure on the new president to advance reforms. So many cities and states have passed reforms, the business coalitions and the churches have spoken out, and he or she will have just won a campaign centered on what they are going to do about the middle class and inequality.

Perhaps the Democrats will have won back the Senate and made gains in the House, and Republicans will feel some pressure to give way on some issue or show a more bipartisan spirit. Perhaps the business community will pressure the GOP establishment to bite the bullet and allow immigration reform. Yet it is more than likely that Republicans will have dug their heels in even deeper in resistance to the ascendant trends and necessary reforms. And Republicans will still hold considerable power in the states and in the Congress.

The new Democratic president then might learn from what Teddy Roosevelt did as he faced such conservative roadblocks.

First, he used these messages to Congress to assert a clear and expanded role for government to check the power of industrial concentration and excess.

> *The fortunes amassed through corporate organization are now so large, and vest such power in those that wield them, as to make it a matter of necessity to give to the sovereign—that is, to the Government, which represents the people as a whole—some effective power of supervision over their corporate use.*

He was forthright about the need for government to be the counterbalance.

> *In order to insure a healthy social and industrial life, every big corporation should be held responsible by, and be accountable to, some sovereign strong enough to control its conduct.*[2]

Second, Roosevelt used his message to repeatedly call for Washington, D.C., to become a "model city." While he was uncomfortable with the rush to enact reforms by La Follette in Wisconsin, he urged the Congress to do just that in Washington, where the federal government had uncontested authority to affect working and living conditions:

> *The National Government has control of the District of Columbia and it should see to it that the City of Washington is made a model city in all respects, both as regards parks, public playgrounds, proper regulation of the system of housing, so as to do away with the evils of alley tenements, a proper system of education, a proper system of dealing with truancy and juvenile offenders, [and] a proper handling of the charitable work of the District.*

Roosevelt went further, saying that Washington should send a message on what is a proper agenda for the times:

> *There should be proper factory laws to prevent all abuses in the employment of women and children in the District. These will be useful chiefly as object lessons, but even this limited amount of usefulness would be of real National value.*

Our next Democratic president's State of the Union address will no doubt draw inspiration from the successful reformers in Seattle, San Francisco, and Los Angeles who enacted a living wage; in Chicago and New York City, who are pressing toward universal pre-K; and in Connecticut and California, where paid sick days are now law and a remarkable number of citizens now have health insurance for the first time. He or she might well point to Mayor Bill de Blasio and Mayor Rahm Emanuel sitting in the gallery, leaders of cities that should be an "object lesson to the nation."

Returning to Roosevelt's considered use of his messages to Congress, the third goal he set to Congress in 1904 and 1905 was to enact laws to expand the president's ability to take executive action to protect public lands, create national parks, and limit commercial use of national forests—and to do so urgently or regret the consequences. In both messages, he made clear his intention to protect the Yosemite Valley, the Grand Canyon, and Yellowstone. He praised the state of California for gifting Yosemite Valley and Mariposa Big Tree Grove, encouraged the government to immediately appropriate funds for their inclusion in the National Park Service, and called on other states to do the same so that the national government could see to their proper supervision as national public resources.

In his or her speech, the next Democratic president will no doubt thank President Obama for using his executive powers in the face of Washington dysfunction to reduce emissions from coal-fired plants by requiring major cuts in emissions by 2030 and to ensure that America is on a path to reducing greenhouse gases, which will remain his or her commitment as well. He or she will thank him for his executive order on pay equity that empowered women to challenge for equal pay in businesses contracting with the federal government and establishing reliable data to enforce all equal pay laws. And he or she will thank President Obama for laying the groundwork for similar action with regard to paid sick days and paid family leave and overtime.[5]

With the next Democratic president's likely mandate to address the challenges facing working women and families, he or she should pay a lot of attention to how Roosevelt approached such issues in his 1905 message.

Roosevelt concentrated repeatedly on what was happening to women, families, and children in the new industrial economy of his time. He educated the country on the new economic realities:

> The introduction of women into industry is working change and disturbance in the domestic and social life of the Nation. The decrease in marriage, and especially in the birth rate, has been coincident with it. We must face accomplished facts, and the adjustment of factory conditions must be made, but surely it can be made with less friction and less harmful effects on family life than is now the case. This whole matter in reality forms one of the greatest sociological phenomena of our time.

Even without any prospect of enacting a national law to correct the emerging abuses, Roosevelt simply asserted that there must be an "an effective system of factory laws to prevent the abuse of women and children." And to that end, he instructed the Department of Commerce and Labor to help create the "full knowledge on which to base action looking toward State and municipal legislation for the protection of working women."

America's next Democratic president will face a Supreme Court fully committed to the free-speech rights of corporations, and that makes it almost impossible to make fundamental reforms and disrupt the close bond of special interests and government, though here, too, he or she will do well to note the fifth task Roosevelt took on in his message to Congress.

Roosevelt had been elected to a second term in 1904 with massive financial support from the industrialists and New York elites, though without the remotest prospect of a legislative hearing, he asserted almost gratuitously a challenge to the corruption at the heart of the Gilded Age:

> All contributions by corporations to any political committee or for any
> political purpose should be forbidden by law; directors should not be
> permitted to use stockholders' money for such purposes; and, moreover,
> a prohibition of this kind would be, as far as it went, an effective
> method of stopping the evils aimed at in corrupt practices acts.

The next Democratic president will have to say categorically that he or she will campaign for a constitutional amendment to enable this modern democracy to regulate this unacceptable flood of private and secret money into politics and challenge Congress to move urgently to enact a law that requires all donations to all organizations influencing elections be disclosed in full and immediately on the Internet. Like Roosevelt he or she will say, "This is the defining threat to our democracy and acting now will empower our citizens, workers, and consumers to have their say."

President Woodrow Wilson began his inaugural address on the East Portico on March 4, 1913, the way contemporary progressives should when they finally achieve the political breakthrough necessary to enact the full reform agenda. Then they will have the wind at their backs and the freedom to realize all that we have learned.

"There has been a change of government," President Wilson's speech began. He continued:

> It began two years ago, when the House of Representatives became
> Democratic by a decisive majority. It has now been completed. The
> Senate about to assemble will also be Democratic. The offices of

President and Vice-President have been put into the hands of Democrats. What does the change mean?

And he declared his intention "to interpret the occasion."[4]

For Wilson and the country in 1913, this was a triumph of party that he was about to use for the country as an instrument "for a large and definite purpose." It is difficult to imagine such a moment when today's Democrats will govern politically and self-consciously with a partisan agenda to bring the radical reforms that began with first steps in the cities and states, communities and parishes, then coalitions and corporate America until their ideas and values became hegemonic.

That tipping point was deeply political and partisan, as it will have to be for Democratic presidents who make a breakthrough on enacting reforms.

At that moment, President Wilson had the security to give voice to the contradictions and dark side of our progress and speak of these reforms as releasing America's inherent potential, as he did in his first inaugural address.

"We see that in many things that life is very great," President Wilson said at the outset:

> *[America] is incomparably great in its material aspects, in its body of wealth, in the diversity and sweep of its energy, in the industries which have been conceived and built up by the genius of individual men and the limitless enterprise of groups of men.*

America has also "built up . . . a great system of government, which has stood through a long age as in many respects a model for those who seek to set liberty upon foundations that will endure against fortuitous change, against storm and accident."

Then, he redirected his focus to speak directly and eloquently of the contradictions that motivate the urgency to bring change. "With riches has come inexcusable waste," he declared:

> *We have squandered a great part of what we might have used, and have not stopped to conserve the exceeding bounty of nature, without which our genius for enterprise would have been worthless and impotent, scorning to be careful, shamefully prodigal as well as admirably efficient.*

> *We have been proud of our industrial achievements, but we have not hitherto stopped thoughtfully enough to count the human cost, the cost of lives snuffed out, of energies overtaxed and broken, the fearful physical and spiritual cost to the men and women and children upon whom the dead weight and burden of it all has fallen pitilessly the years through.*

The groans and agony of it all had not yet reached our ears, the solemn,
moving undertone of our life, coming up out of the mines and factories, and
out of every home where the struggle had its intimate and familiar seat.

When a Democratic president assumes office at a comparable tipping-point moment, he or she will speak of the contradictions that have left so many people struggling, so much potential wasted by the accumulation of wealth in the hands of the few and not used toward any public purpose, and declare the necessity to act. Let's hope that president brings the same eloquence to the core wrongs that demand bold changes.

Wilson, too, lamented how America's great experiment in democracy and government also brings a dark side we are hard pressed to address:

> [M]any deep secret things which we too long delayed to look into
> and scrutinize with candid, fearless eyes. The great Government we
> loved has too often been made use of for private and selfish purposes,
> and those who used it had forgotten the people.

The country is "stirred by the knowledge of wrong, of ideals lost, of government too often debauched and made an instrument of evil."

When such a Democrat assumes the nation's highest office in our new progressive era, what diminishes government will hardly be a secret as the top 1 percent exercises its "freedom of speech" to make sure government advances its interests, without regard to the middle class whose voices and values get crowded out along with policies that would allow them to rise again.

"The scales of heedlessness have fallen from our eyes," President Wilson observed. That leaves us with a duty to "to cleanse, to reconsider, to restore, to correct the evil without impairing the good, to purify and humanize every process of our common life without weakening or sentimentalizing it."

"Here muster, not the forces of party, but the forces of humanity," the president concluded his address. Knowing he needed to rally big forces if the progressive reformers were to prevail, he challenged the nation to join him in this mission: "Men's hearts wait upon us; men's lives hang in the balance; men's hopes call upon us to say what we will do."

President Wilson used this political moment to create the momentum for a cascading set of reforms that renewed America. He believed in America's promise and values. He was angry that corruption and greed had allowed our democratic and Industrial Revolution to be soiled, and the task now was "to cleanse, to reconsider, to restore, to correct the evil."

Today, the vast majority of Americans believe in the country's promise. They identify with this changing America, its diversity and multiculturalism, and identify strongly with cities where they live and the quality of life there.

Many of the new immigrants may be working in low-wage jobs in restaurants and hotels, but they have faith and strong neighborhoods and networks of family and friends from their native countries. Today's working women would not trade for an instant today's frustrations for their role in the traditional breadwinner household. Millennials have different economic prospects and too much debt, though they have their own strategies and goals and friends and gravitate to the new urbanism.

At the core, though, they think that their promise and America's promise are being eroded by so many things that are just wrong. The American people are deeply frustrated with an economy that leaves them always on the edge. They live with the changes to the family and in parenting, and many are on their own. They resent the fact that CEOs and the richest play by different rules and use their money to buy a government that works for them, not the hardworking middle class. And with all of these problems, they are angry at the political class for not figuring out how to address them.

Their anger will become poignant and reach a tipping point that compels the nation's leaders to get to work, right the wrong, and address the deepest problems. The citizenry is ready for a cleansing era of reform that allows America to realize its promise.

ACKNOWLEDGMENTS

I could not have written this book but for the leaders and party activists and for the ordinary citizens whom I have listened to in different countries across the globe. That must seem odd, since this book is about America. Yet they allowed me to see an America unobscured by the deadening partisan gridlock and the average American's daily struggle to get by.

Do you know the original title of my book plan accepted by the publisher was "America Without Dreams"? At least it was posed as a question.

I was in Bilbao, Spain, giving a keynote address at a conference on "political communication," and I was using it to test out the arguments of this book. I was asking, "What is the consequence of a younger generation that no longer expects to follow their parents' path to the middle class?" I literally just stopped myself in mid-speech and went silent for a moment. "Look, I get that America's unemployment rate is nearing 8 percent and here, half the youth are out of work and in revolt against failed political leaders. You must think I'm from Mars," I said, or something to that effect.

Over wine that evening with one of the discussants, I soon realized they were not at all upset with what must have seemed like my obvious insensitivity to what they were living through. They were upset about what I was saying about America. They believe America is economically and culturally dynamic, and they need it as a model of how a country can be a success. They just believed more than I did at the time that America would figure out how to fix what is broken and find a way to renew itself like it has done in the past.

I think about Armando Briquet, the campaign manager for Henrique Capriles Radonski, who worked to unite the opposition to challenge Hugo Chavez for the presidency of Venezuela and then nearly defeated Nicolas Maduro, both of whom were aided by the immense machinery of Chavez's party and state. Henrique's manager would encourage thousands of activists to march through the streets of Chavista-controlled towns to show they were not afraid to go to the polling place and vote. With red flags draped on the balcony and Chavez supporters peering down, it was a brave statement.

Yet there was no meeting, coffee, or dinner where the manager didn't ask, "How is Obama doing?" Or, "How is Hillary doing?" As you know from having read this book, I am modestly critical of President Obama for not educating the country about the big structural economic problems that leave the middle class struggling. And they just ignored me. The president's doing well, right?

Well, with the official inflation rate at 69 percent, no toilet paper, medicines rationed, and key opposition leaders in jail in Venezuela, you first tell yourself to have some perspective on the American condition.

You also realize very soon how important America is for them, and how important it is for America to be successful and exceptional.

You should never lose track of how much America means to aspirant people in countries everywhere.

They see an America continually renewed by new immigrants and that welcomes people like nowhere else. Some want their children to live there. They travel there to breathe its dynamism. They think America is the future.

As I worked in country after country, I began to realize how unique is America's openness to new immigrants, its growing racial and religious diversity and multiculturalism, and its framework for bringing unity out of diversity.

That understanding of America changed the book, obviously.

It also took a huge toll on my timetable for the book. It took me four and a half years to turn in the manuscript—roughly three years late.

The book also took longer because I decided that my historic project of making Bill Clinton's "forgotten middle class" front and center was no longer the formula for Democratic hegemony. That stopped me as I began to think through the implications. After all, I had paused writing this book to write with James Carville, *It's the Middle Class, Stupid!* I threw out the planned chapter on the "Reagan Democrats."

I realize now that people are living through revolutionary changes, and they want a politics relevant to their lives. And they want to see reforms of such scale that they can address the deep problems the country faces. This is new territory, and you see the ordinary citizen has little patience with the leaders who don't get it.

And only late in the writing did I come to a realization that America is building a demand for bold reforms that could produce a new progressive era, which led me to write a book with more historical perspective. I wanted to signify what I believe is happening with my country and progressive politics.

So, I have to thank Thomas Dunne, the editor and soul of Thomas Dunne Books at St. Martin's Press, who has remained patient as the months and years ticked by and who understood the new scope of the book and its implications. Bob Barnett remained a faithful agent and advocate. And Anne Brewer took ownership, understood the timing, and produced a book we are all proud of. Joe Rinaldi was the publicist for my previous books, and he understood how this one could help make history.

Many patient people reacted to the book plan, listened to me drone on at conferences, and read chapters or even the whole manuscript. I want to thank Robert Borosage, James Carville, Rosa DeLauro, Paul Glastris at *Washington Monthly*, Ed Kilgore and Andrew Levison at *Democratic Strategist*, Robert Kuttner at *The American Prospect*, Gara LaMarche, Theda Skocpol, Douglas Sosnik, and George Stephanopoulos. My brother, Edward Greenberg, at the University of Colorado, whose own books educate generations to bring a critical eye to American political institutions, took an especially critical pen to multiple drafts of the book.

James Carville and I created Democracy Corps sixteen years ago, with the sustained financial support of Steve Bing in its first decade. He believed in our collaboration to create an independent and respected public-opinion-based organization that would not be afraid to be bold and offer strategies for change. *America Ascendant* was possible because of Democracy Corps' polls and focus groups, carried on with new partners who are battling for reform too.

Democracy Corps is vital and engaged because of the long-term partners who support the innovative research that allowed this book to explore new vistas. I am especially grateful to Page Gardner, head of Women's Voices Women Vote and the Voter Participation Project, who has constantly evolved her strategy, expanded her partnerships, and demanded effectiveness; to David Donnelly, head of Every Voice, who is redefining what reform means in the face of unlimited money; to Anna Burger and Felicia Wong and to the Roosevelt Institute, which is redefining the liberal economic agenda in the face of financialization; to William and David Harris, who are always there; to Rahm Emanuel, Chris van Hollen, and Steve Israel, chairs of the Democratic Congressional Campaign Committee; and to Kelly Ward and Alixandria Lapp. They allowed Democracy Corps to remain engaged and make a difference.

The economy project was possible because of the original collaboration of John Podesta and the Center for American Progress; Jeffrey Katzenberg provided start-up funds for the Republican Party Project; and Robert Borosage and Roger Hickey and Campaign for America's Future supported many of the key post-election surveys reported in this book.

I am grateful to The Markle Foundation, which supported a bipartisan research project conducted by Greenberg Quinlan Rosner and North Star Opinion Research that provided new insights into the thinking of college graduates on technology and challenges of the new economy.

I took full advantage of the bipartisan polls conducted by Greenberg Quinlan Rosner and American Viewpoint for *The Los Angeles Times* that allowed this book to pay a lot of attention to California.

And Mara Liasson and Ron Elving at National Public Radio have welcomed conducting their election-year polls jointly with Democracy Corps and Resurgent Republic—our Republican counterpart, created at the urging of Karl Rove. I also want to thank Whit Ayres for his contribution to this book. I trust he will enjoy it.

None of this would have been possible without Greenberg Quinlan Rosner, which continues to lead as a company finding research-based strategies for campaigns, businesses, and NGOs in the United States and around the world. It is a company that wears its values on its sleeve, is engaged, and works for leaders of integrity. It provided amazing support while writing this book, including ideas and input from the partners. I am indebted to Anna Greenberg and Jeremy Rosner, who run the company, as well as to my partners, Al Quinlan and James Morris.

With great conviction, Erica Seifert headed up Democracy Corps while a great deal of the research was done for this book, and she was aided in that work by Scott Tiell and Laura Swartz. Mathew Groch was my expert project coordinator. Nancy Zdunkewicz now leads Democracy Corps and has taken it to a new level, including critical research done for this book. The key studies were overseen by the talented analysts and vice presidents at Greenberg Quinlan Rosner, including Missy Egelsky, Angela Kuefler, Drew Lieberman, Chloe Mullins, Dave Walker, and Ben Winston.

Nancy Zdunkewicz's deep commitment to the quality of this book, her professionalism, her understanding of the underlying issues, her writing and editing skills, her bravery in exposing my unconvincing arguments, and her willingness to work unimaginable hours to get this done did make this book possible. Nancy was aided on the book by a small army of interns whom I wish I could thank by name, and also by Jiore Craig, Kate McCarthy, and Katrina Avila of GQR Digital.

Libby Green is my project coordinator, and she allows me to carry on my work for clients while protecting my writing time and time with the grandkids. She, too, pitched in to get the book done.

My family plays a special role for me, though I know how important family is for all of us. All of our children are engaged in their own ways in bringing change and contributing to their communities—and we spend a lot of time helping each other. Kathryn Greenberg advises progressive groups on how to be effective, and her husband, Ari Zentner, does the same for businesses. Amazingly, Anna Greenberg and I work together, and she now leads all the U.S. domestic teams and has elected great leaders on her own. Jonathan Greenberg has built a successful pizzeria, Rosco's, in Brooklyn, and his wife, Justine, copyedits books, of all things.

The book is dedicated to our grandchildren Jasper Samuel Delicath, Teo Isaac Zentner, Sadie Liberty Delicath, and Rigby Maya Zentner, who give life purpose. It is for them and their generation that our country and others need to tackle our deepest problems and allow America to lead this century.

My wife, Congresswoman Rosa DeLauro, read this book through multiple drafts and offered comments; the book was a way we shared our thinking and helped each other in the ways we battle for change. I am in awe of what she has accomplished on food stamps, food safety and nutrition, food labeling, equal pay for women and paid leave, on tax credits for low-wage workers, and in her principled battles for the most vulnerable and against America's new trade agreements. While I write on, she really is one of those creating the momentum for an era of reform.

Washington, DC
August 30, 2015

NOTES

1 AMERICA AT A TIPPING POINT

1. Joseph S. Nye Jr., *Is the American Century Over?* (Malden: Polity Press, 2015), Kindle location 191, 871.

2. "A More Diverse Nation: For the First Time, More Than 50 Percent of Children Under Age 5 Are Minorities," U.S. Census Bureau, 2015; New York City Department of City Planning, "The Newest New Yorkers; Characteristics of the City's Foreign-Born Population, 2013 Edition," December 2013; U.S. Census Bureau, State and County QuickFacts, last revised January 7, 2014; Vivek Wadhwa, AnnaLee Saxenian, and F. Daniel Siciliano, *Then and Now: America's New Immigrant Entrepreneurs*, Part VII (Duke University and University of California at Berkeley, October 2012), p. 2; national survey of 2,566 adults conducted by Gallup, May 2–7 and December 5–8, 2013, cited by Frank Newport, "In U.S., Four in 10 Report Attending Church in Last Week," Gallup, December 24, 2013; migration data released by the United Nations, September 2013, cited in "Changing Patterns of Global Migration and Remittances: More Migrants in U.S. and Other Wealthy Countries: More Money to Middle-Income Countries," Pew Research Center, December 2013, pp. 4–7; Wendy Wang, "The Rise of Intermarriage," Pew Research Center, February 16, 2012, pp. 1, 5.

3. Democracy Corps projections of composition of the 2016 presidential electorate. Projections reflect internal and external analysis of demographic and voter trends; David Madland and Ruy Teixeira, "New Progressive America: The Millennial Generation," *Center for American Progress*, May 2009, p. 5.

4. Robert Putnam and David Campbell, *American Grace* (New York: Simon & Schuster, 2012), Kindle location 1945, 331, 1500–1571; Robert P. Jones, Daniel Cox, and Juhem Navarro-Rivera, "A Shifting Landscape," Public Religion Research Institute, February 26, 2014, p. 11.

5. Mark J. Perry, "Stunning College Degree Gap: Women Have Earned Almost 10 Million More College Degrees Than Men Since 1982," American Enterprise Institute, May 13, 2013; Wendy Wang, Kim Parker, and Paul Taylor, "Breadwinner Moms," Pew Research Center, May 29, 2013, p. 6; Pew Research Center analysis of Decennial Census (1960–2000) and American Community Survey data (2008, 2010) cited in "Barely Half of U.S. Adults Are Married—A Record Low," *Pew Research Center*, December 14, 2011, pp. 1–2; Leigh Gallagher, *The End of the Suburbs: Where the American Dream Is Moving* (New York: Penguin Group, 2013), pp. 19, 146.

6. Joe Cortright, "The Young and Restless and the Nation's Cities," City Report, City Observatory, October 2014, p. 1.

7. Lawrence Mishel and Alyssa Davis, "CEO Pay Continues to Rise as Typical Workers Are Paid Less," Economic Policy Institute, June 12, 2014.

8. Nicholas Kristof, "Where the G.O.P Gets It Right," *The New York Times*, April 10, 2014; Nick Schulz, *Home Economics: The Consequences of Changing Family Structure* (Washington, D.C.: AEI, 2013), Kindle location 470–83; Charles Murray, "The New American Divide," *The Wall Street Journal*, January 21, 2012.

9. Andrew J. Cherlin, *Labor's Love Lost: The Rise and Fall of the Working-Class Family in America* (New York: Russell Sage Foundation, 2014), p. 117.

10. Walter Isaacson, *The Innovators: How a Group of Hackers, Geniuses, and Geeks Created the Digital Revolution* (New York: Simon & Schuster, 2014), Kindle location 239; Ian Morris, *Why the West Rules—for Now: The Patterns of History, and What They Reveal About the Future* (New York: Farrar, Straus & and Giroux, 2014), Kindle location 8034–8039; Thomas Piketty, "Table S2.4. World output growth rate 0-2100," technical appendix in *Capital in the Twenty-first Century* (Cambridge, Mass.: Belknap Press of Harvard University, March 2014).

11. Thomas Piketty, *Capital in the Twenty-first Century*, pp. 59, 91; Morris, *Why the West Rules*, Kindle location 8013–8023, 439–45.

12. Cherlin, *Labor's Love Lost*, pp. 48–49.

13. Piketty, *Capital in the Twenty-first Century*, p. 349.

14. Matthew O'Brien, "The Most Expensive Election Ever . . . 1896?," *The Atlantic*, November 6, 2012.

15. Michael Wolraich, *Unreasonable Men: Theodore Roosevelt and the Republican Rebels Who Created Progressive Politics* (New York: Palgrave Macmillan, 2014), p. 200.

16. The GOP Conservative Heartland includes Alabama, Alaska, Arkansas, Georgia, Idaho, Kansas, Kentucky, Louisiana, Mississippi, Montana, Nebraska, North Dakota, Oklahoma, South Carolina, South Dakota, Texas, Tennessee, Utah, West Virginia, and Wyoming.

17. "Political Polarization in the American Public," Pew Research Center, June 12, 2014, p. 12.

18. Evan Halper, "Voters See Some Good in Grim Budget," *The Los Angeles Times*, July 22, 2011; statewide survey of fifteen hundred registered voters in California conducted by Greenberg Quinlan Rosner and Public Opinion Strategies for *The Los Angeles Times* and the USC College of Letters, Arts, and Sciences, October 27–November 3, 2009; Adam Nagourney, "California Faces a New Quandary, Too Much Money," *The New York Times*, May 25, 2013; Rory Carroll, "Jerry Brown, Version 2.0: 'California's the Healthiest It's Been in a Decade,'" *The Guardian*, December 18, 2013.

19. University of California Budget News, "UC to Get Modest Boost from State Budget," January 11, 2013, http://budget.universityofcalifornia.edu/?p=1765; Phil Oliff, Vincent Palacios, Ingrid Johnson, and Michael Leachman, "Recent Deep State Higher Education Cuts May Harm Students and the Economy for Years to Come," Center on Budget and Policy Priorities, March 19, 2013.

20. Halper, "Voters See Some Good in Grim Budget."

21. Rory Carroll, "Jerry Brown, Version 2.0"; Robin Respaut, "California Sees Reserves Growing More Than $4 Billion over Two Years," Reuters, November 19, 2014; Ed Coghlan, "U.S. Jobs Numbers Sluggish, California Economy Out-pacing National Growth," California Economic Summit, August 2, 2013.

22. Sharon Bernstein, "California to Raise Minimum Wage to $10 an Hour by 2016," Reuters, September 25, 2013; "Paid Sick Leave," National Conference of State Legislatures, December 9, 2014; Jerry Geisel, "California Expands Paid Family Leave Law," *Business Insurance,* September 25, 2013.

23. Matthew A. Winkler, "Best State for Business? Yes, California," *Bloomberg View*, March 12, 2015.

24. David Brooks, "Capitalism for the Masses," *The New York Times*, February 20, 2014.

25. Henry Goldman, "Bloomberg Proposes $20 Billion NYC Flood Plan After Sandy," *Bloomberg News,* June 11, 2013; "Climate Action in Megacities," C40 Cities Baseline and Opportunities, Vol. 2.0, February 2014; "City of San Francisco," C40 Cities Report, 2013.

26. "De Blasio Unveils Greenhouse Gas Reduction Plan," CBS New York, September 21, 2014.

27. Ronald Brownstein, "America's Coal-Fired Divide," *National Journal,* September 6, 2014.

28. Pope Francis, *Apostolic Exhortation Evangelii Gaudium of the Holy Father Francis to the Bishops, Clergy, Consecrated Persons, and the Lay Faithful on the Proclamation of the Gospel in Today's World* (Rome: Vatican Press, English ed., 2014), p. 45.

29. U.S. Census Bureau, State and County QuickFacts, last revised February 5, 2015.

30. Richard V. Burkhauser, Jeff Larrimore, and Kosali I. Simon, "A 'Second Opinion' on the Economic Health of the American Middle Class," National Bureau of Economic Research, Working Paper No. 17164, June 2011.

31. Ibid., pp. 33–34.

32. Elisabeth Rosenthal, "How the High Cost of Medical Care Is Affecting Americans," *The New York Times*, December 18, 2014; Jenna Levy, "In U.S., Uninsured Rate Sinks to 13.4% in Second Quarter," Gallup, July 10, 2014.

33. Remarks by President Barack Obama to a joint session of Congress at the Capitol, Washington, D.C., January 21, 2015.

2   AMERICA'S ECONOMIC ASCENDANCY

1. Michael Levi, *The Power Surge: Energy, Opportunity, and the Battle for America's Future* (New York: Oxford University Press, 2013), p. 24.

2. "Game Changers: Five Opportunities for U.S. Growth and Renewal," *McKinsey Global Institute*, July 2013, p. 7; "Natural Gas Annual with Data for 2013," U.S. Energy Information Administration, October 31, 2014.

3. Ed Crooks, "U.S. Oil Reserves at Highest Since 1975," *Financial Times*, December 4, 2014; Steven Mufson, "As Oil Prices Plunge, Wide-Ranging Effects for Consumers and the Global Economy," *Washington Post*, December 1, 2014; Myles Udland, "Oil Prices Are Cratering—but So Is the Price of Gas," *Business Insider*, December 10, 2014.

4. James B. Stewart, "Steep Slide in Oil Prices Is Blessing for Most," *The New York Times*, December 5, 2014; Tom Bemis, "Iran, Venezuela, Russia May Face Pain from Cratering Oil Prices," MarketWatch, December 1, 2014.

5. Sherle R. Schwenninger and Samuel Sherraden, "The Promise of (and Obstacles to) America's Emerging Growth Story," New America Foundation, July 2012, p. 7; Gwynne Taraska, "U.S. Liquefied Natural Gas: A Primer on the Process and the Debate," Center for American Progress, November 5, 2013.

6. Levi, *The Power Surge*, p. 55.

7. Ibid., pp. 23–24.

8. Daniel Yergin, *The Quest: Energy, Security, and the Remaking of the Modern World* (New York: Penguin, 2011), Kindle locations 5409–5477; Levi, *The Power Surge*, pp. 22–24.

9. Yergin, *The Quest*, Kindle locations 5478, 5486.

10. Levi, *The Power Surge*, pp. 26–27.

11. Game Changers," McKinsey Global Institute, July 2013, pp. 7–8; Levi, *The Power Surge*, p. 28.

12. John Kemp, "Fracking Safely and Responsibly," Reuters, March 13, 2012; Brad Quick and Morgan Brennan, "Inside North Dakota's Latest Fracking Problem," CNBC, August 22, 2014; Susan Phillips, "Maryland Governor Proposes Stringent Fracking Regulations," NPR, state impact, November 25, 2014.

13. Jennifer A. Dlouhy, "Feds Work Through Millions of Comments on Fracking Rules," Fuel Fix, April 4, 2014; Eric Lipton, "Energy Firms in Secretive Alliance with Attorneys General," *The New York Times*, December 6, 2014; national survey of one thousand registered voters conducted by Greenberg Quinlan Rosner on behalf of the American Lung Association, November 13–18, 2014.

14. Stephen Lacey, "Nine More Dirty, Aging Coal Plants Set to Close, Bringing Total U.S. Retirements to 106 Plants Since 2010," ThinkProgress, February 29, 2012; "How Many Dirty

Coal-Burning Plants Have We Retired?," Sierra Club, "Beyond Coal Victories," visited March 20, 2014.

15. Yergin, Kindle location 5434; "Nonconventional Fuels Tax Credit," Independent Petroleum Association of America, February 2005.

16. Levi, *The Power Surge,* p. 122; U.S. Congress, Energy Independence and Security Act of 2007, 110th Cong., 1st sess., 2007, H.R. 6, Sections 131, 301, 411–12, 421; U.S. Environmental Protection Agency, Renewable Fuel Standard (RFS), last updated December 10, 2013, http://www .epa.gov/otaq/fuels/renewablefuels/.

17. Levi, *The Power Surge,* p. 122.

18. Ibid., p. 110.

19. National survey of 1,530 adults conducted by Pew Research Center, March 7–11, 2012, cited in "Those Aware of Fracking Favor Its Use: As Gas Prices Pinch, Support for Oil and Gas Production Grows," Pew Research Center, March 19, 2012, p. 2. The most popular energy policies were requiring better fuel efficiency for vehicles (78 percent favor) and increasing federal funding for research on wind, solar, and hydrogen technology (69 percent favor); national survey of 1,024 adults conducted by Gallup, March 8–11, 2012, cited by Frank Newport in "Americans Endorse Various Energy, Environment Proposals," Gallup.com, April 9, 2012. The most popular energy and environmental proposals were setting higher emissions and pollution standards (70 percent favor), spending government money to develop solar and wind power (69 percent favor), and spending government funds to develop alternative fuel sources for cars (66 percent favor).

20. U.S. Department of Energy, Successes of the Recovery Act, January 2012, http://energy .gov/sites/prod/files/RecoveryActSuccess_Jan2012final.pdf; Diane Cardwell, "Solar and Wind Energy Start to Win on Price vs. Conventional Fuels," *The New York Times,* November 23, 2014; "Renewable Portfolio Standard Policies," Database of State Incentives for Renewables and Efficiency, March 2013, http://www.dsireusa.org/documents/summarymaps/RPS_map.pdf.

21. U.S. Energy Information Administration, "Most States Have Renewable Portfolio Standards," February 3, 2012; Office of Governor Edmund G. Brown Jr., Executive Order B-16-2012, May 23, 2012.

22. Matthew A. Winkler, "Best State for Business? Yes, California," Bloomberg, March 12, 2015.

23. Battleground survey of sixteen hundred likely voters conducted in fifty Republican-held competitive districts conducted by Greenberg Quinlan Rosner for Democracy Corps, October 13–16, 2008. Nearly one in seven (69 percent) said this statement made them more likely to vote for the Democratic candidate; swing districts survey of twelve hundred likely voters in forty-nine Republican-held competitive districts conducted by Greenberg Quinlan Rosner for Democracy Corps, October 10–12, 2006. Almost half (52 percent) said a candidate who says "I will be a member of Congress who works with Democrats as well as Republicans and President Bush to do whatever needs to be done to create alternative energy and move America toward energy independence" comes closer to their view.

24. Elizabeth Shogren, "EPA Plan Targets New Coal-Fired Plants," NPR, March 27, 2012; Coral Davenport, "McConnell Urges States to Help Thwart Obama's 'War on Coal,'" *The New York Times,* March 19, 2015.

25. Morgan Winsor, "Sen. Mitch McConnell 'Going to War' with Obama Over Coal," *International Business Times,* November 15, 2014.

26. Clifford Krauss and Stanley Reed, "Surge Seen in U.S. Oil Output, Lowering Gasoline Prices," *The New York Times,* December 16, 2013; Brian M. Carney, "Why This European Is Bullish on America," *The Wall Street Journal,* January 10, 2014; Levi, p. 3.

27. Trip Gabriel, Michael Wines, and Coral Davenport, "Chemical Spill Muddies Picture in a State Wary of Regulations," *The New York Times,* January 18, 2014.

28. Migration data released by the United Nations, September 2013, cited in "Changing Patterns of Global Migration and Remittances: More Migrants in U.S. and Other Wealthy Countries: More Money to Middle-Income Countries," Pew Research Center, December 2013, pp. 4–7.

29. New York City Department of City Planning, "The Newest New Yorkers: Characteristics of the City's Foreign-Born Population, 2013 Edition," December 2013; U.S. Census Bureau, State and County QuickFacts, last revised January 7, 2014.

30. New York City Department of City Planning, "The Newest New Yorkers"; Kirk Semple, "Immigration Remakes and Sustains New York, Report Finds," *The New York Times,* December 18, 2013.

31. U.S. Census Bureau: State and County QuickFacts; Alan Ehrenhalt, *The Great Inversion and the Future of the American City* (New York: Alfred A. Knopf, 2012), pp. 92–225.

32. Vivek Wadhwa, AnnaLee Saxenian, and F. Daniel Siciliano, *Then and Now: America's New Immigrant Entrepreneurs,* Part VII (Duke University and University of California at Berkeley, October 2012), pp. 3, 25–26; Josef Joffe, *The Myth of America's Decline: Politics, Economics, and a Half Century of False Prophecies* (New York: Liveright, 2014), p. 202.

33. Joffe, *The Myth of America's Decline,* p. 202. Between 1989 and 2009, American universities awarded 223,245 PhDs to foreign-born students. Students from China, India, South Korea, and Taiwan earned 150,000 of those degrees; Jon Bruner, "American Leadership in Science, Measured in Nobel Prizes [Infographic]," *Forbes,* October 5, 2011. Of the 314 people who won a Nobel Prize while working in the United States, more than in any other country, 32 percent or 102 of them were foreign-born.

34. Joffe, *The Myth of America's Decline,* pp. 165–69.

35. Federal Statistical Office, "Population Estimate 2013: Number of Inhabitants Increased to Just Under 80.8 million," 2013; Federal Statistical Office, "Germany's Population by 2060; Results of the Twelfth Coordinated Population Projection," November, 18, 2009, p. 5; National Institute of Statistics and Economic Studies, "Population Forecasts 2005–2050 for Metropolitan France," July 2006.

36. Joffe, *The Myth of America's Decline,* pp. 168–70.

37. Grayson Vincent and Victoria Velkoff, "The Next Four Decades: The Older Population in the United States: 2010 to 2050," U.S. Census Bureau, May 2012.

38. "The Economic Impact of S.744, The Border Security, Economic Opportunity, and Immigration Modernization Act," Congressional Budget Office, June 2013, p. 1; Jeffrey Passel, D'Vera Cohn, and Ana Gonzalez-Barrera, "Population Decline of Unauthorized Immigrants Stalls, May Have Reversed," Pew Research Center, September, 23, 2013; U.S. Senate, The Border Security, Economic Opportunity, and Immigration Modernization Act, 113th Cong., 1st sess., 2013, S.744; American Immigration Council, "Guide to S.744: Understanding the 2013 Senate Immigration Bill," Immigration Policy Center, July 2013.

39. U.S. Senate, The Border Security, Economic Opportunity, and Immigration Modernization Act; American Immigration Council, "Guide to S.744."

40. "The Economic Impact of S.744," pp. 12–14.

41. Ibid., pp. 3, 7, 9.

42. Ibid., p. 3.

43. Joffe, *The Myth of America's Decline,* pp. 189–90; "2014 Global R&D Funding Forecast," Battelle, December 2013, http://www.battelle.org/docs/tpp/2014_global_rd_funding_forecast.pdf.

44. Joffe, *The Myth of America's Decline,* pp. 174–75.

45. "Academic Ranking of World Universities," Institute of Higher Education, Shanghai Jiao Tong University, 2014; Fareed Zakaria, *In Defense of a Liberal Education* (New York: W. W. Norton & Company, Inc., 2015).

46. Kevin Carey, "Americans Think We Have the World's Best Colleges. We Don't," *The New York Times,* June 28, 2014.

47. Joffe, *The Myth of America's Decline,* pp. 191–94.

48. Walter Isaacson, *The Innovators,* Kindle locations 1359–1372, 3840.

49. Ibid., Kindle location 2785.

50. Greg Satell, "The True Secrets of Silicon Valley," *Forbes,* July 8, 2013; Vinod Khosla, "Maintain the Silicon Valley Vision," *The New York Times,* July 13, 2012.

51. McKinsey Global Institute, "Game Changes: Five Opportunities for U.S. Growth and Renewal," McKinsey & Company, July 2013, pp. 11–12.

52. Joseph B. White, "New Chapter for Detroit Auto Makers," *The Wall Street Journal,* January 12, 2014; Colum Murphy, "Detroit's Plan: Export Cars and Import Chinese Investment," *The Wall Street Journal,* January 13, 2014; Neal E. Boudette, "Auto Makers Dare to Book Capacity: North American Factories Will Build One Million More Cars a Year," *The Wall Street Journal,* January 14, 2014.

53. Federal Reserve Bank of St. Louis Economic Data, "Graph: All Employees: Manufacturing (MANEMP),"accessed February 2014; U.S. Department of Commerce Bureau of Economic Analysis, "Widespread Growth Across Industries in 2012 Revised Statistics of Gross Domestic Product by Industry for 1997–2012," January 23, 2014; "U.S. International Trade in Goods and Services 2013 Highlights for Congress," U.S. Census Bureau and U.S. Bureau of Economic Analysis, December 2013; Kiran Moodley, "'Made in USA' on the Rise as Manufacturing Costs Drop," NBC News, February 3, 2014; Pilita Clark and Christian Oliver, "EU Energy Costs Widen Over Trade Partners," *Fortune,* January 21, 2014.

54. Joffe, *The Myth of America's Decline,* pp. 158–60.

55. "Offshoring: Welcome Home," *The Economist,* January 19, 2013.

56. Brian M. Carney, "Why This European Is Bullish on America," *The Wall Street Journal,* January 10, 2014; Amy Myers Jaffe, "The Experts: Countering the Biggest Misconceptions People Have About U.S. Manufacturing," *The Wall Street Journal,* June 14, 2013.

57. Angelo Young, "Global Defense Budget Seen Climbing in 2014; First Total Increase Since 2009 as Russia Surpasses Britain and Saudi Arabia Continues Its Security Spending Spree," *International Business Times,* February 6, 2014; Kristina Wong and Cristina Marcos, "House Passes $585B Defense Bill," *The Hill,* December 4, 2014.

58. "About Us," Boeing.com, accessed April 2014, http://www.boeing.com/boeing/companyoffices/aboutus/brief.page.

59. Paul Bond, "Study: Global Entertainment Industry Poised to Top $2 Trillion in 2016," *The Hollywood Reporter,* June 4, 2013; "2013 Economic Contribution of the Motion Picture & Television Industry to the United States," Motion Picture Association of America, 2011, http://www.mpaa.org/wp-content/uploads/2014/01/2013-Economic-Contribution-Fact-Sheet.pdf; "Hollywood Has Blockbuster Impact on U.S. Economy That Tourism Fails to Match," *The Guardian,* December 5, 2013.

60. Michael Cieply, "Hollywood Works to Maintain Its World Dominance," *The New York Times,* November 3, 2014.

61. "The Economic Contribution of the Motion Picture & Television Industry to the United States," Motion Picture Association of America, 2013.

62. I unabashedly stole the title from Bruce Katz and Jennifer Bradley, *The Metropolitan Revolution: How Cities and Metros Are Fixing Our Broken Politics and Fragile Economy* (Washington, D.C.: The Brookings Institution, 2013).

63. Ibid., p.1; Parag Khanna, "When Cities Rule the World," McKinsey & Company, February 2011.

64. James Manyika, Jaana Remes, Richard Dobbs, Javier Orellana, and Fabian Schaer, "Urban America: U.S. Cities in the Global Economy," McKinsey Global Institute, April 2012, pp. 2, 7, 11.

65. "Cities of Opportunity," 6th ed., Pricewaterhouse Coopers, 2014, p. 55.

66. Manyika et al., pp. 3, 5, 9.

67. Erin Carlyle, "Washington, D.C., Tops Forbes 2014 List of America's Coolest Cities," *Forbes,* August 6, 2014.

68. Katz and Bradley, *The Metropolitan Revolution,* p. 1.

69. Brenda Cronin, "Seattle v. Denver: Who's Got the Better Job Market?," *The Wall Street Journal,* January 31, 2014.

70. Pamela Druckerman, "Miami Grows Up. A Little," *The New York Times*, August 8, 2014; Seth Motel and Eileen Patten, "The 10 Largest Hispanic Origin Groups: Characteristics, Rankings, Top Counties," Pew Research Center, July 12, 2012; Kevin Gray, "Cash-Rich Latin Americans Help Resuscitate Miami Real Estate," Reuters, February 23, 2012.

71. Lizette Alvarez, "Influx of South Americans Drive Miami's Reinvention," *The New York Times*, July 19, 2014.

72. Leigh Gallagher, *The End of the Suburbs: Where the American Dream Is Moving* (New York: Penguin Group, 2013), Kindle locations 18–20, 118, 311–321; Claire Cain Miller, "More New Jobs Are in City Centers, While Employment Growth Shrinks in the Suburbs," *The New York Times*, February 24, 2015.

73. Alan Ehrenhalt, *The Great Inversion and the Future of the American City* (New York: Vintage Books, 2012); Gallagher, *The End of the Suburbs*, p. 5, Kindle locations 2272–2280; Lauren Weber, "Companies Say Goodbye to the 'Burbs," *The Wall Street Journal*, December 4, 2013.

74. Gallagher, *The End of the Suburbs*, pp. 6, 14–17; Ehrenhalt, *The Great Inversion*, Kindle location 199; Matthew Yglesias, "Single-Family Homes Are Going Out of Style. Thanks, Millennials!," *Vox*, October 19, 2014.

75. Pew Research Center analysis of Decennial Census (1960–2000) and American community survey data (2008, 2010) cited in "Barely Half of U.S. Adults Are Married—a Record Low," Pew Research Center, December 14, 2011, pp. 1–2; Gallagher, *The End of the Suburbs*, pp. 19, 146.

76. Douglas Quenqua, "Millennials Set to Outnumber Baby Boomers," *The New York Times*, January 19, 2015; Gallagher, *The End of the Suburbs*, pp. 19–20; Katz and Bradley, *The Metropolitan Revolution*, p. 120.

77. Joe Cortright, "The Young and Restless and the Nation's Cities," City Report, City Observatory, October 2014, p. 1.

78. Mark Oppenheimer, "Technology Is Not Driving Us Apart After All," *The New York Times Magazine*, January 17, 2004.

79. The first four paragraphs in this section are adapted from my book with James Carville, *It's the Middle Class, Stupid!* (New York: Blue Rider Press, Penguin Group, 2012), pp. 230–35; Fiscal Year 2014 Budget Resolution, "The Path to Prosperity: A Responsible, Balanced Budget," House Budget Committee, March 2013, p. 14.

80. "The Budget and Economic Outlook 2014 to 2024," Congressional Budget Office, February 2014, pp. 7, 9; Paul Krugman, "The Dwindling Deficit," *The New York Times*, May 8, 2013.

81. Carville and Greenberg, *It's the Middle Class, Stupid!*, p. 118.

82. Jason Furman, "Six Economic Benefits of the Affordable Care Act," White House Council of Economic Advisers, February 6, 2014; Sarah Kliff, "The Amazing News Buried Inside a 283-Page Medicare Report," *Vox*, July 28, 2014.

83. Margot Sanger-Katz and Kevin Quealy, "Medicare: Not Such a Budget-Buster Anymore," *The New York Times*, August 27, 2014.

84. Sarah Kliff, "Good News! Health Spending as a Share of the Economy Is Shrinking," *The Washington Post*, January 6, 2014; "National Health Expenditures; Aggregate and Per Capita Amounts, Annual Percent Change and Percent Distribution: Selected Years 1960–2012," Centers for Medicare and Medicaid Services, Office of the Actuary, National Health Statistics Group, http://www.cms.gov/Research-Statistics-Data-and-Systems/Statistics-Trends-and-Reports/NationalHealthExpendData/downloads/tables.pdf.

85. "Trends in Health Care Costs and the Role of the Affordable Care Act," White House Council of Economic Advisers, November 2013, pp. 1, 4; Jason Millman, "Here's Exactly How the United States Spends $2.9 Trillion on Health Care," *The Washington Post*, December 3, 2014.

86. Margot Sanger-Katz, "More Good News on the Deficit, This Time Because of Private Insurance Health Premiums Numbers," *The New York Times*, March 9, 2015.

87. Ezekiel J. Emanuel, "Insurance Companies as We Know Them Are About to Die," *The New Republic,* March 2, 2014.

3 AMERICA'S CULTURAL EXCEPTIONALISM

1. U.S. Census Bureau, State and County QuickFacts, last revised January 7, 2014; "Millennials in Adulthood," Pew Research Center, March 7, 2014, pp. 3, 9; "An Older and More Diverse Nation by Midcentury," U.S. Census Bureau, August 14, 2008; "Most Children Younger Than Age 1 Are Minorities, Census Bureau Reports," U.S. Census Bureau, May 17, 2012; Tallese Johnson and Rose Kreider, "Mapping the Geographic Distribution of Interracial/Interethnic Married Couples in the United States: 2010," U.S. Census Bureau, SEHSD Working Paper 2013–19, April 2013; Wendy Wang, "The Rise of Intermarriage," Pew Research Center, February 16, 2012, pp. 1, 5.

2. U.S. Census Bureau, State and County QuickFacts, last revised January 7, 2014.

3. Michael Hout, Claude Fischer, and Mark Chaves, "More Americans Have No Religious Preference: Key Finding from the 2012 General Social Survey," Institute for the Study of Societal Issues, University of California at Berkeley, March 7, 2013; national survey of 2,566 adults conducted by Gallup, May 2–7 and December 5–8, 2013, cited by Frank Newport, "In U.S., Four in 10 Report Attending Church in Last Week," Gallup, December 24, 2013.

4. Inaugural Address by President William J. Clinton at the West Front Capitol, January 20, 1997.

5. Daniel Proussalidis, "2011 Census: Nearly One in Five Canadians Are Visible Minorities, StatsCan Reports," *Toronto Sun,* May 8, 2013; "Welcoming More New Canadians," Department of Canadian Immigration and Citizenship, February 28, 2014; Jonathan L. Black-Branch, *Making Sense of the Canadian Charter of Rights and Freedoms* (Toronto: Canadian Education Association, 1995), p. 38; Irene Bloemraad, "Understanding Canadian Exceptionalism in Immigration and Pluralism Policy," Migration Policy Institute Transatlantic Council on Migration, July 2012.

6. Simon Romero, "Rio's Race to Future Intersects Slave Past," *The New York Times,* March 8, 2014; Mimi Whitehead, "Brazil: In the Market for Millions of Immigrants," *The Christian Science Monitor,* March 28, 2013; Linsey Davis and Eric Noll, "Interracial Marriage More Common Than Ever, but Black Women Still Lag," ABC News, June 4, 2010; "Characteristics of the Population and Households of the 2010 Population Census," table 1.3.1, Brazilian Institute of Geography and Statistics, 2010; Marcelo Paixão, "Analysis of Conclusions and Recommendations Made by the Working Group in Previous Sessions: Millennium Development Goals," Human Rights Council, seventh session of the Working Group of Experts on People of African Descent, January 14–18, 2008.

7. Kirk Spitzer, "Japan Looks for a Few Good Women to Revive Economy," *USA Today,* January 15, 2014.

8. Thomas Friedman, "Not Just About Us," *The New York Times,* January 7, 2014; Thomas Friedman, "1; 5,000; 500,000," *The New York Times,* January 25, 2014; Megan Price, Anita Gohdes, and Patrick Ball, "Updated Statistical Analysis of Documentation of Killings in the Syrian Arab Republic," Human Rights Data Analysis Group commissioned by the Office of the UN High Commissioner for Human Rights, August 2014.

9. Aryn Baker, "ISIS Claims Massacre of 1,700 Iraqi Soldiers," *Time Magazine,* June 15, 2014; Sudarsan Raghavan, "Tens of Thousands of Muslims Flee Christian Militias in Central African Republic," *The Washington Post,* February 7, 2014; Deborah Amos, "With Each New Upheaval in Iraq, More Minorities Flee," NPR, December 27, 2014.

10. Council on Foreign Relations, Nigeria Security Tracker, accessed December 2015; James Verini, "The War for Nigeria," *National Geographic,* November 2013.

11. Jonathan Lis, "Knesset Passes New Draft Law, Which Includes Haredi Conscription," *Haaretz,* March 12, 2014; Yaniv Kubovich, Shirly Seidler, and Yair Ettinger, "Thousands of Ultra-Orthodox Jews Protest Cut in Yeshiva Funding for Draft-Dodgers," *Haaretz,* February 6, 2014;

Akiva Novick, "Haredim Threaten Huge Demonstration Against Legislation," *Yedioth Ahronoth*, February 20, 2014.

12. Jonathan Lis, "Government Backs Bill Requiring Schools to Teach Israel Is the Jewish Nation-State," *Haaretz*, February, 9, 2014.

13. See Gideon Rachman, "Obama Is a Lonely Western Liberal on Immigration," *The Financial Times*, December 1, 2014; Pini Herman, "President Rivlin: In Israel, There Is a Word Which Has Long Since Turned into a Weapon: 'Demography,'" *Jewish Journal*, June 11, 2015.

14. Catherine Boyle, "Why Crimea Matters," CNBC, March 3, 2014.

15. The Scottish independence referendum results were 45 percent "yes" and 55 percent "no." See "Scottish Referendum: Scotland Votes 'No' to Independence," BBC, September 19, 2014.

16. Twenty-eight-nation survey of 27,829 adults from E.U. countries conducted by TNS opinion and social for the European Commission, November 2–17, 2013, cited in "Public Opinion in the European Union," European Commission, Directorate-General for Communication, Standard Eurobarometer 80, Autumn 2013; national survey of 986 adults in Great Britain conducted by Ipsos MORI, January 31–February 10, 2014; 34 percent said race relations/immigration was the most important issue facing the country, second only to the economy, with 39 percent.

17. Dr. Cinzia Rienzo and Dr. Carlos Vargas-Silva, "Migrants in the UK: An Overview," the Migration Observatory at the University of Oxford, December 17, 2013; national survey of 1,005 adults conducted by ICM Research for *The Guardian*, January 10–12, 2014; 36 percent say that immigration from the E.U. is "good for Britain, because its immigrants claim fewer benefits and help the country pay its way"; Zack Beauchamp, "Map: What Countries Around the Globe See as 'the Greatest Threat in the World,'" *Vox*, October 18, 2014.

18. Richard Ford, "Britain Leads Europe in Giving Out New Passports," *The Times*, November 19, 2014.

19. David Cameron, "Speech on Radicalisation and Islamic Extremism," *The New Statesman*, February 5, 2011; "David Cameron Urges EU Support for Migration Plans," BBC News, November 28, 2014.

20. National survey of 1,005 French adults conducted by Ipsos/Steria for *Le Monde*, France Inter, and Cevipof, January 8–14, 2014; national survey of 1,021 French voters conducted by TNS-Sofres for *Le Monde* and Canal+, January 30–February 3, 2014.

21. "French Secularism on Trial," *The New York Times*, December 2, 2013.

22. "Terror in Paris: A Blow Against Freedom," *The Economist*, January 10, 2015; Elise Vincent, "France's Political Elite Never Champions Virtues of a Multicultural Nation," *The Guardian*, January 10, 2015.

23. James Fontanella-Khan and Hugh Carnegy, "Eurosceptics Storm Brussels," *The Financial Times*, May 26, 2014; Cas Mudde, "The Far Right in the 2014 European Elections: Of Earthquakes, Cartels and Designer Fascists," *The Washington Post*, May 30, 2014; "The Eurosceptics' Victory," *The Economist*, October 5, 2013; Kim Willsher, "Marine Le Pen's Confidence Vindicated by Front National Election Triumph," *The Guardian*, May 25, 2014.

24. Bethany Bell, "Austria's Freedom Party Sees Vote Rise," BBC News, May 25, 2014; Steven Erlanger, "Amid Debate on Migrants, Norway Party Comes to Fore," *The New York Times*, January 23, 2014; the Editors, "Sweden's Chill on Immigration," *Bloomberg View*, September 15, 2014; Rachman, "Obama Is a Lonely Western Liberal on Immigration."

25. Andrew Sparrow, "Nigel Farage: Parts of Britain Are 'Like a Foreign Land,'" *The Guardian*, February 28, 2014; Robert Ford and Matthew Goodwin, *Revolt on the Right: Explaining Support for the Radical Right in Britain* (New York: Routledge, 2014); U.K. 2015 Election Results, UKIP received 12.6 percent of the national vote.

26. John Jay, "The Federalist No. 2: Concerning Dangers from Foreign Force and Influence," *The Independent Journal*, October 31, 1787; John Higham, *Strangers in the Land: Patterns of American Nativism, 1860–1925* (New Brunswick, N.J.: Rutgers University Press, 1983), Kindle locations 1206–1209.

27. Higham, *Strangers in the Land,* Kindle locations 109, 1206–1209; Stanley Feldstein and Lawrence Costello, eds., *The Ordeal of Assimilation: A Documentary History of the Working Class* (Garden City, N.Y.: Anchor Books, 1974), pp. 1–3.

28. Ibid., Kindle locations 96, 158–159, 182–188, 252–283.

29. Ibid., Kindle locations 202–208; Erik Brynjolfsson and Andrew McAfee, *The Second Machine Age: Work Progress, and Prosperity in a Time of Brilliant Technologies* (New York: W. W. Norton, 2014), p. 6.

30. Higham, *Strangers in the Land,* Kindle locations 215, 257, 262.

31. Ibid., Kindle locations 259–265.

32. Ibid., Kindle locations 265–277.

33. Jacob A. Riis, *How the Other Half Lives* (New York: Hill & Wang, 1957), pp. 37, 76–78, 176–82.

34. Higham, *Strangers in the Land,* Kindle locations 286–294.

35. Ibid., Kindle locations 50–56.

36. Ibid., Kindle locations 65–85; Feldstein and Costello, *The Ordeal of Assimilation,* p. 153.

37. Feldstein and Costello, *The Ordeal of Assimilation,* p. 144; Higham, *Strangers in the Land,* Kindle location 89; Declaration of Principles of the Native American Convention Assembled at Philadelphia, July 4, 1845, pp. 4–7.

38. Feldstein and Costello, *The Ordeal of Assimilation,* pp. 164–68, 170–71.

39. Higham, *Strangers in the Land,* Kindle locations 989–1074.

40. Address of Senator John F. Kennedy to the Greater Houston Ministerial Association at the Rice Hotel in Houston, Texas, September 12, 1960.

41. Higham, *Strangers in the Land,* Kindle locations 311, 600, 1239–1245.

42. Ibid., Kindle locations 1375–1386, 1465–1470, 1607–1613.

43. Ibid., Kindle locations 885–892, 1257–1313, 1187–1201, 1264–1269.

44. Ibid., Kindle locations 1254–1321.

45. Ibid., Kindle locations 1325, 1540, 1583, 2361–2367.

46. Ibid., Kindle locations 2865–2921, 3856–3863.

47. Ibid., Kindle locations 3885, 4049–4054.

48. Stanley B. Greenberg, *Politics and Poverty: Modernization and Response in Five Poor Neighborhoods* (New York: John Wiley, 1974), pp. 15–16.

49. Ibid., p. 27.

50. Ibid., pp. 16–18; Ezra Klein, "Everything You Know About Immigration Is Wrong," *The Washington Post,* August 10, 2013.

51. Greenberg, *Politics and Poverty,* pp. 17, 24–25; Klein, "Everything You Think You Know About Immigration Is Wrong."

52. Klein, "Everything You Think You Know About Immigration Is Wrong"; Greenberg, *Politics and Poverty,* p. 18.

53. Greenberg, *Politics and Poverty,* p. 17.

54. Ibid., p. 16.

55. Nathan Glazer and Daniel P. Moynihan, *Beyond the Melting Pot: The Negroes, Puerto Ricans, Jews, Italians, and Irish of New York City* (Cambridge, Mass.: MIT Press, 1963), p. 1; Herbert Gans, *The Urban Villagers: Group and Class in the Life of Italian-Americans* (New York: The Free Press, 1962), pp. 3–6, 241–75, 293.

56. Kent Germany, "Lyndon B. Johnson and Civil Rights: Introduction to the Digital Version," Presidential Recordings at the University of Virginia.

57. "Three Decades of Mass Immigration: The Legacy of the 1965 Immigration Act," Center for Immigration Studies, September 1995.

58. Ibid.

59. Remarks by President Lyndon B. Johnson at the Signing of the Immigration Bill, Liberty Island, New York, October 3, 1965.

60. Klein, "Everything You Think You Know About Immigration Is Wrong."

61. Remarks by President Ronald Reagan at Fudan University in Shanghai, China, April 30, 1984.

62. "Three Decades of Mass Immigration"; Klein, "Everything You Think You Know About Immigration Is Wrong."

63. U.S. Census Bureau, State and County QuickFacts, last revised January 7, 2014; Thom File, "The Diversifying Electorate—Voting Rates by Race and Hispanic Origins in 2012 (and Other Recent Elections)," U.S. Census Bureau, Population Characteristics, Current Population Survey, May 2013.

64. Gebe Martinez, "Learning from Proposition 187," Center for American Progress, May 5, 2010.

65. Ian Gordon and Tasneem Raja, "164 Anti-Immigration Laws Passed Since 2010? A MoJo Analysis," *Mother Jones*, March/April 2012.

66. "Growth and Opportunity Project," Republican National Committee, 2013, p. 8.

67. National survey of 1,010 registered voters conducted by ORC International for CNN, January 31–February 2, 2014.

68. Address by President Barack Obama to a joint session of Congress at the U.S. Capitol in Washington, D.C., January 28, 2014.

69. Ibid.; Max Ehrenfreund, "Your Complete Guide to Obama's Immigration Executive Action," *The Washington Post*, November 20, 2014.

70. Keynote address by candidate for the U.S. Senate Barack Obama at the Democratic National Convention in Boston, July 27, 2004.

71. National survey of 2,973 adults by Pew Research Center, June 28–July 9, 2012, cited in "'Nones' on the Rise: One-in-Five Adults Have No Religious Affiliation," Pew Research Center, October 9, 2012, pp. 13, 17, 22; Robert D. Putnam and David E. Campbell, *American Grace: How Religion Divides and Unites Us* (New York: Simon & Schuster, 2010), Kindle locations 179–81.

72. Putnam and Campbell, *American Grace*, Kindle location 205.

73. Ibid., Kindle locations 200–206; survey of 14,760 adults in fourteen nations by Pew Research Center, August 27–September 24, 2009, cited in "Two Decades After the Wall's Fall," Pew Research Center, November 2, 2009; Putnam and Campbell, *American Grace*, Kindle location 200.

74. Putnam and Campbell, *American Grace*, Kindle location 205; national survey of 1,015 Russian adults by International Social Survey Program, January 2–26, 2008, cited in "Russians Return to Religion, but Not to Church," Pew Research Center, February 10, 2014, pp. 1–2; national Survey of 700 Japanese adults by Pew Research Center, 2012, cited in "Asian Americans: A Mosaic of Faiths," Pew Research Center, July 19, 2012.

75. National survey of 2,303 adults by Princeton Survey Research Associates International for Pew Research Center, November 23–December 21, 2010, cited by Jim Jansen in "The Civic and Community Engagement of Religiously Active Americans," Pew Research Center, December 23, 2011, p. 5; Putnam and Campbell, *American Grace*, Kindle locations 520–539.

76. Putnam and Campbell, *American Grace*, Kindle locations 506–542.

77. Ibid., Kindle location 7893.

78. National survey of 1,504 adults by Pew Research Center, May 1–5, 2013, cited in "After Boston, Little Change in Views of Islam and Violence," Pew Research Center, May 7, 2013, p. 2.

79. National survey of 4,006 adults by Pew Research Center, March 21–April 8, 2013, cited in "Living to 120 and Beyond," Pew Research Center, August 6, 2013, p. 74. Seventy-seven percent of respondents reported believing in heaven "where people who have led good lives are eternally rewarded" and 62 percent reported believing in hell "where people who have bad lives and die without being sorry are eternally punished"; Putnam and Campbell, *American Grace*, Kindle locations 8136–8157.

80. Putnam and Campbell, *American Grace*, Kindle locations 191, 7733–7743.

81. Ibid., Kindle location 8807.

82. Ibid., Kindle locations 333, 4215–4263.

83. Ibid., Kindle locations 4279–4354.

84. Ibid., Kindle locations 4363–4621.

85. Ibid., Kindle location 108.

86. Ibid., Kindle locations 331, 1945.

87. Ibid., Kindle locations 1500–1571.

88. Ibid., Kindle locations 1289, 1977; based on Pew Research Center surveys of the general public in 2014 cited in "Millennials in Adulthood," Pew Research Center, March 7, 2014, p. 4; "America's Changing Religious Landscape: Christians Decline Sharply as Share of Population; Unaffiliated and Other Faiths Continue to Grow," *The Pew Research Center*, May 2015.

89. Putnam and Campbell, *American Grace*, Kindle locations 1877–1879; Robert P. Jones, Daniel Cox, and Juhem Navarro-Rivera, "A Shifting Landscape: A Decade of Change in American Attitudes About Same-Sex Marriage and LGBT Issues," Public Religion Research Institute, February 26, 2014, pp. 1, 10–11; national survey of 3,338 adults by Pew Research Center, February 12–26, 2014, cited by Michael Lipka and Elizabeth Sciupac in "Support for Gay Marriage Up Among Black Protestants in Last Year, Flat Among White Evangelicals," Pew Research Center, March 17, 2014; Carol Kuruvilla, "Meet The Evangelicals Who Cheered the SCOTUS Gay Marriage Ruling," *The Huffington Post*, June 29, 2015.

90. "American Jews and the Current Challenges of Church-State Separation," Pew Research Center, October 19, 2004; Jones, Cox, and Navarro-Rivera, "A Shifting Landscape," p. 11.

91. Tallese Johnson and Rose Kreider, "Mapping the Geographic Distribution of Interracial/ Interethnic Married Couples in the United States: 2010," U.S. Census Bureau, SEHSD Working Paper 2013–2019, April 2013.

92. Decennial Census and American Community Surveys Integrated Public Use Microdata Sample Files, 2008–2010, analyzed by Wendy Wang in "The Rise of Intermarriage," Pew Research Center, February 16, 2012, pp. 5, 8, 9; Helen Marrow and Tomás Jiménez, "Mexican American Mobility," *The Los Angeles Times*, July 2, 2013.

93. "A More Perfect Union," address of Senator Barack Obama to the National Constitution Center in Pittsburg, Pennsylvania, March 18, 2008. "Multiracial in America: Proud, Diverse and Growing in Numbers," *Pew Research Center*, June 11, 2015, pp. 5, 8, 10.

94. Note that Anna Greenberg of Greenberg Quinlan Rosner was the pollster for Bill de Blasio during his primary and general election; inaugural address of Mayor Bill de Blasio at City Hall in New York City, January 1, 2014.

95. Jonathan Allen and Sebastien Malo, "Angry Police Shun NYC Mayor at Funeral for Slain Officer," Reuters, December 28, 2014.

96. Campbell Gibson and Kay Jung, "Historical Census Statistics on Population Totals by Race, 1790 to 1990, and by Hispanic Origin, 1970 to 1990, for the United States, Regions, Divisions, and States," U.S. Census Bureau, Working Paper Series No. 56, September 2002; Karen R. Humes, Nicholas A. Jones, and Roberto R. Ramirez, "Overview of Race and Hispanic Origin: 2010," U.S. Census Bureau, 2010 Census Briefs, March 2011; Sean Trende, "Minority Turnout & the Racial Breakdown of Polls," Real Clear Politics, August 29, 2012; *The New York Times* presidential exit polls from 2012 and 2008.

97. "Young Voters Supported Obama Less, but May Have Mattered More," Pew Research Center, November 26, 2012; David Madland and Ruy Teixeira, "New Progressive America: The Millennial Generation," Center for American Progress, May 2009, p. 9; Ruy Teixeira, "When Will Your State Become Majority-Minority?," ThinkProgress, May 8, 2013.

98. Stanley B. Greenberg, "The Last Test," *Politico Magazine*, November 2013.

99. Frank Newport, "In U.S., 87% Approve of Black-White Marriage, vs. 4% in 1958," Gallup, July 25, 2013.

100. National survey of 2,003 adults by Pew Research Center, September 1–15, 2011, cited by Wendy Wong in "The Rise of Intermarriage," Pew Research Center, February 16, 2012, p. 33; national survey of 2,884 adults by Pew Research Center, October 28–November 30, 2009, cited by Wendy Wong in "The Rise of Intermarriage," Pew Research Center, February 16, 2012, p. 37.

101. Madland and Teixeira, "New Progressive America," p. 5; national survey of 1,815 U.S. residents ages 16+ by *Pew Research Center*, July 20–August 2, 2009, cited in "Forty Years After Woodstock, A Gentler Generation Gap," Pew Research Center, August 12, 2009.

102. Ryan Faughnder, "Super Bowl XLVIII Draws a Record 111.5-Million Viewers, *The Los Angeles Times,* February 3, 2014; Journey Staff, "'It's Beautiful': Coke Debuts Inspiring Ad During Big Game," Coca-ColaCompany.com, February 14, 2014.

4 CONTRADICTIONS OF THE NEW ECONOMY

1. Address by President Barack Obama to a joint session of Congress at the U.S. Capitol in Washington, D.C., January 28, 2014.

2. Remarks on the economy by President Barack Obama at the Port of Wilmington, Wilmington, Del., July 17, 2104.

3. Jeffrey M. Jones, "Bush Approval Ratings: Foreign Policy and the Economy," Gallup, May 27, 2003.

4. "Table H-6. Regions—All Races by Median and Mean Income: 1975 to 2012," U.S. Census Bureau, Current Population Survey, Annual Social and Economic Supplements, Historical Income Tables: Households, accessed August 7, 2014; survey of 1,501 adults by Pew Research Center, August 20–24, 2014, cited in "Views of Job Market Tick Up, No Rise in Economic Optimism," Pew Research Center, September 4, 2014; "Consumer Expenditures Midyear Update—July 2013 Through June 2014 Average," Bureau of Labor Statistics, April 2, 2015.

5. Michael Greenstone and Adam Looney, "Unemployment and Earnings Losses: A Look at Long-Term Impacts of the Great Recession on American Workers," the Hamilton Project, Economic Studies, The Brookings Institution, November 4, 2011.

6. Annie Lowrey, "Living on Minimum Wage," *The New York Times,* June 15, 2013; "Myth and Reality: The Low-Wage Job Machine," Federal Reserve Bank of Atlanta, August 9, 2013.

7. John Coughlan, "Restaurants Help Feed Job Growth: How the Leisure and Hospitality Industry Fared After the Recent Employment Downturn," Bureau of Labor Statistics, U.S. Department of Labor, Vol. 3, no. 16, July 2014; Ben Casselman, "Recovery Redraws Labor Landscape," *The Wall Street Journal,* January 4, 2012.

8. Claire Cain Miller, "As Robots Grow Smarter, American Workers Struggle to Keep Up," *The New York Times*, December 15, 2014.

9. Steven Rattner, "The Myth of Industrial Rebound," *The New York Times*, January 25, 2014; Harold Meyerson, "The Forty-Year Slump," *The American Prospect,* November 12, 2013.

10. Meyerson, "The Forty-Year Slump."

11. Tyler Cowen, *Average Is Over: Powering America Beyond the Age of the Great Stagnation* (New York: Penguin Group, 2013), p. 4.

12. Steven Rattner, "America Is 2013, as Told in Charts," *The New York Times,* December 30, 2013.

13. Lowrey, "Living on Minimum Wage"; Bill Marsh, "The Low Wage Americans," *The New York Times,* July 27, 2013; Kevin Drum, "The Minimum Wage in America Is Pretty Damn Low," *Mother Jones,* December 2, 2013.

14. Annie Lowrey, "Why Are Americans Staying Put?" *The New York Times,* December 10, 2013.

15. Stephen Greenhouse, "A Push to Give Steadier Shifts to Part-Timers," *The New York Times,* July 15, 2014; Mortimer Zuckerman, "The Full-Time Scandal of Part-Time America," *The Wall Street Journal,* July 13, 2014.

16. "Carl Camden: Full-Time Employment May Give Way to a Free Agent Economy," Next

New Deal, the Roosevelt Institute, July 23, 2014; Cowen, *Average Is Over,* p. 61; Robert Kuttner, "The TaskRabbit Economy," *The American Prospect,* October 10, 2013.

17. Union affiliation data from the current population survey, Bureau of Labor Statistics, accessed August 11, 2014.

18. Meyerson, "The Forty-Year Slump."

19. Emmanuel Saez, "Striking It Richer: The Evolution of Top Incomes in the United States (updated with 2012 preliminary estimates)," September 2013; Joseph E. Stiglitz, *The Price of Inequality: How Today's Divided Society Endangers Our Future* (New York: W. W. Norton, 2013), p. 3.

20. Thomas Piketty, *Capital in the Twenty-first Century* (Cambridge, Mass.: Harvard University Press, March 2014), pp. 432–33; "The World's Billionaires," *Forbes,* accessed August 12, 2014; Luisa Kroll and Kerry A. Dolan, "The Forbes 400 Richest People in America," *Forbes,* September 16, 2013.

21. Robert J. Samuelson, "Robert Samuelson: Capitalists Wait, While Labor Loses Out," *The Washington Post,* September 8, 2013.

22. Ibid.; Nelson D. Schwartz, "The Middle Class Is Steadily Eroding. Just Ask the Business World," *The New York Times,* February 2, 2014.

23. Stiglitz, *The Price of Inequality,* p. 8; Paul Krugman, "Why We're in a New Gilded Age," *The New York Times,* May 8, 2014.

24. Ibid.

25. Robert Thoeren and Polly James (screenwriters), *Mrs. Parkington,* MGM Studios, 1944.

26. Piketty, *Capital in the Twenty-first Century,* pp. 292–93, 298; Krugman, "Why We're in a New Gilded Age."

27. Krugman, "Why We're in a New Gilded Age"; Lawrence Mishel and Alyssa Davis, "CEO Pay Continues to Rise as Typical Workers Are Paid Less," Economic Policy Institute, June 12, 2014.

28. Mishel and Davis, "CEO Pay Continues to Rise as Typical Workers Are Paid Less"; Gretchen Morgenson, "An Unstoppable Climb in C.E.O. Pay," *The New York Times,* June 29, 2013.

29. Susan Holmberg and Mark Schmitt, "The Overpaid CEO," *Democracy Journal,* pp. 61–64, 66–68; J. W. Mason, "Disgorge the Cash: The Disconnect Between Corporate Borrowing and Investment," the Roosevelt Institute, February 25, 2015.

30. Mike DeBonis, "Report: D.C. Is Among Most Unequal U.S. Cities by Income," *The Washington Post,* March 13, 2104.

31. Raj Chetty, Nathaniel Hendren, Patrick Kline, Emmanuel Saez, and Nicholas Turner, "Is the United States a Land of Opportunity? Recent Trends in Intergenerational Mobility," National Bureau of Economic Research, Working Paper 19844, January 2014; Miles Corak, "Inequality from Generation to Generation: The United States in Comparison," University of Ottawa Graduate School of Public and International Affairs, January 2012, p. 10.

32. Derek Thompson, "Get Rich, Live Longer: The Ultimate Consequence of Income Inequality," *The Atlantic,* April 18, 2014.

33. Stiglitz, *The Price of Inequality,* p. 28.

34. "History of Federal Individual Income Bottom and Top Bracket Rates," National Taxpayers Union, accessed August 13, 2014; Piketty, *Capital in the Twenty-first Century,* pp. 499, 508–10.

35. Stiglitz, *The Price of Inequality,* pp. 72–73; Danielle Kurtzleben, "Corporations Used to Pay Almost One-Third of Federal Taxes. Now It's One-Tenth," *Vox,* July 25, 2014; Thomas L. Hungerford, "Corporate Tax Rates and Economic Growth Since 1947," Economic Policy Center, June 4, 2013; Kenneth F. Scheve Jr. and David Stasavage, "Is the Estate Tax Doomed?," *The New York Times,* March 24, 2013; Darien B. Jacobson, Brian G. Raub, and Barry W. Johnson, "The Estate Tax: Ninety Years and Counting," SOI Bulletin, Internal Revenue Service, U.S. Department of the Treasury, 2007, pp. 118–28.

36. Tom Edsall, "Milking the Money Machine," *The New York Times,* July 23, 2014.

37. Rebecca Riffkin, "U.S. Consumer Spending Increases Slightly in July to $94," Gallup, August 4, 2014; national survey of 950 2012 voters by Democracy Corps for the Roosevelt Institute, October 16–21, 2014.

38. From focus groups in Columbus, Ohio, on May 10, 2011, and Denver, Colorado, on May 12, 2011. The Ohio groups were conducted among non-college-educated men, swing voters, and college-educated women, swing voters, with a household income of more than $50,000. The Denver groups were conducted among non-college-educated women, swing voters, and college-educated men, swing voters, with a household income of more than $50,000.

39. National survey of 950 2012 voters by Greenberg Quinlan Rosner for Democracy Corps and the Roosevelt Institute, October 16–21, 2014.

40. Survey of 1,501 adults by Pew Research Center, August 20–24, 2014, cited in "Views of Job Market Tick Up, No Rise in Economic Optimism," Pew Research Center, September 4, 2014.

41. Eight focus groups were conducted by Greenberg Quinlan Rosner and North Star Opinion Research for the Markle Foundation and American Greetings in May 2014—two online; two in Austin, Texas; two in Portland, Oregon; and two in Cleveland, Ohio. The online focus groups, one among male respondents and one among female respondents, were recruited nationally and the survey was conducted on May 19–20, 2014, among college-educated, where "college-educated" was defined broadly to include those with a post-high-school education (some college education, a two-year or technical degree), a four-year college degree, or a postgraduate degree. The Austin focus groups were conducted on May 27, 2014, the first among college-educated Hispanic men and women and the second among white college-educated men and women. The Portland focus groups were conducted on May 21, 2014, the first among college-educated men and women and the second among only post-high-school-educated men and women without a four-year degree. The Cleveland focus groups were conducted on May 22, 2014, the first among college-educated men and women and the second among high-school-graduate men and women.

42. National survey of 950 2012 voters by Greenberg Quinlan Rosner for Democracy Corps and the Roosevelt Institute, October 16–21, 2014.

43. Ibid.

44. Wendy Wang, Kim Parker, and Paul Taylor, "Breadwinner Moms," Pew Research Center, May 29, 2013.

45. Alissa Quart, "Crushed by the Cost of Child Care," *The New York Times,* August 17, 2013; Christopher Ingraham, "Start Saving Now: Day Care Costs More Than College in 31 States," *The Washington Post,* April 9, 2014.

46. Neil Shah, "Consumer Borrowing Picks Up," *The Wall Street Journal,* November 14, 2013; Jeff Cox, "It's Back with a Vengeance: Private Debt," CNBC, October 12, 2013.

47. National survey of 950 2012 voters by Democracy Corps.

48. Survey of 1,000 adults by Hart Research Associates for Public Opinion Strategies and NBC News/*The Wall Street Journal,* July 30–August 3, 2014.

49. Cherlin, pp. 156–58.

50. Survey of 1,000 adults by Hart Research Associates for Public Opinion Strategies and NBC News/*The Wall Street Journal,* July 30–August 3, 2014.

51. Andrew Levison, *The White Working Class Today* (Washington, D.C.: Democratic Strategist Press, 2013), pp. 46–72.

52. Bonnie Kavoussi, "Recession Killed 170,000 Small Businesses Between 2008 and 2010: Report," *The Huffington Post,* July 26, 2012.

53. Natasha Singer, "In the Sharing Economy, Workers Find Both Freedom and Uncertainty," *The New York Times,* August 16, 2014.

54. Survey of 950 2012 voters by Greenberg Quinlan Rosner for Democracy Corps and the Roosevelt Institute, October 16–21, 2014.

55. Survey of 1,485 adults by Pew Research Center, October 9–12, cited in "Public Not Desperate About Economy or Personal Finances," Pew Research Center, October 15, 2008; survey of

1,000 adults by Hart Research Associates for Public Opinion Strategies and NBC News/Wall Street Journal, conducted July 30–August 3, 2014.

56. Survey of 1,000 adults by Hart Research Associates for Public Opinion Strategies and NBC News/Wall Street Journal, conducted July 30–August 3, 2014; Rebecca Riffkin, "Public Faith in Congress Falls Again, Hits Historic Low," Gallup, June 19, 2014.

57. National survey of 950 2012 voters by Greenberg Quinlan Rosner for Democracy Corps and the Roosevelt Institute, October 16–21, 2014; national survey of 950 likely 2016 voters at 60 percent cell conducted by Greenberg Quinlan Rosner for Democracy Corps and Women's Voices Women Vote Action Fund, June 13–17, 2015.

58. Time series (January 10–14, 2010, to January 5–8, 2014) provided by Gallup Historical Trends, Big Business, Gallup, accessed August 27, 2014.

59. Survey of 1,651 U.S. registered voters by Hart Research Associates for Center for American Progress, November 15–December 2, 2013.

60. National survey of 950 2012 voters by Greenberg Quinlan Rosner for Democracy Corps and the Roosevelt Institute, October 16–21, 2014.

5   CONTRADICTIONS OF THE NEW SOCIETY

1. Richard Reeves, "How to Save Marriage in America," *The Atlantic,* February 13, 2014.

2. Nick Schulz, *Home Economics: The Consequences of Changing Family Structure* (Washington, D.C.: AEI, 2013), Kindle locations 39–69.

3. U.S. Department of Labor, "The Negro Family: The Case for National Action," Office of Policy Planning and Research, March 1965.

4. Stanley B. Greenberg, *Politics and Poverty: Modernization and Response in Five Poor Neighborhoods* (New York: John Wiley, 1974).

5. Nicholas Kristof, "Where the G.O.P. Gets It Right," *The New York Times,* April 10, 2014; Schulz, *Home Economics,* Kindle locations 470–483; Charles Murray, "The New American Divide," *The Wall Street Journal,* January 21, 2012.

6. Jonathan Rauch, "The No Good, Very Bad Outlook for the Working-Class American Man," *National Journal,* December 5, 2012; Andrew J. Cherlin, *Labor's Love Lost: The Rise and Fall of the Working-Class Family in America* (New York: Russell Sage, 2014), p. 4.

7. Michael Kimmel, *Angry White Men: American Masculinity and the End of an Era* (New York: Nation Books, 2013), Kindle location 138.

8. "For Richer, for Smarter," *The Economist,* June 23, 2011; D'Vera Cohn, "Marriage Rate Declines and Marriage Age Rises," Pew Research Center, December 14, 2011; Claire Cain Miller, "The Divorce Surge Is Over, but the Myth Lives On," *The New York Times,* December 2, 2014.

9. "King's Dream Remains an Elusive Goal; Many Americans See Racial Disparities," Pew Research Center, August 22, 2013, p. 29; Charles Murray, *Coming Apart: The State of White America, 1960–2010* (New York: Crown Forum, 2012), pp. 154–56.

10. "The Decline of Marriage and Rise of New Families," Pew Research Center, November 18, 2010, p. 10; Belinda Luscombe, "How Shacking Up Before Marriage Affects a Relationship's Success," *Time,* March 12, 2014; Jason DeParle and Sabrina Tavernise, "For Women Under 30, Most Births Occur Outside Marriage," *The New York Times,* February 17, 2012.

11. David T. Ellwood and Christopher Jencks, "The Spread of Single-Parent Families in the United States Since 1960," John F. Kennedy School of Government, Harvard University, October 2002, pp. 25–32; Reeves, "How to Save Marriage in America."

12. Reeves, "How to Save Marriage in America."

13. State of Our Union, "When Marriage Disappears: The New Middle America," National Marriage Project at University of Virginia and Center for Marriage and Families at Institute for American Values, 2010; "The Decline of Marriage and Rise of New Families," p. 23; survey of 2,003 adults nationwide by Pew Research Center, May 22–25 and May 29–June 1, 2014, cited in

"Record Share of Americans Have Never Been Married," Pew Research Center, September 24, 2014, p. 29.

14. "The Decline of Marriage and Rise of New Families," p. 23; survey of 2,003 adults nationwide by Pew Research Center, pp. 19, 21, 28.

15. Charles Murray, *Coming Apart: The State of White America, 1960–2010* (New York: Crown Forum, 2012), pp. 154–56.

16. Ibid., pp. 156–57, 203; Annie Lowrey, "Can Marriage Cure Poverty?," *The New York Times,* February 14, 2014.

17. Binyamin Appelbaum, "Out of Trouble, but Criminal Records Keep Men Out of Work," *The New York Times,* February 28, 2015; "King's Dream Remains an Elusive Goal; "Black Lives Matter: The Schott 50 State Report on Public Education and Black Males," The Schott Foundation for Public Education, 2015. The national high school graduation rate for black males is 59 percent; Reniqua Allen, "For Black Men, A Permanent Recession," *Al Jazeera America,* October 9, 2014; "Many Americans See Racial Disparities," Pew Research Center, August 22, 2013.

18. Justin Wolfers, David Leonhardt, and Kevin Quealy, "1.5 Million Missing Black Men," *The New York Times,* April 20, 2015.

19. "The Reversal of the College Marriage Gap," Pew Research Center, October 7, 2010, p. 3; "The Decline of Marriage and Rise of New Families."

20. Lowrey, "Can Marriage Cure Poverty?" ; Carol Graham, "The High Costs of Being Poor in America: Stress, Pain, and Worry," Brookings Social Mobility Project, Brookings Institution, February 19, 2015.

21. Sara McLanahan and Chistopher Jencks, "Was Moynihan Right?," *Education Next,* Vol. 15, No. 2., Spring 2015.

22. Raj Chetty, Nathaniel Hendren, Patrick Kline, and Emmanuel Saez, "Where Is the Land of Opportunity? The Geography of Inequality," National Bureau of Economic Research, June 2014.

23. Kathleen Gerson, *The Unfinished Revolution: How a New Generation Is Reshaping Family, Work, and Gender in America* (New York: Oxford University Press, 2010), p. 9; Reeves, "How to Save Marriage in America."

24. James J. Heckman, "The American Family in Black and White: A Post-racial Strategy for Improving Skills to Promote Equality," National Bureau of Economic Research, March, 2011, pp. 14, 20.

25. Heckman, "The American Family in Black and White."

26. Survey of 600 likely voters in Chicago by Greenberg Quinlan Rosner, March 11-14, 2013. Fifty-two percent of all residents, 44 percent of white residents, 60 percent of black residents, and 55 percent of Hispanic residents said this statement made them much more positive about the city's direction and future goals. Seventy-five percent of all residents, 71 percent of white residents, 78 percent of black residents, and 74 percent of Hispanic residents said this made them much more or somewhat more positive about the city's direction and future goals.

27. Remarks on strengthening the economy for the middle class by President Barack Obama at Hyde Park Career Academy, Chicago, Illinois, February 15, 2013.

28. Jonathan Rauch, "The No Good, Very Bad Outlook"; Pew Research Center analysis of the 1960–2000 decennial censuses and 2010–2012 American Community survey, Integrated Public Use Microdata Series (IPUMS), cited in "Record Share of Americans Have Never Been Married," p. 9.

29. Janet Beer, "White Working-Class Males Need Our Attention, but So Do Wider Issues," *The Guardian,* January 11, 2013; Mark J. Perry, "Stunning College Degree Gap: Women Have Earned Almost 10 Million More College Degrees Than Men Since 1982," American Enterprise Institute, May 13, 2013; "The Condition of Education 2012 (NCES 2012-045), Indicator 47," U.S. Department of Education, National Center for Education Statistics, 2012; Christina Hoff Sommers, "The Boys at the Back," *The New York Times,* February 2, 2013.

30. Data from David Autor and Melanie Wasserman, "Wayward Sons: The Emerging Gender Gap in Labor Markets and Education," *Third Way,* March 2013, p. 12, presented in "Diverging

Fortunes for Men and Women," *The New York Times,* March 20, 2013; Stephanie Coontz, "How Can We Help Men? By Helping Women," *The New York Times,* January 11, 2014.

31. Coontz, "How Can We Help Men?"

32. David Brooks, "Why Men Fail," *The New York Times,* September 10, 2012; Heartland Monitor Poll XII of 1,000 adults nationwide for Allstate and the *National Journal,* March 3–6, 2012, cited by Ronald Brownstein in "Door Opening," *National Journal,* March 15, 2012.

33. Cherlin, *Labor's Love Lost.* pp. 156–58.

34. Hanna Rosin, *The End of Men: And the Rise of Women* (New York: Penguin Group, 2012), pp. 107, 124; Brooks, "Why Men Fail."

35. "Janet Yellen's Husband on Men, Marriage, and the Family," Institute for Family Studies, October 10, 2013; Kay S. Hymowitz, "Where Have the Good Men Gone?," *The Wall Street Journal,* February 19, 2011; Rauch, "The No Good, Very Bad Outlook."

36. Coontz, "How Can We Help Men?"; "Janet Yellen's Husband."

37. Michael Jindra, "Why Working-Class Men Are Falling Behind," *Family Studies,* January 2, 2014; Tyler Cowen, *Average Is Over: Powering America Beyond the Age of the Great Stagnation* (New York: Penguin Group, 2013), p. 52.

38. Survey of 2,511 adults nationwide by Pew Research Center, November 29–December 5, 2012, cited in "Modern Parenthood," Pew Research Center, March 14, 2013, pp. 9–14; "Women in the Labor Force: A Databook," U.S. Bureau of Labor Statistics, Report 1040, February 2013, p. 15; Wendy Wang, Kim Parker, and Paul Taylor, "Breadwinner Moms," Pew Research Center, May 29, 2013, pp. 1, 4.

39. Kim Parker and Wendy Wang, "Modern Parenthood," Pew Research Center, March 14, 2013, p. 1.

40. Ibid., pp. 10, 36–37, 44; "On Pay Gap, Millennial Women Near Parity—for Now," Pew Research Center, December 11, 2013, pp. 20–21.

41. Parker and Wang, "Modern Parenthood," pp. 13, 22.

42. Survey of 2,002 adults nationwide by Pew Research Center, October 7–27, 2013, reported in "On Pay Gap, Millennial Women Near Parity—for Now," pp. 11–12.

43. Ibid., p. 3; Claire Cain Miller, "The Motherhood Penalty vs. the Fatherhood Bonus," *The New York Times,* September 6, 2014.

44. President Bill Clinton, "Bill Clinton: Why I Signed the Family and Medical Leave Act," *Politico,* February 5, 2013.

45. Gretchen Livingston, "Among 38 Nations, U.S. Is the Outlier When It Comes to Paid Parental Leave," Pew Research Center, December 12, 2013.

46. OECD Family Database, Social Policy Division, Directorate of Employment, Labour, and Social Affairs, May 2014, pp. 1–2; Child Care Aware of America Web site, "About Child Care," accessed September 24, 2014; Christopher Ingraham, "Start Saving Now: Day Care Costs More Than College in 31 States," *The Washington Post,* April 9, 2014.

47. Brigid Schulte, "The U.S. Ranks Last in Every Measure When It Comes to Family Policy, in 10 Charts," *The Washington Post,* June 23, 2014.

48. Bryce Covert, "Help for Families Who Can't Afford Childcare Hits Decade Low," *Think-Progress,* February 25, 2014.

49. Rosin, *The End of Men,* p. 2.

50. Brooks, "Why Men Fail."

51. Rosin, *The End of Men,* p. 2.

52. Gerson, *The Unfinished Revolution,* pp. 10–11, 105; survey of 1,821 adults nationwide, including 617 Millennial adults by Pew Research Center, February 14–23, 2014, cited in "Millennials in Adulthood," Pew Research Center, March 7, 2014, p. 5.

53. Gerson, *The Unfinished Revolution,* pp. 11, 127–28.

54. Survey of 2,002 adults nationwide by Pew Research Center, p. 9; Rosin, *The End of Men,* pp. 19–21.

55. "One-Third of Fathers with Working Wives Regularly Care for Their Children, Census Bureau Reports," U.S. Census Bureau, press release, December 5, 2011. Pew Research Center analysis of March Current Population surveys Integrated Public Use Microdata Series (IPUMS-CPS), 1990 and 2013, cited by Gretchen Livingston in "Growing Number of Dads Home with the Kids," Pew Research Center, June 5, 2014, pp. 6–9; Pew Research Center analysis of Decennial Census and American Community Survey data cited by Gretchen Livingston, "The Rise of Single Fathers," Pew Research Center, July 2, 2013. p. 1.

56. Gerson, *The Unfinished Revolution,* p. 105; Pew Research Center analysis of March Current Population surveys, p. 6; survey of 1,003 adults nationwide conducted by Pew Research Center, April 25–28, 2013 cited by Wang, Parker, and Taylor in "Breadwinner Moms," p. 11.

57. Joan Entmacher, "Women in Low-Wage Jobs Are Underpaid and Overlooked," *National Journal,* July 30, 2014; Ginia Bellafante, "When Living on Tips Means Putting Up with Harassment," *The New York Times,* October 17, 2014.

58. "Occupational Employment and Wages—May 2013," Bureau of Labor Statistics, April 1, 2014.

59. "Table 11: Percent of Faculty in Tenure-Track Appointments and Percent of Faculty with Tenure, by Affiliation, Academic Rank, and Gender, 2011–2012," American Association of University Professors, 2012; Claire Cain Miller, "Women on Boards: Where the U.S. Ranks," *The New York Times,* March 10, 2015.

60. Claire Cain Miller, "Even Among Harvard Graduates, Women Fall Short of Their Work Expectations," *The New York Times,* November 28, 2014.

61. Danielle Paquette, "When Companies Know More but Say Less About Their Gender Gap," *The Washington Post,* March 13, 2015.

62. "On Pay Gap, Millennial Women Near Parity—for Now." Pew Research Center, December 11, 2013, p. 2; Lisa Rapaport, "Even In Nursing, No Equal Pay For Women," Reuters, March 24, 2015.

63. Survey of 2,002 adults nationwide by Pew Research Center, pp. 8, 29.

64. "Table 11: Percent of Faculty."

65. Heartland Monitor Poll XII.

6 REVOLUTIONS AND COUNTERREVOLUTION: THE BATTLE FOR AMERICAN VALUES

1. Cheryl Wetzstein, "Condoms Reign Supreme for Birth Control; Pill Second Most Popular," *The Washington Times,* February 14, 2013; Linda Greenhouse, "Doesn't Eat, Doesn't Pray and Doesn't Love," *The New York Times,* November 27, 2013.

2. Antonio Gramsci, *Selections from Prison Notebooks: State and Civil Society* (London: Electric Book, 1999), p. 556.

3. National survey of 2,943 Americans age eighteen or older with oversamples of African Americans, Hispanics, and Asian Americans, by Latino Decisions for the Center for American Progress and PolicyLink, June 11–July 10, 2013, cited by Ruy Teixeira, John Halpin, Matt Barreto, and Adrian Pantoja in "Building an All-in Nation: A View of the American Public," Center for American Progress, October 2013, pp. 3–4, 35.

4. Paul Taylor, *The Next America: Boomers, Millennials, and the Looming Generational Showdown* (New York: PublicAffairs, 2014), Kindle location 1855; 60 percent of Millennials say that President Obama is of mixed race.

5. Teixeira et al., "Building an All-in Nation," p. 12.

6. National survey of 2,943 Americans age eighteen or older.

7. PRRI polls in 2012–2013 cited in Racial Attitudes graphic posted May 8, 2014, on http://publicreligion.org/research/graphic-of-the-week/racial-attitudes/.

8. National survey of 2,943 Americans age eighteen or older.

9. Ibid.

10. Ibid.

11. Ibid.; John Hawkins, "5 Reasons America Is in Decline," Townhall.com, May 15, 2012.

12. Todd S. Purdum, *An Idea Whose Time Has Come: Two Presidents, Two Parties, and the Battle for the Civil Rights Act of 1964* (New York: Henry Holt, 2014).

13. Lou Cannon, *President Reagan: The Role of a Lifetime* (New York: Touchstone /Simon & Schuster, 1991), p. 520.

14. "Election 2012: Voting Laws Roundup," Brennan Center for Justice, October 11, 2012.

15. "Voting Laws Roundup 2013," Brennan Center for Justice, December 19, 2013.

16. Steven Yaccino and Lizette Alvarez, "New GOP Bid to Limit Voting in Swing States," *The New York Times,* March 29, 2014.

17. Michael McAuliff, "Republicans Explain They Filibustered Unemployment Aid on Principle," *The Huffington Post,* January 25, 2014.

18. Yaccino and Alvarez, "New GOP Bid"; Sarah Childress, "'Unprecedented' Number of Restrictive Voting Laws Being Introduced," PBS, May 31, 2012; Ryan J. Reilly, "Pennsylvania GOP Leader: Voter ID Will Help Romney Win State," *Talking Points Memo,* June 25, 2012.

19. Michael McAuliff, "Republicans Explain They Filibustered Unemployment Aid on Principle"; "The War on Poverty: 50 Years Later," House Budget Committee, majority staff, March 3, 2014, pp. 3–9.

20. Terence P. Jeffrey, "Obamacare Puts Families Making $192,920 on Welfare," CBS News, August 19, 2009; Michael Syder, "Obamacare Is Going to Be the Biggest Expansion of the Welfare State in U.S. History," Endoftheamericandream.com, November 21, 2013.

21. Jonathan Chait, "How Obamacare Became the New Welfare," *New York,* February 10, 2014.

22. Drew Magary, "What the Duck?," *GQ,* January 2014; David Corn, "More Evidence of Paul Ryan's 'Inner Cities' Problem," *Mother Jones,* March 27, 2014; Brad Heath, "Racial Gap in U.S. Arrest Rates: 'Staggering Disparity,'" *USA Today,* November 19, 2015; "Report of The Sentencing Project to the United Nations Human Rights Committee Regarding Racial Disparities in the United States Criminal Justice System," The Sentencing Project, August 2013; Remarks by President Barack Obama in Eulogy for the Honorable Reverend Clementa Pinckney, Charleston, South Carolina, June 26, 2015.

23. Yaccino and Alvarez, "New GOP"; Jan E. Leighley and Jonathan Nagler, *Who Votes Now? Demographics, Issues, Inequality, and Turnout in the United States* (Princeton, N.J.: Princeton University Press, 2014); William H. Frey, "Minority Turnout Determined the 2012 Election," The Brookings Institution, May 10, 2013.

24. Carrie Dann, "Where Were All the Dems? Here's Who Turned Up to Vote," NBC News, November 5, 2014.

25. Remarks by President William J. Clinton on signing memorandums on medical research and reproductive health and an exchange with reporters in the White House, January 22, 1993.

26. James C. Dobson, Focus on Family newsletter, February 2001; James Davison Hunter, *Culture Wars: The Struggle to Define America* (New York: Basic Books, 1991), pp. 112–13, 130.

27. William V. D'Antonio, Steven A. Tuch, and Josiah R. Baker, *Religion, Politics, and Polarization: How Religiopolitical Conflict Is Changing Congress and American Democracy* (Lanham, Md.: Rowman & Littlefield, 2013), pp. 35, 40, 49–50.

28. Alan Cooperman, "Openly Religious, to a Point," *The Washington Post,* September 16, 2004; Tim Griffin, "What Went Wrong in 2012? The Case of the 4 Million Missing Voters," *RedState,* November 14, 2012; Alan Cooperman and Thomas B. Edsall, "Evangelicals Say They Led Charge for the GOP," *The Washington Post,* November 8, 2004; Bob Allen, "Miers Withdraws as Supreme Court Nominee," *Ethics Daily,* October 27, 2005.

29. Brian Faler, "Election Turnout in 2004 Was Highest Since 1968," *The Washington Post,* January 15, 2005; Stanley B. Greenberg, *The Two Americas: Our Current Political Deadlock and How to Break It* (New York: Thomas Dunne Books/St. Martin's Press, 2005), pp. 321–25; Griffin, "What Went Wrong in 2012?"

30. Greenberg, *The Two Americas,* p. 314.

31. Robert D. Putnam and David E. Campbell, *American Grace: How Religion Divides and Unites Us* (New York: Simon & Schuster, 2012), Kindle location 5935.

32. Juliet Lapidos, "Mike Huckabee's War for Women," *The New York Times,* January 24, 2014.

33. National survey of 1,301 adults by NORC at the University of Chicago, March 20–September 5, 2012, cited by Tom Smith and Jaesok Son, "Trends in Public Attitudes About Sexual Morality," NORC General Social Survey 2012 final report, April 2013, p. 10; national survey of 1,001 adults by Pew Research Center, March 25–April 14, 2011, cited by Jacob Poushter in "What's Morally Acceptable? It Depends on Where in the World You Live," Pew Research Center, April 15, 2014; Putnam and Campbell, *American Grace,* Kindle location 1876.

34. National survey of 1,010 adults by ORC International for CNN, January 31–February 2, 2014; survey of 1,502 adults by Pew Research Center, January 9–13, 2013, cited in *"Roe v. Wade* at 40: Most Oppose Overturning Abortion Decision," Pew Research Center, January 16, 2013, p. 3.

35. Survey of 1,502 adults by Pew Research Center. p. 3.

36. Jeffrey W. Peters, "Parties Seize on Abortion Issues in Midterm Race," *The New York Times,* January 20, 2014.

37. Survey of 1,644 adults by *The New York Times* and CBS News, February 19–23, 2014. Carol Kuruvilla, "Meet The Evangelicals Who Cheered the SCOTUS Gay Marriage Ruling," *The Huffington Post,* June 29, 2015.

38. Ibid.; survey of 1,821 adults with an oversample of eighteen-to-thirty-three-year-olds by Pew Research Center, February 14–23, 2014, cited in "Millennials in Adulthood," Pew Research Center, March 7, 2014, p. 14.

39. Michael Lipka and Elizabeth Sciupac, "Support for Gay Marriage Up Among Black Protestants in Last Year, Flat Among White Evangelicals," Pew Research Center, March 17, 2014.

40. Eric Kelsey, "'Duck Dynasty' Star Phil Robertson Critical of Gays in 2010 Speech," Reuters, December 20, 2013.

41. Zack Ford, "How a Federal Judge in Utah Adeptly Dismantled All of the Arguments Against Marriage Equality," *Think Progress,* December 21, 2013; Sandhya Somashekhar, "Texas AG: County Workers Don't Have to Issue Same-Sex Marriage Licenses," *The Washington Post,* June 28, 2015; Sheryl Gay Stolberg, "Jubilation and Weddings, but Also Confusion, Delay and Denunciation," *The New York Times,* June 26, 2015.

42. Eyder Peralta, "Virginia's New Attorney General Will Not Defend Gay-Marriage Ban," NPR, January 23, 2014; Matt Apuzzo, "Holder Sees Way to Curb Bans on Gay Marriage," *The New York Times,* February 24, 2014.

43. David Bailey, "Michigan Must Recognize Legal Marriages of 300 Same-Sex Couples," Reuters, January 15, 2015.

44. Survey of 1,005 adults by United Technologies for the *National Journal*/Congressional Connection, June 20–23, 2013.

45. Nathan Koppel, "Obama Administration Appeals Texas Judge's Immigration Order," *The Wall Street Journal,* April 17, 2015.

46. Bilingual national survey of 800 Hispanic adults, 470 also registered voters, by Latino Opinions, June 5–16, 2013; survey of 1,220 Hispanic adults by Pew Research Center, November 9–December 7, 2011, cited in "When Labels Don't Fit: Hispanics and Their Views of Identity," Pew Research Center, April 4, 2012, p. 23; Cristina Costantini, "Study: Latinos Learn English Faster Than Past Immigrants," Fusion.net, June 18, 2013.

47. National survey of 1,000 adults by Rasmussen Reports, May 10–11, 2013.

48. Address to the nation on immigration by President Barack Obama in the White House, Washington, D.C., November 20, 2014.

49. Carrie Dann, "Immigration Reform Activists Seize on 'Moral Tone' of Civil Rights Movement," NBC News, August 27, 2013.

50. "Growth and Opportunity Project," Republican National Committee, 2013, pp. 8, 15.

51. Ronald Brownstein, "How Essential Is a College Education?," *National Journal,* November 9, 2013.

52. Ibid.

53. Survey of 1,502 adults by Pew Research Center, p. 3.

54. Hawkins, "5 Reasons America Is in Decline."

55. John T. Jost, "The End of the End of Ideology," *American Psychologist* 61, no. 7 (October 2006): 655, 661–62.

56. Peter Rentfrow, John Jost, Samuel Gosling, and Jeffrey Potter, "Statewide Differences in Personality Predict Voting Patterns in 1996–2004 U.S. Presidential Elections" in John Jost, Aaron Kay, and Hulda Thorisdottir, eds., *Social and Psychological Bases of Ideology and System Justification* (New York: Oxford University Press, 2009), Kindle locations 4570–4577.

57. Rentfrow et al., "Statewide Differences in Personality," Kindle location 4305.

58. Jonathan Haidt and Jesse Graham, "Planet of the Durkheimians, Where Community, Authority, and Sacredness Are Foundations of Morality," *Social and Psychological Bases of Ideology and System Justification* (New York: Oxford University Press, 2009), Kindle locations 5092–5148; Jeffrey M. Jones, "On Social Ideology, the Left Catches Up to the Right," Gallup, May 22, 2015.

59. Ibid., Kindle locations 5174–5186.

60. "Political Polarization in the American Public," Pew Research Center, June 12, 2014, p. 83; Jeffrey M. Jones, "Conservative Lead on Social and Economic Ideology Shrinking," Gallup, May 28, 2014.

61. "Political Polarization in the American Public," Pew Research Center, June 12, 2014, pp. 41–42.

62. Ibid., p. 45.

63. Ibid., p. 12.

64. Ibid., p. 34.

65. Ibid., p. 33.

66. Ibid., p. 22–24.

7 THE DEMOCRATIC ASCENDANCY

1. National election night survey of 1,429 likely 2016 voters, including 1,030 2014 voters, by Greenberg Quinlan Rosner for Democracy Corps, November 3–5, 2014.

2. The GOP conservative heartland includes Alabama, Alaska, Arkansas, Georgia, Idaho, Kansas, Kentucky, Louisiana, Mississippi, Montana, Nebraska, North Dakota, Oklahoma, South Carolina, South Dakota, Texas, Tennessee, Utah, West Virginia, and Wyoming.

3. Pew Hispanic Center analysis on national exit poll data, 1980–2012, cited in "Latino Voters in the 2012 Election," Pew Research Center, November 7, 2012, pp. 4, 13; national survey of 1,765 Hispanic adults by Pew Research Center, September 7–October 4, 2012, cited by Eileen Patten and Mark Hugo Lopez in "Are Unauthorized Immigrants Overwhelmingly Democrats?," Pew Research Center, July 22, 2013; analysis of 7,901 Hispanic respondents interviewed in daily national tracking surveys by Gallup, January 3–June 27, 2013, cited by Frank Newport and Joy Wilke in "Hispanics of All Ages Tilt Democratic," Gallup Politics, July 15, 2013.

4. Jens Manuel Krogstad and Mark Hugo Lopez, "Hispanic Voters in the 2014 Election: Democratic Advantage Remains, but Republicans Improve Margin in Some States," Pew Research Center, November 7, 2014.

5. David A. Bositis, "Blacks & the 2012 Democratic National Convention," Joint Center for Political and Economic Studies, September 2012, p. 9; "National Exit Poll Tables," *The New York Times*, November 5, 2008.

6. Thom File, "The Diversifying Electorate—Voting Rates by Race and Hispanic Origin in 2012 (and Other Recent Elections)," U.S. Census Bureau, May 2013, pp. 3–5; "Exit Polls: Va. Governor," *The New York Times,* November 6, 2013.

7. "Election 2012: President Exit Polls," *The New York Times,* updated November 29, 2012; multilingual exit poll of 9,096 Asian American voters in fourteen states and Washington, D.C., by The Asian American Legal Defense and Education Fund, 2012, cited in the slide show "The Asian American Vote," The Asian American Legal Defense and Education Fund, January 17, 2013.

8. "Grand Old Party for a Brand New Generation," College Republican National Committee, June 2013, pp. 2, 69; "Young Voters Supported Obama Less, but May Have Mattered More," Pew Research Center, November 26, 2012; based on totals from all Pew Research surveys of the general public between 2004 and 2014, cited in "Millennials in Adulthood," Pew Research Center, March 7, 2104; "How Americans Voted in House Elections, Based on Exit Polls Conducted by Edison Research," *The New York Times,* November 4, 2014; projections made by Democracy Corps based on Census data and past election turnout; Nate Cohn, "Democrats Keep Lead in Party Identification," *The New York Times*, April 10, 2015; David Madland and Ruy Teixeira, "New Progressive America: The Millennial Generation," Center for American Progress, May 2009, p. 1; national survey of 950 likely 2016 voters at 60 percent cell conducted by Greenberg Quinlan Rosner for Democracy Corps and Women's Voices Women Vote Action Fund, June 13–17, 2015.

9. Projections made by Democracy Corps based on Census data and past election turnout.

10. Jonathan Vespa, Jamie M. Lewis, and Rose M. Kreider, "America's Families and Living Arrangements: 2012," U.S. Census Bureau, August 2013; based on 7,004 interviews from national surveys by Greenberg Quinlan Rosner for Democracy Corps, July 2013–January 2015; national election night survey of 1,429 likely 2016 voters, including 1,030 2014 voters, by Greenberg Quinlan Rosner for Democracy Corps and Women's Voices Women Vote Action Fund, November 3–5, 2014.

11. National election night survey of 1,429 likely 2016 voters.

12. Based on 7,004 interviews from national surveys by Greenberg Quinlan Rosner for Democracy Corps, July 2013–January 2015.

13. National survey of 950 likely 2016 voters by Greenberg Quinlan Rosner for Democracy Corps and Women's Voices Women Vote Action Fund, January 7–11, 2015.

14. Ruy Teixeira, "Why Democrats Win the Presidency but Lose the House," *Think Progress,* May 29, 2013.

15. Based on analysis of the 2012 presidential election results by county.

16. Based on 2012 presidential election results by county, the U.S. Census Bureau's definition of metro statistical areas, and McKinsey Global Institute's analysis of GDP generated by global cities: "Urban World: Cities and the Rise of the Consuming Class," McKinsey Global Institute, June 2012.

17. Teixeira, "Why Democrats Win the Presidency but Lose the House"; Richard Florida, "What Is It Exactly That Makes Big Cities Vote Democratic?," *The Atlantic,* February 19, 2013; analysis of the county level 2012 presidential election results.

18. Based on 7,004 interviews from national surveys by Greenberg Quinlan Rosner for Democracy Corps, July 2013–January 2015.

19. Florida, "What Is It Exactly That Makes Big Cities Vote Democratic?"; analysis of 2012 presidential election results for the San Jose and Seattle metro statistical areas as defined by the U.S. Census Bureau.

20. Florida, "What Is It Exactly That Makes Big Cities Vote Democratic?"

21. Based on 2012 presidential election results by county and the U.S. Census Bureau's definition of metro statistical areas; Robert Gebeloff and David Leonhardt, "The Growing Blue-State Diaspora," *The New York Times*, August 23, 2014.

22. National survey of 950 respondents and an oversample of 760 Republicans by Greenberg Quinlan Rosner for Democracy Corps' Republican Party Project, July 10–15, 2013.

23. National survey of 950 likely 2016 voters by Greenberg Quinlan Rosner for Democracy Corps and Women's Voices Women Vote Action Fund, January 7–11, 2014.

24. Survey of 1,008 by Selzer & Company for Bloomberg Politics, April 6–8, 2015; "A Deep Dive into Party Affiliation," Pew Research Center, April 7, 2015; Nate Cohn, "Democrats Keep

Lead in Party Identification," *The New York Times*, April 10, 2015; national survey of 950 likely 2016 voters at 60 percent cell conducted by Greenberg Quinlan Rosner for Democracy Corps and Women's Voices Women Vote Action Fund, June 13–17, 2015; Janet Hook, "Liberals Make Big Comeback in 2015, Poll Analysis Finds," *The Wall Street Journal*, June 7, 2015.

25. Ron Brownstein, "Shellacking, the Sequel," *National Journal*, November 8, 2014.

26. National election night survey of 1,429 likely 2016 voters, including 1,030 2014 voters, by Greenberg Quinlan Rosner for Democracy Corps and Women's Voices Women Vote Action Fund, November 3–5, 2014; Brownstein, "Shellacking, the Sequel."

27. "How Americans Voted in House Elections, Based on Exit Polls by Edison Research."

28. National survey of 1,000 likely 2012 voters by Greenberg Quinlan Rosner for Democracy Corps and the Center for American Progress, October 15–18, 2011.

29. National election night survey of 1,429 likely 2016 voters, including 1,030 2014 voters, by Greenberg Quinlan Rosner for Democracy Corps, November 3–5, 2014; based on 7,004 interviews conducted by Democracy Corps nationally, July 2013–January 2015.

30. National survey of 950 likely 2016 voters by Greenberg Quinlan Rosner for Democracy Corps and Women's Voices Women Vote Action Fund, January 7–11, 2015; national survey of 950 likely 2016 voters at 60 percent cell conducted by Greenberg Quinlan Rosner for Democracy Corps and Women's Voices Women Vote Action Fund, June 13–17, 2015; from focus groups conducted by Greenberg Quinlan Rosner for Democracy Corps and Women's Voices Women Vote Action Fund on May 19, 2015 in Jacksonville, Florida, among older white unmarried women and young white non-college-educated women and on June 4, 2015 in Orlando, Florida, among white non-college-educated women and white non-college-educated men.

31. National election night survey of 1,429 likely 2016 voters, including 1,030 2014 voters, by Greenberg Quinlan Rosner for Democracy Corps, November 3–5, 2014; national survey of 950 likely 2016 voters by Greenberg Quinlan Rosner for Democracy Corps and Women's Voices Women Vote Action Fund, January 7–11, 2015. National survey of 950 likely 2016 voters at 60 percent cell conducted by Greenberg Quinlan Rosner for Democracy Corps and Women's Voices Women Vote Action Fund, June 13–17, 2015.

32. Jonathan Chait, "The Color of His Presidency," *New York*, April 6, 2014; Avidit Acharya, Matthew Blackwell, and Maya Sen, "The Political Legacy of American Slavery," University of Rochester, February 13, 2014.

33. Based on 13,197 interviews from national surveys by Greenberg Quinlan Rosner for Democracy Corps throughout 2012, overall margin of error of ±3 percent. The actual 2012 election results were within the margin of error.

34. Ibid.

35. Ibid.

36. Kyle Kondik, "Size Matters When It Comes to U.S. House Districts, That Is," *Sabato's Crystal Ball*, May 23, 2013; Charlie Cook, "The Republican Advantage," *National Journal*, April 11, 2013.

37. Markos Moulitsas, "The 2020 Redistricting Battle Begins in 2014," *Daily Kos*, August 29, 2013; Jowei Chen and Jonathan Rodden, "Don't Blame the Maps," *The New York Times*, January 24, 2014.

38. Teixeira, "Why Democrats Win the Presidency but Lose the House."

39. Nicholas Confessore, "A National Strategy Funds State Political Monopolies," *The New York Times*, January 11, 2014.

40. Chris Cillizza, "Republicans Have Gained More Than 900 State Legislative Seats Since 2010," *The Washington Post*, January 14, 2015.

41. "2014 State and Legislative Partisan Composition," National Conference of State Legislatures, December 2, 2014; "2010 State and Legislative Partisan Composition Prior to the Election," National Conference of State Legislatures, November 1, 2010.

42. Florida Department of State Division of Elections, November 4, 2014, general election results; State of Kansas Office of the Secretary of State, 2014 general election official results; North Carolina State Board of Elections 2014 statewide official general election results.

43. Nate Cohn, "The GOP Has Problems with White Voters, Too," *The New Republic*, November 12, 2012.

44. Bob Burnett, "Scott Walker: Mobilizing Resentment," *Daily Kos*, April 23, 2015.

45. Ron Brownstein, "Bad Bet: Why Republicans Can't Win with Whites Alone," *The New Republic*, September 5, 2013.

46. Ruy Teixeira and John Halpin, "The Political Consequences of the Great Recession," Center for American Progress, November 6, 2014.

47. Based on 7,004 interviews from national surveys by Greenberg Quinlan Rosner for Democracy Corps, July 2013–January 2015.

48. Based on combined data from national surveys conducted by Greenberg Quinlan Rosner Research for Democracy Corps, 2010–2012.

49. Ibid.

50. Based on 13,197 interviews from national surveys by Greenberg Quinlan Rosner for Democracy Corps throughout 2012, overall margin of error of ±3 percent. The actual 2012 election results were within the margin of error. Working class is defined by education as those without a four-year college degree.

51. Based on 13,197 interviews from national surveys by Greenberg Quinlan Rosner for Democracy Corps in 2012.

52. National survey of 950 likely 2016 voters by Greenberg Quinlan Rosner for Democracy Corps and Women's Voices Women Vote Action Fund, January 7–11, 2015.

53. Ben Highton, "A Big Electoral College Advantage for Democrats Is Looming," *The Washington Post*, April 28, 2014.

54. Ronald Brownstein, "Playing Their Hand," *National Journal*, May 10, 2012.

55. Highton, "A Big Electoral College Advantage for the Democrats Is Looming."

56. Nate Cohn, "The Swing State Where the GOP Desperately Needs Hispanics," *The New Republic*, July 11, 2013.

8 THE END OF THE REPUBLICAN PARTY AS WE KNOW IT

1. Based on 7,004 interviews from national surveys by Greenberg Quinlan Rosner for Democracy Corps, July 2013–January 2015.

2. This is based on findings from the first phase of research for Democracy Corps' Republican Party Project. We conducted six focus groups among Republican partisans—divided into Evangelicals, Tea Party adherents, and moderates—between July 30 and August 1, 2013. All participants indicated that they voted only or mostly for Republican candidates and were screened on a battery of ideological and political indicators. The groups were conducted in Raleigh, North Carolina (moderate and Tea Party), Roanoke, Virginia (Tea Party and Evangelical), and Colorado Springs, Colorado (moderate and Evangelical).

3. Merrill Knox, "April 2014 Ratings: *Fox News* Marks 148 Straight Months at No. 1," Mediabistro.com, April 30, 2014.

4. A factor analysis of Democracy Corps' June 2013 national survey identified a "homosexuality-traditional-values-pro-life" dimension that explained 8.2 percent of variance in survey responses among Republicans.

9 THE CONSERVATIVE INTERREGNUM

1. Thomas E. Mann and Norman J. Ornstein, *It's Even Worse Than It Looks: How the American Constitutional System Collided with the New Politics of Extremism* (New York: Basic Books, 2012), p. 52.

2. Kenneth P. Vogel, "4 GOP Hopefuls Expected to Attend Koch Event," *Politico*, January 19, 2015; Nicholas Confessore, "Koch Brothers' Budget of $889 Million for 2016 Is on Par With Both Parties' Spending," *The New York Times*, January 26, 2015; Nicholas Confessore, "David Koch Signals a Favorite: Scott Walker," *The New York Times*, April 20, 2015; Philip Blump, "Scott Walker's Monday: A Semi-endorsement, Paired with an 'Olympics-Quality Flip-Flop,'" *The Washington Post*, April 20, 2015.

3. Mara Liasson, "Political Necessity Forces GOP into Middle-Class Income Debate," NPR, February 13, 2015; Drew MacKenzie, "Republicans Putting Forward Own Plans to Aid Middle Class," *Newsmax*, January 22, 2015; *The Washington Post*, July 27, 2015.

4. Catherine Rampell, "Republicans Have Started to Care About Income Inequality," *The Washington Post*, January 22, 2015.

5. Jonathan Weisman and Ashley Parker, "Talk of Wealth Gap Prods the G.O.P. to Refocus," *The New York Times*, January 21, 2015; Rory Carroll, "Mitt Romney Looks to 2016 Run and Wants to 'Lift People out of Poverty,'" *The Guardian*, January 17, 2015; William A. Galston, "When Right and Left Agree on Inequality," *The Wall Street Journal*, January 14, 2015; E. J. Dionne, *Our Divided Political Heart: The Battle for the American Idea in an Age of Discontent* (New York: Bloomsbury, 2012), p. 45.

6. Sam Tanenhaus, "Can the GOP Be a Party of Ideas?," *The New York Times*, July 2, 2014; E. J. Dionne, "The Reformicons," *Democracy Journal*, Summer 2014.

7. Michael Tomasky, "2016: The Republicans Write," *The New York Review of Books*, March 19, 2015.

8. Tanenhaus, "Can the GOP Be a Party of Ideas?"

9. Albert R. Hunt, "The Republican Schism Over Taxes," *Bloomberg View*, April 19, 2015; Matt O'Brien, "The New Republican Tax Plan Is Just the Bush Tax Cuts on Steroids" *The Washington Post*, March 12, 2015; Josh Marro, "Marco Rubio's Puppies-and-Rainbows Tax Plan," *The New York Times*, March 12, 2015.

10. Kimberley A. Strassel, "Searching for Rubio the Reformer," *The Wall Street Journal*, April 16, 2015; Ben Kamisar, "Bush Would Overturn Obama's Executive Actions on Immigration," *The Hill*, April 21, 2015.

11. Remarks by Governor Rick Perry of Texas at the CPAC Conference in Washington, D.C., March 7, 2014.

12. Ibid.

13. Luncheon keynote by Governor Bobby Jindal of Louisiana at the Texas Public Policy Foundation's Policy Orientation for the Texas Legislature in Austin, Texas, January 9, 2014.

14. Governor Bobby Jindal, "GOP Needs Action, Not Navel-Gazing," *Politico*, June 18, 2013.

15. Ibid.

16. Ibid.; Governor Bobby Jindal, "How Republicans Can Win Future Elections," CNN Opinion, November 15, 2012.

17. Jindal, "GOP Needs Action, Not Navel-Gazing."

18. Luncheon keynote by Governor Bobby Jindal of Louisiana.

19. Dionne, *Our Divided Political Heart*, p. 124.

20. Ibid., p. 105.

21. Ibid., p. 5.

22. Mann and Ornstein, *It's Even Worse Than It Looks*, Kindle locations 119, 139; Jonathan Chait, "Anarchists of the House," *New York*, July 21, 2013.

23. Molly Hennessy-Fiske, "Rick Perry, Rand Paul Take Aim at Obama, Hillary Clinton at Koch Event," *The Los Angeles Times*, August 29, 2014; Joe Scarborough, *The Right Path: From Ike to Reagan, How Republicans Once Mastered Politics—and Can Again* (New York: Random House, 2013).

24. Peggy Noonan, "Don't Do It, Mr. Romney," *The Wall Street Journal*, January 16, 2015.

25. Dionne, *Our Divided Political Heart*, pp. 154, 244.

26. Ronald Brownstein, "The State of Conflict," *National Journal,* March 1, 2014.

27. "Slide Show: The State Budget Crisis and the Economy," Center for Budget and Policy Priorities, http://www.cbpp.org/slideshows/?fa=stateFiscalCrisis, December 19, 2011, slide 5; David Callahan, "89,000 Government Workers Have Been Laid Off Since September," *Demos,* January 4, 2013; Heidi Shierholz, "Six Years from Its Beginning, the Great Recession's Shadow Looms over the Labor Market," Economic Policy Institute, January 9, 2014; Gordon Lafer, "The Legislative Attack on American Wages and Labor Standards, 2011–2012," Economic Policy Institute, October 31, 2013.

28. Carolyn Barta, "Eighty-second Legislature Cuts School Funds, State Jobs," *Texas Almanac,* Texas State Historical Association; calculated based on data for 2008–2014 from the Center on Budget and Policy Priorities, accessed February 13, 2014, http://www.offthechartsblog.org/mapping-higher-ed-funding-cuts-and-tuition-hikes/.

29. Lafer, "The Legislative Attack on American Wages and Labor Standards, 2011–2012."

30. Ibid.

31. Charles M. Blow, "Poverty Is Not a State of Mind," *The New York Times,* May 18, 2014.

32. Nancy Folbre, "The Color of Affordable Care," *The New York Times,* October 7, 2013; Robert Pear, "States' Policies on Health Care Exclude Some of the Poorest," *The New York Times,* May 24, 2013.

33. Lafer, "The Legislative Attack on American Wages and Labor Standards, 2011–2012."

34. Ibid.

35. Ibid.; Amanda Terkel, "Rep. Jack Kingston Proposes That Poor Students Sweep Floors in Exchange for Lunch," *The Huffington Post,* December 18, 2013.

36. Annual State of the State address by Governor Sam Brownback to a joint session of the Kansas State Legislature at the State House Chamber in Topeka, Kansas, January 15, 2014.

37. John Gramlich, "In Kansas, Governor Sam Brownback Drives a Rightward Shift," Stateline, Pew Charitable Trusts, January 25, 2012.

38. Governor Sam Brownback, "Gov. Sam Brownback: Tax Cuts Needed to Grow Economy," *The Wichita Eagle,* July 29, 2012.

39. "Under Gov. Sam Brownback, Kansas Lags Neighboring States and the Nation in Job Growth," *The Kansas City Star,* May 16, 2014; Alan Pyke, "Kansas Anti-poverty Task Force Recommends Stronger Families, Weaker Safety Net," *Think Progress,* September 9, 2013.

40. Survey of 693 Kansas voters, including 375 Republican primary voters, by Public Policy Polling, February 18–20, 2014.

41. Adam Nagourney and Shaila Dewan, "Republican Governors Buck Party Line on Raising Taxes," *The New York Times,* January 24, 2015; Max Ehrenfreund, "Kansas Lawmakers Want the Poor to Pay for Tax Cuts for the Rich," *The Washington Post,* April 21, 2015.

42. Trip Gabriel, "Pennsylvania Governor Faces an Uphill Battle for a Second Term," *The New York Times,* May 10, 2014; "Under Gov. Tom Corbett, 'Pennsylvania Ranks 49th in Job Creation,'" PolitiFact.com, July 15, 2014.

43. Laura Bassett, "Tom Corbett, Pennsylvania Governor, on Ultrasound Mandate: Just 'Close Your Eyes,'" *The Huffington Post,* March 15, 2012.

44. Survey of 1,308 registered Pennsylvania voters by Quinnipiac, May 29–June 2, 2014.

45. Steve Singiser, "In an Election Year, North Carolina Republicans Flog a Phony 'Teachers Raise,'" *Daily Kos,* May 30, 2014.

46. Annie Lowrey, "States Cutting Weeks of Aid to the Jobless," *The New York Times,* January 21, 2014; Jeanne Sahadi, "North Carolina's Republican Tax Experiment," CNN Money, August 8, 2013; Lee Weisbecker, "McCrory Signs Bill Eliminating Tax Credit," *Triangle Business Journal,* March 13, 2013; "A Look at Unemployment Benefits by State," Associated Press, January 7, 2014; Evan Soltas, "North Carolina Shows How to Crush the Unemployed," *Bloomberg View,* December 17, 2013.

47. Survey of 672 registered North Carolina voters by Elon University, April 25–28, 2014; survey of 1,076 registered North Carolina voters by Public Policy Polling, June 12–15, 2014;

North Carolina State Board of Elections 2014 statewide official general election results, accessed February 11, 2015, http://enr.ncsbe.gov/ElectionResults/?election_dt=11/04/2014.

48. Survey of 600 Louisiana voters by Southern Media & Opinion Research, September 11–20, 2012. Fifty-four percent of the respondents disapproved of the voucher.

49. Rachel Weiner, "What Happened to Bobby Jindal?," *The Washington Post,* April 9, 2013.

50. Survey of 664 Louisiana voters by Public Policy Polling, June 26–29, 2014; survey of 750 2014 likely Louisiana voters by Rasmussen, July 8–9, 2014.

51. Campbell Robinson, "As Jindal's G.O.P. Profile Grows, So Do Louisiana's Budget Woes," *The New York Times,* February 6, 2015; The Editorial, "Governors Can Run, but They Can't Hide," *The New York Times,* February 28, 2015.

52. David Leonhardt, "Is College Worth It? Clearly, New Data Say," *The New York Times,* May 27, 2014.

53. Matt O'Brien, "The Good News: We're Back to 2008 Job Levels. That's Also the Bad News," *The Washington Post,* June 6, 2014.

54. Andrew P. Kelly, "Does College Really Improve Social Mobility?," The Brookings Institution, February 11, 2014.

55. Neil Irwin, Claire Cain Miller, and Margot Sanger-Katz, "America's Racial Divide, Charted," *The New York Times,* August 19, 2014.

56. Next America survey of 1,272 adults by Princeton Survey Research Associates International for National Journal and College Board, October 14–24, 2013.

57. Ibid.

58. Michael Leachman and Chris Mai, "Most States Funding Schools Less Than Before the Recession," Center on Budget and Policy Priorities, May 20, 2014; Editorial Board, "Governors Can Run, but They Can't Hide," *The New York Times,* February 28, 2015; Julie Bosman, "2016 Ambitions Seen in Walker's Push for University Cuts in Wisconsin," *The New York Times,* February 16, 2015; Fareed Zakaria, *In Defense of a Liberal Education* (New York: W. W. Norton & Company, Inc., 2015).

59. Sarah Ayres and Adam Hersh, "New Ryan Budget Cuts Investments in America's Future," Center for American Progress, March 13, 2013; "Fact Sheet: GOP Budget Cuts to Non-defense Discretionary Programs," House Budget Committee Democrats, April 8, 2014.

60. Jerry M. Melillo, Terese Richmond, and Gary W. Yohe, "Climate Change Impacts in the United States: The Third Climate Assessment," U.S. Global Change Research Program, 841, pp. 7–8.

61. "Red News/Blue News: Climate Change," CNN, *Reliable Sources,* May 11, 2014.

62. National survey of 1,200 adults by Greenberg Quinlan Rosner for Democracy Corps' Republican Party Project, July 10–15, 2013.

63. David Gutman, "McKinley Amendment Bars Defense Fund for Climate Change," *WV Gazette,* May 25, 2014; Ryan Koronowski, "House Votes to Deny Climate Science and Ties Pentagon's Hands on Climate Change," *Think Progress,* May 22, 2014.

64. Jamie Fuller, "Environmental Policy Is Partisan. It Wasn't Always," *The Washington Post,* June 2, 2014.

65. Rebecca Leber, "What Happens If Congress Doesn't Deliver on Obama's Climate Promises?," *The New Republic,* February 4, 2015.

66. Benjamin Bell, "Sen. Marco Rubio: Yes, I'm Ready to Be President," ABC News, May 11, 2014.

67. Paul Waldman, "Where the 2016 GOP Contenders Stand on Climate Change," *The Washington Post,* May 12, 2014.

68. Philip Bump, "Why Don't GOP Presidential Candidates Address Climate Change? Because They Want to Win," *The Washington Post,* April 22, 2015. Pope Francis, *Encyclical Letter of the Holy Father Francis on Care of Our Common Home* (Rome: Vatican Press, English ed., 2015); Max Ehrenfreund, "Pope Francis's Views on Climate Change Put Catholic GOP Candidates in a Bind," *The Washington Post,* June 18, 2015; Jessica Mendoza, "Why Rick Santorum

Doesn't Want Pope Francis Talking About Climate Change," *The Christian Science Monitor*, June 3, 2015.

69. Motoko Rich, "Science Standards Divide a State Built on Coal and Oil," *The New York Times,* May 18, 2014.

70. Ibid.; Ashton Edwards and Dallas Franklin, "UPDATE: Oklahoma Governor Announces Decision on Common Core Measure," KFOR.com, May 23, 2014.

71. Remarks by President Barack Obama on the economy in Osawatomie, Kansas, December 6, 2011.

72. Scott Winship, "Stop Feeling Sorry for the Middle Class! They're Doing Just Fine," *The New Republic,* February 7, 2012; Reihan Salam, "Guest Post: Scott Winship on the Obama Administration's Questionable Mobility Claims," *National Review,* January 17, 2012.

73. Richard V. Burkhauser, Jeff Larrimore, and Kosali I. Simon, "A 'Second Opinion' on the Economic Health of the American Middle Class," National Bureau of Economic Research, Working Paper 17164, June 2011; Ron Haskins, "The Myth of the Disappearing Middle Class," *The Washington Post,* March 29, 2012; Winship, "Stop Feeling Sorry for the Middle Class!"; Bruce D. Meyer and James X. Sullivan, "Sorry, Mr. Biden, Most Middle Class Americans Are Better Off Now Than They Were Thirty Years Ago," *Fox News,* October 24, 2011.

74. Burkhauser, Larrimore, and Simon, "A 'Second Opinion,' " p. 4; Meyer and Sullivan, *Fox News;* remarks by President Barack Obama on the economy in Osawatomie, Kansas; remarks by Alan Krueger in "The Rise and Consequences of Inequality in the United States," Center for American Progress, Washington, D.C., January 12, 2012.

75. Burkhauser, Larrimore, and Simon, "A 'Second Opinion,' " pp. 33–34.

76. Ibid.

77. Haskins, "The Myth of the Disappearing Middle Class."

78. Sabrina Tavernise, "Education Gap Grows Between Rich and Poor, Studies Say," *The New York Times,* February 9, 2012.

79. Haskins, "The Myth of the Disappearing Middle Class"; Burkhauser, Larrimore, and Simon, "A 'Second Opinion,' " pp. 31–34.

80. Winship, "Stop Feeling Sorry for the Middle Class!"

81. Charles M. Blow, "Paul Ryan and His Poverty Prophet," *The New York Times,* July 23, 2014.

82. Nicholas Eberstadt, "American Exceptionalism and the Entitlement State," *National Affairs*, Issue Number 2, Winter 2015.

83. Philip Bump, "Why Hillary Clinton Should (And Will) Embrace Obamacare," *The Washington Post*, April 13, 2015.

84. House Budget Committee, "The War on Poverty: 50 Years Later," March 3, 2014, p. 4; Glenn Kessler, "A Story Too Good to Check: Paul Ryan and the Tale of the Brown Paper Bag," *The Washington Post,* March 6, 2014.

85. The Editors, "Paul Ryan Is Right," *National Review,* March 17, 2014.

86. Andrew J. Cherlin, *Labor's Love Lost: The Rise and Fall of the Working-Class Family in America* (New York: Russell Sage, 2014), p. 196.

87. Ibid., p. 178; Rob Stein, "Premarital Abstinence Pledges Ineffective, Study Finds," *The Washington Post,* December 29, 2008.

88. National survey of 950 2012 voters (840 likely 2014 voters) by Greenberg Quinlan Rosner for Democracy Corps and Women's Voices Women Vote Action Fund, March 19–23, 2014.

89. Ibid.; this will be discussed at length in chapter 10.

90. Abby M. McCloskey, "Clearing the Way for Working Women," *National Affairs*, Issue Number 22, Winter 2015.

91. Steven Swinford, "David Cameron Pledges 600,000 Childcare to 'Make Work Pay,' " *The Telegraph*, April 22, 2015.

92. K. J. Dell'Antonia, "For Younger Mothers, Out-of-Wedlock Births Are the New Normal,"

The New York Times, February 19, 2012; George A. Akerlof, "Men Without Children," *The Economic Journal*, 108, Royal Economic Society, 1998.

93. Ross Douthat, "Is Marriage Promotion Possible?," *The New York Times*, January 14, 2014.

94. Ross Douthat, "For Poorer and Richer," *The New York Times*, March 14, 2015. David Brooks, "The Next Culture War," *The New York Times*, July 1, 2015.

95. Scott Winship, "Whither the Bottom 90 Percent, Thomas Piketty?," *Forbes*, April 17, 2014; Avik Roy, "Thomas Piketty's Impoverished Debate About Inequality—and Ours," *Forbes*, May 26, 2014.

96. Rush Limbaugh, "The Left Is Giddy over New Marxist Book," *The Rush Limbaugh Show*, April 24, 2014.

97. Danny Vinik, "Meet the Man Who Wants to Help Paul Ryan Solve Poverty," *Business Insider*, November 26, 2013.

98. Jared Bernstein, "Piketty's Arguments Still Hold Up, After Taxes," *The New York Times*, May 9, 2014.

99. Alan Reynolds, "The Truth About the 1 Percent," *National Review*, November 11, 2013.

100. Chris Giles, "Piketty Findings Undercut by Errors," *The Financial Times*, May 23, 2014; "Picking Holes in Piketty," *The Economist*, May 31, 2014.

101. Roy, "Thomas Piketty's Impoverished Debate."

102. David Brooks, "The Piketty Phenomenon," *The New York Times*, April 24, 2014; David Brooks, "The Inequality Problem," *The New York Times*, January 16, 2014.

103. James Pethokoukis, "The New Marxism," *National Review*, March 24, 2014.

104. Ross Douthat, "Piketty, Doom Loops, and Haymarket," *The New York Times*, April 22, 2014.

10   FROM REAGAN DEMOCRATS TO THE NEW AMERICA

1. National survey of 950 likely 2016 voters for Democracy Corps, Women's Voice Women Vote Action Fund, and the Voter Participation Center, January 7–11, 2015; national election survey of 1,001 likely 2012 voters by Greenberg Quinlan Rosner for Democracy Corps and the Voter Participation Center, November 5–7, 2012. Survey results were weighted to reflect the national exit survey.

2. National survey of 950 2012 voters (827 likely 2014 voters) by Greenberg Quinlan Rosner for Democracy Corps and Women's Voice Women Vote Action Function, June 10–15, 2014.

3. National survey of 950 likely 2016 voters by Greenberg Quinlan Rosner for Democracy Corps and Women's Voice Women Vote Action Fund and the Voter Participation Center, January 7–11, 2015. This is the average of the top six policies.

4. Ibid.; "The Moment of Truth," Report of the National Commission on Fiscal Responsibility and Reform, December 1, 2010.

5. Statewide survey of 456 white persuadable likely voters in Louisiana by Greenberg Quinlan Rosner for Democracy Corps.

6. National survey of 950 likely 2016 voters by Greenberg Quinlan Rosner for Democracy Corps and Women's Voice Women Vote Action Fund and the Voter Participation Center.

7. House battleground survey of 1,105 likely 2014 voters in the 66 most competitive House districts (280 interviews in the 17 most competitive Republican districts and 200 interviews in the next 16 most competitive Republican districts and 625 interviews in the 33 most competitive Democratic-held districts) by Greenberg Quinlan Rosner for Democracy Corps, October 4–9, 2014.

8. Survey of 1,000 likely voters in the 12 most competitive Senate races across the country by Greenberg Quinlan Rosner for Democracy Corps and Women's Voice Women Vote Action Function, September 20–24, 2014, including an oversample of 1,200 voters across Georgia, Iowa, North Carolina, and Colorado conducted September 12–October 1, 2014.

9. North Carolina State Board of Elections 2014 statewide official general election results, accessed February 11, 2015, http://enr.ncsbe.gov/ElectionResults/?election_dt=11/04/2014.

10. State of the Union research was conducted on January 20, 2015, by Greenberg Quinlan Rosner for Democracy Corps and Women's Voices Women Vote Action Fund. Participants were 61 white swing voters nationwide who split their votes fairly evenly between Democratic and Republican candidates over the past several presidential and congressional elections, though there were slightly more Obama voters than Romney voters. The group's self-identified partisanship was 33 percent Democratic, 34 percent independent, and 33 percent Republican. The group included 27 women and 34 men, including 13 unmarried women.

11. Focus groups by Greenberg Quinlan Rosner for Democracy Corps and Women's Voice Women Vote Action Fund in Virginia Beach, January 8, 2015, among white non-college-educated men and women from Virginia Beach. These men and women have household incomes under $50,000 a year, were roughly half Obama voters, and weak partisans or independents.

12. Greenberg Quinlan Rosner conducted 31 double-blind qualitative interviews, 30–45 minutes long, with thought leaders in the infrastructure field spanning functions, asset class, and geography for McKinsey in the fall of 2012. All participants were in infrastructure-focused roles within organizations with revenues or budgets in excess of $2 billion; 9 have truly global roles, 9 focus on EMEA, 7 on the United States, 3 LATAM, and 3 APAC; across the value chain from government and developers, through finance and construction to operations; across sectors, but with a focus on transport and energy.

13. Focus groups by Greenberg Quinlan Rosner for Democracy Corps and Women's Voice Women Vote Action Fund in Virginia Beach, January 8, 2015.

14. James Carville and Stanley B. Greenberg, *It's the Middle Class Stupid!* (New York: Blue Rider Press, Penguin Group, 2012), pp. 108–25; national survey of 1,000 2008 voters (866 likely 2010 voters) by Greenberg Quinlan Rosner for Democracy Corps and Campaign for America's Future, July 26–29, 2010; survey of 1,000 likely 2012 voters by Greenberg Quinlan Rosner for Democracy Corps and Center for American Progress, October 15–18, 2011.

15. Web survey of 1,500 2010 voters by Greenberg Quinlan Rosner for Democracy Corps' Economic Media Project, March 1–7, 2013; 52 percent favored an infrastructure investment plan and 48 percent favored an austerity/spending cut plan for growth: "*Given where our economy is, we should invest now in infrastructure, education, and technology, and rehiring teachers and firefighters to get people back to work to make our country stronger in the long-term*"; survey of 1,012 British adults and 1,025 German adults by Pew Research Center's Global Attitudes Project, March 4–27, 2013. When asked if the best way to solve the country's economic problems is to reduce government spending to reduce public debt or spend more to stimulate the economy, 67 percent of Germans said cuts while 26 percent said stimulus, and 52 percent of Britons said cuts while 37 percent said stimulus. Survey of 1,710 adults. Conducted by YouGov for *The Sun*, July 21–22, 2013. Asked about the way the government is cutting spending to reduce the deficit, 39 percent said it is good for the economy, 44 percent said it was bad for the economy, and 17 percent said they don't know; 57 percent said the cuts are necessary, 29 percent said unnecessary, and 14 percent said they don't know. http://cdn.yougov.com/cumulus_uploads /document/vu1qujpx35/YG-Archive-Pol-Sun-results-220713.pdf.

16. Survey of 800 adults by Greenberg Quinlan Rosner and Public Opinion Strategies for Building America's Future, June 30–July 2, 2009. A majority of Americans said the most used infrastructure items (bridges, sidewalks/bike paths, roads, and highways) were in good condition, but there was little intensity driving this sentiment.

17. Survey of 800 adults by Greenberg Quinlan Rosner and Public Opinion Strategies for Building America's Future, June 30–July 2, 2009.

18. "Recovery Act Fourth Quarterly Report—the Public Provisions of the Recovery Act," White House Council of Economic Advisers, 2010; survey of 1,001 adults nationwide by GfK Roper Public Affairs & Media for the Associated Press, February 12–17, 2009; 34 percent said infrastructure spending will help the economy a great deal and 34 percent said it will help some.

19. President Barack Obama, address by the president to a joint session of Congress, September

8, 2011; survey of 1,000 likely voters in 60 battleground districts by Greenberg Quinlan Rosner for Democracy Corps, September 14–19, 2011; 45 percent favored the American Jobs Act (without information) and 41 percent opposed it.

20. Survey of 800 adults by Greenberg Quinlan Rosner and Public Opinion Strategies for Building America's Future, June 30–July 2, 2009; 58 percent supported public-private partnerships and 57 percent supported a national infrastructure bank as acceptable ways to fund new infrastructure projects.

21. Web survey of 1,000 likely voters by Greenberg Quinlan Rosner for Democracy Corps, September 8–12, 2012; 68 percent agreed, including 38 percent who strongly agreed with the statement.

22. Survey of 1,000 2008 voters (866 likely voters and 134 drop-off voters) by Greenberg Quinlan Rosner for Democracy Corps and Campaign for America's Future, July 26–29, 2010. Nearly three-quarters (74 percent) said that they felt more positive about a leader who said this about government investment, the economy, and deficits; 54 percent said the statement made them feel much or somewhat more positive.

23. Thomas B. Edsall, "How Democrats Can Compete for the White Working Class," *The New York Times,* March 11, 2014; national survey of 950 likely 2016 voters by Greenberg Quinlan Rosner for Democracy Corps, Women's Voice Women Vote Action Fund and the Voter Participation Center, January 7–11, 2015.

24. Rebecca Shabad, "Obama Proposes $4T Budget with Tax Hikes on the Wealthy," *The Hill,* February 2, 2015.

25. Lori Montgomery and Paul Kane, "Democrats, in a Stark Shift in Messaging, to Make Big Tax-Break Pitch for Middle Class," *The Washington Post,* January 11, 2015.

26. Carville and Greenberg, *It's the Middle Class, Stupid!*, Kindle location 2185.

27. Bill Clinton, acceptance speech at the Democratic National Convention, New York, July 16, 1992; Bill Clinton, "A Partnership for Opportunity," remarks by Governor Clinton at Montgomery College, Rockville, Md., September 2, 1992.

28. "Ad Watch: Campaign '92," *The Los Angeles Times*, September 19, 1992, and May 23, 1992.

29. Survey of 1,000 likely 2008 voters by Greenberg Quinlan Rosner for Democracy Corps, October 21–23, 2008.

30. An important academic study by Kate Kenski, Bruce W. Hardy, and Kathleen Hall Jamieson, "The Obama Victory: How Media, Money, and Message Shaped the 2008 Election," unfortunately gets this piece of their groundbreaking work wrong. They label the period after McCain joined the issue in the debates as "the McCain Surge" (October 15–28). Just to be clear, there was no McCain surge. Obama's vote did not drop after the third debate, in fact it went up over the coming days. Confidence in Obama to handle the economy remained unaffected, dropping not even a point. Indeed, Obama's small advantage on handling "taxes"—the subject of the debate—surged to 10 points with Joe the Plumber and the debate and locked in, Obama's lead on taxes growing further on election day, 13 points.

31. Kenski, Hardy, and Jamieson in "The Obama Victory" asked instead whether Obama would raise your taxes—but that wording accepts the conservative terms of the debate. That could shift perceptions of what he would do, but not necessarily shift voters to the Republicans on their approach to taxes. A more neutral wording—"better job on taxes"—allows the respondent to champion their overall posture on taxes, including the prospect of increased taxes. Sure, McCain's distortion of Obama's tax plans produced more people saying Obama would raise their taxes, but not more people saying McCain would do a better job on taxes. There was no surge on this more neutral wording.

32. House battleground survey of 1,105 likely 2014 voters in the 66 most competitive House districts (280 interviews in the 17 most competitive Republican districts and 200 interviews in the next 16 most competitive Republican districts and 625 interviews in the 33 most competitive

Democratic-held districts) by Greenberg Quinlan Rosner for Democracy Corps, October 4–9, 2014.

33. Paul Krugman, "In Defense of Obama," *Rolling Stone,* October 8, 2014.

34. Web survey of 2,671 adults nationwide by Greenberg Quinlan Rosner for Citizen Opinion and the Center for American Progress, April 18–19, 2010.

35. National election night survey of 1,429 likely 2016 voters, including 1,030 2014 voters, by Democracy Corps for Every Voice, November 3–5, 2014.

36. National survey of 1,004 adults nationwide for ABC News/*The Washington Post,* February 4–8, 2010.

37. National election night survey of 1,000 2012 voters by Greenberg Quinlan Rosner for Democracy Corps and Public Campaign Action Fund, November 6–7, 2012—the night of and night after the election.

38. National election night survey of 1,429 likely 2016 voters, including 1,030 2014 voters, by Greenberg Quinlan Rosner for Democracy Corps for Every Voice, November 3–5, 2014.

39. Outside Spending, Total by Type of Spender, 2014, Open Secrets, accessed February 12, 2015, http://www.opensecrets.org/outsidespending/fes_summ.php.

40. National election night survey of 1,000 2012 voters conducted by Greenberg Quinlan Rosner for Democracy Corps and Public Campaign Action Fund, November 6–7, 2012; survey of 1,000 likely 2014 voters across the 12 most competitive Senate battleground states by Greenberg Quinlan Roser for Democracy Corps and Every Voice, July 12–16, 2014.

41. National election night survey of 1,429 likely 2016 voters including 1,030 2014 voters, by Greenberg Quinlan Rosner for Democracy Corps and Every Voice, November 3–5, 2014.

42. Survey of 1,000 likely 2014 voters across the 12 most competitive Senate battleground states by Greenberg Quinlan Rosner for Democracy Corps and Every Voice, July 12–16, 2014.

43. Ibid.; among the half sample who heard the constitutional amendment to overturn *Citizens United* and the proposal to publicly fund campaigns, the net change in the vote was 5 points among all voters, 8 points among independents, 8 points among moderate Republicans, and 6 points among the white non-college-educated.

44. National survey of 950 likely 2016 voters by Greenberg Quinlan Rosner for Democracy Corps and Women's Voice Women Vote Action Fund and the Voter Participation Center, January 7–11, 2015.

45. Statewide survey of 456 white persuadable likely voters in Louisiana by Greenberg Quinlan Rosner for Democracy Corps; survey of 1,000 likely voters in the 12 most competitive Senate races across the country by Greenberg Quinlan Rosner for Democracy Corps and Women's Voice Women Vote Action Function, September 20–24, 2014, including an oversample of 1,200 voters across Georgia, Iowa, North Carolina, and Colorado conducted September 12–October 1, 2014.

46. Thomas B. Edsall, "Can the Government Actually Do Anything About Inequality?," *The New York Times,* September 10, 2013.

47. Based on surveys with a total of 13,197 adults by Greenberg Quinlan Rosner for Democracy Corps throughout 2012, overall margin of error of ±3 percent. The actual 2012 election results were within the margin of error. Working class is defined by education as those without a four-year-college degree.

48. Based on time series from national surveys conducted by Democracy Corps.

49. State of the Union address by President Barack Obama to a joint session of Congress, the Capitol, Washington, D.C., January 20, 2015.

11   THE PROGRESSIVE ERA: "TO CLEANSE, TO RECONSIDER, TO RESTORE, TO CORRECT THE EVIL"

1. Thomas Piketty, "Table S2.4; world output growth rate 0-2100," technical appendix of *Capital in the Twenty-first Century* (Cambridge, Mass.: Harvard University Press, 2014).

2. Ian Morris, *Why the West Rules—for Now: The Patterns of History, and What They Reveal About the Future* (New York: Farrar, Straus & Giroux, 2014), Kindle locations 7825–7831.

3. Ibid., Kindle location 8053; Michael Wolraich, *Unreasonable Men: Theodore Roosevelt and the Republican Rebels Who Created Progressive Politics* (New York: Palgrave MacMillan, 2014), p. 32.

4. Morris, *Why the West Rules*, Kindle locations 8034–8039.

5. Thomas Piketty, Directory of Figure and Tables for *Capital in the Twenty-first Century*, "Table S1.1a. The distribution of world output, 0-2012," Paris School of Economics, March 2014.

6. Morris, *Why the West Rules*, Kindle location 8013.

7. Ibid., Kindle location 8023; Piketty, *Capital in the Twenty-first Century*, pp. 59, 91.

8. Wolraich, *Unreasonable Men*, p. 14; Jackson Lears, *Rebirth of a Nation: The Making of Modern America, 1877–1920* (New York: HarperCollins, 2009), pp. 166–69, 222.

9. Morris, *Why the West Rules*, Kindle locations 7926–7949.

10. Ibid., Kindle locations 8022–8027.

11. Ibid., Kindle locations 439–445.

12. Ibid., Kindle locations 410–447.

13. Lears, *Rebirth of a Nation*, pp. 75, 84–85.

14. Ibid., pp. 79–80; Doris Kearns Goodwin, *The Bully Pulpit: Theodore Roosevelt, William Howard Taft, and The Golden Age of Journalism* (New York: Simon & Schuster, 2013), p. 158; "It Is Estimated That 132,000 Men Will Go Out at Noon," *The New York Times*, April 20, 1894.

15. Wolraich, *Unreasonable Men*, pp. 22–23.

16. Lears, *Rebirth of a Nation*, pp. 59–60.

17. Ibid., p. 61.

18. Ida M. Tarbell, *The History of The Standard Oil Company* (Houston: Halcyon Press, 2009), Kindle locations 27–32, 823, 1017.

19. Ibid., Kindle locations 12–34.

20. Lears, *Rebirth of a Nation*, pp. 177, 179–80.

21. Wolraich, *Unreasonable Men*, p. 4.

22. Piketty, *Capital in the Twenty-first Century*, p. 349.

23. Lears, *Rebirth of a Nation*, p. 188; Paul Krugman, "The Deflation Caucus," *The New York Times*, September 4, 2014.

24. Lears, *Rebirth of a Nation*, pp. 290–92.

25. Wolraich, *Unreasonable Men*, Kindle location 60.

26. Ibid., Kindle location 125; Goodwin, *The Bully Pulpit*, pp. 168–70, 178.

27. Goodwin, *The Bully Pulpit*, pp. 195, 375–76, 747; Wolraich, *Unreasonable Men*, pp. 11–12.

28. Franklin Foer, "The Story of How *The New Republic* Invented Modern Liberalism," *The New Republic*, November 9, 2014.

29. Wolraich, *Unreasonable Men*, Kindle locations 53, 326, 5138.

30. Lears, *Rebirth of a Nation*, pp. 199, 309.

31. Wolraich, *Unreasonable Men*, pp. 46–48.

32. Ibid., p. 28; Goodwin, *The Bully Pulpit*, p. 696.

33. Lears, *Rebirth of a Nation*, p. 160; Digital History, "Overview of the 1920s," Digital History ID 2920.

34. Lears, *Rebirth of a Nation*, pp. 313–14.

35. Wolraich, *Unreasonable Men*, p. 210.

36. Ibid., p. 200.

37. Ibid., p. 201.

38. The first inaugural address of President Woodrow Wilson at the U.S. Capitol, Washington, D.C., March 4, 1913.

39. Ibid.

40. Wolraich, *Unreasonable Men*, pp. 255–56.

12   MOMENTUM FOR REFORM

1. National survey of 2,943 Americans age 18 or older with oversamples of African Americans, Hispanics, and Asian Americans, conducted by Latino Decisions for the Center for American Progress and PolicyLink, June 11–July 10, 2013, cited in "Building an All-in Nation," Center for American Progress, October 2013, p. 11; Robert P. Jones, Daniel Cox, William A. Galston, and E. J. Dionne, "What It Means to Be American: Attitudes in an Increasingly Diverse America Ten Years After 9/11," Public Religion Research Institute and the Governance Studies Program at The Brookings Institution, September 2011, p. 2.

2. Martin Wolf, *The Shifts and Shocks: What We've Learned—and Have Still to Learn—from the Financial Crisis* (New York: Penguin Press, 2014), pp. 193–95, 430, 493.

3. "Inequality for All (2013)," IMDB.com.

4. Articles in *The New York Times* by Paul Krugman: "Return of the Bums on Welfare," September 20, 2014; "Those Lazy Jobless," September 21, 2014; "The Deflation Caucus," September 4, 2014; "The Fiscal Fizzle: An Imaginary Budget and Debt Crisis," July 20, 2014; "Addicted to Inflation," July 17, 2014; and "Obamacare Fails to Fail," July 13, 2014.

5. Danielle Kurtzleben, "Corporations Used to Pay Almost One-Third of Federal Taxes. Now It's One-Tenth," *Vox*, July 25, 2014; Libby Nelson, "Boosting School Funding 20 Percent Erased the Graduation Gap Between Rich and Poor Students," *Vox*, May 18, 2014; Patricia Cohen, "Among the Poor, Women Feel Inequality More Deeply," *The New York Times*, August 18, 2014; Anna Bernasek, "The Typical Household, Now Worth a Third Less," *The New York Times*, July 26, 2014; David Leonhardt and Kevin Quealy, "The American Middle Class Is No Longer the World's Richest," *The New York Times*, April 22, 2014; Kevin Drum, "Chart: The Minimum Wage in America Is Pretty Damn Low," *Mother Jones*, December 2, 2013; Erika Eichelberger, "The Head of the IMF Says Inequality Threatens Democracy. Here Are Seven Charts Proving She's Right," *Mother Jones*, May 28, 2014; Michael Massing, "Digital Journalism: The Next Generation," *New York Review of Books*, June 25, 2015.

6. Merrill Knox, "May 2014 Ratings: *Fox News* #1 for 149 Straight Months," *TVNewser*, May 28, 2014.

7. Survey of 1,000 adults by YouGov for *The Huffington Post*, July 18–19, 2013; 53 percent view Planned Parenthood favorably.

8. Human Rights Campaign, "Marriage Center," accessed February 11, 2015, http://www.hrc .org/campaigns/marriage-center; Jen McGregor, "Wal-Mart CEO Speaks Out Against 'Religious Freedom' Bill in Arkansas," *The Washington Post*, April 1, 2015.

9. Pope Francis, *Apostolic Exhortation*, p. 45.

10. Raj Chetty, Nathaniel Hendren, Patrick Kline, and Emmanuel Saez, "Where Is the Land of Opportunity? The Geography of Inequality," National Bureau of Economic Research, Working Paper 19843, June 2014.

11. "The Effects of a Minimum Wage Increase on Employment and Family Income," Congressional Budget Office, February 18, 2014, pp. 1–2; David Cooper and Doug Hall, "Raising the Federal Minimum Wage to $10.10 Would Give Working Families, and the Overall Economy, a Much-Needed Boost," Economic Policy Institute, March 13, 2013; Paul Krugman, "Better Pay Now," *The New York Times*, December 1, 2013; Ron Unz, "Raise the Minimum Wage to $12 an Hour," *The New York Times*, December 4, 2013; Arindrajit Dube, "The Minimum We Can Do," *The New York Times*, November 30, 2013.

12. Pamela Prah, "Next Wave of State Minimum Wage Proposals Would 'Index' to Inflation," Pew Stateline, March 15, 2013; GOP conservative heartland: Alabama, Alaska, Arkansas,

Georgia, Idaho, Kansas, Kentucky, Louisiana, Mississippi, Montana, Nebraska, North Dakota, Oklahoma, South Carolina, South Dakota, Texas, Tennessee, Utah, West Virginia, and Wyoming.

13. "2014 Minimum Wage Ballot Measures," National Conference of State Legislatures, November 16, 2014. Four states passed initiatives to raise the minimum wage (Alaska, Arkansas, Nebraska, and South Dakota), and one state, Illinois, passed an advisory question on raising the minimum wage.

14. Harold Meyerson, "Labor's New Groove: Taking the Struggle from Streets to Legislatures," *The American Prospect,* September 1, 2014; David Zahniser and Emily Alpert Reyes, "L.A. Lawmakers Lay Out Path to $15.25 Minimum Wage by 2019," *The Los Angeles Times,* October 7, 2014.

15. Mayor's Press Office, "Mayor Emanuel Signs Executive Order Requiring City Contractors to Pay a Minimum Wage of $13," City of Chicago, September 3, 2014; Hal Dardick and Alejandro Cancino, "Emanuel Task Force: Raise Chicago Minimum Wage to $13 an Hour by 2018," *Chicago Tribune,* July 7, 2014.

16. Steven Greenhouse, "Fighting Back Against Wretched Wages," *The New York Times,* July 27, 2013; Meyerson, "Labor's New Groove" ; Brian Mahoney, "Corporate America Strikes a Liberal Note on Wages," *Politico,* April 2, 2015.

17. Brian Mahoney, "Corporate America Strikes a Liberal Note on Wages."

18. Patricia Cohen, "One Company's New Minimum Wage," *The New York Times*, April 13, 2015.

19. Noam Scheiber, "Democrats Are Rallying Around $12 Minimum Wage," *The New York Times*, April 22, 2015; "Progressive Caucus Supports Low-Wage Workers Striking for Higher Wages," press release from the Congressional Progressive Caucus. April 15, 2015.

20. Stephen Singer, "Connecticut 1st State to Require Paid Sick Time," *The Washington Post,* July 5, 2011; Mark Pazniokas, "Connecticut Becomes First State to Pass $10.10 Minimum Wage," *The CT Mirror,* March 26, 2014; "Connecticut's Statewide Uninsured Rate Cut in Half: Nearly 140,000 Enrollees Were Previously Uninsured," press release from the Office of Governor Dannel P. Malloy, State of Connecticut, August 6, 2014; Michelle Andrews, "California Passes Law to Require Paid Sick Leave as Legislation Lingers in D.C.," PBS, October 3, 2014.

21. Richard Pérez-Peña and Motoko Rich, "Preschool Push Moving Ahead in Many States," *The New York Times,* February 3, 2014.

22. Dorothy Tucker, "Chicago Expanding Pre-K Programs for Next Fall," CBS Chicago, April 24, 2014; Elizabeth A. Harris and Kate Taylor, "51,000 Answer de Blasio's Bell for New Pre-K," *The New York Times,* September 4, 2014.

23. Raj Chetty, Nathaniel Hendren, Patrick Kline, and Emmanuel Saez, "Where Is the Land of Opportunity? The Geography of Inequality," National Bureau of Economic Research, Working Paper 19843, June 2014.

24. David Leonhardt, "In Climbing Income Ladder, Location Matters," *The New York Times,* July 22, 2013.

25. Kirk Johnson, "Targeting Inequality, This Time on Public Transit," *The New York Times,* February 28, 2015.

26. Editorial Board, "Can New York Be Affordable Again?," *The New York Times,* February 6, 2015; Editorial Board, "Yes to Housing in Our Backyards," *The New York Times,* August 29, 2014; Editorial Board, "Mr. de Blasio's Moon Shot," *The New York Times,* May 5, 2014; Editorial Board, "Setting Up a Better Domino Plan," *The New York Times,* March 4, 2014; Editorial Board, "New York's Affordable Housing Shortage," *The New York Times,* February 7, 2014; Monique Madan, "$350 Million for New York's Affordable Housing Effort," *The New York Times,* July 30, 2014.

27. Pope Francis, *Apostolic Exhortation,* pp. 3, 31–39.

28. Ibid., pp. 45–46.

29. Ibid., pp. 45–46, 164.

30. Ibid., p. 47.

31. Ibid., p. 160.

32. Ibid., pp. 44–45.

33. Ibid., pp. 61, 164.

34. Ibid., p. 61.

35. Ibid., pp. 55–56.

36. Ibid., pp. 161–64.

37. Ibid., p. 161.

38. Robert D. Putnam, *Our Kids: The American Dream in Crisis* (New York: Simon & Schuster, 2015), pp. 77, 231–32.

39. Jasmine Garsd, "Pope Francis Says Catholics Don't Need to Breed 'Like Rabbits,'" NPR, January 20, 2015; Andrew J. Cherlin, *Labor's Love Lost: The Rise and Fall of the Working-Class Family in America* (New York: Russell Sage, 2014), pp. 179–82; Isabel V. Sawhill and Joanna Venator, "Part 3: Changing the Default to Improve Families' Opportunity," The Brookings Institution, Social Mobility Memos, October 20, 2014.

40. Putnam, *Our Kids*, pp. 75–76, 243; "'Red' States Have Higher Divorce Rates Than 'Blue' States, And Here's Why," *Huffington Post*, January 21, 2014; Cherlin, *Labor's Love Lost*, p. 179.

41. Isabel V. Sawhill and Joanna Venator, "Part 3: Changing the Default to Improve Families' Opportunity," The Brookings Institution, October 20, 2014.

42. Ibid; Putnam, *Our Kids*, p. 245.

43. Emily Cuddy and Richard V. Reeves, "Teen Moms: The Difference Two Years and a Diploma Make," The Brookings Institution, August 18, 2014.

44. Ron Haskins, "Social Programs That Work," *The New York Times*, December 31, 2014.

45. Putnam, *Our Kids*, p. 247.

46. Ibid, p. 246.

47. "The Economic Impact of S.744, The Border Security, Economic Opportunity, and Immigration Modernization Act," Congressional Budget Office, June 2013, p. 1; Jeffrey Passel, D'Vera Cohn, and Ana Gonzalez-Barrera, "Population Decline of Unauthorized Immigrants Stalls, May Have Reversed," Pew Research Center, September, 23, 2013; U.S. Senate, Border Security, Economic Opportunity, and Immigration Modernization Act, 113th Cong., 1st sess., 2013, S.744; American Immigration Council, "Guide to S.744: Understanding the 2013 Senate Immigration Bill," Immigration Policy Center, July 2013.

48. U.S. Senate, Border Security, Economic Opportunity, and Immigration Modernization Act; American Immigration Council, "Guide to S.744."

49. "The Economic Impact of S.744," pp. 3, 12–14.

50. U.S. Chamber of Commerce, Issues, Immigration, accessed February 12, 2015, https://www.uschamber.com/immigration.

51. Susan Lund, James Manyika, Scott Nyquist, Lenny Mendonca, and Sreenivas Ramaswamy, "Game Changers: Five Opportunities for U.S. Growth and Renewal," McKinsey Global Institute, p. 15.

52. "2013 Report Card for America's Infrastructure," American Society of Civil Engineers, March 2013; "2009 Report Card for American Infrastructure," American Society of Civil Engineers, March 25, 2009.

53. World Economic Forum 2015 competitiveness rankings, accessed Feb. 22, 2015. http://reports.weforum.org/global-competitiveness-report-2014-2015/rankings/.

54. Chris Mooney, "The Gas Tax Has Been Fixed at 18 Cents for Two Decades. Now Would Be a Great Time to Raise It," *The Washington Post*, December 3, 2014.

55. James Carville and Stanley B. Greenberg, *It's the Middle Class, Stupid!* (New York: Blue Rider Press, Penguin Group, 2012), Kindle location 3811; Adam Hersh and Sarah Ayres, "New Ryan Budget Disinvests in America," Center for American Progress, March 20, 2009.

56. "Game Changers," p. 15.

57. Remarks by Thomas J. Donohue, president and CEO of the U.S. Chamber of Commerce, on the state of American business, delivered January 12, 2012; Leo Hindery and Leo Gerard, "The Task Force on Job Creation: A Vision for Economic Renewal," New America Foundation, July 2011, pp. 42–43.

58. Congresswoman Rosa L. DeLauro, comments, New America Foundation I-Bank event, "A Bank to Renew America," June 8, 2011.

59. H.R. 402: National Infrastructure Development Bank Act of 2011, 112th Cong. First Session, sponsored by Congresswoman Rosa DeLauro.

60. "Pre-K to 12 Education Policy," U.S. Chamber of Commerce, August 4, 2010.

61. Jennifer Steinhauer, "Cuts to Head Start Show Challenge of Fiscal Restraint," *The New York Times,* March 10, 2011; Adrienne Lu, "Head Start Hit with Worst Cuts in Its History," *USA Today,* August 20, 2013.

62. Caitlin Emma and Philip Ewing, "Obama Fund Binds Pre-K, Defense Money," *Politico,* February 28, 2014; David Brooks, "When Families Fail," *The New York Times,* February 14, 2013; Caitlin Emma, "Business Community Urging Action on Pre-K Plan," *Politico,* September 24, 2013.

63. "13 Things That Business Can Do to Support Early Childhood Education," Center for Education and Workforce, U.S. Chamber of Commerce Foundation, August 7, 2014.

64. Josh Baugh, "Seven Chambers Backing Pre-K Proposal," *My San Antonio,* September 13, 2012.

65. Kimberly Howard and Richard V. Reeves, "Early Childhood Achievement Gaps and Social Mobility (Part 3)," The Brookings Institution, September 26, 2013.

66. Darrell M. West, *Billionaires: Reflections on the Upper Crust* (Washington, D.C.: The Brookings Institution, 2014), Kindle location 282.

67. Derek Willis, "Super PACs Are Gobbling Up Even More Power, Jeb Bush Edition," *The New York Times,* April 21, 2015.

68. Thomas Beaumont, "Jeb Bush Prepares to Turn Key Campaign Functions Over to Super PAC," Associated Press, April 21, 2015; Jeremy Diamond, "Network of Cruz Super PACs Boasts Big Haul," *CNN,* April 8, 2015; M. J. Lee and Jeremy Diamond, "Ted Cruz Super PACs: A New Era of Political Fundraising," *CNN,* April 9, 2015; Tribune wire reports, "Super PAC Formed to Help Wisconsin's Scott Walker in 2016 Campaign," *Chicago Tribune,* April 16, 2015; Ed O'Keefe, "Marco Rubio Gets a Super PAC," *The Washington Post,* April 9, 2015.

69. Emily Badger, "Why Early Voting Is About So Much More Than Convenience," *The Washington Post,* September 30, 2014.

70. Thomas B. Edsall, "Milking the Money Machine," *The New York Times,* July 22, 2014.

71. West, *Billionaires,* Kindle location 208.

72. Joseph E. Stiglitz, "Democracy in the Twenty-first Century," Project Syndicate, September 1, 2014, p. 31.

73. Paul Lewis, "Hillary Clinton Signals Break with Past In Iowa Call to End 'Uncontrolled Money,'" *The Guardian,* April 14, 2015; Conversation with John Podesta, April 21, 2015.

74. The battleground states include: New Hampshire, Iowa, Colorado, Nevada, Florida, Ohio, Pennsylvania, North Carolina, Wisconsin, and Michigan.

75. Joseph E. Stiglitz, "Democracy in the Twenty-first Century," Project Syndicate, September 1, 2014.

76. Remarks of Congresswoman Rosa DeLauro, "Financing Infrastructure in Tough Times," delivered at the CT Voices State Budget Forum, Hartford, Connecticut, January 12, 2012.

77. Richard Burkhauser, Jeff Larrimore, and Kosali Simon, "A 'Second Opinion' on the Economic Health of the American Middle Class," NBER Working Paper Series, June 2011.

78. Stiglitz, "Democracy," p. 114; Thomas Piketty, *Capital in the Twenty-first Century* (Cambridge, Mass.: Harvard University Press, March 2014), p. 498.

79. Neil Irwin, "Obama's Tax Proposal Is Really About Shaping the Democratic Party After

Obama," *The New York Times*, January 18, 2015; Thomas B. Edsall, "Can Capitalists Save Capitalism?," *The New York Times*, January 20, 2015; Lawrence H. Summers and Ed Balls, "Report of the Commission on Inclusive Prosperity," Center for American Progress, January 15, 2015, p. 124; Thomas B. Edsall, "Establishment Populism Rising," *The New York Times*, March 4, 2015.

80. Ezra Klein, "The Doom Loop of Oligarchy," *Vox*, April 11, 2014.

81. Coral Davenport, "Industry Awakens to Threat of Climate Change," *The New York Times*, January 23, 2014; Coral Davenport, "President's Drive for Carbon Pricing Fails to Win at Home," *The New York Times*, September 27, 2014.

82. "The Budget and Economic Outlook: 2015 to 2025," Congressional Budget Office, January 2015, p. 92; graphs from the Office of Congressman Chris Van Hollen, "The Budget: Democratic vs. Republican Approaches to Growing the Economy and Paychecks," February 2015.

83. Lawrence H. Summers and Ed Balls, "Report of the Commission on Inclusive Prosperity," Center for American Progress, January 15, 2015, p. 124.

84. Graphs from the Office of Congressman Chris Van Hollen; Lori Montgomery and Paul Kane, "Democrats, in a Stark Shift in Messaging, to Make Big Tax-Break Pitch for Middle Class," *The Washington Post*, January 11, 2015.

85. Lawrence H. Summers and Ed Balls, "Report of the Commission on Inclusive Prosperity," Center for American Progress, January 15, 2015, p. 34.

86. See chapter 5; Joseph E. Stiglitz, *The Price of Inequality: How Today's Divided Society Endangers Our Future* (New York: W. W. Norton, 2013), p. 35.

87. Suzanne Berger, "How Finance Gutted Manufacturing," *Boston Review*, April 1, 2014; Lawrence H. Summers and Ed Balls, "Report of the Commission on Inclusive Prosperity," Center for American Progress, January 15, 2015, p. 124.

88. Lawrence H. Summers and Ed Balls, "Report of the Commission on Inclusive Prosperity," Center for American Progress, January 15, 2015, p. 124.

89. Susan Holmberg and Mark Schmitt, "The Overpaid CEO," *Democracy Journal*, Fall 2014, pp. 70–72.

90. "Policy Basics: Top Ten Facts About Social Security," Center on Budget and Policy Priorities, November 6, 2012.

91. Heather Boushey, "A New Agenda for American Families and the Economy," *Dissent*, Summer 2014.

92. Office of the Press Secretary, "Fact Sheet: Helping All Working Families with Young Children Afford Child Care," the White House, January 21, 2015.

93. H.R. 1286: Healthy Families Act, 113th Cong. First Session, sponsored by Congresswoman Rosa DeLauro; Boushey, "A New Agenda."

94. Editorial Board, "Silicon Valley's Diversity Problem," *The New York Times*, October 4, 2014; Claire Cain Miller, "Women on the Board: Quotas Have Limited Success," *The New York Times*, June 19, 2014.

95. Pansy Yau, "Shanghai: Market Profile," HKTDC Research, January 3, 2014; Josef Joffe, *The Myth of America's Decline: Politics, Economics, and a Half Century of False Prophecies* (New York: Liveright, 2014), pp. 175–76; Tino Sanandaji, "The Amazing Truth About PISA Scores: USA Beats Western Europe, Ties with Asia," *New Geography*, December 28, 2010.

96. "Game Changers."

97. Suzanne Mettler, "College, the Great Unleveler," *New York Times*, March 1, 2014.

98. Eduardo Porter, "A Simple Equation: More Education=More Income," *The New York Times*, September 10, 2014; "Game Changers," p. 111.

99. Ibid., p. 124.

100. Ibid., p. 125. I should note that I conduct polling for the National Education Association.

101. Joe Nocera, "Imagining Successful Schools," *The New York Times*, August 29, 2014.

102. Editorial Board, "Why Other Countries Teach Better," *The New York Times*, December 17, 2013; "Game Changers," p. 127.

103. Ibid., pp. 145–46.

104. Allie Grasgreen, "Obama to Propose Two Free Years of Community College for Students," *Politico*, January 18, 2015.

105. Ibid; Shahien Nasiripour and Sam Stein, "Obama to Endorse Elizabeth Warren's Student Loan Proposal," *Huffington Post*, June 6, 2014; Shahien Nasiripour, "Senate Blocks Elizabeth Warren's Student Loan Refinancing Proposal," *Huffington Post*, June 11, 2014; Danielle Kurtzleben, "CHARTS: Just How Fast Has College Tuition Grown?" *U.S. News & World Report*, October 23, 2013.

106. Paul Krugman, "Secular Stagnation, Coalmines, Bubbles and Larry Summers," *The New York Times*, November, 16, 2013; remarks by Lawrence H. Summers at the IMF Fourteenth Annual Research Conference in Honor of Stanley Fischer, Washington, D.C., November, 8, 2013; Martin Wolf, *The Shifts and Shocks*, pp. 260, 274; Ferdinando Giugliano, "IMF Warns of Long Period of Lower Growth," *Financial Times*, April 7, 2015.

107. Lawrence H. Summers and Ed Balls, "Report of the Commission on Inclusive Prosperity," Center for American Progress, January 15, 2015, pp. 53, 111, 123; Robert Kuttner, "Are the Elites Catching Up with the People?" *The American Prospect*, January 28, 2015; Martin Wolf, *The Shifts and Shocks*, p. 166.

108. Lawrence H. Summers and Ed Balls, "Report of the Commission on Inclusive Prosperity," Center for American Progress, January 15, 2015, p. 109; Ferdinando Giugliano, "IMF Warns of Long Period of Lower Growth," *Financial Times*, April 7, 2015.

109. Martin Wolf, *The Shifts and the Shocks*, Kindle locations 921–942.

13 THE STATE OF THE UNION

1. Fourth annual message of President Theodore Roosevelt to the U.S. Senate and House of Representatives, on December 6, 1904; fifth annual message of President Theodore Roosevelt to the U.S. Senate and House of Representatives, on December 5, 1905.

2. For the remainder of the chapter, quotes attributed to President Theodore Roosevelt may be found in the fifth annual message of President Theodore Roosevelt to the U.S. Senate and House of Representatives, on December 5, 1905.

3. Coral Davenport, "Obama to Take Action to Slash Coal Pollution," *The New York Times*, June 1, 2014; Office of the Press Secretary, "Fact Sheet: President Obama Announces New Actions to Strengthen Global Resilience to Climate Change and Launches Partnerships to Cut Carbon Pollution," the White House, September 23, 2014; Office of the Press Secretary, "Presidential Memorandum—Advancing Pay Equality Through Compensation Data Collection," the White House, April 8, 2014.

4. This and all quotes for the remainder of the chapter attributed to President Woodrow Wilson are from the first inaugural address of President Woodrow Wilson, at the U.S. Capitol, Washington, D.C., March 4, 1913.

INDEX